P9-CRN-983

Praise for *The New Rules of Marketing & PR*

"The silos that marketing and PR have been operating in are crumbling. This monumental shift has redefined the ways that brands target, engage, and build relationships with their audiences. David Meerman Scott's visionary approach started a chain reaction whose effects can still be felt today. The legend that is *The New Rules of Marketing & PR* continues to be one of the most influential books in the hybrid marketer's library."

—Jason A Miller, Global Content Marketing Leader at
LinkedIn and Author of *Welcome to the Funnel*

"This excellent look at the basics of new-millennial marketing should find use in the hands of any serious PR professional making the transition."

—*Publishers Weekly* (starred review)

"This is absolutely the *best* book on the new world of marketing and PR. David Meerman Scott is 'the teacher's teacher in the world of social media.' I get all my best stuff from him. In fact, I buy each new edition because, in the ever-changing world of online marketing, if you don't stay current, you die a fast death. This edition is so *new* that it includes tools I hadn't even heard of yet. You'll love it."

—Michael Port, *New York Times* Bestselling
Author of *Book Yourself Solid*

"Most professional marketers—and the groups in which they work—are on the edge of becoming obsolete, so they'd better learn how marketing is really going to work in the future."

—BNET, "The Best & Worst Business Books"

"*The New Rules of Marketing & PR* has inspired me to do what I have coached so many young artists to do, 'Find your authentic voice, become vulnerable, and then put yourself out there.' David Meerman Scott expertly and clearly lays out how to use many great new tools to help accomplish this. Since reading this book, I have been excited about truly connecting with people without the filter of all the 'old PR' hype. It has been really energizing for me to speak about things that I really care about, using my real voice."

—Meredith Brooks, Multi-Platinum Recording Artist,
Writer, Producer, and Founder of record label
Kissing Booth Music

"I've relied on *The New Rules of Marketing & PR* as a core text for my New Media and Public Relations course at Boston University for the past eight years. David's book is a bold, crystal-clear, and practical guide toward a new (and better) future for the profession."

—Stephen Quigley, Boston University

"What a wake-up call! By embracing the strategies in this book, you will totally transform your business. David Meerman Scott shows you a multitude of ways to propel your company to a thought leadership position in your market and drive sales—all without a huge budget. I am a huge fan and practitioner of his advice."

—Jill Konrath, Author of *Snap Selling* and Chief Sales Officer,
SellingtoBigCompanies.com

"David is a leading expert on how the digital age has dramatically changed marketing and PR. A great guide for large and small companies alike to navigate the 'new rules.'"

—Martin Lindstrom, *New York Times*
Bestselling Author of *Buyology:
The Truth and Lies about Why We Buy*

"When I read the *New Rules* for the first time, it was a 'eureka' moment for me at HubSpot. David nailed the fundamental shifts going on in the buyer-seller relationship and wrote the classic text to help marketers take advantage of them."

—Brian Halligan, HubSpot CEO and
Co-Author of *Inbound Marketing*

"The Internet is not so much about technology as it is about people. David Meerman Scott, in his remarkable *The New Rules of Marketing & PR*, goes far beyond technology and explores the ramifications of the web as it pertains to people. He sets down a body of rules that show you how to negotiate those ramifications with maximum effectiveness. And he does it with real-life case histories and an engaging style."

—Jay Conrad Levinson, Father of
Guerrilla Marketing and Author,
Guerrilla Marketing series of books

"*The New Rules of Marketing & PR* teaches readers how to launch a thought leadership campaign by using the far-reaching, long-lasting tools of social media. It is an invaluable guide for anyone who wants to make a name for themselves, their ideas, and their organization."

—Mark Levy, Co-Author, *How to Persuade People
Who Don't Want to Be Persuaded*, and Founder of
Levy Innovation: A Marketing Strategy Firm

"*Revolution* may be an overused word in describing what the Internet has wrought, but revolution is exactly what David Meerman Scott embraces and propels forward in this book. He exposes the futility of the old media rules and opens to all of us an insiders' game, previously played by a few well-connected specialists. With this rule book to the online revolution, you can learn how to win minds and markets, playing by the new rules of new media."

—Don Dunnington, President, International
Association of Online Communicators (IAOC);
Director of Business Communications, K-Tron International;
and Graduate Instructor in Online Communication,
Rowan University, Glassboro, New Jersey

"The history of marketing communications—about 60 years or so—has been about pushing messages to convince prospects to take some action we need. Now marketing communications, largely because of the overwhelming power and influence of the web and other electronic communications, is about engaging in conversation with prospects and leading/persuading them to take action. David Meerman Scott shows how marketing is now about participation and connection, and no longer about strong-arm force."

—Roy Young, Chief Revenue Officer, MarketingProfs.com,
and Co-Author, *Marketing Champions: Practical Strategies for Improving Marketing's Power, Influence, and Business Impact*

"David Meerman Scott not only offers good descriptions of digital tools available for public relations professionals, but also explains strategy, especially the importance of thinking about PR from the public's perspectives, and provides lots of helpful examples. My students loved this book."

—Karen Miller Russell, Associate Professor,
Grady College of Journalism and Mass Communication,
University of Georgia

"This is a must-read book if you don't want to waste time and resources on the old methods of Internet marketing and PR. David Meerman Scott reviews the old rules for old times' sake while bridging into the new rules for Internet marketing and PR for your cause. He doesn't leave us with only theories, but offers practical and results-oriented how-tos."

—Ron Peck, Executive Director,
Neurological Disease Foundation

"*The New Rules of Marketing & PR* is all about breaking the rules and creating new roles in traditional functional areas. Using maverick, nontraditional approaches to access and engage a multiplicity of audiences, communities, and thought leaders online, PR people are realizing new value, influence, and outcomes. We're now in a content-rich, Internet-driven world, and David Meerman Scott has written a valuable treatise on how marketing-minded PR professionals can leverage new media channels and forums to take their stories to market. No longer are PR practitioners limited in where and how they direct their knowledge, penmanship, and perception management skills. The Internet has multiplied and segmented a wealth of new avenues for directly reaching and activating key constituencies and stakeholders. A good book well worth the read by all marketing mavens and aging PR flacks."

—Donovan Neale-May, Executive Director,
CMO Council

"*The New Rules of Marketing & PR* provides a concise action plan for success. Rather than focusing on a single solution, Scott shows how to use multiple online tools, all directed toward increasing your firm's visibility and word-of-mouth awareness."

—Roger C. Parker, Author of *The Streetwise Guide to Relationship Marketing on the Internet* and *Design to Sell*

"Once again we are at a critical inflection point on our society's evolutionary path, with individuals wresting away power and control from institutions and traditional gatekeepers who control the flow of knowledge and maintain the silo walls. As communications professionals, we have little time to figure out what has changed, why it changed, and what we should be doing about it. If you don't start doing things differently and start right now, you may as well start looking for your next career path. In a world where disruption is commonplace and new ways of communicating and collaborating are invented every day, what does it take for a hardworking, ethical communications professional to be successful? David Meerman Scott's book, *The New Rules of Marketing & PR*, is an insightful look at how the game is changing as we play it and some of the key tactics you need to succeed in the knowledge economy."

—Chris Heuer, Co-Founder, Social Media Club

The NEW RULES of MARKETING & PR

Also by David Meerman Scott

Fanocracy: Turning Fans into Customers and Customers into Fans (with Reiko Scott)

The New Rules of Sales and Service: How to Use Agile Selling, Real-Time Customer Engagement, Big Data, Content, and Storytelling to Grow Your Business

Marketing the Moon: The Selling of the Apollo Lunar Program (with Richard Jurek)

Real-Time Marketing & PR: How to Instantly Engage Your Market, Connect with Customers, and Create Products That Grow Your Business Now

Marketing Lessons from the Grateful Dead: What Every Business Can Learn from the Most Iconic Band in History (with Brian Halligan)

Newsjacking: How to Inject Your Ideas into a Breaking News Story and Generate Tons of Media Coverage

World Wide Rave: Creating Triggers That Get Millions of People to Spread Your Ideas and Share Your Stories

Tuned In: Uncover the Extraordinary Opportunities That Lead to Business Breakthroughs (with Craig Stull and Phil Myers)

Cashing in with Content: How Innovative Marketers Use Digital Information to Turn Browsers into Buyers

Eyeball Wars: A Novel of Dot-Com Intrigue

The NEW RULES of MARKETING & PR

HOW TO USE CONTENT MARKETING, PODCASTING, SOCIAL MEDIA, AI, LIVE VIDEO, AND NEWSJACKING TO REACH BUYERS DIRECTLY

SEVENTH EDITION

DAVID MEERMAN SCOTT

WILEY

Cover design: Wiley

Cover Image: © Barsoom Design

Copyright © 2020 by David Meerman Scott. All rights reserved.

Published by John Wiley & Sons, Inc., Hoboken, New Jersey.
Published simultaneously in Canada.

No part of this publication may be reproduced, stored in a retrieval system, or transmitted in any form or by any means, electronic, mechanical, photocopying, recording, scanning, or otherwise, except as permitted under Section 107 or 108 of the 1976 United States Copyright Act, without either the prior written permission of the Publisher, or authorization through payment of the appropriate per-copy fee to the Copyright Clearance Center, Inc., 222 Rosewood Drive, Danvers, MA 01923, (978) 750-8400, fax (978) 646-8600, or on the Web at www.copyright.com. Requests to the Publisher for permission should be addressed to the Permissions Department, John Wiley & Sons, Inc., 111 River Street, Hoboken, NJ 07030, (201) 748-6011, fax (201) 748-6008, or online at http://www.wiley.com/go/permissions.

Limit of Liability/Disclaimer of Warranty: While the publisher and author have used their best efforts in preparing this book, they make no representations or warranties with respect to the accuracy or completeness of the contents of this book and specifically disclaim any implied warranties of merchantability or fitness for a particular purpose. No warranty may be created or extended by sales representatives or written sales materials. The advice and strategies contained herein may not be suitable for your situation. You should consult with a professional where appropriate. Neither the publisher nor author shall be liable for any loss of profit or any other commercial damages, including but not limited to special, incidental, consequential, or other damages.

For general information on our other products and services or for technical support, please contact our Customer Care Department within the United States at (800) 762-2974, outside the United States at (317) 572-3993, or fax (317) 572-4002.

Wiley publishes in a variety of print and electronic formats and by print-on-demand. Some material included with standard print versions of this book may not be included in e-books or in print-on-demand. If this book refers to media such as a CD or DVD that is not included in the version you purchased, you may download this material at http://booksupport.wiley.com. For more information about Wiley products, visit www.wiley.com.

Library of Congress Cataloging-in-Publication Data:

Names: Scott, David Meerman, author.
Title: The new rules of marketing & PR : how to use content marketing, podcasting, social media, AI, live video, and newsjacking to reach buyers directly / David Meerman Scott.
Description: Seventh edition. | Hoboken, New Jersey : John Wiley & Sons, [2020] | Includes index.
Identifiers: LCCN 2019053589 (print) | LCCN 2019053590 (ebook) | ISBN 9781119651543 (paperback) | ISBN 9781119651611 (adobe pdf) | ISBN 9781119651604 (epub)
Subjects: LCSH: Internet marketing. | Internet in public relations.
Classification: LCC HF5415.1265 .S393 2020 (print) | LCC HF5415.1265 (ebook) | DDC 658.8/72—dc23
LC record available at https://lccn.loc.gov/2019053589
LC ebook record available at https://lccn.loc.gov/2019053590

Printed in the United States of America

10 9 8 7 6 5 4 3 2 1

For the Scott women

my mother, Carolyn J. Scott;
my wife, Yukari Watanabe Scott;
and my daughter, Allison C.R. Scott

Contents

Introduction

A few years ago I was considering buying a new surfboard. I've been mainly riding an 8'0" Spyder Wright over the past several years, and I wanted to get a smaller board. In an article in *Surfer* magazine, I read about a trend back to wooden surfboards, so I thought I'd do a little research on wood as an option for my next purchase. Like billions of other consumers, I headed over to Google to start my research. I entered the phrase "wooden surfboard." Then I followed the link at the top search result to Grain Surfboards at grainsurfboards.com.

I was not disappointed. The Grain Surfboards site drew me in immediately with beautiful images of the boards and excellent descriptions of how the company makes them. No wonder Grain Surfboards had the top search result for the most important phrase in their business.

I learned that while surfboards were originally made of solid wood a hundred or more years ago in Hawaii, for the past 60 years machine-made materials such as polyurethane or polystyrene foam have all but replaced wood. After all, wood is heavier and harder to work with.

However, along came Grain Surfboards. The company pioneered the idea of applying boatbuilding techniques to make a hollow wooden board that is light, beautiful, and eco-friendly. The Grain Surfboards site wasn't just talking up their products. It was educating me about the history of my sport.

The lessons didn't stop with history. In fact, the company details its building process on the web for all to see. The idea of sharing your best ideas is foreign to many marketers and entrepreneurs, because people don't want their competitors to understand their business. Yet the more you educate a consumer, the more likely they are to buy.

Along the way, I learned that at Grain Surfboards, you can buy a build-it-yourself wooden surfboard kit that has everything you need, including detailed plans. I also learned that the company conducts classes most months in its Maine workshop and also has a traveling course (held recently in California). If building your own board doesn't appeal to you, you can have the artisans at Grain Surfboards craft one for you.

Grain Surfboards perfectly illustrates a different way of doing business—the very method we will discuss in this book. Grain Surfboards understands that when you share your work on the web, you spread your ideas and grow your business as a result. Throughout these pages, we'll discuss how to create content that educates and informs, just like Grain Surfboards does.

As I was poking around on the site, I found my way to the Grain Surfboards Facebook page (12,000+ likes) and the @GrainSurfboards Instagram feed (50,000+ followers). Grain Surfboards engages with fans and shares what's new. Because fans are excited to be engaged, they naturally help spread the company's ideas—without even being asked. On Instagram, for example, Grain Surfboards posts get hundreds of likes and many comments and shares. The team regularly posts images of the boards they are building, of customer-created work, and, of course, images of surfing enthusiasts shredding atop the company's gorgeous boards.

In this book, you'll learn how to use tools like Instagram and Facebook in your business too. Social networking platforms are easy, fun, and powerful to use. It just takes a minute or two to shoot a photo, manipulate it with the filters, and share it with your network. With Instagram, images and videos do the talking, so even writing-challenged people can create awesome content.

In about 10 minutes of research on the Grain Surfboards site, as well as their Facebook and Instagram feeds, I made up my mind to purchase one of their boards. But I did more than that. I signed up for the four-day class on building a wooden surfboard held at the factory in York, Maine. When I read this description, I just couldn't refuse this empowering opportunity: *"Four days in, beautiful board out! You'll get right down to it in this four-day class, beginning on Day 1 with a board that has pre-installed (by us) frames, chine and one railstrip. You'll pair up with another student to build the rails of your board in the morning and your classmate's that afternoon. Spend the remaining three days completing, shaping and sanding your board. It's fast, but it's fun and in only four days, you've got a shaped and sanded board ready for glass."* Sign me up!

It was an fantastic experience to build my own board. Many others share my enthusiasm, and they tell the story of their Grain Surfboards workshop via the company's Facebook page. These posts further spread the word about the brand. My story? Four days to a beautiful 6′4″ Wherry fish model board, which I left behind to be finished with a fiberglass coating.

When I went back to pick it up, I signed up for a second course to build yet another board.

The company has me hooked. Grain Surfboards has built a thriving business and become number one in its marketplace. And the online content is a primary reason for its success. The company doesn't resort to paying for expensive ads in surfing magazines. It doesn't focus on trying to get retailers to carry its product. Instead, it reaches potential buyers directly—at the precise moment when those buyers are looking for what it sells.

I did a search on Google for "wooden surfboard." Less than a half-hour later, I had my credit card out to book a class in another state! Had it not been for Grain Surfboards' content-rich website, beautiful images, detailed process information, and happy customer showcase, I would have quickly clicked away to check out other manufacturers. Instead, I spent thousands of dollars, rewarding a company that had treated me with respect and invited me into the wooden surfboard world.

The web provides tremendous opportunities to reach buyers directly, and you will learn how to harness that power. What was science fiction just a few years ago is common, even expected, today. Take a moment to acknowledge how incredible it is that you can instantly create a video stream using that small device in your pocket and connect to a service like Facebook Live, Instagram, or Snapchat to reach thousands of interested people who pay attention to what you are broadcasting. Or you can have a two-way video conversation with a potential customer on the other side of the planet. For free! Your mobile device is much more powerful than what the creators of *The Jetsons* imagined decades ago. Each of us has the ability to reach almost any human on the planet in real time. You can publish content—a blog post, video, infographic, photo—to reach potential customers who will be eager to do business with you.

There used to be only three ways to get noticed: Buy expensive advertising, beg the mainstream media to tell your story for you, or hire a huge sales staff to bug people individually about your products. Now we have a better option: publishing interesting content on the web, content that your buyers *want* to consume. The tools of the marketing and PR trade have changed. The skills that worked offline to help you buy or beg or bug your way into opportunity are the skills of interruption and coercion. Online success comes from thinking like a journalist and publishing amazing content that will brand you as an organization or person it would be a pleasure to do business with. You are in charge of your own success.

The New Rules

At the height of the dot-com boom, I was vice president of marketing at NewsEdge Corporation, a NASDAQ-traded online news distributor with more than $70 million in annual revenue. My multimillion-dollar marketing budget included tens of thousands of dollars per month for a public relations (PR) agency, hundreds of thousands per year for print advertising and glossy brochures, and expensive participation at a dozen trade shows per year. My team put these things on our marketing to-do list, worked like hell to execute, and paid the big bucks for it all because that's what marketing and PR people did. These efforts made us feel good because we were *doing something*, but the programs were not producing significant, measurable results. We were working based on the rules of the past.

At the same time, drawing on experience I had gained in my previous position as Asia marketing director for the online division of Knight-Ridder (then one of the largest newspaper and information companies in the world), my team and I quietly created content-based marketing and PR programs on the web.

Against the advice of the PR agency professionals we had on retainer (who insisted that press releases were only for the press), we wrote and sent dozens of releases ourselves. Each time we sent a release, it appeared at online services such as Yahoo! and *resulted in sales leads*. Even though our advertising agency told us not to put the valuable information "somewhere where competitors could steal it," we created a monthly newsletter called *The Edge*, about the exploding world of digital news. We made it freely available on the homepage of our website *because it generated interest from buyers, the media, and analysts*.

Way back in the 1990s, when web marketing and PR were in their infancy, my team and I ignored the old rules, drawing instead on my online publishing experience, and created a marketing strategy using content to reach buyers directly on the web. The homegrown programs we created at virtually no cost consistently generated more interest from qualified buyers, the media, and analysts—and resulted in more sales—than the big-bucks programs that the "professionals" were running for us. People we never heard of were finding us through search engines. We had discovered a better way to reach buyers.

In 2002, after NewsEdge was sold to the Thomson Corporation (now Thomson Reuters), I started my own business to refine my ideas and teach others through writing, speaking at conferences, and conducting seminars for corporate groups. The objective in all this work was to help others reach buyers directly with web content. Since then, many new forms of online media have burst onto the scene, including social networks like Twitter, Facebook, Instagram, Snapchat, and Pinterest, plus blogs, podcasts, video, and virtual communities. But what all the new web tools and techniques have in common is that they are the best way to communicate *directly* with your marketplace.

This book actually started as web marketing on my blog more than a decade ago. I published an e-book called *The New Rules of PR*, immediately generating remarkable enthusiasm (and much controversy) among marketers and businesspeople around the world. Since the e-book was published, it has been downloaded several million times and commented on by thousands of readers on my blog and many others. (To those of you who have read and shared the e-book, thank you!) The first edition of this book was much more than just an expansion of that work, because I made its subject marketing *and* PR and because I included many different forms of online media and incorporated years of additional research.

This book contains much more than just my own ideas, because I blogged the book, section by section, as I wrote the first edition. As I have worked on revisions, including this seventh edition, I've continued to blog the stories that appear here. Thousands of you have followed along, and many have contributed to the writing process by offering suggestions through comments on my blog, via Twitter, and by email. Thank you for contributing your ideas. And thank you for arguing with me when I got off track. Your enthusiasm has made the book much better than it would have been if I had written in isolation.

The web has changed not only the rules of marketing and PR, but also the template for business books. *The New Rules of Marketing & PR* is an interesting example. My online content (the e-book and my blog) led me directly to a print book deal. Other publishers would have freaked out if an author wanted to put parts of his book online (for free!) to solicit ideas. The people at John Wiley & Sons encouraged it. So my thanks go to them as well.

Life with the New Rules

The New Rules of Marketing & PR has sold remarkably well since the initial release in June 2007. The first edition made the *BusinessWeek* bestseller list for multiple months. Since then, the revised editions have remained a top title for well more than a decade among thousands of books about marketing and public relations. Want to know the amazing thing? I didn't spend a single penny advertising or promoting it.

Here's what I did do when I launched the first edition: I offered advance copies to approximately 130 important bloggers, I sent out nearly 20 news releases (you'll read later in the book about news releases as a tool to reach buyers directly), and my publisher alerted contacts in the media. That's it. Thousands of bloggers have written about the book over the years (thank you!), significantly driving its sales. And the mainstream media have found me as a result of this blogger interest. The *Wall Street Journal* called several times for interviews that landed me quotes in the paper because the journalists had first read about my ideas online. I've appeared on international and local television and radio, including MSNBC, Fox Business, and NPR. I've been interviewed on hundreds of podcasts. Magazines and newspaper reporters email me all the time to get quotes for their stories. How do they find me? Online, of course! And it doesn't cost me a single penny. I'm not telling you all this to brag about my book sales or my media appearances. I'm telling you to show you how well these ideas work and to assure you that you can achieve a similar result in your business.

But the coolest part of my life since the book was published isn't that I took advantage of the new rules of marketing and PR, nor that this book has been selling like hotcakes as a result. No, the coolest part of my life right now is that people like you contact me every day to say that the ideas in these pages have transformed their businesses and changed their lives. Really! That's the sort of language people use. They write just to thank me for putting the ideas into a book so that they could tap into the new realities of marketing and PR.

Take Jody. He sent me an email to tell me the book had an unexpected effect on him and his wife. Jody explained that, to them, the really exciting and hopeful idea is that they can actually use their genuine voices online; they've left behind the hype-inflated, PR-speak their agencies had used so tediously.

Jim wrote to tell me, "More powerful than saying I read your book twice, I used it to innovate a new writing model. I've been building my audience from scratch on LinkedIn ahead of publication of my first novel and I've now got over 70,000 subscribers."

Jorge, who lives in Portugal, commented on LinkedIn that "it was because of this book that I started blogging. It took me one entire day to do my first blog post. Now I use content marketing in a regular basis and all my business comes from Mr. Google! Thanks David and thanks *New Rules* . . . (and Mr. Google)!"

Andrew left a comment on my blog: "David, your book so inspired me, I decided to start a brand-new business (launching shortly) based around the principles you espouse. You cogently expressed many of the things that I'd been grappling with myself. So your book has certainly changed one life."

Mark said, "I took your advice back in 2006 and started a blog. If you Google 'fix sales problems,' you will find 42 million listings, and I am number one in the world! Thanks again for the advice years ago, and I forced myself to do it and I am glad I did."

Julie, who is a senior executive at a PR firm, handed out copies to all 75 of her staff members. Mike wrote to say that his company takes advantage of all the trends and techniques described in the book. He purchased a bunch of copies to share with everyone in his organization. Larry bought copies for all the members of his professional association. Robin, who works for a company that offers public relations services, purchased 300 copies for clients. People approach me at conferences asking me to sign wonderfully dog-eared, coffee-stained, Post-it-noted copies of the book. Sometimes they tell me some funny secrets, too. Kathy, who works in PR, said that if everyone read it, she'd be out of a job! David told me he used what he learned to find a *new* job.

While all this incredible feedback is personally flattering, I am most grateful that my ideas have empowered people to find their own voices and tell their own stories online. How cool is that?

Now let me disclose a secret of my own. As I was writing the first edition of this book, I was a bit unsure of the global applicability of the new rules. Sure, I'd found a number of anecdotal stories about online marketing, blogging, and social networking outside North America. But I couldn't help but wonder at the time: Are organizations of all kinds reaching their buyers directly, with web content written in languages other than English and for cultures other than my own?

I quickly learned that the answer is a resounding yes! About 25 percent of the book's English-language sales have come from outside the United States. And as I write this, the book has been or is being translated into more than 29 other languages, including Bulgarian, Finnish, Korean, Vietnamese, Serbian, and Turkish. I'm also receiving invitations from all over the world to speak about the new rules. I've traveled for talks to Bulgaria, Sweden, Saudi Arabia, India, Japan, the United Kingdom, Spain, Estonia, Latvia, Turkey, Egypt, Italy, Croatia, the Netherlands, Australia, New Zealand, Malaysia, Trinidad, Colombia, and the Dominican Republic. So I can say with certainty that the ideas in these pages do resonate worldwide. We are indeed witnessing a global phenomenon.

What's New

This seventh edition of the book builds on the completely revised sixth edition with another extensive rewrite. I have checked every story, fact, and figure. But I've also listened. In the past decade, I've met thousands of people like you, people who have shared their stories with me. I have drawn from those experiences and included in these pages many new examples of success. For those of you who have read earlier editions, you'll still find many fresh ideas in these pages.

I've made some more significant additions as well. The tools of marketing and public relations are constantly evolving. Consider this: When I wrote the first edition of the book, Twitter didn't even exist and Facebook was available only to students. Now Twitter is an essential tool of marketing, and as of March 31, 2019, Facebook had 2.38 billion monthly active users around the world. And those are just two examples.

Here's another example of how the ideas in this book have become mainstream: I first wrote about newsjacking, the art and science of injecting your ideas into a breaking news story to generate tons of media coverage, get sales leads, and grow business, back in 2011. I'm honored and grateful that because of people like you who learned about my pioneering ideas around newsjacking in previous editions of this book, the concept has become incredibly popular.

In fact, Oxford Dictionaries listed "newsjacking" in the Oxford English Dictionary in 2017 and named it to the short list of contenders for word of the year. In their announcement, Oxford Dictionaries said: "In the space of a few short years, newsjacking has gone from an experimental technique to a staple in every social media-savvy marketing department's arsenal. Brands from across industry sectors fully embraced the strategy this year, increasingly taking advantage of current events to not only push their brand into the public consciousness, but to align themselves with certain ethical or moral positions. Blending 'news' and 'hijacking,' the word itself dates back to the 1970s with reference to the theft of newspapers in order to sell them to scrap dealers. Its contemporary iteration, however, dates from the early twenty-first century, as first popularized by marketing and sales strategist David Meerman Scott." You will learn about Newsjacking in Chapter 21, where I have added several new examples in this edition of the book.

Since the last edition of the book was published, the number of people using voice assistants from the likes of Amazon, Google, and Apple has dramatically increased. That means understanding how people use voice to ask questions has become an important aspect of Search Engine Optimization, and I've added a section about this.

In early 2019 Google shut down its social networking service Google Plus (G+), so I needed to remove that section from the book. Google Plus launched in mid-2011 to great excitement. Initially available by invitation only—a clever ploy to get early adopters like me to sign on—G+ became the fastest growing social network in history when it opened to everybody in September 2011. However, once people started to use the service, it didn't seem much different than Facebook. Most didn't stick around. Less than a decade after launch, the service was abruptly shut down. We can learn several lessons from this saga: (1) "Me too" social networks never succeed, and (2) never tie the majority of your personal brand to a single social network.

I used my scalpel to cut other stories and concepts that I felt were no longer appropriate, including an entire chapter on viral marketing that was in previous editions. With the tremendous rise of social media, newsjacking, and real-time connections between people around the world, the fact that information travels quickly and grows in reach is an aspect of many ideas in various chapters in the book. The idea no longer needs its own chapter.

Finally, this edition includes a brand-new chapter on artificial intelligence (AI) and machine learning. Since the last edition of the book was published, the rise of AI in marketing and public relations has become an important way to automate routine tasks to save time and money as well as to increase the success of marketing initiatives. The chapter explores ways that AI can help marketers, such as analyzing which blog or email newsletter topics have the greatest chance of getting seen and shared, the best ways to write headlines for maximum exposure, the best time and day to post it, which channels are the best to share it on, and what hashtags are appropriate to use. As you consider AI in your organization, think about the routine tasks that drive business value that might be possible to automate. Even if you're not using AI yet, you need to know what's possible in this, perhaps fastest changing aspect of marketing.

Writing Like on a Blog, but in a Book

Because the lines between marketing and PR have blurred so much that the distinction is now virtually unrecognizable, the best online media choice is often not as obvious as it was in the old days. I had to organize the book by chapters for the various tools, including blogs, video, social networking, and so on. The truth is that all these techniques intersect and complement one another.

These online media are evolving very rapidly, and by the time you read these words, I'll no doubt have come across new techniques that I'll wish I could have put in the seventh edition. Still, I believe that the fundamentals are important, which is why Chapter 10 (where you'll start to develop your own online marketing and PR plan) is steeped in practical, commonsense thinking.

The book is organized into three parts. Part I is a rigorous overview of how the web has changed the rules of marketing and PR. Part II introduces and provides details about each of the various media. Part III contains detailed how-to information and an action plan to help you put the new rules to work for your organization.

While I think this sequence is the most logical way to present these ideas, there's no reason why you shouldn't flip from chapter to chapter in any order that you please. Unlike a mystery novel, you won't get lost in the story if you skip around. And I certainly don't want to waste your time. As I was writing, I found myself wishing that I could send you from one chapter to another chapter with hyperlinks, like on a blog. Alas, a printed book doesn't allow that, so instead I have included more old-fashioned references where I suggest you skip ahead or go back to review specific topics.

When I mention people and organizations, I frequently mention their Twitter IDs, which are preceded by the "@" sign. So if I were to reference my name and Twitter ID, you'd see it like this: David Meerman Scott @dmscott. This way, you can quickly learn more about the person or organization by checking them out on Twitter.

You'll notice that I write in a familiar and casual tone, rather than the more formal and stilted voice of many business books. That's because I'm using my "blog voice" to share the new rules with you. It's how I like to write, and I believe it also makes things easier for you, the reader.

When I use the words *company* and *organization* throughout this book, I'm including all types of organizations and individuals. Feel free to mentally insert *nonprofit*, *government agency*, *political candidate*, *church*, *school*, *sports team*, *legal firm*, or other entity in place of *company* and *organization*. Similarly, when I use the word *buyers*, I also mean subscribers, voters, volunteers, applicants, and donors, because the new rules work for reaching all these groups. Are you a leader of a nonprofit organization that needs to increase donations? The new rules apply to you as much as to a corporation. Ditto for political campaigns looking for votes, schools that want to increase applications, consultants hunting for business, and churches seeking new members.

This book will show you the new rules and how to apply them. For the people all over the world interacting on the web, the old rules of marketing and PR just don't work. Today, all kinds of organizations communicate directly with their buyers online. According to the International Telecommunications Union, an agency of the United Nations, 51.2 percent of the global population, or 3.9 billion people, were using the Internet at the end of 2018. Even more remarkably, there were 107 cell phone subscriptions for every 100 people in the world. Yes, there are more mobile phones than people in the world! So it's no surprise that, in order to reach the individuals who would be interested in their organizations, smart marketers everywhere have altered the way they think about marketing and PR.

Showcasing Success

The most exciting aspect of the book is that, throughout these pages, I have the honor of showcasing some of the best examples of building successful programs on the web. There are more than 50 profiles throughout the book, many of them featuring the marketers' own words from interviews with me. These profiles bring the concepts to life. You'll learn from people at Fortune 500 companies and at businesses with just a handful of employees. These companies make products ranging from racing bicycles to jet helicopters and from computer software to men's hair accessories. Some of the organizations are well known to the public, while others are famous only in their own market niches. I profile nonprofit organizations, political advocacy groups, and an inner city school district. I tell the stories of independent consultants, churches, rock bands, and lawyers, all of whom successfully use the web to reach their target audiences.

I can't thank enough the people who shared their time with me, on the phone and in person. I'm sure you'll agree that they are the stars of the book. My favorite part is that many of them are people who read earlier editions and shared their success with me. How cool is that? You can read this edition and be equipped to create programs that could grow your business and lead you to achievements that might inform readers of *future* editions!

As you read the stories of successful marketers, remember that you will learn from them even if they come from a very different market, industry, or type of organization from your own. Nonprofits can learn from the experiences of corporations. Consultants will gain insights from the successes of rock bands. In fact, I'm absolutely convinced that you will learn more by emulating successful ideas from outside your industry than by copying what your nearest competitor is doing. Remember, the best thing about new rules is that your competitors probably don't know about them yet.

Thank you for your interest in the new rules. I hope that you too will be successful in implementing these strategies and will improve your life as a result.

—David Meerman Scott
davidmeermanscott.com
@dmscott

How the Web Has Changed the Rules of Marketing and PR

1

The Old Rules of Marketing and PR Are Ineffective in an Online World

As I write this, I am considering buying a new car. As it is for billions of other global consumers, the web is my primary source of information when I consider a purchase. So I sat down at the computer and began poking around.

Figuring they were the natural place to begin my research, I started with some major automaker sites. That was a big mistake. I was assaulted on the homepages with a barrage of TV-style broadcast *advertising*. And most of the one-way messages focused on price. For example, at Ford, the all-capital-letters headline screamed, "YEAR END EVENT FINAL DAYS. UP to $1,500 TOTAL CASH." Dodge announced a similar offer: "BIG FINISH 2016. GET 20% OFF MSRP." Other manufacturers touted similar flashy offers.

I'm not planning to buy a car in the next 100 hours, thank you. I may not even buy one within 100 days! I'm just kicking the virtual tires. These sites and most others assume that I'm ready to buy a car *right now*. But I actually just wanted to learn something. Sure, I got graphics and animation, TV commercials, pretty pictures, and low financing offers on these sites, but little else.

I looked around for some personality on these sites and didn't find much, because the automaker websites portray their organizations as nameless, faceless corporations. In fact, the sites I looked at are so similar that they're effectively interchangeable. At each site, I felt as if I was being marketed to with a string of messages that had been developed in a lab or via focus groups. It just didn't feel authentic. If I wanted to see car TV ads, I would have flipped on the TV. I was struck with the odd feeling that all large auto-makers' sites were designed and built by the same Madison Avenue ad guy. These sites were advertising *to* me, not building a relationship *with* me. They were luring me in with one-way messages, not educating me about the companies' products. Guess what? When I arrive at a site, you don't need to grab my attention; you already have it!

Automakers have become addicted to the crack cocaine of marketing: big-budget TV commercials and other offline advertising. Everywhere I turn, I see automobile ads that make me think, "This has got to be really freakin' expensive." The television commercials, the "sponsored by" stuff, the sales "events," and other high-ticket Madison Avenue marketing might make you feel good, but is it effective?

These days, when people are thinking of buying a car (or any other product or service), they usually go to the web first. Even my 85-year-old mother does it! When people come to you online, they are not looking for TV commercials. They are looking for information to help them make a decision.

Here's the good news: I did find some terrific places on the web to learn about cars. Unfortunately, the places where I got authentic content and where I became educated and where I interacted with humans weren't part of the automakers' sites. Edmunds Forums is a free, consumer-driven, social networking and personal pages site. It features photo albums, user groups based on make and model of car, and favorite links. The site was excellent in helping me narrow down choices. For example, in the forums, I could read hundreds of messages about each car I was considering. I could see pages where owners showed off their vehicles. This is where I was making my decision, *dozens of clicks removed from the big automaker sites.*

Since I first wrote about automaker sites on my blog, hundreds of people have jumped in to comment or email me with similar car-shopping experiences and frustrations with automaker websites. And while I certainly recognize that the automakers have improved their sites since I first wrote about them, the focus is still on advertising. Something is seriously broken in the automobile business if so many people tell me they are unable to find, directly on a company site, the information they need to make a purchase decision.

But it's not just automakers.

Think about your own buying habits. Do you make purchase decisions based on your independent research, via information you find with search engines like Google? Of course you do! Do you contact your friends and colleagues via social media like Facebook and ask them about products and services you're interested in? If so, you are not alone. And yet many sellers fail to reach you in this process.

In the years before she headed to college, my daughter researched appropriate schools by searching online and connecting with her friends. Over the course of her high school years, she carefully narrowed her choices down to a handful of schools that were a good fit for her. When applications were due, she was all set.

Yet in the months leading up to the application deadline, she received hundreds of very expensive direct-mail packages from universities around the world. Many sent large, thick envelopes containing glossy brochures with hundreds of pages. These efforts were completely wasted, because my daughter had already made up her mind by doing her own research on the web. This huge investment in direct-mail advertising simply didn't work.

> Before the web, organizations had only two significant options for attracting attention: Buy expensive advertising or get third-party ink from the media. But the web has changed the rules. The web is not TV. Organizations that understand the New Rules of Marketing and PR develop relationships directly with consumers like you and me.

I'd like to pause here a moment for a clarification. When I talk about the new rules and compare them to the old rules, I don't mean to suggest that all organizations should immediately drop their existing marketing and PR programs and use this book's ideas exclusively. Moreover, I'm not of the belief that the only marketing worth doing is on the web. If your newspaper advertisements, telephone directory listings, media outreach, and other programs are working for you, that's great! Please keep going. There is room in many marketing and PR programs for traditional techniques.

That being said, there's no doubt that today people solve problems by turning to the web. I'm sure you do too. Just reflect on your own habits as you contemplate a purchase.

Consider another form of marketing, the art of finding a new job. Several times per month, I receive email or phone calls from people who are searching for work. They usually send their resume (CV) to me and want to network with me to find a job. What these people are doing is advertising a product (their labor) by sending me an unsolicited email message. Like the auto companies and the universities, the typical job seeker is advertising a product. Yet the vast majority of these people are not positioning themselves to be found on the web, because they don't have a personal website, they aren't blogging or creating online videos, and, except for maybe a Facebook or LinkedIn profile, they aren't active in social networking. They are not creating the content that will help an employer to find them when a company needs new staff.

If you aren't present and engaged in the places and at the times that your buyers are, then you're losing out on potential business—no matter whether you're looking for a job or marketing your company's product or your organization's service. Worse, if you are trying to apply the game plan that works in your mainstream-media-based advertising and public relations (PR) programs to your online efforts, you will not be successful.

So take a minute to ask yourself this simple question: *How are my existing advertising and media relations programs working?*

Advertising: A Money Pit of Wasted Resources

In the old days, traditional, nontargeted advertising via newspapers, magazines, radio, television, and direct mail was the only way to go. But these media make it very difficult to target specific buyers with individualized content. Yes, advertising is still used for megabrands with broad reach and probably still works for some organizations and products (though not as well as before). Guys watching football on TV drink a lot of beer, so perhaps it makes sense for mass marketer Budweiser to advertise on NFL broadcasts (but not for small microbrews that appeal to a small niche customer base to do so). Advertising also works in many trade publications. If your company makes deck sealant, then you probably want to advertise in *Professional Deck Builder* magazine to reach your buyers (but that won't allow you to reach the do-it-yourself market). If you run a local real estate agency in a smaller community, it might make sense to do a direct mailing to all of the homeowners there (but that won't let you reach people who might be planning to move to your community from another location).

However, for millions of other organizations—for those of us who are professionals, musicians, artists, nonprofit organizations, churches, and niche product companies—traditional advertising is generally so wide and broad that it is ineffective. A great strategy for Procter & Gamble, Disney, and a U.S. presidential candidate—reaching large numbers of people with a message of broad national appeal—just doesn't work for niche products, local services, and specialized nonprofit organizations.

> The web has opened a tremendous opportunity to reach niche buyers directly with targeted information that costs a fraction of what big-budget advertising costs.

One-Way Interruption Marketing Is Yesterday's Message

A primary technique of what Seth Godin calls the TV-industrial complex is interruption. Under this system, advertising agency creative people sit in hip offices dreaming up ways to interrupt people so that they pay attention to a one-way message. Think about it: You're watching your favorite TV show, so the advertiser's job is to craft a commercial to get you to pay attention, when you'd really rather be doing something else, like quickly grabbing some ice cream before the show resumes. You're reading an interesting article in a magazine, so the ads need to jolt you into reading an ad instead of the article. Or you're flying on American Airlines (which I do frequently), and during the flight, the airline deems it important to interrupt your nap with a loud advertisement announcing its credit card offer. The goal in each of these examples is to get people to stop what they are doing and pay attention to a message.

Moreover, the messages in advertising are product-focused, one-way spin. Advertisers can no longer break through with dumbed-down broadcasts about their wonderful products. The average person now sees hundreds of seller-spun commercial messages per day. People just don't trust them. We turn them off in our minds, if we notice them at all.

> The web is different. Instead of one-way interruption, web marketing is about delivering useful content at just the precise moment a buyer needs it. It's about interaction, information, education, and choice.

Before the web, good advertising people were well versed in the tools and techniques of reaching broad markets with lowest-common-denominator messages via interruption techniques. Advertising was about great "creative work." Unfortunately, many companies rooted in these old ways desperately want the web to be like TV, because they understand how TV advertising works. Advertising agencies that excel in creative TV ads simply believe they can transfer their skills to the web.

They are wrong. They are following outdated rules.

The Old Rules of Marketing

- Marketing simply meant advertising (and branding).
- Advertising needed to appeal to the masses.
- Advertising relied on interrupting people to get them to pay attention to a message.
- Advertising was one-way: company to consumer.
- Advertising was exclusively about selling products.
- Advertising was based on campaigns that had a limited life.
- Creativity was deemed the most important component of advertising.
- It was more important for the ad agency to win advertising awards than for the client to win new customers.
- Advertising and PR were separate disciplines run by different people with separate goals, strategies, and measurement criteria.

> None of this is true anymore. The web has transformed the rules, and you must transform your marketing to make the most of the web-enabled marketplace of ideas.

Public Relations Used to Be Exclusively about the Media

For nearly a decade, I was a contributing editor at *EContent* magazine. I occasionally write for the *HuffPost*, contribute guest articles to many other publications, and maintain a popular blog. As a result, I receive hundreds of broadcast email press releases and pitches per month from well-meaning PR people who want me to write about their products and services. Guess what? In 10 years, I have *never* written about a company because of a non-targeted broadcast press release or pitch that somebody sent me. Think about that: tens of thousands of press releases and pitches; zero stories.

Discussions I've had with journalists in other industries confirm that I'm not the only one who doesn't use unsolicited press releases. Instead, I think about a subject that I want to write about, and I check out what I can find on blogs, on Twitter, and through search engines. If I find a press release on the subject through Google or a company's online media room, great! But I don't wait for press releases to come to me. Rather, I go looking for interesting topics, products, people, and companies. And when I do feel ready to write a story, I might try out a concept on my blog first, to see how it flies. Does anyone comment on it? Do any PR people jump in and email me?

Here's another amazing figure: In more than 10 years, only a tiny number of PR people have commented on my blog or reached out to me as a result of a blog post or a story I've written in a magazine. How difficult can it be to read the blogs and Twitter feeds of the reporters you're trying to pitch? It teaches you precisely what interests them. Then you can email them with something interesting that they are likely to write about rather than spamming them with unsolicited press releases. When I don't want to be bothered, I get hundreds of press releases a month. But when I do want feedback and conversation, I get silence.

Something's very wrong in PR land.

> Reporters and editors use the web to seek out interesting stories, people, and companies. Will they find you?

Public Relations and Third-Party Ink ═══

Public relations was once an exclusive club. PR people used lots of jargon and followed strict rules. If you weren't part of the in crowd, PR seemed like an esoteric and mysterious job that required lots of training, sort of like being an astronaut or a court stenographer. PR people occupied their time by writing press releases targeted exclusively to reporters and editors and by schmoozing with those same reporters and editors. And then they crossed their fingers and hoped that the media would give them some ink or some airtime ("Oh, please write about me!"). The end result of their efforts—the ultimate goal of PR in the old days—was the press clip, which proved they had done their job.

Only the best PR people had personal relationships with the media and could pick up the phone and pitch a story to the reporter for whom they had bought lunch the month before.

Prior to 1995, outside of paying big bucks for advertising or working with the media, there just weren't any significant options for a company to tell its story to the world.

> The web has changed the rules. Today, organizations are communicating directly with buyers.

Yes, the Media Are Still Important ═══

Allow me to pause again for a moment to say that the mainstream and trade media are still important components of a great public relations program. On my blog and on the speaking circuit, I've sometimes been accused of suggesting that the media are no longer relevant. That is not my position. The media are critically important for many organizations. A positive story in *Rolling Stone* propels a rock band to fame. An article in the *Wall Street Journal* brands a company as a player. A consumer product talked about on the *Today* show gets noticed. In many niche markets and vertical industries, trade magazines and journals help decide which companies are important. However, I do believe that, while all these outlets are important aspects of a larger PR program, there are easier and more efficient ways to reach your buyers. And here's something really neat: If you do a good job of telling your story directly, the media will find out. And then they will write about you!

Public relations work has changed. PR is no longer just an esoteric discipline where companies make great efforts to communicate exclusively to a handful of reporters who then tell the company's story, generating a clip for the PR people to show their bosses. These days, great PR includes programs to reach buyers directly. The web allows direct access to information about your products, and smart companies understand and use this phenomenal resource to great advantage.

> The Internet has made public relations public again, after years of almost exclusive focus on media. Blogs, online video, news releases, and other forms of web content let organizations communicate directly with buyers.

Press Releases and the Journalistic Black Hole

In the old days, a press release was actually a release to the press, so these documents evolved as an esoteric and stylized way for companies to issue their "news" to reporters and editors. Because it was assumed that nobody saw the actual press release except a handful of reporters and editors, these documents were written with the media's existing understanding in mind.

In a typical case, a tiny audience of several dozen media people got a steady stream of product releases from a company. The reporters and editors were already well versed on the niche market, so the company supplied very little background information. Jargon was rampant. *What's the news?* journalists would think as they perused the release. *Oh, here it is—the company just announced the Super Techno Widget Plus with a New Scalable and Robust Architecture.* While this might mean something to a trade magazine journalist, it is just plain gobbledygook to the rest of the world. Since press releases are now seen by millions of people who are searching the web for solutions to their problems, these old rules are obsolete.

The Old Rules of PR

- The only way to get ink and airtime was through the media.
- Companies communicated to journalists via press releases.
- Nobody saw the actual press release except a handful of reporters and editors.
- Companies had to have significant news before they were allowed to write a press release.
- Jargon was okay because the journalists all understood it.
- You weren't supposed to send a release unless it included quotes from third parties, such as customers, analysts, and experts.
- The only way buyers would learn about the press release's content was if the media wrote a story about it.
- The only way to measure the effectiveness of press releases was through clip books, which noted each time the media deigned to pick up a company's release.
- PR and marketing were separate disciplines run by different people with separate goals, strategies, and measurement techniques.

> The web has transformed the rules, and you must transform your PR strategies to make the most of the web-enabled marketplace of ideas.

The vast majority of organizations don't have instant access to mainstream media for coverage of their products. People like you and me need to work hard to be noticed in the online marketplace of ideas. By understanding how the role of PR and the press release has changed, we can get our stories known in that marketplace.

There are some exceptions. Very large companies, very famous people, and governments might all still be able to get away with using the media exclusively, but even that is doubtful. These name-brand people and companies may be big enough, and their news just so compelling, that no effort is required of them. For these lucky few, the media may still be the primary mouthpiece.

- If you are J. K. Rowling and you issue a press release about a new book, the news will be picked up by the media.
- If Apple Computer CEO Tim Cook announces the company's new iPhone, the news will be picked up by the media.
- If the president of the United States announces a pick to fill a vacancy on the U.S. Supreme Court, the news will be picked up by the media.

If you are smaller and less famous but have an interesting story to tell, you need to tell it yourself. Fortunately, the web is a terrific place to do so.

Learn to Ignore the Old Rules

To harness the power of the web to reach buyers directly, you must ignore the old rules. Public relations is not just about speaking through the media, although the media remain an important component. Marketing is not just about one-way broadcast advertising, although advertising can be part of an overall strategy.

I've noticed that some marketing and PR professionals have a very difficult time changing old habits. These new ideas make people uncomfortable. When I speak at conferences, people sometimes fold their arms in a defensive posture and look down at their shoes. Naturally, marketing and PR people who learned the old rules resist the new world of direct access. It means that to be successful, they need to learn new skills. And change is not easy.

But I've also noticed that many enlightened marketing executives, CEOs, entrepreneurs, nonprofit executives, and professionals jump at the chance to tell their stories directly. These people love the new way of communicating with buyers and are eager to learn. Smart marketers are bringing success to their organizations each and every day by communicating through the web.

Here's how to tell if the new rules are right for you. Consider your goals for communicating via marketing and public relations. Are you buying that Super Bowl ad to score great tickets to the game? Are you designing a creative magazine ad to win an award for your agency? Do you hope to create a book of press clips from mainstream media outlets to show to your bosses? Does your CEO want to be on TV? If the answers to these questions are yes, then the new rules (and this book) are not for you.

However, if you're like millions of smart marketers and entrepreneurs whose goal is to communicate with buyers directly, then read on. If you're working to make your organization more visible online, then read on. If you want to drive people into your company's sales process so they actually buy something (or apply or donate or join or submit their names as leads), then read on. I wrote this book especially for you.

2 The New Rules of Marketing and PR

My wife, Yukari, was checking out her Twitter stream one day and noticed that someone she follows tweeted about Hotel & Igloo Village Kakslauttanen. Yukari clicked the link and learned that the resort is located in the Saariselkä Fell area of Lapland in northern Finland. In winter, you can stay there in a private glass igloo, which means that from bed you can check out the stars (or, if you are lucky, the aurora borealis). She found this terribly exciting, so she tweeted a response from her Twitter ID, @yukariwatanabe: "I want to go there!"

We discussed the resort that evening over dinner. Why not go? Our daughter was off to university, so we had the time. The next day we booked the trip for several months later. Done deal.

Now, I know that a winter vacation above the Arctic Circle might seem like a punch line to a bad joke. Heck, the sun didn't even rise when we were there in mid-December (the "day" consists of just four hours of twilight at that time of year). But for us it seemed perfect, because we've traveled all over the world and are always looking for unusual adventures.

How did we know that we wanted to go? By the resort's website, of course. The site lists all sorts of winter activities for guests. When I saw "Husky Sledding Safari," I was ready to pack my bags (bucket list . . .). But Yukari wanted to do a little more checking, so she Googled the resort, looked at the reviews on TripAdvisor, and also read about it in a *New York Times* article.

Everybody I know has a story like this. Somebody makes a comment via a social network site. It leads someone else to a website where the content educates and informs. And that person ends up becoming a customer of a company that he or she had never heard of moments before. We're living in a new world of marketing and PR.

If you are the seller in this transaction, it all comes down to content: What are you creating, compared to what others are saying about you?

You're in control. You create the content. You bring in the business.

Our time in Lapland was amazing. We had all kinds of wonderful adventures. The dogsledding was especially fun, because I got to drive (well, more like hang on). And we never would have had this amazing experience if the Hotel & Igloo Village Kakslauttanen only marketed their property using the old rules. We never would have heard about it.

The Most Important Communications Revolution in Human History

I'd like to step way back and look at the big picture. This is not a view, to use the cliché, from 30,000 feet. It's more like the view from the moon. The new rules of marketing and public relations are part of the much bigger and more important communications revolution we're currently living through—the most important communications revolution in human history.

Johannes Gutenberg's invention of printing with mechanical movable type (circa 1439) was the second most important communications breakthrough in history. It meant books could be mass-produced, rather than painstakingly copied by hand. It meant ordinary people could refer to things in books, like laws. These used to have to be committed to memory.

The printing press created the first important communications revolution by freeing people's minds from memorization and allowing them to use that extra brainpower to be creative. At the same time, this first communications revolution (which took many decades) helped large numbers of people become literate and raised living standards along the way. It brought humanity out of the medieval period and into the Renaissance.

Some 556 years later, in 1995, an even more important communications revolution began. I choose 1995 because it was the year that Netscape went public on the success of Netscape Navigator, the first popular product to allow easy web browsing.

We're fortunate to be living in this time in history, the time of another important communications revolution. I figure we're about halfway through it. The first 25 years or so were fast-paced, and things changed very quickly. Usage went from a few million people online to billions. But many organizations still aren't communicating in real time on the web.

The next few decades will bring a continuation of the revolution. The pace of that change means that I need to update this book every few years. Soon, this seventh edition will be replaced by the eighth. And then the ninth. We need to be constantly learning and updating our skills to reach buyers as they're looking for the products and services we sell.

Are you one of the revolutionaries? Or do you support the old regime? Are you marketing your product or service like Hotel & Igloo Village Kakslauttanen? Or are you failing to produce content that will do well in the search engines and social networks? For your sake, I hope it's the former— or soon will be with the help of this book.

Open for Business

Gerard Vroomen will tell you that he is an engineer, not a marketer. He will tell you that the companies he co-founded, Cervélo Cycles and Open Cycle (aka OPEN), do not have any marketing experts. But Vroomen is wrong. Why? Because he is obsessed with the buyers of racing bikes from Cervélo and mountain bikes from OPEN. And he's obsessed with the engineering-driven products he offers them.

Cervélo Cycles, which Vroomen sold in 2011 but for which he remains an advisor, is a Canadian manufacturer of racing bicycle frames. He focused Cervélo to help his customers win races—and they do. In the 2005 Tour de France, David Zabriskie rode the fastest time trial in the race's history on a Cervélo P3C at an average speed of 54.676 kph (33.954 mph). The winner of the 2008 Tour de France, Carlos Sastre, did so on a Cervélo. And at the three most recent Olympics, Cervélo bikes were ridden by dozens of athletes, resulting in multiple gold, silver, and bronze medals. Besides building excellent bikes, Vroomen also excels at using the web to tell cycling enthusiasts compelling stories, to educate them, to engage them in conversation, and to entertain them. Vroomen is a terrific marketer because he uses web content in interesting ways and sells a bunch of bikes in the process.

"In marketing, if the point is for our company to get noticed, we can't do it the same as everybody else," Vroomen says. "A big part of that is to do something unexpected and being remarkable. For example, we were the first to blog at the Tour de France and the first to do video there."

The Cervélo site works extremely well because it includes perfect content for visitors who are ready to buy a bike and also for people who are just browsing. The content is valuable and authentic compared to the marketing messages that appear on so many other sites. "Our goal is education," Vroomen says. "We have a technical product, and we're the most engineering-driven company in the industry. Most bike companies don't employ a single engineer, and Cervélo has eight. So we want to have that engineering focus stand out with the content on the site. We don't sell on the newest paint job. So on the site, we're not spending our time creating fluff. Instead, we have a good set of content."

Ryan Patch is an amateur triathlon competitor on the Vortex Racing team—just the sort of customer Cervélo wants to reach. "On the Cervélo site, I learned that Bobby Julich rides the same bike that is available to me," Patch says. "And it's not just that they are riding, but they are doing really well. I can see how someone won the Giro de Italia on a Cervélo. That's mind-blowing, that I can get the same bike that the pros are riding. I can ride the same gear. Cervélo has as much street cred as you can have with shaved legs."

Patch says that if you're looking to buy a new bike, if you are a hard-core consumer, then there is a great deal of detailed information on the Cervélo site about the bikes' technology, construction, and specs. "What I really like about this website is how it gives off the aura of legitimacy, being based in fact, not fluff," he says.

Search engine marketing is important for Cervélo. Because of the keyword-rich cycling content available on the site, Vroomen says, Cervélo gets the same amount of search engine traffic as many sites for bike companies that are 10 times larger. As a result, Cervélo has grown quickly into one of the most important bike companies in the world.

In 2011, Vroomen shifted gears and now spends the majority of his time at Open Cycle, the mountain bike company he co-founded with Andy Kessler and launched in mid-2012. Now OPEN sells via over 100 stores in dozens of countries, its own office/showroom in Basel, and an online store. He took to heart what he learned at Cervélo, making every aspect of the company "open" to customers. Right from the start, OPEN focused on social engagement throughout the site, with community aspects and social networking links. Anyone can comment on anything.

The OPEN site also features a blog. What's interesting is that Vroomen and Kessler had been blogging for a year as they secretly developed the technology for their new bike, but the blog posts went unpublished until launch. "We talk not only about the product but also about how we're running the company," Vroomen says. "So a part of that was publishing that blog after we launched, so people could see what we'd been doing the year leading up to us becoming visible."

Vroomen is committed to having the community of enthusiasts help them, and that's a big reason why they chose the name Open Cycle. "Every page on the site has a question and answer section at the bottom," he says. "So it's very easy, as soon as you've read something, to say, 'Hey, I don't quite understand this.' We answer all of those as soon as we can, time zone permitting, but certainly within a day, usually sooner. People see that when they ask something, they actually get a response. But the crazy part is that consumers don't expect it. So we said, 'How about if we ask people to talk to us, and we respond?' That's the basic premise of OPEN."

The company's use of questions and answers on every page of the OPEN site, the comment feature on the OPEN blog, and social networks like Instagram (@opencycle has 40,000+ followers) serves as a terrific way to market the new company. "I don't think of it as marketing," Vroomen says. "It feels simply like talking to people. And networks like Facebook, Twitter, et al. have given us some interesting ways to do that. They turn companies such as Open Cycle into the global version of the village baker of yesteryear. You know your customers and they know you, so you want to treat them well. You want to give them good quality, and they tell their neighbors. That's the opposite of what's happening at many companies today. And, of course, the flip side is that if you don't treat them well they'll tell the rest of the village."

All signs point to OPEN being on a trajectory to replicate the tremendous success of Cervélo—with the site, the blog, and social networking leading the way forward. And that's no coincidence. As Vroomen would tell you, the ideas you'll read about in this book work.

"This is the future for companies like us," Vroomen says. "You can be very small and occupy a niche and still sell your products all over the world. It's amazing, when we go into a new country, the amount of name recognition we have. The Internet gives you opportunities you never had before. And it's not rocket science. It's pretty easy to figure out."

The Long Tail of Marketing

The theory of the long tail as popularized by Chris Anderson in his book of the same name is that our culture and economy are increasingly shifting away from a focus on a relatively small number of major hits (mainstream products and markets) at the head of the demand curve and toward a huge number of niches in the tail. As the costs of production and distribution fall, especially online, there is now less need to lump products and consumers into one-size-fits-all containers. In an era without the constraints of physical shelf space and other bottlenecks of distribution, narrowly targeted goods and services can be as economically attractive as mainstream fare.

Some of today's most successful Internet businesses leverage the long tail to reach underserved customers and satisfy demand for products not found in traditional physical stores. Examples include Amazon, which makes available at the click of a mouse hundreds of thousands of books and other products not stocked in local chain stores; Spotify and other services that legally bring niche music not found in record stores to people who crave artists outside the mainstream; and Netflix, which exploited the long tail of demand for movie rentals beyond the blockbuster hits found at the local DVD rental shop. The business implications of the long tail are profound and illustrate that there's much money to be made by creating and distributing at the long end of the tail. Yes, big hits are still important. But as these businesses have shown, there's a huge market beyond the latest *Batman* movie, U2, Taylor Swift, and *Top Gear*.

So, what about marketing? While Anderson's book focuses on product availability and selling models on the web, the concepts apply equally well to marketing. There's no doubt that there is a long-tail market for web content created by organizations of all kinds—corporations, nonprofits, churches, schools, individuals, rock bands—and used for directly reaching buyers—those who buy, donate, join, apply. As consumers search the Internet for answers to their problems, as they browse blogs and chat rooms and websites for ideas, they are searching for what organizations like yours have to offer. Unlike in the days of the old rules of interruption marketing with a mainstream message, today's consumers are looking for just the right product or service to satisfy their unique desires at the precise moment they are online. People are looking for what you have to offer right now.

> Marketers must shift their thinking away from the short head of the demand curve—mainstream marketing to the masses—and toward the long tail—a strategy of targeting vast numbers of underserved audiences via the web.

As marketers understand the web as a place to reach millions of micro-markets with precise messages just at the point of consumption, the way they create web content changes dramatically. Instead of a one-size-fits-all website with a mass-market message, we need to create just-right content—each aimed at a narrow target constituency. As marketing case studies, the examples of Netflix, Amazon, and Spotify are also fascinating. The techniques pioneered by the leaders of long-tail retail for reaching customers with niche interests are examples of marketing genius.

Tell Me Something I Don't Know, Please

Amazon.com has been optimized for browsing. At a broad level, there are just two ways that people interact with web content: They search and they browse. Most organizations optimize sites for searching, which helps people answer their questions but doesn't encourage them to browse. But people also want a site to tell them something they didn't think to ask. The marketers at Amazon understand that when people browse the site, they may have a general idea of what they want (in my case, perhaps a book for my daughter about surfing) but not the particular title. So if I start with a search on Amazon for the phrase "surfing for beginners," I get 99 titles in the search results. With this list as a starting point, I shift into browse mode, which is where Amazon excels. Each title has a customer ranking where I instantly see how other customers rated the book. I see reader-generated reviews, together with reviews from other media. I can see "Customers who bought this item also bought" lists and also rankings of "What other items do customers buy after viewing this item?" I can poke around the contents of the book itself. After I purchase the perfect book for my daughter (*The Girl's Guide to Surfing*), I might get an email from Amazon weeks or months later, suggesting, based on this purchase, another book that I might find useful. This is brilliant stuff.

The site is designed to work for a major and often-ignored audience: people who do their own research and consider a decision over a period of time before making a commitment. Smart marketers, like the folks at Amazon and Cervélo, unlike those at the Big Three automakers we saw in Chapter 1, know that the most effective web strategies anticipate needs and provide content to meet them, even before people know to ask.

Marketing on the web is not about generic banner ads designed to trick people with neon color or wacky movement. It is about understanding the keywords and phrases that our buyers are using, and creating the content that they seek.

Bricks-and-Mortar News

The new rules are just as important for public relations. In fact, I think that online content in all of its forms is causing a convergence of marketing and PR that does not really exist offline. When your buyer is on the web browsing for something, content is content in all of its manifestations. And in an interconnected web world, content drives action.

I often hear people claim that online content such as blogs, photos, and infographics doesn't work as a marketing strategy for traditional bricks-and-mortar industries. But I've always disagreed. Great content brands an organization as a trusted resource and calls people to action—to buy, subscribe, apply, or donate. And great content means that interested people return again and again. As a result, the organization succeeds, achieving goals such as adding revenue, building traffic, gaining donations, or generating sales leads.

For instance, The Concrete Network provides information about residential concrete products and services and helps buyers and sellers connect with each other. The company targets consumers and builders who might want to plan and build a concrete patio, pool deck, or driveway—this audience makes up the business-to-consumer (B2C) component of The Concrete Network—as well as the concrete contractors who make up the business-to-business (B2B) component. The Concrete Network's Find a Contractor service links homeowners and builders who need a project done with contractors who specialize in several dozen different services located in hundreds of metropolitan areas in the United States, Canada, and Australia. The company's web content drives business for The Concrete Network. Yes, ladies and gentlemen, web content sells concrete! (You can't get any more bricks-and-mortar than, well, mortar.)

"The new rules of PR are that anybody who wants to be the leader has to have news coming out," says Jim Peterson, president of The Concrete Network. The company's ongoing marketing and PR program includes a series of articles on the site; free online catalogs for categories such as countertops, pool decks, patios, and driveways; and photo galleries for potential customers to check out what is available. As a result of all of the terrific content, The Concrete Network gets more than 10 times the traffic of any other site in the concrete industry, according to Peterson. An important component of the site's content is the beautiful photos drawn from "Earth's largest collection of decorative concrete photos." For example, there are dozens of photos of just concrete patios.

As president of The Concrete Network, Peterson is that rare executive who understands the power of content marketing, search engine optimization, and images to reach buyers directly and drive business. What is his advice to other company presidents and CEOs? "Every business has information that can contribute to the education of the marketplace. You need to ask yourself, 'How can I get that information out there?' You have to have a bit longer view and have a sense of how your business will be better down the line. For example, we created an entire series of buyer guides, because we knew that they would be valuable to the market. You need to think about how it will benefit your business and then commit to it, understanding that nothing is an overnight thing."

Peterson also suggests getting help from an expert to get started with a program. "Don't sit there and leave this [as] just a part of your list of good intentions," he says. "Businesses will live or die on original content. If you are creating truly useful content for customers, you're going to be seen in a great light and with a great spirit—you're setting the table for new business. But the vast majority of businesses don't seem to care. At The Concrete Network, we're on a mission. Get down to the essence of what your product solves and write good stories about that and publish them online."

You've got to love it. If content sells concrete, content can sell what you have to offer, too!

The Long Tail of PR

In PR, it's not about clip books. It's about reaching our buyers.

I was vice president of marketing and PR for two publicly traded companies, and I've done it the old way. It doesn't work anymore. But the new rules do work—really well.

Instead of spending tens of thousands of dollars per month on a media relations program that tries to convince a handful of reporters at select magazines, newspapers, and TV stations to cover us, we should be targeting the plugged-in bloggers, online news sites, micropublications, public speakers, analysts, and consultants who reach the targeted audiences who are looking for what we have to offer. Better yet, we no longer even need to wait for someone with a media voice to write about us at all. With social media, we communicate directly with our audience, bypassing the media filter completely. We have the power to create our own media brand in the niche of our own choosing. It's about being found on Google, Yahoo!, Bing, and niche content sites. Instead of writing press releases only when we have big news—releases that reach just a handful of journalists—we should be using techniques like newsjacking that highlight our expert ideas and stories. You will learn about newsjacking in Chapter 21.

To succeed in long-tail marketing and PR, we need to adopt different criteria for success. In the book world, everyone used to say, "If I can only get on *Oprah*, I'll be a success." Sure, I would have liked to be on *The Oprah Winfrey Show*, too. But instead of focusing countless (and probably fruitless) hours on a potential blockbuster of a TV appearance, wouldn't it be a better strategy to have lots of people reviewing your book in smaller publications that reach the specific audiences who buy books like yours? Oprah was a long shot, but right now bloggers would love to hear from you. Oprah ignored 100 books a day, but bloggers run to their mailboxes to see what interesting things might be in there. Sure, it would be great to have your business profiled in *Fortune* or the *Financial Times*. But instead of putting all of your public relations efforts into that one potential PR blockbuster (a mention in the major business press), wouldn't it be better to get dozens of the most influential bloggers and analysts to tell your story directly to the niche markets that are looking for what you have to offer?

The New Rules of Marketing and PR

If you've been nodding your head excitedly while reading about what some of these companies are up to, then the new rules are for you. In the next chapter, I offer interesting case studies of companies that have been successful with the new rules. In each case example, I've interviewed a particular person from that organization so we can learn directly from them. Following are chapters on specific areas of online content (such as blogging, online video, and social networking) and then more detailed how-to chapters. But before we move on, let me explicitly state the new rules of marketing and PR that we'll discuss throughout the rest of the book:

- Marketing is more than just advertising.
- PR is for more than just a mainstream media audience.
- You are what you publish.
- People want authenticity, not spin.
- People want participation, not propaganda.
- Instead of causing one-way interruption, marketing is about delivering content at just the precise moment your audience needs it.
- Marketers must shift their thinking from mainstream marketing to the masses to a strategy of reaching vast numbers of underserved audiences via the web.
- PR is not about your boss seeing your company on TV. It's about your buyers seeing your company on the web.
- Marketing is not about your agency winning awards. It's about your organization winning business.
- The Internet has made public relations public again, after years of almost exclusive focus on media.
- Companies must drive people into the purchasing process with great online content.
- Blogs, online video, e-books, news releases, and other forms of online content let organizations communicate directly with buyers in a form they appreciate.
- Buyers want information in language they understand, not gobbledygook-laden jargon.
- Social networks like Twitter, Facebook, and LinkedIn allow people all over the world to share content and connect with the people and companies they do business with.
- In our always-on world, buyers expect instant, 24/7 communications.
- On the web, the lines between marketing and PR (and sales and service, too) have blurred.

The Convergence of Marketing and PR on the Web

As I originally wrote this list and edited it down, I was struck by how important one particular concept was to any successful online strategy to reach buyers directly: This concept is the convergence of marketing and PR. In an offline world, marketing and PR are separate departments with different people and different skill sets, but this is not the case on the web. What's the difference between what Amazon, Spotify, and Netflix are doing to reach customers via online marketing and what The Concrete Network does? There's not much difference. How is the news that Open Cycle creates itself and posts on the site different from a story on *Bicycling* magazine's website? It isn't. And when a buyer is researching your product category by using a search engine, does it really matter if the first exposure is a hit on your website, a news release your organization sent, a magazine article, or a post on your blog? I'd argue that it doesn't matter. Whereas I presented two separate lists for The Old Rules of Marketing and The Old Rules of PR, now there is just one set of rules: The New Rules of Marketing and PR. Great content in all forms helps buyers see that you and your organization get it. Content drives action.

3

Reaching Your Buyers Directly

The frustration of relying exclusively on the media and expensive advertising to deliver your organization's story is long gone. Yes, mainstream media are still important, but today smart marketers craft compelling information and tell the world directly via the web. The tremendous expense of relying on advertising to convince buyers to pay attention to your organization, ideas, products, and services is yesterday's headache.

Chip McDermott founded ZeroTrash as a nonprofit organization to rid the streets and beaches of Laguna Beach, California, of trash. Population and tourism had exploded, and the city had not kept up in providing sufficient infrastructure for public trash collecting and recycling. McDermott used the web to rally the community with a grassroots movement.

"The spark of the idea was that trash was becoming commonplace on the streets and the sidewalks of Laguna Beach," McDermott says. "We started to tackle the problem with a Facebook page for ZeroTrash Laguna and quickly built it to hundreds of members."

People use the ZeroTrash Facebook page to organize events and to connect local store owners with residents. Facebook was instrumental in launching the ZeroTrash First Saturday movement, where store owners and volunteers walk the city and pick up trash on the first Saturday of each month. The store owners love it because people support local stores and keep the shopping areas clean. In turn, McDermott has tapped store owners as sponsors who fund the purchase of supplies and tools like trash pickers, trash bags, T-shirts, and gloves.

Facebook serves to keep people updated about what ZeroTrash is up to. For example, on a recent First Saturday, the Laguna Beach community helped to remove another 590 pounds of trash and 375 pounds of recyclables from the streets; McDermott used the social media sites to report these totals to interested people.

After the initial success in Laguna Beach, ZeroTrash now also serves Newport Beach and Dana Point in Southern California and Chico in Northern California, and is launching in Seattle, Washington, soon. "We want people to take individual ownership of each new local ZeroTrash community," he says. "How can they get people with a passion to take control and start in their own communities? The obvious answer is to use social media to influence people."

There's no doubt that getting the word out about an idea, a product, or a service is much simpler when you can rely on social media sites like blogs, Facebook, and Twitter. The web allows any organization (including nonprofits like ZeroTrash, as well as companies large and small, government agencies, and schools) and any individual (including candidates for public office, artists, and even job seekers) to reach buyers directly. This power is clear to nearly everyone these days, but many executives and entrepreneurs still struggle to find the right mix of traditional advertising and direct communication with buyers.

The Right Marketing in a Wired World

Century 21 Real Estate LLC is the franchisor of the world's largest residential real estate sales organization, an industry giant with approximately 8,000 offices in 45 countries. The company had been spending on television advertising for years but, in a significant strategy change, pulled its national television advertising and invested those resources into online marketing.

Wow! I've seen Century 21 TV ads for years. We're talking millions of dollars shifting from TV to the web. This is a big deal.

"We are moving our advertising investments to the mediums that have the greatest relevance to our target buyers and sellers, and to where the return on our investment is most significant," says Bev Thorne, chief marketing officer at Century 21. "We found that our online investments provided a return that was substantively higher than our more traditional TV media investments."

Thorne and her team learned that people who are in the market to buy or sell a home rely heavily on the web and that the closer they get to a real estate transaction, the more they use online resources. "We are embracing LinkedIn, Facebook, Twitter, ActiveRain, and others," Thorne says. "YouTube is a central component of our activities, and we seek to utilize it even more."

Many companies spending large amounts of money on television advertising (and other offline marketing such as direct mail, magazine and newspaper advertising, and Yellow Pages listings) are afraid to make even partial moves away from their comfort zones and into online marketing and social media. But the evidence describing how people actually research products overwhelmingly suggests that companies must tell their stories and spread their ideas online, at the precise moment that potential buyers are searching for answers.

It's an exciting time to be a marketer, no matter what business you're in. We have been liberated from relying exclusively on buying access through advertising or convincing mainstream media to talk us up. Now we can publish information on the web that people are eager to pay attention to.

Let the World Know about Your Expertise

All people and organizations possess the power to elevate themselves on the web to a position of importance. In the new e-marketplace of ideas, organizations highlight their expertise in online media that focus on buyers' needs. The web allows organizations to deliver the right information to buyers, right at the point when they are most receptive to the information. The tools at our disposal as marketers are web-based media to deliver our own thoughtful and informative content via websites, blogs, e-books, white papers, images, photos, audio content, video, and even things like product placement, games, and virtual reality. We also have the ability to interact and participate in conversations that other people begin on social media sites like Twitter, blogs, chat rooms, and forums. What links all of these techniques together is that organizations of all types behave like *publishers*, creating content that people are eager to consume. Organizations gain credibility and loyalty with buyers through content, and smart marketers now think and act like publishers in order to create and deliver content targeted directly at their audience.

The Lodge at Chaa Creek, an eco-resort on a 265-acre rain-forest reserve in western Belize in Central America, is a publisher of valuable content about rain-forest wildlife, nearby destinations such as ancient Mayan cities, and the country of Belize itself. This content marketing effort helps the Lodge at Chaa Creek achieve high search engine rankings for many important phrases associated with travel to Belize. This work generates a remarkable 80 percent of new business for the lodge. Its story is among the best I know for learning how content drives business.

As anyone who has built a website knows, there is much more to think about than just the content. Design, color, navigation, and appropriate technology are all important aspects of a good website. Unfortunately, these other concerns often dominate. Why is that? I think it's easier to focus on a site's design or technology than on its content.

The global hotel chains fall into this trap: big-budget design and poor content. If you visit the sites of any of the majors (Hilton, Starwood, Marriott, etc.), you'll notice they all look the same. The content is all created by corporate headquarters, so individual property pages rarely contain original content about the location of each hotel. The result is that most hotel sites are just big brochures that pull product features like room types and food offerings from a global database.

The Lodge at Chaa Creek's website couldn't be more different. The team behind it includes co-owner Lucy Fleming, who oversees marketing; Australia-based writer and former newspaper editor Mark Langan, who creates most of the written content; and an on-site marketer who focuses on social media and search engine optimization. The team researches what people are searching on—terms like "Belize honeymoon" and "Belize all-inclusive vacation"—and then works to craft content for the Lodge at Chaa Creek's site, as well as its Belize Travel Blog. The goal is to offer content that is valuable for those researching a Belize vacation, content that will be ranked highly in the search engines.

Can you see what's happening here? Somebody goes to Google and wants to learn about bird-watching in Belize. And because the content on the Chaa Creek site and blog includes stories about the birds of Belize, this searcher ends up on the Chaa Creek site or blog. For people searching for information on planning a wedding trip to Belize, Chaa Creek publishes content such as "Ten Reasons Why Belize Makes for Honeymoon Bliss" on the Belize Travel Blog.

Notice that this kind of information is not about the lodge itself. Instead, the Chaa Creek publishing program focuses on delivering information to people planning a trip to Belize. Then, when they are ready to book a place to stay, they're likely to consider the Lodge at Chaa Creek, the place where they learned about traveling in the country.

My favorite examples of this technique are the team's articles about the Mayan sites located in the vicinity of the Lodge at Chaa Creek, such as the Xunantunich Maya Temples. Anyone using a search engine to find information on "Xunantunich Maya Temples" will see the article on the Chaa Creek site at the top of the search results. Clicking through, they learn that the temples are located near the village of San Jose Succotz and that the lower temple is famous for its stucco frieze (a band of sculpture along the facade). Let me remind you that this is a hotel website. The team even created content about the Tikal Mayan site, located about two hours from Chaa Creek in Guatemala, a whole different country!

All this content drives people from the search engines to the hotel site. Many of them will then choose to stay at the Lodge at Chaa Creek. Indeed, some 80 percent of new bookings to the lodge come directly from this content marketing effort. This reduces the lodge's reliance on the old-fashioned techniques of its competitors, which get a large percentage of their bookings from online travel sites (for which they must pay a commission) or advertising in travel magazines (which is very expensive). And it all starts by providing would-be travelers with the information they're looking for when they begin researching a trip.

Develop Information Your Buyers Want to Consume

Companies with large budgets can't wait to spend the big bucks on slick TV advertisements. It's like commissioning artwork. TV ads make marketing people at larger companies feel good. But broadcast advertisements dating from the time of the TV-industrial complex don't work so well anymore. When we had three networks and no cable, it was different. In the time-shifted, multichannel, web-centric world of the long tail, YouTube, DVRs,

Twitter, and blogs, spending big bucks on TV ads is like commissioning a portrait back in the nineteenth century: It might make you feel good, but does it bring in any money?

Instead of deploying huge budgets for dumbed-down TV commercials that purport to speak to the masses and therefore appeal to nobody, we need to think about the information that our niche audiences want to know. Why not build content specifically for these niche audiences and tell them an online story that is created especially for them? Once marketers and PR people tune their brains to think about niches, they begin to see opportunities for being more effective at delivering their organization's message.

Big Birge Plumbing Company Grows Business in a Competitive Market

Plumbers and other tradespeople used to generate business through the print telephone directory (when I was growing up we called it the Yellow Pages). I remember my parents both turned to it when they needed, say, a house painter or an electrician.

We're in a new world now. People go to search engines and consumer review sites like Yelp to research companies. In this new world, it's not the expensive half-page Yellow Pages ad that grows business. It's the best website—especially in a highly competitive market like plumbing.

When I was in Omaha, Nebraska, for a speaking engagement, I had an opportunity to speak with Lallenia Birge, who with her husband Brad Birge operate Big Birge Plumbing Company. Lallenia goes by a wonderful title: "A Plumber's Wife to Big Birge Plumbing Co."

"Don't let your money go down the drain! Call Big Birge Plumbing Company. For all your plumbing needs!" The clever, if punny, writing personalizes Big Birge Plumbing Company, making it stand out from the rest of the market. When the vast majority of plumbers either don't have a site or just maintain a basic one with straightforward facts and contact info, being different gets you noticed. The Big Birge Plumbing Company site uses fun original photos, has a great design, and showcases the company's humorous personality.

Here's how Lallenia introduces herself on the Meet Big Birge page: "Hi! Unlike my husband, I do NOT have years and years of plumbing experience nor have I dug ditches in 100-degree weather. Honestly I'm pretty sure my husband has had to use our drain cleaner at our house more than most of his 'regular' customers (pun intended). I did not realize you aren't supposed to flush wax down the toilet or not place all the food scrapes [sic] off the plate into the garbage disposal! (Whoops!)"

The fun carries over to the design of their trucks (Lallenia with a "gasp" expression, peering into a toilet filled with money) and to their social media presence, including Facebook.

In a crowded market—there are more than 400 plumbing companies in the Omaha area—Big Birge Plumbing Company has grown very quickly in less than five years in business.

"Our very first year, we received Best of Omaha due to our marketing online via social media and the image we display," Lallenia says. "This is a major award in our city, and we came out of nowhere. We have won it two years in a row now."

Big Birge Plumbing Company shows that anyone with a smartphone and a focus on reaching buyers online can grow a business, even in a very competitive market. When I checked recently, Big Birge Plumbing was ranked on the first page of the Google results for "Omaha Plumber." That's amazing, considering the company is only a few years old. You can achieve the same result in your market.

Buyer Personas: The Basics

Smart marketers understand buyers, and many build formal buyer personas for their target demographics. (I discuss buyer personas in detail in Chapter 10.) It can be daunting for many of us to consider who, exactly, might be interested in our products and services and is visiting our site and checking out our content. But if we break the buyers into distinct groups and then catalog everything we know about each one, we make it easier to create content targeted to each important demographic.

For example, a college website usually has the goal of keeping alumni happy so that they donate money to their alma mater on a regular basis. A college might have two buyer personas for alumni: younger alumni (those who graduated within the past 10 or 15 years) and older alumni. Universities also have a goal of recruiting students by driving them into the application process. The effective college site might have a buyer persona for the high school student who is considering college. But since the parents of the prospective student have very different information needs, the site designers might build another buyer persona for parents. A college also has to keep its existing customers (current students) happy.

That means a well-executed college site might target five distinct buyer personas, with the goals of getting younger and older alumni to donate money, high school students to complete the application process, and parents to make certain their kids complete it. The goals for the current students aspect of the site might be making certain they come back for another year, plus answering routine questions so that staff time is not wasted.

By truly understanding the needs and the mind-sets of the five buyer personas, the college will be able to create appropriate content. Once you understand these audiences very well, then (and only then) you should set out to satisfy their informational needs by focusing on your buyers' problems and creating and delivering content accordingly. Website content too often simply describes what an organization or a product does from an egotistical perspective. While information about your organization and products is certainly valuable on the inner pages of your site, what visitors really want is content that first describes the issues and problems they face and then provides details on how to solve those problems.

Once you've built an online relationship, you can begin to offer potential solutions that have been defined for each audience. After you've identified target audiences and articulated their problems, content is your tool to show off your expertise. Well-organized web content will lead your visitors through the sales cycle all the way to the point when they are ready to buy from or otherwise commit to your organization.

Understanding buyers and building an effective content strategy to reach them are critical for success. And providing clear links from the content to the place where action occurs is critical.

"Slacker." "Hippie." "Freak." "Get a job." "You look like a girl." "Unprofessional!"

After hearing these and all sorts of other snide comments about their atypical personal grooming choices, Chris Healy and Lindsay Barto founded The Longhairs. This global community advocates for, educates, and celebrates men with long hair.

Why? "Because longhairs are badass," their site says. "From Samson to Jesus to George Washington, real men let it ride. Don't let 'em convince you otherwise." Healy and Barto realized early on that women are taught from birth on how to care for, style, and manage long hair. But men haven't had that luxury. So the duo created a blog to serve this unmet need. And now that they've gathered a vibrant community on their popular blog, they are starting to sell products, initially Hair Ties for Guys.

"Content is absolutely the cornerstone of our community," Healy says. "In fact, we began with no product—or really almost anything at all. We just started with three or four blog posts, and we had a pretty good idea that there would be lots of content that we could come up with. I think the first four blog posts were 'Long Hair at High Speed,' 'Six Tips for Guys with Long Hair,' and a couple of other really basic ones. But we decided from the very beginning that content was going to be the backbone of our community and our business."

The site is beautifully designed. That's not surprising when you learn that Healy and Barto also run Round Two Creative Group, a creative studio in San Diego, California. But consistency is their key to success. As I write this, they've blogged every week for more than 100 weeks.

"The blog content is written within the three categories of our mission," Healy says. "We advocate for men with long hair. For millennia men who are leaders, warriors, scientists, and politicians have all had long hair. Only in the past century has it become 'unprofessional' to have long hair. There are employers who won't hire men with long hair, and the stereotypes are well documented. One of our content categories is the Longhairs Professional Series. We interview CEOs, business owners, and other successful professionals with long hair to illustrate that you can in fact be a successful professional."

For example, there is a conversation with Dave Littlechild, a successful business professional from the United Kingdom. Littlechild has lived around the world building businesses, most recently as executive vice president for dotmailer, the largest email marketing software firm in the UK.

The educational content of the blog is focused on addressing that male knowledge gap about long hair. "We've got no idea what to do or how to brush it," Healy says. "Is it okay to do a ponytail? How do I braid it? None of these things we know about. Before The Longhairs, the only place to learn was women's blogs, websites, magazines, or asking our moms and our sisters about it. And frankly, some of the videos can be a little uncomfortable for men to watch. We help guys by teaching them, 'Hey, you don't need to be a hair expert, but there are a few things every guy with long hair needs to know. We got it. You need it. Here it is. Let us help you out and show you how to do these things.'

"And you know, since probably very few people are encouraging you to grow your hair out, you're probably not celebrating it with your mom or with your buddies or your sister. So we have some fun by celebrating on the blog with 'Hair Whip Wednesdays' and 'Famous Long Hair Fridays.' You know, it's a club and it's a community. We should celebrate it. So we do that with our Celebrate Style content."

Many of the new visitors to the community come through search. As Healy and Barto pored through their stats, they realized that people were coming for some of their more unusual posts. "We wrote a blog post about a year and a half ago called 'The Uncomfortable Truth about Awkward-Stage Hair' that documented that phase when guys start to grow out their hair between about four, five, six months until about a year and a half," Healy says. "Man, it just looks bad. There's nothing you can do about it. But that's part of why long hair is a minority among men, because you have to get through that awkward phase. It turns out a lot of guys are searching for information on awkward-stage hair: how to deal with it, how to accelerate it, how to make it go faster. Now, if you Google 'awkward-stage hair,' we show up in the number one position."

While the blog posts are the primary content on the site, Healy and Barto also publish videos, record podcasts, and use photography. The content drives people to where they can get updates via email and become part of the community of Longhairs.

The flagship product of the Longhairs community is Hair Ties for Guys. "That was the original idea before The Longhairs even existed or was an idea," Healy says. "We were thinking 'Hair Ties for Guys'—man, we need that. It tells you what it is. It's sticky. You're not going to forget that!"

Once the community launched, they started work on Hair Ties for Guys. The process involved a great deal of product testing and searching for manufacturing sources, but after more than a year they released the first offerings. Today they have six collections of Hair Ties for Guys.

"We have some fun names, including the Outdoorsmen, the Kokomos, and the Up All Nighters," Healy says. "Instead of what you would find in the women's hair care aisle (pastel colors and maybe some more feminine designs with flowers), we do rocket launchers and shotgun shells, camouflage, surfboards, fishing rods, and stuff that guys are into. And guys love them. The reach has been extraordinary. We have now shipped Hair Ties for Guys to 47 states in the U.S. and 36 countries around the world."

Now that the Hair Ties for Guys product is doing well, Healy says he is looking at new products to offer the community.

The potential market for his products is huge. Healy estimates that men with long hair make up somewhere between 3 and 5 percent of the population of the United States. If you also include men who live in other countries and have disposable income, the target market is in the tens of millions. Guys with long hair is a distinct buyer persona that had been ignored by nearly all other companies.

As Healy and Barto say in their introductory video, "In the end, long hair is about more than just hair itself. It's commitment. It's identity. It's a lifestyle. It's all of those things and more. So even if you're not a guy with long hair, if you're a mother of a boy with long hair, if you're a wife or a girlfriend of a man with long hair, if you're a few months removed from your last haircut and you're ready to press on, if you have an ailment and you're not capable of growing hair, The Longhairs are here for you. Because long hair lives in the heart."

Content sells products to guys with long hair. A well-written blog targeting a specific audience with a well-defined buyer persona has the power to sell your product or service too. It's about tapping into a shared challenge and rallying the community around it.

Think Like a Publisher

The new publishing model on the web is not about hype and spin and messages. It is about delivering content when and where it is needed and, in the process, branding you or your organization as a leader. When you understand your audience—those people who will become your buyers (or those who will join, donate, subscribe, apply, volunteer, or vote)—you can craft an editorial and content strategy just for them. What works is a focus on your buyers and their problems. What fails is an egocentric display of your products and services.

To implement a successful strategy, think like a publisher. Marketers at the organizations successfully using the new rules recognize that they are now purveyors of information, and they manage content as a valuable asset with the same care that a publishing company does. One of the most important things that publishers do is start with a content strategy and *then* focus on the mechanics and design of delivering that content. Publishers carefully identify and define target audiences and consider what content is required to meet their needs. Publishers consider all of the following questions: Who are my readers? How do I reach them? What are their motivations? What are the problems I can help them solve? How can I entertain them and inform them at the same time? What content will compel them to purchase what I have to offer? To be successful, you need to consider these same questions.

Staying Connected with Members and the Community

As the demographics of the United States have changed over the past several decades, many mainline church organizations have struggled to attract and maintain members. Like any business or nonprofit, the churches that succeed are those whose leaders understand the problems buyers (here: churchgoers) face and use the power of publishing valuable information to reach them directly. Trinity Cathedral in Cleveland is a place where ancient church practice has blended with new patterns of social interaction to build a vibrant community both online and offline. Trinity Cathedral is a historic landmark and home to a vibrant, inclusive congregation in the heart of a city struggling to revitalize after decades of decline in manufacturing jobs. The Very Rev. Tracey Lind, dean of Trinity Cathedral, leads the effort.

"The official way you count attendance or membership in the Episcopal Church is to count average Sunday attendance," Lind says. "For a long time, I and a group of my colleagues have been saying that's not an accurate measure of the work we're doing. In fact, our vitality would be better measured by average weekly touch." To touch people regularly outside of Sunday services, Lind publishes an email newsletter, her own blog, audio podcasts, a Facebook page, and a Twitter feed. "Reality is that most people don't go to church every week anymore," she says. "That's just a reality of life. My attitude is that you can fight it, or you can be a part of it."

Lind's publishing efforts help create a virtual community within the congregation. Trinity Cathedral employs a full-time communications person and also relies on Rebecca Wilson and Jim Naughton of Canticle Communications (a firm that serves mainly church organizations) to help with web design and content publishing efforts. "We do everything as if we are running a web business to try to attract people to us," Lind says. "The reality is I'm not going to get everybody to church every week. If you can't get to church on Sunday, you can listen to the service on a podcast or you can read it on my blog. If you're teaching our kids or you're singing in the choir or doing something else at that hour, you can listen to it on a podcast. What we find is we're reaching huge communities of people [with] our podcasting. People are listening to us all over the globe. I get emails from folks in Australia or Germany, thanking me for a sermon that I preached and wanting to engage."

Music is a particularly important aspect of Trinity Cathedral's podcasting efforts. "If you go to England, one of the things that people do is go to the great cathedrals to attend choral Evensong to listen to the men's and boys' choirs sing," Lind says. "Well, we do that at Trinity every week, and we think there's nobody in the country podcasting choral Evensong. So we started podcasting that, which is a way of making us unique. People listen to really extraordinary choral music every week, and they count on the podcast."

Marketers at companies whose buyers include a segment of older people frequently assume that the elders are not online and that they won't engage with a web publishing effort. I've always pushed back on this notion. So does Lind, who has demographic data to show how misguided those conventional ideas can be. "We find that in our 1,000-member congregation, all but about 10 adults are on the Internet," she says. "Only 10 adults are not using the web, and that includes our elders. Most of our elders are actively social networking and on the Internet. When we suspended our print newspaper, I got just one complaint."

Trinity Cathedral attracts a very diverse group of people in the Cleveland area, and the web publishing efforts aid in building the community of people who become members. "Our market is clear," Lind says. "We're trying to attract progressive people of faith who are concerned about the city and who want to be a part of an intentionally inclusive, diverse, engaged congregation. We're trying to attract change agents. We're intentional about trying to attract the 20s and 30s, but there's also great value in the world of the empty-nesters, and also in the 'third half of life': boomers, those reinventing aging. I think of one of our audiences as those who listen to NPR—thoughtful, but not necessarily highly educated. We attract a lot of really thoughtful working-class folks that you wouldn't otherwise think would be coming. We're racially diverse. We are always interested in families that are wanting something other than the bland suburbs for their kids—so a lot of alternative families, blended families, adopted families, LGBT families, single moms, single dads." Lind considers each of these markets as she creates information to publish on the web.

Developing and maintaining the publishing program at Trinity Cathedral is a major effort for an organization tight on resources. But reaching buyers through the blog, podcasting, social networking, and the email newsletter is essential, given the changing ways people relate to their churches. Just like so many leaders of for-profit businesses, Lind has had to convince stakeholders of the importance of online marketing. "When I got to Trinity, there was one computer in the place, and it was barely used. That was in 2000. Part of the dilemma is the amount of money that has to go into communications, which is an enormous paradigm shift for churches. Frankly, my communications director is as valuable as a priest. That is a shift that is sometimes hard to explain to people." But it's one that will be essential for traditional churches to understand if they are to survive and thrive in the age of the social networks.

Know the Goals and Let Content Drive Action

On the speaking circuit and via my blog, I am often asked to critique marketing programs, websites, and blogs. My typical responses—"What's the goal?" and "What problems do you solve for your buyers?"—often throw people off. It is amazing that so many marketers don't have established goals for their marketing programs and for websites and blogs in particular. And they often cannot articulate who their buyers are and what problems they solve for them.

An effective web marketing and PR strategy that delivers compelling content to buyers gets them to take action. (You will learn more about developing your own marketing and PR strategy in Chapter 10.)

Organizations that understand the new rules of marketing and PR have a clearly defined *business* goal—to sell products, to generate contributions, or to get people to vote or join. These successful organizations aren't focused on the wrong goals, things like press clips and advertising awards. At successful organizations, news releases, blogs, websites, video, and other content draw visitors into the sales-consideration cycle and then funnel them toward the place where action occurs. The goal is not hidden, and it is easy for buyers to find the way to take the next step. When content effectively drives action, the next step of the sales process—an e-commerce company's Products button, the B2B corporation's White Paper Download form, or a nonprofit's Donate link—is easy to find.

Working from the perspective of the company's desire for revenue growth and customer retention (the goals), rather than focusing on made-up metrics for things like leads and website traffic, yields surprising changes in the typical marketing plan and in the organization of web content. Website traffic doesn't matter if your goal is revenue (however, the traffic may *lead to* the goal). Similarly, being ranked number one on Google for a phrase isn't important (although, if your buyers care about that phrase, it can lead to the goal).

Ultimately, when marketers focus on the same goals as the rest of the organization, we develop marketing programs that really deliver action and begin to contribute to the bottom line and command respect. Rather than meeting rolled eyes and snide comments about marketing as simply the T-shirt department, we're seen as part of a strategic unit that contributes to reaching the organization's goals.

Real-Time Business at American Airlines Reaches Buyers Directly

While on an American Airlines flight I was introduced to a well-behaved German shepherd named Kobuk. His handler is Elizabeth Fossett of the nonprofit Maine Search & Rescue Dogs team. She told me how Kobuk had searched for hours to find a 77-year-old woman with diabetes and dementia who had been lost in the woods for several nights: no water, no food, and none of her medications. Kobuk had just traveled across the United States with Fossett to attend a ceremony at American Humane. For saving the woman's life, he was being honored with the 2016 Hero Dog Award: Search & Rescue Dog.

Of course, I had to get a photo with Kobuk!

And then, naturally, I had to share it with my followers. So I tweeted the photo with the text "Psyched to meet Kobuk – 2016 @AmericanHumane National search & rescue hero dog – on @AmericanAir." Within a few minutes, American Airlines thoughtfully tweeted back to me: "@dmscott Oh wow! We're sure that was a great moment. #smile." Seeing that response—and many others like it over the years—there was no question in my mind that the airline's people pay attention to every message they receive and, when appropriate, craft a personal response. There are no generic "thanks for sharing" type responses on the @AmericanAir feed.

American Airlines is also fast to respond to Direct Messages on Twitter, and to similar communications in other social networks. As a frequent traveler on the airline, I sometimes tweet questions. A response typically comes within 15 minutes.

I was impressed and wanted to learn more about how the world's largest airline uses real-time communications. I flew to the company's Dallas/Fort Worth headquarters to spend the day with Jonathan Pierce, director of social media and content services, and more than a dozen of his American Airlines colleagues.

I went there expecting to learn how the airline uses real-time social networking to engage with customers and solve their problems. But I hadn't expected to learn how important these interactions are to the entire company and its brand. I was fascinated to learn how real-time customer data is used all the way to the CEO level as a major source of data informing how to run the company. For this, American Airlines is at the forefront of a new way to manage business.

> Rather than living in isolation in marketing, marketers and business leaders benefit from real-time content and social networking. At forward-thinking organizations, salespeople curate real-time content, customer support offers real-time troubleshooting, and management uses real-time engagement metrics to inform business decisions.

"We try to create customer value, and we try to create business value," Pierce says of his company's approach to real-time social media. "We're building relationships with customers through social and building relationships internally through the value provided by our work."

While Pierce was showing me around, I took interest in the team's social media wall, a dashboard of real-time metrics displayed on a series of large video screens. On the day I was there, 5,130 people had mentioned American Airlines on social networks in the past 24 hours, and 2,666 of them geotagged their mentions with their location. The monitors showed a scrolling set of tweets as well as recent images that people posted. The social media wall, as well as reports that are sent to management daily, weekly, and monthly, aren't interesting just to a geeky visitor.

"The CEO walks by and says, 'What's going on today?'" Pierce explains. He'll sit with us and chat. He knows what we do, and he cares about what's going on. Everyone on the executive team also get a daily Social Pulse message, which includes the hot topics of the last 24 hours. And they all get a weekly scorecard with key data, number of mentions, our response time, the top stories of the week, the top proactive posts, and what were the things that bubbled up. We also share stories about our team members, because it's very important to the leadership that we tell them."

The reporting and social data wall have become so important to management that they use it to gauge real-time reaction to new initiatives. "You know you have a good thing when we've launched a product or done an announcement and the VP of marketing will come up here and stand and watch the screens for the first hour to get a sense of what the customer reactions are," Pierce says. "It has gotten to the stage now where leaders know customers will give immediate feedback through these social platforms, and this is where we can gain insight immediately. We can course correct and get a sense of reaction quickly based on the immediate insights that come out." As I was learning about this use of real-time data, I was thinking how the vast majority of large companies would have convened a focus group or hired a team of researchers and then taken months to gather data. At American Airlines, big data in real time provides immediate intelligence that is used up and down the company to run the business.

The real-time social networking at American Airlines is all done in-house. There is no external social agency involved. "That's a very deliberate move, because the process and the time line to brief an agency and getting them up to speed with the business just takes too long," Pierce says. "We've got the luxury of being able to get to market much quicker."

The team operates around the clock with 25 team members, several of whom are fluent in Spanish and another in Portuguese. "Our permanent team come from all different backgrounds at American," Pierce says. "The last time we checked, the average seniority for the team was about 16 years with the company. We like to refer to them as super representatives, because in this job you're going to get every kind of question and comment that you could imagine. They have to know so much about everything. And if they don't know the answer, they have all the resources they need to find the answer."

The real-time social networking team handles all sorts of issues for customers, such as rebooking flights, handling lost bag inquiries, and answering questions. But they also serve as the outward face of the brand, commenting on tweets like mine with Kobuk the hero dog.

Perhaps you noticed that, unlike the large majority of organizations that hire people who are already so-called social media experts or hire young people because they grew up using social media, American Airlines takes people who are experienced in the business and teaches them the social media aspect.

"Training in the first week is tone of voice," Pierce says. "How a reservations rep or an airport rep communicates with you is different than how we talk on social media. We start new hires in the private feed, responding to Direct Messages on Twitter, for example, so they can get their social media legs and build their confidence before they manage the public feed. We can put folks in there who are real pros at helping the customer, while we are developing and training them on being the face of the brand online."

Once a new person on the social team has gotten experience responding via Direct Messages to individual customers, they might begin working on the public feed.

If a customer provides his or her American Airlines AAdvantage frequent flier number when communicating through Direct Messages, as I have done, the team adds the number to the person's internal social profile maintained at the airline. That way, a person's social profile and customer profile are merged. In my case, the team knows me as more than just @dmscott on Twitter, who has more than 125,000 followers. They know I've also been a frequent flier for 20 years and have flown over two million miles on American Airlines, making me among their best customers. All of this information pops up on the social media representatives' screens as they interact with somebody on a network. They can go back and look at the history of all social engagements between the airline and that customer. This is another example of how real-time social networking has become a fully integrated aspect of American Airlines' business, much more than for a typical company that uses social networking just to promote products. I've interacted on Twitter with hundreds of companies I do business with, and I don't know of any besides American Airlines that have merged public social networking feeds with private customer data to understand the total picture of the people they are interacting with.

Besides the global social media team, there are many individual employees who are active on social networks and who serve as unofficial brand ambassadors for American Airlines as a result. For example, @taylortippett is an American Airlines flight attendant with well over 100,000 Instagram followers, and Brad Tate is a Dallas/Fort Worth–based first officer who tweets to his 18,000 followers at @AAfo4ever. "We've got lots of pilots who take great, amazing pictures," Pierce says. "In fact, we use a lot of that content for our own proactive engagement."

Toward the end of the day I visited the American Airlines Integrated Operations Center (IOC), where 1,600 employees operate in one arena-like room. The 150,000-square-foot facility is where real-time flight operations for the entire airline and its one million yearly flights are conducted, including dispatch, crew scheduling, air traffic control, maintenance operation control, customer service, and other functions. It was here, in the nerve center of the largest airline in the world, where it became crystal clear to me how important real-time social networking is to running the airline, or managing any large business. In fact, in the center of the room is what they call "the bridge," which is where the operations manager for the entire American Airlines system sits together with a handful of key staff. And right next to the operations manager is a representative of the social team.

"Every passenger on a plane is a reporter now," says Pierce. "They've got phones, and they are sometimes tweeting about things faster than our team members can tell us what's going on. That's really useful. Maybe there are people arguing on the plane, or it's delayed, or they pulled somebody off, or somebody's not comfortable on board. We find out immediately. We'll let others on the bridge know what we're hearing about the situation on this particular flight."

Having a social media representative sit on the bridge was originally done on a short-term trial basis, but the benefits to the entire airline became obvious very quickly. The arrangement was made permanent after just a week. "It still amazes me to see something going on at the IOC and the operations manager will turn around and say, 'What have we seen on social? Is there anything going on?'" Pierce says. "They're communicating with our team just as much as we're communicating with them. It's a really great partnership."

I went to American Airlines to learn how the airline uses real-time social networking to communicate with customers who tweet cute photos like mine. I wasn't expecting to learn how important real-time customer communications are for running the entire airline. American Airlines is an amazing example of the new rules of marketing and public relations at work throughout an organization. But it's not just large organizations that can operate this way. I'll share many more examples in these pages of companies small and large that are making the new rules work for them, too.

In the following chapters that make up Part II of the book, I introduce social media, blogs, online video, podcasting, content-rich websites, real-time marketing and PR, and artificial intelligence and machine learning. Then Part III presents a guide to creating your marketing and PR plan (Chapter 10), followed by detailed chapters with how-to information on each technique. Content turns browsers into buyers. It doesn't matter whether you're selling premium wine cabinets or a new music CD, or advocating to stop sonar harm to whales, web content sells any product or service and advocates for any philosophy or image.

Web-Based Communications to Reach Buyers Directly

4 Social Media and Your Targeted Audience

As millions of people use the web for conducting detailed research on products and services, getting involved in political campaigns, joining music and film fan clubs, reviewing products, and discussing hobbies and passions, they congregate in all kinds of online places. The technologies and tools, which many people now refer to collectively as *social media*, all include ways for users to express their opinions online:

- **Social networking** sites like Facebook, Twitter, and LinkedIn help people cultivate a community of friends and share information.
- **Blogs**, personal websites written by somebody who is passionate about a topic, provide a means to share that passion with the world and to foster an active community of readers who provide comments on the author's posts.
- **Video and image sharing** sites like YouTube, Vimeo, Flickr, Slide-Share, and Instagram greatly simplify the process of sharing and commenting on photos, graphic images, and videos.
- **Chat rooms and message boards** serve as online meeting places where people meet and discuss topics of interest, with the main feature being that anyone can start a discussion thread.
- **Review sites** such as Yelp, Rotten Tomatoes, Amazon, and TripAdvisor are places where consumers rate products, services, and companies.
- **Wikis** are websites that anybody can edit and update.

- **Social bookmarking** sites like Reddit allow users to suggest content to others and vote on what is interesting.
- **Mobile applications** with GPS-generated location services add the component of identifying exactly where each user is in the world.

What Is Social Media, Anyway?

Since social media is such an important concept (and is so often misunderstood), I'll define it:

> Social media provides the way people share ideas, content, thoughts, and relationships online. Social media differs from so-called mainstream media in that anyone can create, comment on, and add to social media content. Social media can take the form of text, audio, video, images, and communities.

The best way to think about social media is not in terms of the different technologies and tools but, rather, how those technologies and tools allow you to communicate directly with your buyers in places where they are congregating right now.

Just as a point of clarification, note that there are two terms that sound similar here: social media and social networking. *Social media* is the superset and is how we refer to the various media that people use to communicate online in a social way. Social media include blogs, wikis, video and photo sharing, and much more. A subset of social media is *social networking*, a term I use to refer to how people interact on Facebook, Twitter, LinkedIn, and similar sites. Social networking occurs when people create a personal profile and interact to become part of a community of friends and like-minded people and to share information. You'll notice throughout the book that I use both terms. This chapter is about the larger concept of social media, whereas in Chapter 14 we dive into detail about social networking.

I'm fond of thinking of the web as a city—it helps make sense of each aspect of online life and how we create and interact. Corporate sites are the storefronts on Main Street peddling wares. Craigslist is like the bulletin board at the entrance of the corner store; eBay, a garage sale; Amazon, a superstore replete with patrons anxious to give you their two cents.

Mainstream media sites like the *New York Times* online are the newspapers of the city. Chat rooms and forums are the pubs, saloons, cafés, and coffeehouses of the online world. You even have the proverbial wrong-side-of-the-tracks spots: the web's adult-entertainment and spam underbelly.

Social Media Is a Cocktail Party

If you follow my metaphor of the web as a city, then think of social media and the ways that people interact on blogs, forums, and social networking sites as the bars, private clubs, and cocktail parties of the city. To extend the (increasingly tortured) analogy even further, Twitter can be compared to the interlude when the girls go to the ladies' room and talk about the guys, and the guys are discussing the girls while they wait.

Viewing the web as a sprawling city where social media are the places where people congregate to have fun helps us make sense of how marketers can best use the tools of social media. How do you act in a cocktail party situation?

- Do you go into a large gathering filled with a few acquaintances and tons of people you do not know and shout, "BUY MY PRODUCT!"?
- Do you go into a cocktail party and ask every single person you meet for a business card before you agree to speak with them?
- Do you try to meet every single person, or do you have a few great conversations?
- Do you listen more than you speak?
- Are you helpful, providing valuable information to people with no expectation of getting something tangible in return?
- Or do you avoid the social interaction of cocktail parties altogether because you are uncomfortable in such situations?

I find these questions are helpful to people who are new to social media. This analogy is also a good one to discuss with social media cynics and those who cannot see the value of this important form of communication.

The web-as-a-city approach is especially important when dealing with people who have been steeped in the traditions of advertising-based marketing, those skilled at interrupting people to talk up products and using coercion techniques to make a sale. Sure, you can go to a cocktail party and treat everyone as a sales lead while blabbing on about what your company does. But that approach is unlikely to make you popular.

Guess what? The popular people on the cocktail circuit make friends. People like to do business with people they like. And they are eager to introduce their friends to one another. The same trends hold true in social media. So go ahead and join the party. But think of it as just that—a fun place where you give more than you get. Of course, you can also do business there, but the kind you do at a cocktail party and not at the general store. What you get in return for your valuable interactions are lasting friendships, many of which lead to business opportunities.

This chapter is an introduction to the concepts of social media. In subsequent chapters, I go into much greater detail about blogs (Chapters 5 and 15), video (Chapters 6 and 17), and social networking (Chapter 14).

"Upgrade to Canada" Social Program Nabs Tourists from Other Countries

The travel market is crowded. Consumers have lots of places to find information about places to visit. In this environment, the best content and the companies that are most engaged with social networks can win the day.

Canada Tourism engaged travelers with a terrific social networking program called "Upgrade to Canada." Representatives from Canada Tourism intercepted travelers at the Frankfurt and Lyon airports and tried to persuade them to switch their holiday plans, on the spot, to visit Canada instead. People had only a few minutes to consider the offer. Fortunately, many of them were open to the serendipity of a real-time travel change, and they spontaneously changed their travel destinations.

Canada Tourism then created real-time social content about the travelers and their experiences once they arrived in Canada, and the tourists themselves eagerly shared on their own social networks, including Twitter, YouTube, and Facebook.

"The results were extraordinary," says Siobhan Chrétien, regional managing director for Canada Tourism. "Not only were we able to share firsthand the travelers' stories with the world, but online we received further upgrades from over 100 countries by travelers who switched to Canada." Social networking drove awareness of Canada as a destination. Canada's share among competitive destinations increased by a remarkable 21.5 percent.

I love the idea of requiring people to make a decision in just a few minutes. The real-time nature of how people then share their experience separates "Upgrade to Canada" from other social media campaigns from tourism organizations.

"No matter how sexy a destination is, promoting a country for tourism purposes has its challenges," Chrétien says, "especially with the world now being a smaller place with many travel options and competing experiences and destinations. The traveler of today and of the future has a vast array of options. It is not enough to run slick ad campaigns or hope that price alone will drive a sale and convert a tourist. The traveler needs to be inspired, motivated, influenced, and in some cases convinced on the spot that the time is now to make the trip!"

Smart organizations understand this new world and build a buying process around the realities of independent research and the power of social networks. Instead of generic information dreamed up by an advertising agency, they tell authentic stories that interest their customers. Instead of selling, they educate through online content. Instead of ignoring those who have already made a purchase, they deliver information at precisely the moment customers need it.

It's not just travel destinations that can benefit from social engagement. Every market is influenced by what people are saying on social networks: the good, the bad, and, in some cases, nothing.

Social Networking and Agility

Social networking allows companies to communicate instantly with their existing and potential customers. That Canada Tourism built an entire awareness campaign around real-time strategies shows the power of instant communications. Yet many organizations don't respond to people quickly on social networks.

I'm a "Pro" user of the Hightail file sharing and storage service. I've been a loyal customer since January 2009, paying more than $100 a year for my premium services. I received an email offer from Hightail with the subject line "Complete your list with our great discount." The offer promised if I would "Upgrade to Hightail Professional" that day, I'd get 50 percent off the annual subscription price. Hightail subscription plans had confusing names: Hightail Professional is an upgrade from the Hightail Pro service I was using at the time.

The offer sounded good, so I clicked the "Get the deal" button.

However, when I logged into my Hightail account to complete the transaction, I got a nasty error message: "Your account does not meet the prerequisites for using this SKU code."

This was frustrating, so I tweeted a message to Hightail (@HightailHQ) and waited for a response. And I waited some more. When I didn't hear from them for three days, I chose to look into competing product offerings from other companies.

> When responding to a negative comment in a social network, it is best to reply quickly, honestly, and in the same medium.

Not responding quickly is a huge missed opportunity. When you reply to user messages in real time, not only do you keep the customer up to date, but you also show the world through your public feed that you're engaged. When customers are happy, they keep their product longer, they spend more money over time, and they share their happiness with others, either in person or on social networks. Hightail missed an opportunity to engage with me. And there's no doubt that some of my more than 125,000 Twitter followers noticed Hightail's lack of interest in responding to a customer.

The team at Hightail did finally get back to me and worked with me to solve the problem. I remain a customer, but it wasn't a pleasant experience.

Contrast the long delay at Hightail with an experience around the same time with @JetBlue. In this case, I received a reply in just two minutes. Talk about speed! No wonder JetBlue has nearly two million followers on Twitter—it communicates in real time.

When Social Networking Doesn't Work: The Cannabis Business in America

In this chapter and throughout the book I talk a lot about how social networking is a great way to reach buyers. But occasionally a market exists where social networking is not appropriate.

As American voters pass referenda permitting the use of medical marijuana and legalizing it for recreational use, many businesses have cropped up to service this emerging market. As I write this, 33 U.S. states have legalized medical marijuana, while 11, plus Washington, D.C., have legalized recreational use. However, because it is still illegal at the federal level, laws often forbid the use of social networking to market products from this fledgling industry.

"Marijuana from a marketing perspective is fascinating, because you can't market in the usual way. It's illegal," says Larry Schwartz, president of Cannabiz Media, the most comprehensive source for U.S. marijuana licensing information. Data from Cannabiz Media helps journalists, regulators, researchers, businesspeople, and investors understand and operate confidently in the evolving U.S. marijuana marketplace.

When Schwartz first started to market his business, he tried to run Google AdWords and Facebook Ads but was quickly rejected by both companies. Twitter and Instagram also forbid such advertising.

Google's representative emailed Schwartz: "Thank you for calling the Google AdWords Welcome center. I looked into and tried to see if there was a way that I could help you to be able to advertise with AdWords. However I was unsuccessful in my pursuit. Google won't allow your website to be advertised with AdWords. While your Business model is solid and company is legal it does fall into Dangerous products or services. With that being said, your ads can show organically. The Search Console will assist you [sic] Organic ad results."

"We realized we had to go the old-fashioned route," Schwartz says. "In the marijuana business, believe it or not, print magazines are huge. I think there are about 20 magazines in this space, titles like *Cannabis Business Times*, *Marijuana Business Magazine*, and *Marijuana Venture*. So for us, our marketing strategy quickly became trade shows, getting out our own email list, and bartering with these magazines and trade show providers. We've got deals with all the big guys now where we trade them our database for free ads and trade show booth space. This was the way everyone marketed 15 or 20 years ago!"

Most of the online action happens on more specialized marijuana search engines and review sites. "Dispensaries are the ones who need to advertise to consumers," Schwartz told me. "And each state has different laws regulating marketing. For instance, in Connecticut and Massachusetts if you put a website up, the state has to approve it. It gets complicated and there are a lot of really strange laws. Now people are bypassing Google and the other traditional search engines and they're using weed search engines like Leafly and Weed Map to find dispensaries, strains, news, all sorts of information. These are big marijuana search engines, and that's where consumers are going."

Schwartz's business is booming. Whenever companies want to enter the cannabis business in a new state, there is a whole new set of laws to deal with. And those laws are constantly changing. Schwartz's business tracks all of those new and changing laws and regulations.

"This business is going to go through a gold-rush mentality," Schwartz says. "It's like the dot-com boom starting in 1995. When California legalizes marijuana it will double the size of the market. And then we're going to have a big bust. Then we'll come back again, just like the Internet business over the past 20 years."

As new states permit medical marijuana or legalize cannabis for recreational use, there are more and more people who want to grow the plant as a business. And with that an entire industry has grown to service cannabis entrepreneurs. As a marketer, I am fascinated by the business-to-business marketing strategies these companies must use.

"We are witnessing a dramatic shift within the USA. Cannabis can now be grown out in the open and with commercial greenhouse methods," says Tom Springer, founder and president of NurserySource. Springer's company has been selling RediRoot root development containers and GroPro root development fabric bags since 2010. The products help growers' profitability by increasing their yield due to root health.

"The changing state laws have certainly encouraged us," Springer says. "But since we manufacture an agricultural product, we have needed a few years of field testing to make sure our products worked as well in developing cannabis roots as they do developing shade tree and conifer roots."

Springer faced a number of marketing challenges. "Suppliers who service cannabis growers are quickly learning how to service full-scale and open commercial enterprises who are paying hefty tax rates," Springer says. "This is entirely different than servicing a more clandestine, black market group of growers utilizing cash for all their supplies. Cannabis farming is maturing at a rapid rate, and grow equipment suppliers are watching margins shrink and sales channels constrict. The market is hyperdynamic, and numerous people will be getting rich over the next few years. And a ton of people will go broke. Companies wishing to stay in this market long-term must utilize good business principles to survive."

It's rare that a market emerges from nothing and grows into a multibillion-dollar industry in a few short years. And just as we saw in those early Internet days, the rules of marketing in this industry are still being written. I expect that over time the cannabis business will be marketing via social media like so many other industries, but for now marketers like Schwartz and Springer must use more traditional marketing strategies.

The New Rules of Job Search

Company lost its funding. Outsourced. Caught in a merger. Downsized. Fired. It seems like every day I learn of another person who is in the job market. Usually that's because when they need a job, all of a sudden people jump into networking mode, and I hear from them after years of silence. Hey, I'm okay with that; it's always good to hear from old friends. And I've been fired three times, so I certainly know what it's like to be in the job market.

Since looking for a job is all about marketing a product (you), I wanted to include a section in the book for those of you who are currently in the job market, soon to graduate from college or university, or otherwise looking for a career opportunity.

If you're like the vast majority of job seekers, you'd do what everyone knows is the way to find a job: You prepare a resume, obsessing over every entry to make sure it paints your background in the best possible light. You also begin a networking campaign, emailing and phoning your contacts and using networking tools like LinkedIn, hoping that someone in your extended network knows of a suitable job opportunity.

While many people find jobs the traditional way, social media allows a new way to interact and meet potential employers. The old rules of job searches required advertising a product (you) with direct mail (your resume that you sent to potential employers). The old rules of job searches required you to interrupt people (friends and colleagues) to tell them that you were in the job market and to ask them to help you.

As people engage with each other on social media sites, there are plenty of opportunities to network. Just like at a physical cocktail party, if you are unemployed and looking for work, the people you meet may be in a position to introduce you to that perfect employer. The converse is also true: Smart employers look to social networking sites to find the sort of plugged-in people who would fit in at their company or in a certain job. In fact, on the day that I wrote this, a friend asked me to tweet a job opportunity. Had you been watching my Twitter feed that day, perhaps you'd have a new job now.

> To find a job via social networks, you have to stop thinking like an advertiser of a product and start thinking like a publisher of information.

So you want to find a new job via social media? Offer information that people want. Create an online presence that people are eager to consume. Establish a virtual front door that people will happily link to—one that employers will find. The new rules of finding a job require you to share your knowledge and expertise with a world that is looking for what you have to offer.

How to Find a New Job via Social Media

It's not just travel destinations, cosmetics, and air travel that can be promoted via social networks like Twitter. It's also you and your career. Let's look at how people use social networks in the job market. David Murray (@DaveMurr) says that after being laid off, he immediately did the traditional things, updating his resume and calling a bunch of contacts. But he eventually realized that he would also have to change gears and pay attention to blogs, social networks, and online communities. Murray already had a Twitter account, so he reached out to his Twitter followers and publicly announced that he was looking for work.

"I guess you could say I used a new tool for old-school networking," Murray says. "The response was overwhelming, and I received several leads and opportunities that were far more fruitful than my previous attempts."

Murray then hit on a creative way to use Twitter Search in his job hunt. "I came across a comment from Chris Brogan [@ChrisBrogan] on how he used Twitter Search to keep track of his tens of thousands of followers using RSS feeds," Murray says. "So I simply began entering keywords in Twitter

Search like 'Hiring Social Media,' 'Social Media Jobs,' 'Online Community Manager,' 'Blogging Jobs,' and so on. I then pulled the RSS feeds of these keyword conversations and made it a habit to check these first thing in the morning every day."

Bingo. Murray came across lots of conversations related to his keywords, and if something sounded like a good fit for him, he took the liberty of introducing himself via Twitter. "Many times, the jobs had not been officially posted," Murray says.

How cool is it that on Twitter you can express interest in a job opportunity that hasn't even been announced yet? It's like getting inside information!

Hired. It didn't take long at all for Murray to land the ideal job. His example is of someone who had already established himself in his career; he was looking for a new job because of a layoff. But what about new (or soon-to-be) university graduates searching for an entry-level position?

When Lindsey Kirchoff was a graduating senior at Tufts University near Boston, Massachusetts, she started a terrific blog called *How to Market to Me*. In her blog, Kirchoff offers her opinions on how to market to millennials like herself. "The blog is my opinion," she says. "It's about the advertisements that 'get' me as a collegiate and 20-something consumer—the companies that understand my values, participate in my humor, and reach me when/where I'm most likely to need them. It's also about companies that don't do any of those things and how they can better reach me (and people like me) in the future."

She used her comments on other people's blogs, her Twitter feed (@LindseyKirchoff), and other social networking tools to share her ideas about how companies should market to people like her—a focus that also served to showcase her understanding of marketing.

At the time, Kirchoff was on the hunt for a job upon graduation, hopefully at a mid-to-large marketing firm with a strong entry-level program. Soon her active social networking led to discussions both online and in person with marketers at a Boston-based software company. Partly based on her solid understanding of social media as demonstrated by her blog and use of Twitter, Kirchoff was hired full-time and started working soon after graduation.

What Kirchoff and Murray both did was to show potential employers that they were available and ready to contribute. They put their enthusiasm and expertise out there to make themselves stand out from the other candidates, who would simply send a paper application or CV.

Some people might argue that this technique works only to find jobs related to social media and marketing (like Murray and Kirchoff did). While it's true that social-media-savvy people are often the first to use these techniques, I'm convinced that they would work for many other kinds of job seekers. These days, Twitter is used very widely, and tweets like "I'm looking for an accountant to join my London office" appear frequently. You should be monitoring what people are saying in your field. Plus, if you're an accountant, salesperson, or production manager looking for work, then you're really going to stand out from the crowd of 1,000 resumes if you use social media to find a job.

As long as we're discussing social media and job searches, here's an important consideration: *What comes up when you Google your name with the name of your most recent employer?* Potential employers do that all the time. And you can influence what they see! Remember, on the web, you are what you publish.

Social Networking Drives Adagio Teas' Success

As social networks become more important for organizations of all kinds, the challenge becomes how to integrate them effectively. Adagio Teas, a family-owned gourmet tea company founded in 1999, has used social networking to become the most popular online destination for tea enthusiasts. Social sharing and crowdsourced product creation aren't "bolted-on" strategies at Adagio Teas. Unlike at most companies, social networking is a critical component for driving business.

I learned about Adagio Teas from my daughter, Allison. She's a loyal customer and eagerly shared with me how the company works. As of this writing, Adagio Teas sells a remarkable 68,050 blends of tea. The vast majority of blends are created by its customers either for their own enjoyment (think private blends) or as a blend that is sold to others on the site. Creating blends via crowdsourcing is a brilliant strategy for driving social interaction, because people are eager to share their creations on networks like Facebook, Twitter, and Tumblr.

"The idea of customer-created blends came from growing up in a Russian background," says Ilya Kreymerman, chief technology officer and member of the family that founded and runs Adagio Teas. "Tea was always something that was in the house, and when my mom and dad had company over, they would always drink this blend of tea that my mom made herself. So the idea of having people create these unique blends was second nature to us. We found a way that people can not only make it but also share with friends, the same way that my mom would share it when people came over. The idea is not just making it for yourself but making it for yourself *and* for a large community."

Avid tea connoisseurs can search the database for a perfect blend, or, as with Amazon's bestseller list, browse teas based on popularity and customer reviews. That's another important social aspect: Like popular authors on Amazon, those who create delicious blends build a following with Adagio Teas customers, driving sales with their ratings and reviews. If you like a blend, you can see what other blends that creator has made. Repeat customers can create a profile to keep track of teas they enjoy most, and they can also add teas they want to try.

For example, a top-ranked tea as I write this, Sherlock, is a blend by Cara McGee: "All at once exotic and mysterious and perhaps a little bit insane, with a lingering hint of smoke. Inspired by BBC's *Sherlock*, which I am in no way affiliated with. This is created purely for my own enjoyment. Ingredients: Lapsang souchong, Assam melody, Oriental spice."

McGee uploaded a video where she talks about the blend. There are also customer reviews and social sharing tools that include Facebook (with over 1,000 likes), Twitter, Tumblr, and Pinterest. The Sherlock blend is part of a theme that Adagio calls Fandom Signature Blends, which also include such teas as Avatar, Big Lebowski, Doctor Who, Harry Potter, and many more blends based on popular movies, TV shows, and books.

"A lot of what drives people to buy the tea is not really the tea itself—it's this story around the tea," Kreymerman says. "You take a pot of tea and infuse it with a character or TV show or video game and suddenly people have an attachment. You're piggybacking on their love for a specific character. Instead of it just being a cup a tea, it's now got all of this background and emotion baked in." And people are naturally eager to talk on Facebook, Twitter, and other social networks about tea that has a connection to the books, movies, and TV shows they love.

Another social aspect kicks in when customers add friends to their profiles. If you log in to Adagio Teas with a Gmail account, you can instantly find out whether one of your contacts also has an Adagio Teas profile. Or if you're reading a review and like someone's taste in tea, you can friend that person.

With all the sharing going on with customers at Adagio Teas, it's no surprise that the company itself is active on social networks. It has an excellent Tumblr blog ("The official blog from the people behind Adagio"), and is active on Twitter (@AdagioTeas, 29,000+ followers), on Facebook (72,000+ likes), and on other social sites.

"People historically have spent a lot of money to advertise products," Kreymerman says. "But we never use traditional marketing, advertising, things like that because it's incredibly expensive. You're kind of shooting in the dark. I think the more interesting thing is to provide customers with value by putting the money towards a really interesting site or really interesting idea or making their experience better instead of just kind of directing them towards your store. We listen to the audience, and a lot of our good ideas come from listening to what people are talking about on Twitter and Tumblr. And once in a while, we hear the same question coming up over and over again and realize that we have to address it."

And Adagio Teas really is active, using social networks to communicate with customers. The mistake made by so many other companies is just using social media like Twitter as a one-way broadcast advertising channel. For example, @AdagioTeas tweeted: "We are developing a wish list feature & would love feedback. Would you use it as a bookmark for yourself, or as a list to help guide others?" A follow-up tweet thanked customers for their suggestions, announced the launch of the wish list, and prompted further discussion.

People love this kind of interaction and happily talk up organizations that provide it. For example, @jamieworley tweeted: "It's so cool that @AdagioTeas sends me twitter DMs to let me know where my tea shipment is!" And it is cool. I wish some of the companies I frequently do business with used Twitter Direct Messages (DMs) to communicate.

Over the Thanksgiving holiday, Allison made her own blend because she wanted to have interesting Christmas and holiday gifts for family and friends. The "Create a Blend" widget is really easy to use. Many people love mixing teas, and Adagio has made it fun and easy to mix different flavors to create a unique and tasty blend: You name your creation and choose the types of teas and the percentages of each. You then have an opportunity to create a custom label, either simple text or something much more elaborate.

Here social networking pops up yet again, because you can upload a Facebook photo to be part of your custom label. Instead, Allison made a hand drawing for her label, which she scanned and saved as a JPEG and then imported into Adobe Photoshop. There she added text before uploading the image to the Adagio Teas app. Her "scottea dog" blend is "Just a cute jumpy Christmas blend of assam melody, hazelnut, and peppermint."

Another fun social aspect of Adagio Teas is that the creator of a custom tea earns points whenever a customer buys that blend. Points can be used to get discounted or free tea. This encourages social sharing by people who create blends—when their new blends are ready to be sold, many people will tweet about them, or post an image of the label with a link on Facebook, or make a Tumblr post talking about the blend. After all, it's in their best interest to do so.

By building social networking features into all aspects of the customer experience, Adagio Teas drives business success. As customers talk about teas on social networks, fan their favorite blends, or even create their own to share with their friends, new people learn about the company. It sure beats traditional advertising to get the word out.

Social media sites are places where people congregate to discuss things that are important to them. Where are people discussing your industry and the products and services you offer? If that place already exists, you should monitor it and participate as appropriate. If it doesn't yet exist, consider starting a place for colleagues and customers to meet and revel in information that is important to your market.

Now let's turn to blogs, another form of social media.

Blogs: Tapping Millions of Evangelists to Tell Your Story

Blogging is my front door. Since 2004, my blog has been where I post my ideas, both big and small. There's no doubt that my blog is the most important marketing and PR tool I have as a professional speaker, writer, and advisor to companies. Even after more than a decade and some 1,500 blog posts, I'm always surprised at how effectively this tool helps me accomplish my goals.

My blog allows me to push ideas into the marketplace as I think of them, generating instant feedback. Sure, many blog posts just sit there with little feedback, few comments, and no results. But I learn from these failures, too; when my audience doesn't get excited about something, it's probably either a dumb idea or poorly explained. On the other hand, some posts have had truly phenomenal results, quite literally changing my business in the process. I'll admit that my ravings about the importance of my blog may sound over the top. But the truth is that blogging really has changed my life.

The first time I shared my ideas about the new rules of PR, in a post on my blog that included a link to an e-book I had written, the reaction was dramatic and swift. In the first week, thousands of people viewed the post. To date, more than a million people have seen the ideas, hundreds of bloggers have linked to them, and thousands of people have commented on them, on my blog and others' blogs. That one blog post—and the resulting refinement of my ideas after receiving so much feedback, both positive and negative—created the opportunity to write the book you are now reading. As I was writing the first edition of the book during much of 2006, and the six subsequent editions since then, I continually posted parts of the book, which generated even more critical feedback—many thousands of comments—that made the book much better.

Thanks to the power of search engines, my blog is also the most vital and effective way for people to find me. Every word of every post is indexed by Google, Bing, Yahoo!, and the other search engines, so when people look for information on the topics I write about, they find me. Journalists find me through my blog and quote me in newspaper and magazine articles *without my having to pitch them*. Conference organizers book me to speak at events as a result of reading my ideas on my blog. I've met many new virtual friends and created a powerful network of colleagues.

As I write and talk to these corporate audiences and other professionals about the power of blogging, many people want to know about the return on investment (ROI) of blogging. In particular, executives want to know, in dollars and cents, what the results will be. The bad news is that this information is difficult to quantify with any degree of certainty. For my small business, I determine ROI by asking people who contact me for the first time, "How did you learn about me?" That approach will be difficult for larger organizations with integrated marketing programs that include blogs. The good news is that blogging most certainly generates returns for anyone who creates an interesting blog and posts regularly to it.

So what about me? My blog has gotten my ideas out to tons of people who had never heard of me before. It has helped me get booked for important speaking gigs around the world. I've determined that about 25 percent of the new speaking business I've brought in during the past 10 years has been either through the blog directly or from purchasers who cited the blog as important to their decision to hire me. Consider this: If I didn't have a blog, you literally wouldn't be reading these words, because I couldn't have been writing this book without it.

Will writing a blog change your life, too? I can't guarantee that. Blogging is not for everyone. But if you're like countless others, your blog will reap tremendous rewards, both for you personally and for your organization. Yes, the rewards may be financial. But your blog will most certainly serve you as a valuable creative outlet, perhaps a more important reward for you and your business.

Why You Still Need a Blog in the Age of Social Networking

Before we go deeply into blogging examples and how-to, I want to answer a common question about whether blogs are still relevant. Social networking sites are excellent ways to market your products and services, and I will be discussing them in detail in upcoming chapters. Depending on your marketplace, Facebook, Twitter, YouTube, LinkedIn, Tumblr, Snapchat, or any of the many thousands of other social networks might be right for you. But for long-term marketing success for your business and your personal brand, you need a blog or similar permanent content site that you own and control.

The problem with social networks is they come and they go. You simply cannot rely on the companies behind social networks to be there forever. And you can't trust that those companies will be active over the long haul to display your content in the way you originally intended (Facebook comes to mind here). Always remember, the social network owns your content on each platform, not you.

As I mentioned in the introduction, Google Plus launched in mid-2011 and became the fastest growing social network in history. However, in 2019, less than a decade after launch, the service shut down. All the content tens of millions of people had posted on G+ disappeared. That's not the first time a popular social network closed. Several years ago, Twitter announced it would shut down its social video app, Vine. Rats. I had used Vine a number of times and found it to be a fun way to share six-second videos. But many people invested way more time than I did, some spending hundreds of hours creating and curating a social presence there. All that work was lost in an instant.

Many people have said to me, "Blogs are dead." Nonsense. Your blog, or similar informational site with content you own and curate, is never going to go away. If you have a custom URL, it's your content real estate that you can own forever.

Unlike most social networks, the search engines index content from your blog—and that traffic goes to you. For example, people visit my blog every day from search engine hits on posts I wrote more than a decade ago! How cool is that?

Your content on most social sites like Facebook and Snapchat simply won't appear in search engine results. (A notable exception is YouTube, which is owned by Google.) Don't give all your content resources to the social networking companies, which can do with them anything they choose.

The rest of this chapter describes more about blogs and blogging. You will meet successful bloggers who have added value to their organizations and benefited themselves by blogging. I'll describe the basics of getting started with blogs, including what you should do first—monitor the blogosphere and comment on other people's blogs—before even beginning to write your own. The nitty-gritty stuff of starting a blog, what to write about, the technology you will need, and other details are found in Chapter 15.

Blogs, Blogging, and Bloggers

Weblogs (blogs) are a popular way to create content because the technology is such an easy and efficient way to get personal (or organizational) viewpoints out into the market. With easy-to-use blog software, anyone can create a professional-looking blog in just minutes. Most marketing and PR people monitor what's being said about their company, products, and executives in this important medium. A significant number of people are also blogging for marketing purposes, some with amazing success.

I have found writing (and revising) this chapter to be a challenge because there is great variance in people's knowledge of blogs and blogging. So with apologies in advance to readers who already understand them, I'd like to start with some basics.

A blog is just a website. But it's a special kind of site that is created and maintained by a person who is passionate about a subject and wants to tell the world about his or her area of expertise. A blog is almost always written by one person who has fire in the belly and wants to communicate with the world. There are also group blogs (written by several people) and even corporate blogs produced by a department or entire company (without individual personalities at all), but these are less common. The most popular form by far is the individual blog.

A blog is written using software that puts the most recent update, or post, at the top of the site (reverse chronological order). Posts are tagged to appear in selected information categories on the blog and often include identifiers about the content of the post to make it easy for people to find what they want on the blog and via search engines. Software for creating a blog functions essentially as an easy-to-use, personal *content management system* that allows bloggers to become authors without any HTML experience. If you can use Microsoft Word or buy a product online from Amazon, you have enough technical skills to blog! In fact, I often suggest that small companies and individual entrepreneurs create a blog rather than a standard website because a blog is easier to create for someone who lacks technical skills. As the lines between what is a blog and what isn't blur, today there are thousands of smaller companies, consultants, and professionals who have a blog but no regular website.

Many blogs allow readers to leave comments. But bloggers often reserve the right to remove inappropriate comments (spam or profanity, for example). Most bloggers tolerate negative comments on their blogs and don't remove them. I actually like some controversy on my blog because it can spark debate. Opinions that are different from mine on my blog are just fine! This might take some getting used to, especially for a traditional PR department that likes to control messaging. However, I strongly believe that comments from readers offering different viewpoints from the original post are actually a good thing on a blog, because they add credibility to your viewpoint by showing two sides of an issue and by highlighting that your readership is passionate enough to want to contribute to a debate on *your blog*. How cool is that?

A Blog (or Not a Blog)

Before we look at some examples, I'd like to comment for just a moment on the term *blog*. The term sometimes carries negative connotations among people who have heard of blogs but do not make an effort to read them regularly. These folks assume that blogs are frivolous and without value. When I ask people in my live presentations if they read blogs, the show of hands tells me that half the audience does. I am certain that this number is wrong. Many more of them, I'm convinced, do read blogs but don't realize what kind of content they are reading when they land on one. They usually find their way there via a Google search or a link suggested by a friend, colleague, or family member, but since they didn't seek out blog content intentionally, it doesn't occur to them that that's what they've found.

What's more, too many people are still hung up with outdated, artificial demarcations between "mainstream media" and "blogs," arguing that one is more legitimate. This leads to flawed marketing and PR strategic decisions.

This is especially true of many (but not all) public relations agencies whose representatives do their clients a disservice by focusing on one form of media over another.

That's nonsense. The distinctions have nearly disappeared, and smart individuals and firms have already eliminated this prejudice.

Whenever this subject pops up, I'm prompted to ask a series of questions that I hope illustrate the changes afoot:

- What is a blog?
- What is an online news site, like the *HuffPost*?
- What do we call it when a print newspaper like the *New York Times* or a television network like the BBC publishes an online news site?
- What do we call it when readers can post comments on an online story from a magazine?
- What do we call it when a reporter for the BBC maintains a blog?

Guess what? It's all just media—real-time media in this case.

The *Huffington Post* is technically a blog. It is written on a blogging platform, so there is no significant difference between when I write an article for the *Huffington Post* and when I write a post on my personal blog (no difference but the size of the audience, that is).

The *Huffington Post* is a blog. But it's one of the most important news sites on the web, with an Alexa ranking as I write this of 200. That ranking places the blog in the top 200 most popular sites of any kind in the world.

The *Huffington Post* is a blog. But it won the Pulitzer Prize in the category of national reporting for senior military correspondent David Wood's 10-part series about wounded veterans, "Beyond the Battlefield."

The BBC is mainstream media, but readers can comment on stories. Thousands do, just like on the *Huffington Post*.

The *New Yorker* is a magazine, but people can share links to stories within the magazine's website, using widgets for Facebook, Twitter, LinkedIn, Pinterest, and Tumblr.

The difference between mainstream media and the blogosphere has blurred, and this blurring has important implications for your business.

When your buyers search Google or another search engine for information related to your business, they don't really care if the top results come from a "news site" like the BBC, a "blog" like the *Huffington Post*, or your own blog or content-rich website. So you need to eliminate the bias.

When buyers ask a question on social media, they are happy when someone sends a valuable link to information on the web. They don't scrutinize what's recommended to them and dismiss the blog content and only read newspaper and magazine articles. They're happy for an article that educates and entertains, wherever it comes from.

The best marketing and PR strategies must include creating your own content, including text, video, and images, and should also include strategies for getting noticed by important voices so they write about you. And getting noticed comes back to the content you create.

If you find in your company that you're encountering resistance to starting a blog, perhaps you shouldn't call it a blog at all. Instead, you could speak with your managers about starting a regularly updated information site or creating ongoing content for your buyers in order to help drive sales. I'd say this renaming could even apply to the links from your main site to your blog. Rather than a link on your homepage to "Our Blog," you could link to the name of the blog (without using the actual word *blog*) or to something like "Our Industry Commentary" or "Our Latest News."

Content is content, no matter what it is called. If you are creating valuable information to market your business, don't let the term *blog* hold you back.

California Lawyer Blogs to Build Authority and Drive More Business

Mitch Jackson, senior partner and trial lawyer at Jackson and Wilson, uses his blog as a way to connect with his existing clients, to reach the marketplace of people who are considering hiring an attorney, and to provide information on legal cases to journalists looking for expert opinions.

"We've been online since 1996 with our first site, and I started blogging soon after," Jackson says. "I find it's really important to post with the perspective of 'How is this helping the client? How is this helping the customer?' So instead of blogging about a legal issue or rule, that same blog post has to be written in more of a story fashion that immediately connects with potential clients and solves problems."

For example, Jackson wrote a powerful blog post titled "How This California Law Firm Handles Bullying Cases." The post was inspired by stories such as that of 12-year-old Rebecca Sedwick, who was bullied and terrorized relentlessly for months both online and offline. After texting a friend that she couldn't take it anymore, Rebecca jumped to her death from a cement factory tower.

In the blog post, Jackson shares several methods and suggestions to help people deal with bullies. In particular he focuses on the legal issues for those whose families are affected and how you can work with the police and perhaps hire a lawyer. As Jackson explains in his post, "What this post is about is how to come down hard on a bully and shut things down. It's a no-nonsense approach to taking control and playing hardball to stop the bully from harming your child, or, if something has already happened, how to hold a bully legally responsible for his or her misguided and wrongful conduct."

Jackson says that his ideas often come from interaction with clients. "A good source of blog material comes from prospective clients asking the same questions, and so we use that as an opportunity to turn it around and try to provide a detailed response," he says. "The bullying issue started to get lots of attention a couple of years ago, and we took the time to put together that blog post. Now, several years later, we probably get two or three contacts a day on this bullying issue." Because Jackson's firm can't help the vast majority of people who read the post and contact him, he has a list of resources he points people to for more information.

News stories are another source of posting ideas. Jackson likes to write about things that are on people's minds. "It seems like every single moment, something happens on the news that has a legal angle to it, where I can share my two cents' worth on the blog," he says. "People with legal questions now turn to Google to get answers. Blogging allows us to be the firm that helps and provides solutions. It's all about client engagement and meeting the expectations of the online consumer. Blogging allows us to do just that."

Jackson says many members of the general public have an incorrect preconceived notion of who lawyers are. "Blogging allows us to show our human side and share our families and passions," he says. "My blog is a digital resume for clients, referring attorneys, insurance claims adjusters, and opposing counsel to review and base their interactions on. They need to know we're established, have a successful track record, and are willing to take our cases to trial. And reporters searching for information, interviews, and quotes land on blog posts and then [reach out to us]."

Jackson is one of very few lawyers who blog. Most businesspeople make excuses for why they can't get involved in blogging. Not Jackson. "How can you not find the time?" he asks. "This is what's necessary to connect with consumers, with potential clients today. This is what customers and clients are looking for. They're looking for information. It's an opportunity to strengthen the business, to strengthen my connections with existing clients and potential clients. It's an opportunity that I'm not willing to let fall by the wayside."

There's no doubt that for Jackson and for many other bloggers, the effort pays off in new business. "We have cases right now, and we've had cases in the past, where clients have come to us because of a blog post that they read," he says. "There are a couple of cases that stand out in my mind where, because of a blog post, the clients came in, retained us, and we were able to obtain seven-figure settlements and verdicts for the clients."

Jackson uses his blog to help others and build relationships with his existing and potential clients, as well as the community and the media. He provides answers, resources, and solutions to the public. And it grows his business as a result.

The remainder of this chapter provides more information on blogging and how to understand blogs as a marketing and PR tool. Then Chapter 15 will be a step-by-step plan for you to create your own blog.

Understanding Blogs in the World of the Web

Blogs are independent, web-based journals containing opinions about anything and everything. *However, blogs are often misperceived by people who don't read them.* Journalists as well as public relations and marketing professionals are quick to dismiss the importance of blogs, because they often insist on comparing blogs to magazines and newspapers, with which they are comfortable. But the blogger's usual focus of promoting a single point of view is dramatically different from the journalist's goal of providing a balanced perspective. In my experience, blogs are deemed bad or wrong only by people who do not read them regularly. In journalism school and on their first beat assignments when they begin their careers, aspiring reporters and editors are taught that stories are developed through research and interviews with knowledgeable sources. Journalists are told that they can't express their own opinions directly but instead need to find experts and data to support their views. The journalist's craft demands fairness and balance.

Blogs are very different. Blogging provides experts and wannabes with an easy way to make their voices heard in the web-based marketplace of ideas. Companies that ignore independent product reviews and blog discussions about service quality are living dangerously. Organizations that don't have their own authentic and human blog voices are increasingly seen as suspect by many people who pay attention to what's being said on blogs. But as millions of independent voices shout and whisper all over the Internet, certain mainstream media and PR people still maintain rigid defensive postures, dismissing the diverse opinions emerging from the web's Main Streets and roads less traveled.

Many people prefer to box blogs into their existing worldviews rather than understand blogs' and bloggers' unique roles on the web. Often people who don't understand these roles simply react with a cry of "Not real journalism!" But bloggers never claimed to be real journalists; unfortunately, many people continue to think of the web as a sprawling online newspaper, and this mentality justifies their need to (negatively) compare blogging to what journalists and PR people do. But the metaphor of the web as a newspaper is inaccurate on many levels, particularly when you are trying to understand blogs. It is better to think of the web as a huge city teeming with individuals, and blogs as the sounds of independent voices, just like those of the street-corner soapbox preacher or that friend of yours who always recommends the best books.

Should you believe everything you read on blogs? Hell, no! That's akin to believing everything you hear on the street or in a bar. Thinking of the web as a city rather than a newspaper and of bloggers as individual citizen voices provides implications for all Internet citizens. Consider the source (don't trust strangers), and find out if the information comes from the government, a newspaper, a big corporation, someone with an agenda, or some banker's ex-wife who is just dying to give you $20 million.

Blogs and bloggers are now important and valuable sources of information, not unlike your next-door neighbor. Take them with a grain of salt, but ignore them at your peril. Just remember that nobody ever said your neighbor was the same as a newspaper. The challenge for marketers and PR people is to make sense of the voices out there (and to incorporate their ideas into our own). Organizations have the power to become tremendously rich and successful by harnessing the millions of conversations found in Web City.

The Four Uses of Blogs for Marketing and PR

As you get started with blogs and blogging, you should think about four different ways to use them:

1. To easily monitor what millions of people are saying about you, the market you sell into, your organization, and its products.
2. To participate in those conversations by commenting on other people's blogs.
3. To work with bloggers who write about your industry, company, or products.
4. To begin to shape those conversations by creating and writing your own blog.

There are good reasons for jumping into the blog world using these four steps. First, by monitoring what people are saying about the marketplace you sell into as well as your company and products, you get a sense of the important bloggers, their online voices, and blog etiquette. It is quite important to understand the unwritten rules of blogging, and the best way to do that is to read blogs.

Next, you can begin to leave comments on the blogs that are important for your industry or marketplace. That starts you on the way to being known to other bloggers and allows you to present your point of view before you create your own blog. Many organizations cultivate powerful relationships with the bloggers who write about their industry.

You should work with bloggers so they know as much as possible about what you do. Finally, when you feel comfortable with blogs and bloggers, you can take the plunge by creating your own blog.

In my experience, corporate PR departments' concerns about blogs always focus on issues of actually writing them. But if you've monitored blogs and know that there are, say, a dozen influential bloggers writing about your market and that those blogs have thousands of loyal readers, you can show a PR person the importance of simply monitoring blogs. Some of the more popular blogs have readerships that are larger than that of the daily newspaper of a major city. PR people care about the readership of the *Boston Globe*, right? Then they should care about a blog that has a similar number of readers. If you become known within your organization as an expert in monitoring blogs, it is a much smaller leap to gaining permission to create your own.

Monitor Blogs—Your Organization's Reputation Depends on It

"Organizations use blogs to measure what's going on with their stakeholders and to understand corporate reputation," says Glenn Fannick, vice president of business operations at Dow Jones. "Reputation management is important, and media measurement is a key part of what PR people do. Companies are already measuring what's going on in the media; now they need to also measure what's going on with blogs."

Text-mining technologies extract content from millions of blogs so you can read what people are saying; in a more sophisticated use, they also allow for measurement of trends. "You can count massive numbers of blogs and look for words and phrases and see what's being said as a whole," Fannick says. "You really need to rely on technology because of the massive volumes of blogs and blog posts out there. There is an unprecedented amount of unsolicited comments and market intelligence available on blogs. It is a unique way to tap into the mind of the marketplace. It is an interesting and fertile ground."

As a starting point, all marketing and PR people need to go to search engines and run queries on their organization's name, the names of their products and services, and other important words and phrases such as executives' names. I can't imagine an organization that wouldn't find value in knowing what's being said on blogs about it or its products or the industry or market into which it sells.

More sophisticated marketers then start to analyze trends. Is your product getting more or fewer blog mentions than your nearest competitor's product? Are the blog posts about your company positive or negative in tone? How does that compare with the ratios from six months ago? "It's naive to think that what your stakeholders think is not important," Fannick says. "Opinions are offered on blogs, and understanding the sum of those opinions is very important. You can't just make decisions on what you think your products do; you need to make decisions on the perceptions of what people are actually doing with your products. Seeing the blogosphere as a source of market intelligence is now vital for companies."

So become an expert in what's being said about your organization on blogs. There has never been a better time for marketers to get a true feel for what's going on in the real world. Bloggers provide instantaneous and unsolicited comments on your products, and this free information is just waiting for you to tap into it.

Comment on Blogs to Get Your Viewpoint Out There

Once you've got a sense of who is out there blogging about your company, its products, and the industry and marketplace you work in, it's time to think about posting comments. Most blogs have a feature that allows anyone to comment on individual posts. Leaving comments on someone's blog is one of the best ways to participate in a conversation. You have the opportunity to offer your viewpoint, adding to the ongoing discussion. However, it takes an understanding of blogs and blogging etiquette to pull it off without sounding like a corporate shill. The key is to focus on what the blog post says and comment on that. As appropriate, you can point to your blog (if you have one) or your website as your contact information, but make sure that in addition to contact information you provide some content of relevant value.

One of the currencies of social media is that when you participate, people find out who you are. When you leave a comment on someone else's blog post, you can link to your profile on the web. All the blogging tools have a place where you can leave a virtual calling card, your own web URL where people who read your comment (especially the blogger) can find out who you are and perhaps contact you.

If you have a blog, then you're all set—just include your blog URL in that comment field. However, most people don't have a blog. What the heck do you do then?

I've seen many solutions, most very limiting:

- Leave no URL (in which case nobody can find you).
- Leave a LinkedIn or Facebook profile URL (this has limitations, because people must ask to be connected to you to see your full profile).
- Leave a company homepage (this shows your affiliation, but nothing about you personally).

I've found an alternative solution that works very well. Create a public about.me profile for yourself and then use that as the URL that you point people to when you leave a comment on a blog or join a social networking site like Twitter. You can include a photo, a bio, and contact details. It's really cool—and the basic version is free.

Once you've got a public profile, use it as your calling card all over the web. Here's just one example: Link to your profile from your Amazon review page so the authors of the books you review can see who you are.

Bloggers Love Interesting Experiences

Many organizations have had success setting up blogger days, where influential people in their industry get the chance to spend all or part of a day with the company. In fact, any citizen journalist should be invited to attend, including those who have a video series or podcast show. On blogger days, guests are given information about new product releases, treated to lunch with employees, and perhaps given an opportunity to meet with the CEO or other executives.

For example, Christopher Barger, as director of global social media at General Motors, organized an opportunity for bloggers and other influential people to test-drive the not-yet-released Chevy Volt electric car at the South by Southwest conference. This event resulted in hundreds of blog posts and thousands of tweets.

Or consider the U.S. Marine Corps's Marine Week, held at various locations throughout the year. I attended one in Boston where bloggers and members of the media were given an opportunity to take a 20-minute flight in a V-22 Osprey tilt-rotor aircraft. The flight originated at Hanscom Air Force Base in Bedford, Massachusetts, went out into suburban Boston, flew over downtown, and returned. Unlike on commercial aircraft, we were encouraged to use our wireless mobile devices throughout the flight. It was very satisfying to live tweet while flying. I and many other participants blogged about the flight, generating awareness for the Marines.

If you don't have a hot toy to give people rides in, you can still organize a dinner for bloggers to meet with executives at your company. Or perhaps you can invite a small group of them to a special webinar for the exclusive announcement of a new product offering. Some companies offer sample products to influential bloggers. These outreach programs are critical to providing bloggers with the information and sense of connection that will help them tell your story for you.

How to Reach Bloggers around the World

Global technology PR agency Text 100 examined the communications preferences of bloggers across the globe. The agency's web-based survey was designed to clarify bloggers' relationships with PR people and corporations. Some of the findings in the survey of 449 bloggers from 21 countries are worth noting as you contemplate how you will engage with bloggers. The good news is that more than 90 percent of the bloggers surveyed welcome contact from representatives of companies in the area that they write about. However, the way that you approach those bloggers is important.

"Bloggers are united in their desire for distinctive content, particularly around new product developments and reviews, feedback on content posted on their blog, and interviews with key people," says Jeremy Woolf, global social media lead for Text 100. "Photographs are the most frequently used form of supplied content, followed by charts and graphs, and video."

However, Woolf says the study reveals that the bad habits of the PR profession don't work in trying to pitch bloggers. "PR professionals are failing to read the blogs and truly understand their target bloggers' communities," he says. "They seem to expect bloggers to post corporate material, demonstrating a lack of understanding of the medium and the very reason why bloggers blog."

There's no doubt that the vast majority of bloggers welcome contact from organizations. But to be successful, company representatives need to treat bloggers as individuals and to provide them with valuable information that complements the work they're already doing on their blogs. Don't just blindly send them corporate press releases, which are ineffective at best and may even diminish your organization's reputation with the people you're trying to reach out to.

Do You Allow Employees to Send Email? How about Letting Them Blog?

Chapter 15 presents everything you'll need to know to start your own blog. If you already know that you are ready, feel free to jump ahead to learn about how to decide what to blog about, what software you'll need, how to find your voice, and other important aspects. If you're still considering a blog for yourself or your organization, you might be hesitant because of fears that blogging isn't right for your organization.

As I work with companies to help develop a blog strategy, I see much consternation within organizations about the issue of allowing people to blog (or not) and allowing them to post comments on other people's blogs (or not). It's been fascinating to both observe and participate in the debate about blogs in the enterprise. Just like the hand-wringing over personal computers entering the workplace in the 1980s, and also echoing the web and email debates of the 1990s, company executives seem to be getting their collective knickers in a twist about blogs these days. Are you old enough to remember when executives believed email might expose a corporation to the risk of its secrets being revealed to the outside world? Do you recall when only so-called important employees were given email addresses? How about when people worried about employees freely using the public Internet and all of its (*gasp!*) unverified information?

It's the same debate all over again today with blogs and other social media. On one side of the corporate fence, the legal eagles are worried about secrets being revealed by their employees while creating content or commenting on blogs. And on the other, there's the feeling that much of the information being created today is not to be trusted. Corporate nannies want to make certain that their naive charges don't get into trouble in the big, scary world of information.

Well, we're talking about people here. Employees do silly things. They send inappropriate email (and blog posts), and they believe some of the things on TV news. This debate should be centered on people, not technology. As the examples of previous technology waves should show us, attempting to block the technology isn't the answer.

So my recommendation to organizations is simple. I'd suggest implementing corporate policies saying such things as that employees can't sexually harass anyone, that they can't reveal secrets, that they can't use inside information to trade stocks or to influence prices, and that they shouldn't talk ill of the competition *in any way or via any media*. The guidelines should include email, delivering a speech, writing a blog, commenting on blogs (and online forums and chat rooms), and other forms of communication. Rather than focusing on putting guidelines on blogs and other social media like Facebook and Twitter (the technology), it is better to focus on guiding the way people behave. However, as always, check with your own legal advisors if you have concerns.

Some organizations take a creative approach to blogging by saying that all blogs are personal and the opinions expressed are of the blogger, not the organization. That seems like a good attitude to me. What I disagree with is putting in place draconian command-and-control measures saying either that employees cannot blog (or submit comments) or that they must pass all blog posts through the corporate communications people before posting. Freely published blogs are an important part of business and should be encouraged by forward-thinking organizations.

Not Another Junky Blog

Tania Venn is director of PR at 1-800-GOT-JUNK?, the largest full-service professional junk removal company in the world. She oversees a team that creates content with a focus on reaching customers who may not think that they need a junk removal service. "Once they hear about what junk removal could do for them and how it could impact their lives, they become interested in our service," she says.

Venn and her colleagues work to identify the kind of information that would be valuable for buyers as they create content for the 1-800-GOT-JUNK? blog. They then use their Facebook page and Twitter feed (@1800GOTJUNK) to let their followers know about new posts.

"We think about what's relevant," she says. "That could be tips and suggestions for people on getting their space back. It could be about decluttering. We also focus on environmental sustainability: what happens to the stuff we haul away and creative ways to reuse junk."

They also create timely content (I'll talk more about this technique in Chapter 21 about newsjacking). "When the holidays are coming up, we'll post about making space to have your in-laws over and making room for new things you might get as gifts," Venn says. "And with New Year's, everyone has resolutions. We know that the top 10 New Year's resolutions include 'getting organized' and 'simplifying.' We also look at what's trending. For example, there is a trend called 'trashion,' where people make fashion out of trash, so we'll write about that."

Because it is written for buyers, the 1-800-GOT-JUNK? blog focuses on people's real junk problems, rather than egocentric advertising messages. "We know there's an emotional component to getting rid of the stuff that you have," Venn says. "Our customers have an emotional release and an amazing magical feeling of 'That crap is not there anymore' when their junk is taken away. They don't realize until it's gone how good it feels. We hear it time and time and time again from our customers. So we build that into our blog because it's what customers are looking for." The 1-800-GOT-JUNK? business is a franchise model, so the content they create also appeals to franchisees who learn about clever ways to market in their local area.

When you focus on buyers' problems as you create content, you'll often write about something that doesn't relate to what your organization actually does. This is true for 1-800-GOT-JUNK? as well.

"We might talk about how to set up your own garage sale," Venn says. "That wouldn't get us business necessarily, but we've got the experience and we can share that with people. We know that readers may not be able to afford our service right now, but someday they will be able to. They'll have learned something from us that can help them out: something that can help them get rid of some of their junk, but they can do it themselves."

Venn knows that the content published in the 1-800-GOT-JUNK? blog and shared on Facebook and Twitter is working because she uses analytics to measure success. "I look at how many people view our blog on a daily basis and a weekly basis," she says. She also pays attention to any content that becomes particularly popular with readers. "We've learned that we need to create content in order to be recognized on the web. It's a way of engaging with customers. It's a great way to get information directly to whom you want to reach rather than going through the media."

Get Started Today

There's no doubt that every organization should be monitoring blogs to find out what people are saying about it. I find it fascinating that most of the time when I mention a company or product on my blog, I do not get any sort of response from that organization. However, maybe 30 percent of the time, I'll get a comment on my blog from someone at that company or a personal email. These are the 30 percent of companies that monitor the blogosphere and react to what's being said. You should be doing this, too, if you're not already, because you'll instantly be ahead of 70 percent of your competitors.

It's also clear to me that in most industries and product categories, early bloggers develop a reputation of being innovative. There are still opportunities for first-mover advantage in many blog categories. Once you're comfortable with reading and commenting on blogs, get out there and start your own! Chapter 15 contains all the information you'll need to get going.

6 Audio and Video Drive Action

Audio and video on the web are not new. Clips have been available on websites since the early days. But until recently, neither audio nor video was used much online because the content was difficult to locate and impossible to browse, and there was no easy way to get regular updates. And since much audio and video content was lengthy—as much as an hour or more—and people had no idea what was in these files without actually watching or listening to them, not many did.

The migration of audio and video from online backwaters to the forefront with valuable content happened because of sites like YouTube, Vimeo, and iTunes, with easy ways for people to view and listen. In addition, high-speed Internet connections became the norm, and the technology to create and upload audio and video became simple enough that anybody can do it (including you).

Improv with the CIO

Videos use emotion to tell stories in ways that most other forms of marketing cannot. That's a technique that Tim Washer, creative director at Cisco Systems, uses all the time. The videos Washer creates are used to market Cisco's technology products and services to multinational customers—and have a little fun in the process.

"The most interesting stories come from our customers telling us how they use technology to transform their business, create new sources of revenue, or improve their customers' experience," Washer says. "We always try to make these interviews more interesting than a corporate 'talking head' video. At a recent conference for our top customers, we planned to interview some of the CIOs [chief information officers]. We knew we didn't want to film in a conference room, since that environment would send the conversation into a 'talking point' disaster. We wanted a more comfortable, fun space to help create a relaxed, more personable conversation.

"The steak house located at the conference hotel was only open during dinner hours, so we were able to rent it during the day. I played an overly inquisitive waiter, asking the 'customers' what they did for a living, which is how we brought in the business transformation discussion. To add some entertainment value and help us reach a wider YouTube audience, we added a little absurdity by having the waiter sit down at the table, ask if he could finish their drinks, and engage in conversation."

Most companies are afraid to use humor in their videos, especially large business-to-business (B2B) outfits like Cisco. But because videos that tell a story through humor are so rare at these big operations, those who make them get noticed. Washer's videos have been viewed hundreds of thousands of times and serve to humanize a big organization.

"To prepare for the filming, we asked a few CIOs if they would be willing to be part of an improv scene with us," Washer says. "We asked them what customer story they would like to tell, and told them there would be some play along the way. We filmed with three different cameras, including one camera locked on the customer. This approach provided a sense of comfort, since the CIOs knew that if they didn't feel comfortable with the humor, they would still have a straightforward talking-head version of their story to use on social media."

While there are no Cisco products or employees in the videos, they generate tremendous value for the company. The videos are hosted on the Cisco YouTube channel, promoted on Cisco websites and social network channels, and sent to customers by Cisco salespeople.

"Every one of the CIOs jumped into the fun and made the scenes work, and they all had a blast," Washer says. "To promote the blog series, we created a mock movie trailer, *Fast Innovation and the Slow Waiter*. It won the Killer Content award several years ago and earned us coverage from *CIO Magazine*, *The Verge*, and other media, which helped drive views."

If you create an interesting story, others will share it for you.

Many organizations create videos to showcase their expertise and provide valuable information to buyers in an easy-to-understand medium. The interview format is very popular, because it's so easy to interview guests and post the resulting video. Other common forms of online video include humor-based approaches (frequently used to try to garner many views or even go viral), product overviews, and executive speeches. An added benefit of producing videos for your organization is that the media, bloggers, and others in a position to talk you up tend to like to watch videos to get story ideas. See Chapter 17 for more information on video and details about how to create your own.

What University Should I Attend?

Many marketers are reluctant to focus on video because they don't see how a video on YouTube or on their company website will lead to a sale. As I was writing this section of the book, I received an email from a student who attends the University of Pennsylvania. She explained that she chose to apply to the University of Pennsylvania because she saw a Penn video on YouTube as she was researching universities and she fell in love with the school without even having a chance to visit. In the video, singer and five-time Grammy Award winner John Legend explains why he has a deep affection for the University of Pennsylvania, his alma mater.

This story is certainly not unique. People are looking for the products and services that you offer right now. They go to Google and the other search engines, and they ask their friends for advice. Frequently, what they find is a video. Will you be in it?

Many organizations encourage their customers or fans to produce videos for them. These customer-generated video efforts often take the form of contests and can be highly successful, especially for a product or service that has a visual impact. For example, Nalgene bottles are virtually indestructible. If you go to YouTube, you'll find hundreds of videos where people try to break them in creative ways, such as running them over with a lawn mower, throwing them out of buildings, and freezing water in them and then hitting them with a hammer. For the makers of the Nalgene bottle, this is a valuable phenomenon, since the company does not have any part in the videos.

Building a Business One YouTube Video at a Time

Matt Risinger is a builder in Austin, Texas, who specializes in applying building science to fine custom homes designed by architects. He has made YouTube his primary marketing platform and now has more than 400,000 subscribers of his terrific channel, which he uses to introduce potential customers and partners to his work.

Risinger told me that when he was a kid, he loved watching *This Old House* on his local public television station. "My hope is that, just like Tom Silva and the rest of the *This Old House* crew did for me when I was a 12-year-old watching that show, people will see me on my YouTube channel in that same light. I hope they say, 'Risinger is obviously a smart guy, and he's a builder.' That's really been fun for me."

After working with other builders for about 10 years in the Pacific Northwest, Risinger moved to Austin and started Risinger Homes in 2005. "I had a brand-new baby and a brand-new business that was really just me and an idea," Risinger says. "I was trying to figure out how to do this custom building thing. How do I build this business when I'm brand-new to the marketplace? No one knew me, and I'd never built a house in Austin before."

As Risinger considered the daunting challenge of finding clients for his fledgling business, he realized he had to do something different from what everyone else in the Austin building industry was doing. He had learned about using blogs as a marketing strategy and realized that was perfect for him.

"I had no marketing budget," Risinger recalls of his business a decade ago. "I had a pickup truck and a couple of tools and that's all I owned. So the first thing I decided was to forget spending money on advertising. I knew I had to do it myself, to market myself. I didn't really know much about blogging at the time, but I started a blog. And before too long I would come to meetings and people would say things like, 'Hey, I saw your blog post about these windows' or whatever. And it gave me early encouragement that even though I had very few readers, people who mattered were paying attention and were finding me."

Soon people started asking Risinger if he had any videos, so he purchased a cheap Flip Video camera and started his Matt Risinger YouTube channel. "I would hand the camera to whoever was on the job to film me," he says. "I didn't get huge traction at first, but I kept going. Even though I might have only 300 views on a video, one of those people watching might be an architect in Austin who would say something to me. Or maybe it was a potential client who watched before they interviewed me for their project. They felt like they knew me at a meeting—even though I'd never met them before—because they could watch a video of me. I got enough feedback that made me realize this was worthwhile."

As he started to realize that his videos were helping introduce people to his business, Risinger then focused on establishing a regular publishing schedule with upgraded video quality. "Now I publish a video every Tuesday and every Friday," he says. "I try to pick subjects organically. I don't script things. I find a topic that interests me, and I figure that the people watching my channel are probably also going to be interested. The YouTube analytics bear [this] out."

Several years ago, Risinger decided to step up the quality of his videos and ditched the Flip Video camera. "I'm kind of the junior high camera nerd and I've always wanted nice camera equipment," he says. "I thought that since I'm competing for work at high-end, expensive houses in the two- to five-million-dollar range, my videos shouldn't look like a high school student shot them."

Risinger also realized that making better videos created an additional opportunity. "I went out to some manufacturers that I liked and whose products I was using and told them that I'd already made videos about their products. I suggested they pay me on an annual basis to get their logo in my videos, and I'd make a couple a videos about their products through the course of the year."

Through this sponsorship effort, Risinger has been able to turn his YouTube channel into a revenue source, and he has used those funds to hire a full-time video professional as part of his company to shoot and edit his videos and manage the channel.

Today, Risinger's channel covers building product reviews, building science, craftsmanship, and construction best practices that he has learned over the years.

Recent videos on the channel include "Recessed Windows—How to Install & Flash to Prevent Leaks," "3 Tips for Remodel Framing Inside an Old House," and "Marvin Windows & Doors Factory Tour."

"I want to be the YouTube version of *This Old House*," Risinger says. "I control the content, I bring the sponsors in, and I shoot at my job sites. I'm not beholden to HDTV or DIY channels or whatever. I can do what I want."

As we discussed Risinger's business and YouTube channel, I kept thinking of myself as a buyer of Risinger Homes' services. My wife and I are currently involved in our own home renovation project. I'm quite sure that if I were looking for a builder and got three introductions from an architect, I would naturally be predisposed to work with the builder with the YouTube channel; they're out there showing me who they are and how they do their work.

I told Risinger that I'm into the artistic part of our home renovation project. We're living on the job site, and we're in there every day. The builders usually start at 7 a.m., so I almost always catch them on the way to my office. I'll wander in and ask what they are working on because I love the craftsmanship, seeing them do some mundane thing really beautifully.

On the day I wrote this, for example, we talked about what the trim around one particular window will be and the reason why that trim needs to be slightly different from other windows because of the way this window hits a beam. That's something most homeowners probably wouldn't care about, but in my case it ends up being a 15-minute discussion before breakfast. For appealing to potential clients like me, who are really into such details, a YouTube channel like Risinger's is a brilliant asset. He gets to illustrate his work from his builder's perspective.

It's no wonder that Risinger is doing so well in the Austin marketplace!

Risinger is up to 4 million views of his YouTube videos per month. That's impressive enough, but what really interests me is that he also generates revenue directly from the channel. Advertising brings in over $300,000 in revenue per year while sponsorships from building supply companies who pay to have their products featured in videos generates $150,000 per year. Imagine that! *Risinger actually gets paid to do his marketing!* Most important of all, Risinger's YouTube marketing is driving his business.

"YouTube and blogging have put my reputation on steroids," Risinger says. "All my competitors are 60 or even 70 years old, and they've had to work 30 or 40 years to get where they are. They've got really incredible businesses with massive portfolios now, but it took time. But here I start my business in 2005 and I'm competing against them. I'm seen as an equal, and that is incredible. I can point to several specific clients that have come to me because of my videos. They have watched me for six months or six years and then they're ready to pull the trigger and they call me and I'm their perfect fit. With just a couple hours a week investment, I'm able to make giant returns. That's the power of YouTube."

Have Fun with Your Videos

Is there anything more tediously boring than the air safety videos on commercial airliners? Well, it doesn't have to be that way. Video is a great format to use humor, especially when you take on a normally boring topic that the members of your buyer persona all know about. That's what Air New Zealand did with a safety video produced with the New Zealand All Blacks rugby team for use on the airline's Boeing 737 aircraft. The "Air New Zealand—Crazy about Rugby—Safety Video" was released on YouTube and quickly generated nearly a million views. That's right: a million views for an airline safety video. So how did they do it?

In the video, the players, coaches, and commentators of the New Zealand All Blacks rugby team serve as actors, along with Air New Zealand staff. The plane is full of fans in crazy getups. There are even credits at the end. I watched it a bunch of times because I kept missing bits and pieces of the hilarious but often subtle humor. Air New Zealand also posted a companion behind-the-scenes video showing how they created the piece.

The timing of the video's release was significant. The All Blacks had just beaten the South Africa Springboks, 29 to 22. In the riveting final five minutes, the team scored two tries to claim the Tri Nations crown. So the entire country was thinking about rugby!

Sometimes when I talk about using humor, people who work in serious firms like business-to-business (B2B) companies, nonprofits, and government agencies insist that they can't use humor. In particular, I'd like to challenge the assumption that B2B marketing must be dreadfully boring.

I think this attitude came about because B2B marketers hear the word *business* (twice) and think, "I am marketing to a business." This results in an overly serious tone. After all, marketing to, say, technology companies is different from consumer marketing, right?

Wrong.

The B2B marketers seem to forget that what all marketers need to do is communicate to *people*. People want to do business with people, and the B2B companies that understand that develop a following.

National Instruments is a B2B supplier of measurement and automation equipment used by engineers and scientists. The tried-and-true marketing strategy of companies like National Instruments is to focus on feeds and speeds, technical data sheets, specs, and so on. We're talking about the engineering community, right?

Yes, but while National Instruments does provide product specs, the company also realizes that buyers are human beings. "We've always had the motto, both internally and externally, that it's okay to have fun," says John M. Graff, vice president of marketing and customer operations at National Instruments. That fun-loving attitude has produced many ways to communicate with the technical audience that buys National Instruments' products.

For example, I'm a fan of a video blog produced by Todd Sierer, an engineer at National Instruments. It's called *An Engineering Mind*, and it is highly effective. In one episode, he talks about the meaning of the word *marketecture* in a humorous way. It's the sort of thing that an engineer would get a kick out of. Thus, it does exactly what good marketing should do—reach buyers.

"We first debuted these videos two years ago at our annual user conference held in Austin, Texas, where over 3,000 engineers and scientists gather to see and discuss the latest technologies for measurement and automation," Graff says. "In addition to the usual technical product demonstrations, we also try to have some fun, including inviting an engineer from the Spike TV show *Deadliest Warriors* to the stage. We've found that our audience greatly appreciates this approach to communication, since they get plenty of examples of the drab, speeds-and-feeds technical fire hose. We believe it's greatly enhanced our reputation."

Are you a B2B marketer? Are you treating your buyers like human beings? Are you having some fun? Really, it's okay to have some fun. I dare you.

Audio Content Delivery through Podcasting

Moving now to the audio-only side of the spectrum, note that the transformation from static audio downloads to radio station–like podcasts, which are much more valuable to listeners (and also more valuable as marketing vehicles for organizations), occurred because of three developments. The first was the ability to add audio feeds and notifications to Rich Site Summary (RSS, often called really simple syndication). This enables listeners who subscribe to an audio feed to download new updates soon after they are released. When audio content was liberated from the need for one large download and went instead to being offered as a series of continuous audio clips, the concept of sequential or episodic shows took off.

Hosts modeled their shows on radio, producing content on specific subjects catering to distinct audiences. But the podcasting business model is very different from broadcast radio. Radio spectrums can support only a finite number of stations, and radio signals have limited geographic range. To support the technical infrastructure of radio, broadcasters need large audiences and lots of advertising to pay the bills (or donors, in the case of public radio). Contrast that with Internet audio podcasting, which is essentially free (except for minimal hosting fees and some cheap equipment). A podcast show reaches a potentially worldwide audience, allowing anyone both to listen to shows and to create them.

The second major development was the availability of those podcast feeds through iTunes and other services, allowing people to search and browse podcasts. Now people can simply subscribe to a feed (usually at no cost), and then every time they plug their mobile device into their computer, the new shows from the feeds they subscribe to automatically download. People who commute and listen in the car or on the train, or who listen at the gym or around the house, suddenly have access to regularly updated shows from whatever cultural niches they specifically choose. With podcasting, people instantly liberate themselves from the tyranny of mainstream, hit-driven broadcast radio and can listen to shows based on their specific interests.

The third major change has been the rise of mobile listening applications for smartphones, like Stitcher and the Podcasts app that comes standard on iOS. Instead of having to subscribe to podcasts and synchronize to a mobile device, you just open the app and start listening to your favorite shows.

Before we continue, let's back up and talk about the name. The term *podcasting* can confuse people. A podcast is simply audio content, usually delivered through a feed service such as iTunes.

Hack the Entrepreneur Podcast Delivers New Clients for Host's Consulting Business

Podcasting has the potential to jump-start your business. Jon Nastor has built a successful coaching and consulting business directly from listeners to his *Hack the Entrepreneur* podcast. While Nastor uses his podcast to drive new business for his company, he never tries to sell from the podcast. Rather, the exposure from his podcast helps people to learn about him and the services he offers. Many listeners then independently choose to learn more and perhaps do business with him.

"I love to talk business with people," Nastor says. "If I were to just call or email somebody and say, 'Would you like to jump on Skype for half an hour and talk business with me?' most people are too busy and won't do it. But if I'm hitting 'record,' they will. So I decided to launch *Hack the Entrepreneur*. I started by sending out five email requests, and everyone agreed to be on the show." Nastor began recording weekly interviews in 2014 and has aired more than 500 episodes since then.

"My shows are about 30 minutes each, because the average commute in North America is 29 and a half minutes," Nastor says. "I want to provide closure for people, so I try to get below that mark to give listeners a beginning, a middle, and an ending with a conclusion to take to work with them that day."

There are thousands of podcasts targeted at entrepreneurs. Nastor knew that for his show to succeed, he needed to be different. "Rather than talking about the how-to of business and the tactics, which most other shows do, I went strictly for the person," he says. "That's why *Hack the Entrepreneur* is about the entrepreneur. I have guests on because they are doing interesting, cool things, and I do not discuss their business once they're on. We just talk about the person: the struggles, the battles, and the things they go through. I try to humanize the entrepreneur. I take them off the pedestal and bring them back down to earth to show other people who are struggling with business that all these other entrepreneurs have the same struggles, and here is how they got through it. Maybe you can get a hack from there and implement that in your life."

Nastor creates a wish list of people he wants to interview based on books he has read and businesses he is interested in. He has his assistant reach out to potential guests. "You have to be a certain type of personality to be on the show and make it a successful episode," he says. "You have to have a level of confidence. I know what my audience wants, and I have to provide that for them or else they stop listening."

While Nastor spends about an hour before each interview learning about the guest and formulating questions, he has a very conversational approach once the interview begins. Unlike many other podcasts, Nastor doesn't just "stick to the script," and that means he's open to serendipity. This approach frequently allows the discussion to go in interesting, unplanned directions. Perhaps that's why his podcast became successful so quickly. I've been a guest on *Hack the Entrepreneur*, and I can attest that Nastor is a great interviewer, making his guests feel comfortable as he asks probing questions.

Most people find the *Hack the Entrepreneur* podcast through the iTunes search engine. They are looking for the sort of content that Nastor is creating, and they take a chance on an episode. Many like this preview enough to subscribe.

Nastor sells sponsorships on *Hack the Entrepreneur* for more than a thousand dollars for a 30-second spot. How cool is that? He actually gets paid to do marketing for his company. But the real payoff comes from people who become Jon Nastor fans because of the show and naturally want to learn more about his consulting work.

"My mind is blown every day by the success of *Hack the Entrepreneur*," Nastor says. "I will stand on the highest mountaintop and preach the power of podcasting, because the reach you can get from your home or office is absolutely astounding. *Hack the Entrepreneur* has had over seven million downloads to date with sponsorships booked out three months in advance. I get emails every day from people who have been touched in some way by what I'm doing. Nothing I've ever done in the past has ever had this reach so quickly."

Now marketers have a tool to efficiently create and deliver audio content to people who want to listen. Anyone can develop a show that targets their buyer personas, just like Nastor did. And anyone can regularly deliver updated content that is welcome and useful to their audience. Podcasting is important for organizations that want to reach buyers directly. For content that is best delivered via audio or for buyers who prefer to listen to content, podcasting is obviously essential. For example, many politicians and churches podcast so that supporters can keep up with speeches and sermons when they can't hear them live. You'll learn more about podcasting, including tips for setting up your own podcast, in Chapter 17.

As a component of a larger content-marketing strategy, podcasting is also an increasingly important part of the marketing mix. For example, many customer service departments deliver how-to podcast series to keep users of their products informed. Companies that market to people who are frequently on the road (such as traveling salespeople) have had success reaching people with entertaining podcasts for all that car and airplane downtime. For many organizations, podcasting for marketing purposes is not an either-or decision. Instead, podcasting coexists with blogging, a great website, e-books, and other online marketing tools and programs in a cohesive marketing strategy.

Grammar Girl Podcast

Mignon Fogarty, creator of the Grammar Girl podcast and founder of the Quick and Dirty Tips podcast network, has been podcasting since 2006. Grammar Girl provides short, friendly tips to improve writing. Covering the grammar rules and word choice guidelines that can confound even the best writers, Grammar Girl makes complex grammar questions simple. I should know. I never know when I should use *whom*, so I try to avoid it altogether. However, this is exactly the sort of grammar problem the podcast solves.

"I get an overwhelming amount of feedback from my audience," Fogarty says. "I had to hire a part-time assistant to help field my messages because they were taking all my time. I get a lot of grammar questions, which I try to answer; a lot of 'I love you' messages; and a lot of people disagreeing with my recommendations. Grammar can get pretty contentious, and people absolutely love it (in a gotcha kind of way) when I make a mistake or typo."

Creating a podcast show is a great way to get your information into the market. Instead of hyping your products and services, an informational show brands you as someone worthy of doing business with. In Fogarty's case, her sound ideas lead people to want to purchase her book, *Grammar Girl's Quick and Dirty Tips for Better Writing*. The free podcast drives her book sales.

"The fan interaction is definitely different from offline marketing," Fogarty says. "I feel weird even calling the people fans because they feel more like friends with the constant messages that go back and forth. (Someone on Facebook recently said I am 'the most helpful person he doesn't know.')

The immediacy of the feedback is also different from offline marketing. I hear within 24 hours (usually faster) if something I'm doing is working or not. If I post a link or a contest on Twitter, I can usually tell within five minutes whether it's getting traction or not."

When Fogarty was ready to release her book, the podcast and her participation in other social networking sites like Twitter and Facebook allowed her to launch the book to her existing fan base. "When I went out on my book tour, the crowds were much bigger than expected, and I believe it is at least in part because of all the groundwork I laid on social networks for over a year before the book came out," she says. "During the first three or four stops on my book tour, bookstores ran out of books. In Atlanta, they ran out of books before I even arrived. A lot of the people who came out were people I had connected with on Twitter or Facebook, and I had posted messages about where I was going to be to both of those services multiple times."

As of this writing, the 700 episodes of the Grammar Girl podcasts have now been downloaded more than *tens of millions* of times. The Grammar Girl podcast was the winner of best education podcast in the 2017 podcast awards. Fogarty has dispensed grammar tips with Oprah Winfrey and appeared on the pages of the *New York Times*, the *Wall Street Journal*, and *USA Today* and appeared on the *Today* show. *Grammar Girl's Quick and Dirty Tips for Better Writing* is a *New York Times* bestseller, and she has a Grammar Girl tip-a-day calendar. "Having an established network of people is really valuable when you're launching something new," Fogarty says.

Podcasting and online video are great ways to connect with an audience and develop a following who will be eager to buy your products. Chapter 17 provides details on how to start a video or podcast series of your own.

7 The Content-Rich Website

If you've read from the beginning of the book, at this point you might be tempted to think that each of the media that innovative marketers use to reach buyers—blogs, podcasts, news releases, and all the rest—is a stand-alone communications vehicle. And while each certainly could be a self-contained unit (your blog does not need to link to your corporate site), most organizations integrate their online marketing efforts to help tell a unified story to buyers. Each medium is interrelated with all the others. Podcasts work with blogs. Twitter feeds point people to other company information. Multiple websites for different divisions or countries come together on a corporate site. No matter how you choose to deploy web content to reach your buyers, the place that brings everything together in a unified location is a content-rich website.

As anyone who has built a website knows, there is much more to think about than just the content. Design, color, navigation, and appropriate technology are all important aspects of a good website. Unfortunately, in many organizations these other concerns dominate. Why is that? I think it's *easier* to focus on a site's design or technology than on its content. Also, there are fewer resources to help website creators with the content aspects of their sites—hey, that's one of the reasons I wrote this book!

Often the only person allowed to work on the website is your organization's technology expert, who in the early days was called a *webmaster*. At many companies, these kings of technology focus all their attention on cool software plug-ins; on HTML, XML, and all sorts of other 'MLs; and on nitty-gritty stuff like server technology and Internet service providers. But with a technology person in charge, what happens to the content?

In other organizations, technology pros are pushed aside by graphic designers and advertising people who focus exclusively on creating websites that look pretty. At these organizations, well-meaning advertising agencies obsess over hip designs.

I've seen many examples where site owners become so concerned about technology and design that they totally forget that great *content* is the most important aspect of any website.

Thus, the best websites focus primarily on content to pull together their various buyers, markets, media, and products in one comprehensive place where content is not only king but president and pope as well. A great website is an intersection of every other online initiative, including podcasts, blogs, news releases, and other online media. In a cohesive and interesting way, the content-rich website organizes the online personality of your organization to delight, entertain, and—most important—inform each of your buyers.

Political Advocacy on the Web

The Natural Resources Defense Council (NRDC) is the nation's most effective environmental action organization. According to its website, the organization uses law, science, and the support of 2.4 million members and online activists in its work to protect the planet's wildlife and wild places and to ensure a safe and healthy environment for all living things. Some of the things that make the organization interesting are the vast amount of web content available on its site, the various media that its marketers deploy, and the tools it provides to online activists and political bloggers to spread the group's message. The professionals at NRDC, which was named by *Worth* magazine as one of America's 100 best charities, know that more than one million members are the best storytelling asset available. By developing a terrific website to enlist people to donate their online voices, NRDC expands the team and its message-delivery capabilities considerably.

The site includes environmental news, resources, and information on topics such as clean air and energy; clean drinking water and oceans; wildlife and fish; and parks, forests, and wetlands. In addition, it offers online publications, links to laws and treaties, and a glossary of environmental terms. NRDC delivers the organization's message via audio, video, and text and also encourages others to support the cause through giving their time and money and through reusing online content.

"I came to NRDC from NPR initially, doing media relations," says Daniel Hinerfeld, associate director of communications for NRDC. "But because I'm in the L.A. office and we have entertainment industry contacts, I've started creating multimedia content for the site. We have a video called *Lethal Sounds*, narrated by Pierce Brosnan, that was my first big taste of multimedia." The video, which has been a hit on the festival circuit, details evidence linking sonar to a series of whale strandings in recent years. To encourage people to take action, the landing page for the video has multiple widgets and tools. From this page, viewers can easily send messages to elected officials, donate money, and send online postcards to friends. Links to additional content, such as an NRDC press release titled "Navy Sued over Harm to Whales from Mid-Frequency Sonar" and a detailed report titled "Sounding the Depths II," are just a click away. All this well-organized content, complete with easy ways to link to related information and to share content on blogs and with friends, is pulled together on the site and contributes greatly to the NRDC leadership position. And online content experts at NRDC are constantly looking for new ways to deliver their important messages.

"We created a podcast channel with broadcast-quality, journalistic-style packages," Hinerfeld says. "Our communications strategy is not just to reach the media, but to also reach the constituents directly." Hinerfeld draws extensively from his experience at NPR when he produces shows for the NRDC podcasts. "I always try hard to include points of view that are at odds with our own," he says. "I think it makes it more interesting, and it reinforces our own position. For example, when we conduct interviews with our own staff, we challenge people with difficult questions, not just softballs, much like a journalist would. Going this route makes it authentic. People don't want PR; they want something that's real."

Hinerfeld says that multimedia is very exciting because it gives NRDC an opportunity to reach younger constituencies. "I've come across people who are huge consumers of podcasts, and many listen to them during long commutes," he says. "We use this sort of content to bond with people in a different, less wonky way. We also profile our younger staff members, which is a way to personalize the institution." Many staff members have social networking profiles and use them to spread the word as well.

Within the news media that cover environmental issues on Capitol Hill, NRDC is very well known. But the site content, the audio and video, and the site components that are offered to bloggers to spread the message (and cause it to go viral) make the organization much more approachable, especially to online activists and the younger Facebook generation. The NRDC staffers are active participants in the market and on the sites and blogs their constituents read. All these efforts make their content authentic, because it is contextually appropriate for the audiences the group needs to reach.

Content: The Focus of Successful Websites

The NRDC site is an excellent example of a website that is designed to reach buyers. For the NRDC, the buyers are the more than one million members, advocates, and activists who use the site to work to protect the planet's wildlife and wild places and to promote a healthy environment.

Unfortunately, the vast majority of sites are built with the wrong focus. Yes, appearance and navigation are important: Appropriate colors, logos, fonts, and design make a site appealing. The right technologies, such as content management systems, make sites easier to update. But what really matters is the *content* itself, how that content is organized, and how it drives action from buyers.

To move content to its rightful place in driving a successful marketing and PR strategy, content must be the most important component. That focus can be tough for many people, both when their agencies push for hip and stylish design and when their information technology (IT) departments obsess about the architecture. It is your role to think like a publisher and begin any new site or site redesign by starting with the content strategy.

Reaching a Global Marketplace

In recent years, I've delivered presentations in many countries, including New Zealand, Malaysia, India, Turkey, and Trinidad. As I traveled to my keynote speeches in each of the Baltic countries (Latvia, Lithuania, and Estonia), I was struck by how plugged in to the web their residents are. My high-speed connections in this part of the world were much faster than in most parts of the United States.

The incredibly successful marketers I met in each of these small countries impressed me greatly with their outward thinking. When you live in a country like Latvia, your home market is tiny, requiring you to sell your products and services internationally. It also requires that you think deeply about your buyers in the global marketplace.

Consider LessLoss Audio Devices, a company based in Kaunas, Lithuania. LessLoss creates amazing (and fabulously expensive) high-end audio products and has become famous among rabid audiophiles worldwide for power cords, filters, cables, and other equipment. LessLoss sells all over the world, and its site has a deliberately global focus. The e-commerce and search engine optimization (SEO) platform is managed by Globaltus, also a Lithuanian company.

The LessLoss site includes amazingly detailed information about the audio devices, together with terrific photos. For example, there's an essay on "The Concept of Noise," which details why a sound-preserving technique known as power filtering is important. After all, when you sell power cables that can cost a thousand U.S. dollars, they had better be good. (And it's probably a good idea to explain *why* they're so good.)

"It is amazing how people from such a small country can reach customers worldwide and prove to be well respected," says Tomas Paplauskas, CEO of Globaltus. "The power of the Internet gives the opportunity to reach huge markets. Just imagine how few of these amazing power cords you could sell in Lithuania. There are no more local businesses—all businesses are global."

I think there is an important lesson here. We can all learn from the successful companies in these small countries, companies that have created content-rich websites to reach a global audience. And we can all reproduce their success. The marketplace is the outside world, not just your home city, state, or even country.

Make Your Site Mobile Friendly

As people use mobile web browsers on their iPhones, Androids, or other devices, it is important that your site be mobile friendly—displaying content quickly and optimizing it for viewing on smaller screens. Many sites still don't have a mobile-friendly architecture, so those organizations miss out on opportunities to sell to the many people now accessing their sites from wireless devices. Your site should have different sets of HTML code that recognize what kind of device visitors are using (computer or mobile) and display the site in the best format.

"It is important to make sure the mobile content loads quickly," says Jim Stewart, CEO of Stew Art Media, a Melbourne-based web development and SEO firm. "People accessing your site with mobile devices are doing so wirelessly, and it's costing them money in their data plans. You want the site to load quickly for them. And they've got a much smaller screen. We're almost back to the days of the early web, when smaller, 'lightweight' pages were better."

Stewart says that designing pages for mobile display requires rethinking the sort of content you offer. "You should display the most crucial information that you would think someone coming in through a mobile device would want," he says. "It might be the menu if you're a restaurant, or it might be the booking number. In Australia over 25 percent of PayPal users have made a purchase using a smartphone. If you use Google AdWords you can now target mobile users directly and place a clickable phone number in the ad so they simply call through to your business, bypassing your website entirely. We had a car dealership client that used this method and had an amazing result."

As you're developing content for mobile devices, remember that search engines have a separate ranking system for mobile. That means there are implications for the SEO strategies that will get your site ranked highly. "Google has Mobile Google, which is a different version from the normal or classic Google," Stewart says. "It's designed and marked up differently, and Google gives preference to sites that are mobile friendly. For example, make sure that Google understands where your mobile content is by setting up what they call a site map for mobile users. This map will be different from the site map for normal users. And if the site is about a local business, you need to use geographic descriptors. For instance, many buyers just type 'flowers' into Mobile Google, and quite often they will get Google Places information in the results. That's because Google has made an assessment that people want that information locally or close to them, or they want a business that services their particular area."

Here are three things you can do right now:

1. Make sure your site is mobile compliant. You need the pages to load properly in mobile devices.
2. Create a mobile site map so the search engines can index your pages for mobile browsers.
3. Use few words and small graphics. People don't read much on mobile devices and they want the data to come quickly.

The challenge is to understand this new landscape so you can get your business into the mix at that precise moment of decision. I chose to work with experts and it was the right decision for me. Don't miss out on opportunities to sell to the many people now accessing sites and searching for products and services like yours from wireless devices.

Putting It All Together with Content

As you're reading through this discussion of unifying your online marketing and PR efforts on your website, you might be thinking, "That's easy for a smaller organization or one that has only one product line, but I work for a large company with many brands." Yes, it is more difficult to coordinate a wide variety of content when you have to juggle multiple brands, geographic variations, languages, and other considerations common to large companies. But with a large, widely dispersed organization, putting it all together on a corporate site might be even more important because showing a unified personality reaps benefits.

"The key is the collaboration between the different business units, the corporate offices, and the departments," says Sarah F. Garnsey, head of marketing and web communications at Textron Inc. "At Textron, each business has its own independently operated website, which makes coordination difficult because each is a well-defined brand that may be more familiar to people than our corporate brand."

Textron Inc., a global company with yearly revenues of $13 billion and more than 35,000 employees in 33 countries, is recognized for strong brands such as Bell Helicopter, Cessna Aircraft Company, and E-Z-GO (golf carts). The company has several dozen websites, typically for the individual brands, such as Bell Helicopter. "Through search logs we learned that many people were searching for product and business information on the corporate [Textron] site," Garnsey says. "That was a wake-up call for us, because we had thought that people were going to the business sites for this information. So we've built out the corporate site with more content about each of the businesses." On a visit to the site, I was able to watch a video featuring the CEO of Cessna Aircraft, check out a lot of great photos of the products, and read feature stories about employees such as John Delamarter, who's the program manager of Lycoming's Thunderbolt engine and who discussed his pride and pleasure in his work. Textron has a well-organized online media room, and because the company's stock is traded on the New York Stock Exchange, there is also an investor relations section on the site.

"We work with the businesses to showcase interesting things, and we try to have fresh content on the site and update it with new weekly stories," Garnsey says. "But the content is only as good as the management of the content and the processes. With a large site, rigor of process is required that many companies might underestimate. It takes coordination and management. For example, I can't make the content in the recruiting section of the site compelling unless I get the complete cooperation of the human resources department. People had grown to believe that you just throw the content at a webmaster and it all just works. But it doesn't—the days of the guy with the server under the desk are over."

Garnsey has a set of processes and procedures to make certain that the Textron site meets the needs of buyers and that everything on it works well, and she has a small team that works with her to coordinate with the people who manage division and product company websites. "We have a content management process to make sure everything is fresh, has been reviewed, and is passed by legal," she says. "But a primary component is that we make sure that the voice of the customer is captured and built into all of our electronic communications. We work on how to draw users into the content and use the site to form a relationship with them. Even if they don't purchase something from us right away, maybe they will become interested in the company stock or in something from one of the brands like Cessna." To make sure the site follows best practices, Garnsey brings people into a lab for annual usability tests and research. "We also do an audit of all of our dot-com sites every year to make sure that all sites comply with the standards," she says. "And each year we hold a web summit of all the Textron people working on web initiatives from all over the company. We try to foster a community of people who otherwise would have no reason to speak with each other because the individual businesses don't have a lot in common."

Great Websites: More Art Than Science

The more I research websites—and I've checked out thousands over the past several years—the more I realize that the best ones unite many important factors in a way that is difficult to describe. They just feel right—as if the creator of the site cares a great deal and wants that passion to shine through. Like a sprinkling of fairy dust, the effect is important but inde-scribable. However, I'm convinced that the key is to understand buyers (or those who may donate, subscribe, join, or vote) and build content espe-cially for them. So how do you create such a site?

Putting it all together to achieve this effect requires a combination of tal-ents. I've found that the best websites are built by a team of people who col-lectively are skilled in the following areas: graphic design, content creation, platform-specific development, search engine optimization, and project management. Almost nobody can do all this alone, so a team approach really is the best way to build an effective website.

If you're a solopreneur or a small business leader or owner building a website, you're likely going to need to seek some outside help, perhaps hir-ing freelancers to help you.

Here are some notes on the five skills:

1. **Graphic design**: Graphic designers have an eye for the visual ele-ments that make up a site. They are skilled at translating the attri-butes of an organization to the web by working with such elements as color, images, and spatial relationships. I love great graphic design and am in awe of the professionals whose skills leap off the screen.

2. **Content creation**: Content is what goes onto the individual pages, including text, videos, infographics, photos, and other images. It's the primary subject of this book. I've been writing and speaking about the importance of content in marketing for 20 years now, and it is still the most overlooked element of most sites. You can be on top of design, development, and SEO but still let bad content creep onto your site. If you don't have content creation skills on hand, I've long recom-mended you hire a journalist (see Chapter 23 for specific advice).

3. **Platform-specific development**: Your developers' job is to bring the designers' and content creators' work to life via code that will be sent to users' browsers. Usually this happens with the help of particular web publishing platforms. Your developer(s) should have expertise in the platform you will be using. My sites and blog are built on HubSpot, so my developer needs to know the ins and outs of HubSpot's features and peculiarities. Make sure the site they develop looks beautiful on the smaller screens of mobile devices.

4. **Search engine optimization:** People who are skilled in SEO make certain your site sends all the right signals to the search engines. SEO optimization helps your content get indexed and returned in searches related to what your company does or offers. There's much more about SEO in Chapter 22.

5. **Project management:** The person who orchestrates the website project brings together and leads the team with the skills. The best person for this work is somebody who knows intimately how the website will help drive action, such as by educating, selling, or driving donations. A working knowledge of the other four skills is ideal, so that the leader can give clear and sensible directions and feedback.

These five areas of skill are very different, so get the people you need and make sure they're clear on their responsibilities and how they'll work together.

A friend alerted me to one of his favorite companies, saying, "You should check out WaterField Designs." My friend said they make all kinds of bags and sleeves for just about any device. At the time, I was tired of the same old black ballistic nylon bags everybody sells, and I wasn't interested in luggage companies that compete on price and rely on a rudimentary photo or two and some poorly edited copy about a bag's features.

The moment I saw the WaterField Designs site, I was hooked! The company and products were perfectly aligned to my lifestyle and to me. It was as if they knew me.

As I was reviewing the site, I became convinced that this site was created by a team with all of the skills I've identified. It's not a coincidence when a site feels like it was created especially for you. It means somebody understood the buyer persona you belong to, somebody created content tailored to that persona, somebody designed text and visuals to present this content effectively, somebody . . . well, you get the idea. The team did its job, and what they created together is so much more effective than a simple product pitch. When I end up somewhere that educates and informs me with a video, a few blog posts, or maybe a Q&A with some instructive photos, I'm ready to make a buying decision in just a few minutes. And guess where I'm inclined to buy? Yes, with the place that educated me.

The WaterField Designs site is compelling in so many ways. As I name a few of the elements I really like, notice that what draws me in is the content, but also imagine the other work that brought that content to my screen.

Hey Gary: The WaterField Designs founder, Gary Waterfield, is very visible. In fact, a link to his email is on every single page. In the Our Story page, we learn: "Gary Waterfield started the company in 1998 with these principles which still guide us today: Make products you can be proud of, treat people with respect, and exercise kindness—we're all human. You won't find corporate intrigue, shareholder revolt, or venture capital drama at our modest headquarters. Instead you will find pot-luck lunches, group outings, and the occasional employee celebration."

Real-time products and real-time content on the blog: I love the fact that WaterField Designs brings its new iPhone cases to market just hours after Tim Cook and the Apple team unveil the products. WaterField Designs was even featured on *ABC World News Tonight* because it had new model cases ready so quickly. And, of course, it tells the story on its blog.

Six-word reviews: Showcasing happy customers is always a challenge for any company. I love how WaterField Designs has a page with what look to be hundreds of six-word reviews. For example: "Enjoy unholstering your Mac through security.—Raymond S., Australia." I submitted my own: "Note to wife: 'No! It's mine!'"

Photos: The images of the products in use are beautiful, showcasing them in a way that makes me want to buy a bunch of them. Each product has multiple product images, so you can see detail from many different angles.

Videos: The products have videos where a WaterField Designs employee, perhaps Gary himself, describes what goes into the item. The iPad Smart Case video has had almost 80,000 views as I write this. Remarkable.

I was glad to be turned on to WaterField Designs. Not only do I find the web content compelling, but I also love the products. I quickly purchased one of the bags (the Franklin Tote). After having used if for several months, I was still thrilled with my purchase so I went back and purchased a backpack and a small bag for my power cables. Organizations filled with people who take the time to understand the needs of buyers they wish to reach, and then develop information to educate and inform those buyers, are more successful than organizations that just make stuff up.

Effective sites like WaterField Designs draw on the passion of the people who build them, and reflect the personality of someone dedicated to helping others. As you develop content to further your organizational goals, remember that a successful approach is often more art than science. The content you offer must have distinctive qualities, and your personality needs to show. A well-executed website, like a high-quality television program or film, is a combination of content and delivery. But on the web, many organizations spend much more time and money on the design and delivery aspects than on the content itself. Don't fall into that trap. Perfecting that critical mix of content, design, and technology is where the art comes in. Adding personality and authenticity and reaching particular buyer personas make the challenge even more daunting. Just remember: There is no absolute right or wrong way to create a website; each organization has an individual and important story to tell.

8 Marketing and PR in Real Time

In mid-2019, I was flying on the American Airlines shuttle from Boston to New York. Soon after takeoff, we hit a flock of geese.

The pilot declared an emergency, and we landed 11 minutes later back at Boston Logan airport. As soon as I deplaned, I shot from the terminal window a photo showing blood and feathers on the nose and windscreen of the plane. Then I posted it on my Twitter and Instagram feeds: "A first for me in something like 4 million air miles. We hit a goose on takeoff and the skilled @americanair pilots brought us back for an emergency landing."

About 30 minutes later, American Airlines tweeted back to me: "We have some of the best captains in the business! Thanks for hanging in there with us today."

While I was pleased to see American Airlines get back to me in real time, I never imagined that my photo would soon become famous.

I've learned that the news media continually tracks air traffic control chatter. When our pilot declared an emergency, news editors around the world instantly knew something was happening. The word "emergency" gets their attention. Instantly, reporters began scrambling for information, anything that could help tell the story.

Because my tweet used the word "emergency" and I tagged American Airlines, a real-time search let members of the media know we had landed safely. My tweet also provided a photo of the plane with blood and feathers on it, ready for news outlets to publish.

Throughout the day, I received requests to use the photo from CBS-TV, NBC-TV, ABC-TV, WBZ-TV, WPIX, Boston25, The Weather Channel, *USA Today*, the *New York Post*, and others. And after eventually landing in New York, I did a television interview for ABC-TV that aired on *World News Tonight*, the U.S. network's national evening news.

Fortunately, our air emergency was handled skillfully by the American Airlines pilots. Nobody was injured—except the poor geese, who never had a chance.

When we landed back at Logan Airport, American Airlines readied another airplane, transferred our bags, and re-boarded us. The ground staff did a fabulous job getting us moving again with minimal delay.

As the adrenaline of the emergency wore off, I reflected, as I often do, about the power of instant communication. Think about it: The pilots instantly got the support they needed to make an emergency landing, news editors were notified of the emergency as it happened and connected with resources for reporting it, and yours truly happened into a chance to appear on national network television and in national newspapers. Friends and clients around the world saw that, and it grew my reputation as somebody who knows how to get noticed online. That marketers can tap into this power represents an incredible opportunity to grow your business.

Real-Time Marketing and PR

In a world where speed and agility are now essential to success, most organizations still operate slowly and deliberately, cementing each step months in advance and responding to new developments through careful but time-consuming processes. Most companies cannot respond quickly to an opportunity because they are operating under the old rules of controlled engagement planned well in advance. But the Internet has fundamentally changed the pace of business, compressing time and rewarding speed.

Real time means that news breaks over minutes, not days. It's when people watch what's happening on social networks such as Twitter, Facebook, and YouTube and cleverly insert themselves into stories. Real-time urgency is also important in customer service, where organizations fix issues instantly rather than taking the typical days or weeks to respond to a complaint. Real time means companies develop (or refine) products or services instantly, based on feedback from customers or events in the marketplace. In all aspects of business, anyone who sees an opportunity and becomes the first to act on it gains tremendous advantage.

The idea of real time—of creating marketing or public relations initiatives as well as responding to customers *right now*, while the moment is ripe—delivers tremendous competitive advantage. You've got to operate quickly to succeed in this world. These ideas are the subject of my book, *Real-Time Marketing & PR: How to Instantly Engage Your Market, Connect with Customers, and Create Products That Grow Your Business Now*. This chapter highlights some of the tactics that you can use to instantly engage your buyers when they are eager to hear from you. If you've read *Real-Time Marketing & PR*, you might want to read on anyway because the stories here are not in that book.

My first job was on a Wall Street trading desk in the 1980s. I witnessed real-time technology transforming financial trading into a game where instant information informs split-second decisions worth millions of dollars.

Traders desperately search their real-time newsfeeds and analysis tools for an angle, any angle. Who's the president meeting with today? Is there any disruption in the energy markets, perhaps because of unrest in the Middle East? What's happening in Japan? Germany? The United Kingdom? As they pore through data and news, the traders are poised, ready to commit huge sums of money when the moment is right.

It has taken decades, but the impact of the real-time revolution is now being felt in all industries, including marketing and public relations.

We can react instantly to what's happening in the news, just like a bond trader. We can engage members of the media on their timetables, precisely when they are writing stories. But we've got to develop a business culture that encourages speed over sloth. The MBA-style approach of working from spreadsheets that predict what to do months into the future is no help when news is breaking in your industry right now.

In the emerging real-time business environment, size is no longer a decisive advantage. Speed and agility win the moment.

As financial market players know, advantage comes from being the first to react to market opportunities. The same thing is true for all companies. If you're first to engage the market, people notice, and your offering gains valuable attention. If you react early and connect with customers as their concerns arise, they see you as thoughtful and caring. And the mainstream media are always looking to cover the latest trend or fast-moving company, so you're likely to get much more coverage if you operate in real time.

John Green Thumps Tom Cruise

Tom Cruise was everywhere on television the first week of June 2014. He was promoting his new megabudget sci-fi spectacular, *Edge of Tomorrow*. Cruise deployed the tried-and-true method in which the film's star goes on the entertainment television shows and late-night talk shows.

Cruise used old marketing and PR techniques to promote his big-budget film.

Meanwhile, *The Fault in Our Stars* was released that same weekend.

John Green, the author of the *New York Times* bestseller of same name, rallied his fans to become #TFIOS brand ambassadors. These #FaultFanatics talked up the film on social networks in a big way. They drove the small-budget film to number one in the box office on opening weekend.

The Fault in Our Stars earned an estimated $58 million at the box office (against a film budget of $12 million), crushing *Edge of Tomorrow*, which generated about $29 million (a poor opening weekend against a $178 million budget).

John Green fans, who loved *The Fault in Our Stars* book, drove the real-time box office success. And it was thanks to Green's dedicated online outreach.

Throughout the year leading up to the release, Green communicated to his fans as insiders, providing all sorts of details on the process of creating the film version. Whenever anything important happened in production, Green shared the news in real time.

Green had already sold the film rights and told fans that he had no financial incentive in ticket sales. He talked up the movie because he liked it. Through his Tumblr blog, Twitter account (@johngreen), video channel, and websites, Green made fans feel a part of the process.

"I think a big thing is John acted like us, the fans, rather than as a celebrity to promote the fandom involved in the movie," my daughter Allison explained at the time of the release. "He encourages people to make art and music and responses to his book. Some of those he reblogs on Tumblr. He is very open in communicating with his fans like they are his equals, which fosters community."

His video of the movie premiere is a great example of how Green brings fans along on the real-time ride. In the video you are with him as he arrives, walks the (not) red carpet, and mugs for photographers.

Rallying the fans works for any business. When your better-funded competitors are focused on traditional marketing and PR, why not bypass them and talk directly to your audience instead? Get in the moment and communicate instantly. Share what you're up to as it happens, in real time. You can thump your competitors, too—even if they have a lot more money.

Develop Your Real-Time Mind-Set

When I speak with people about the ideas of real-time marketing and public relations, they understand that our access to today's communications tools means we can communicate immediately. Twitter allows instant dialogue with buyers. Blog posts help you get your ideas into the marketplace right now. And monitoring tools like Google Alerts and TweetDeck provide up-to-the-second knowledge of what people are saying about you, your company, and its products. However, while people do generally *understand* the situation, many have difficulty adopting the personal and corporate mind-set and habits required for success. Too many individuals, and the organizations they work for, take the cautious and careful approach: Always wait and see, and always check with the experts before acting on an opportunity. Unfortunately, this typical behavior will lose you the advantage.

As an example of one organization that has developed the mind-set required for success, consider the GolinHarris approach of what the company calls "The Bridge"—a network of real-time storytelling centers staffed in the Americas, Europe, and Asia-Pacific. This Wall Street trading room approach is exactly what I've constantly talked about, and I'm excited to see it being implemented, so I connected with Jim Dowd, executive director of national media for GolinHarris International, a communications firm and part of the Interpublic Group, to learn more. "We use The Bridge as a listening outpost, but we are doing it a little differently because we have the mainstream media folks and the digital folks working side by side," Dowd says. "So we are not just looking at social media, which is obviously the flavor of the day. Digital and mainstream are literally sitting next to each other and they are coming up with ideas and are pitching media together, and that is where we have seen just terrific traction."

For example, on the day that then first lady Michelle Obama announced a new food pyramid called MyPlate, the GolinHarris team watched the press conference live on CNN looking for ways to get their clients into the emerging memes. "We are watching all the activity online and took an idea to Hartz to create a food pyramid for dogs," Dowd says. The client loved the idea and reacted quickly, and the team generated some attention as a result.

With most clients working at a glacially slow pace, requiring lengthy legal and PR client-side reviews, I wondered how GolinHarris is able to get speedy sign-offs on ideas generated from The Bridge. "Yeah, approval is always tricky, particularly with legal departments," Dowd says. Golin-Harris works with clients to develop topics ahead of time in anticipation of potential stories so that they can work quickly. "With clients like McDonald's we have general topics that we predict, like if something comes up about the Happy Meal. McDonald's have preapproved that we can have certain conversations about Happy Meals with language we can go out with."

The Bridge is set up just like a 24-hour Wall Street trading desk, with three regions—Asia, Europe, and North America—passing the work around the globe. "We are truly doing it globally," Dowd says. "We are 24/7 so we will scour the landscape the first few hours of the day here in New York, then we will pass all of our results and insights on to Chicago and Chicago to L.A. And, you know, the whole notion of offices and cubes may go away. It's exciting to be able to walk in The Bridge and literally see what is going on."

When you have a real-time mind-set and the tools of a facility like The Bridge, then newsjacking becomes second nature. (Newsjacking is inserting your ideas into a breaking news story by writing a real-time blog post or shooting a video to interest reporters and generate coverage. I discuss newsjacking in detail in Chapter 21.) "Our client Autotrader.com challenged us to make them the leader in all of the post–Super Bowl auto commercial coverage," Dowd says. Autotrader did not advertise during the Super Bowl but wanted to generate a bunch of attention anyway—a classic newsjacking strategy.

Autotrader's analysts worked with GolinHarris to create data on consumers' real-time search patterns during the Super Bowl. They used data from the Autotrader.com site and correlated that to the times auto commercials aired, looking for lift (how much of a boost in search activity each vehicle got in the hour after its ad appeared). They provided the resulting data to the media, who used it in stories like "Acura NSX Won Big with Super Bowl Spot, Survey Says," which appeared on the *Wall Street Journal* site.

"There are lots of clients who love the notion of The Bridge and real-time marketing and what we are doing but aren't jumping on it out of fear—fear of the unknown, fear of the new," Dowd says. "A lot of our clients are still quite old school and traditional."

There's nothing like success to break down the fear barrier. Dowd cites Dow Chemical as a noteworthy GolinHarris real-time success. The company is very careful with stories related to such topics as chemistry or chemical engineering or stem cell research, but that doesn't mean it can't engage in real time.

"We were in The Bridge tracking that President Obama was going to give the Teacher of the Year Award and we were watching live on CNN," Dowd says. "And it was a chemistry teacher who won that award so we immediately got approval from Dow Chemical to go ahead and offer up public congratulations to the teacher, and that resulted in some nice coverage. Even with the trickier clients there are always topics that will work."

The real-time mind-set recognizes the importance of *speed*. It is an attitude to business (and to life) that emphasizes *moving quickly* when the time is right.

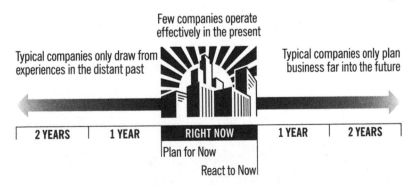

Don't get me wrong. I'm not saying you should focus only on the now and not plan for the future. Developing a real-time mind-set should not feel like an either-or proposition; you can and should do both.

Real-Time Blog Post Drives $1 Million in New Business

Imagine that you're among the first to know that a huge company is about to acquire one of your competitors. What would you do right now?

Not tomorrow. Now!

How about writing a blog post about it in real time?

That's what Eloqua CEO Joe Payne did when he learned that Oracle, a software giant, was to acquire the assets of marketing automation company and Eloqua competitor Market2Lead. A colleague mentioned the acquisition, and as soon as Payne confirmed the news on the Oracle website, he started working on his blog post.

The Oracle announcement, which was located in a difficult-to-find part of the company's website, contained only a terse one-paragraph announcement: *Oracle has acquired the intellectual property assets of Market2Lead, a provider of demand generation and marketing automation software. Market2Lead's technology helps companies improve demand generation to increase sales and marketing effectiveness. Oracle plans to integrate Market2Lead's technology into Oracle CRM applications. The financial details of the transaction were not disclosed.*

Payne realized that there was a tremendous opportunity *right now* to write a blog post. He figured that if *he* hadn't known about the acquisition, then others probably didn't know, either. "The announcement was buried on the Oracle website," he says. "No one else had found it yet." Payne had a unique opportunity to define what the deal meant to the market.

In his post "Oracle Joins the Party," Payne wrote, in part: *I expect Oracle's entry to make a major difference in the attention paid to this sector. It's going to open marketers' eyes, and, as a result, expand the market. This is exactly the type of movement this industry needs. You see, the potential market for lead management systems is less than 10 percent penetrated.*

Payne chose to write a high-level blog post that talks about what the acquisition meant to the market for this kind of software. "We needed to give people information they could sink their teeth into," he says. "And it was picked up very quickly by the media because of what I wrote. News organizations immediately wrote their own stories and blog posts, and they quoted my post as if they had done an interview with me."

Can you see what Payne did? Oracle announces an acquisition but provides almost no details. The media are hungry for something to say and someone to quote. Bingo, a Google search pops up Payne's post, and now reporters, analysts, and bloggers have an authority to cite in their stories.

As a result of this real-time market commentary, Eloqua became an important part of the resulting stories published in outlets that included *Bloomberg Businessweek*, *InfoWorld*, *Customer Experience Matrix*, *PC World*, and *Customer Think*.

But Payne and the Eloqua team didn't stop there. The next step in this real-time outreach was to alert existing and potential Market2Lead clients to Payne's blog post. "Eloqua salespeople who had lost a deal to Market-2Lead immediately sent emails to each customer, linking to the blog post," he says. "In many cases, we broke the news to those clients that their marketing automation company had been acquired. We outlined what the change would likely mean to them. That gave us credibility with the clients and hurt Oracle and Market2Lead, because they were not the first to describe to their buyers what the deal meant."

The Eloqua sales team then offered a money-back guarantee to any Market-2Lead customer who wanted to switch to Eloqua. "We wanted to take away the friction of moving," Payne says. "The tone of the offer was designed to be helpful and informative, to let people know 'We're here, and we would love to have your business.'" And the guarantee meant that if customers were unhappy with the switch, Eloqua would give them their money back.

Eloqua salespeople began hearing back right away. "Market2Lead clients responded by email and said things like, 'We didn't know this—thank you very much' and 'Hey, we should talk.'" Soon these Market2Lead clients were engaged in discussions about moving their business over to Eloqua.

Payne says that within two weeks, Eloqua closed a deal with software company Red Hat that was worth more than $500,000 over two years. It also closed with TRUSTe, a major Internet privacy services company. The half dozen new Eloqua customers gained from this real-time communications effort combined to generate just under $1 million in business—all business directly related to Payne's real-time blog post. "There are other intangible benefits you can't put a price on as a real-time marketer," he says. "We got tremendous credibility in our industry for being a trusted source of news and information. People like that we are straight shooters."

Because Payne's post and the resulting media stories are all indexed by Google and the other search engines, people looking for information about the transaction even months later still found Eloqua in the thick of the discussion. If you're an analyst combing the marketing automation industry, or if you are evaluating marketing automation platforms, Eloqua moves to the head of the pack.

I'm constantly amazed at what a real-time blog post can do. In this case, it generated a million dollars' worth of new business! When everyone else is pitching the media using traditional methods, why not frame the discussion happening right now with your own well-placed commentary on the news?

There's an interesting footnote to this real-time story. Soon after, Oracle acquired Eloqua in a transaction worth $871 million. Based on the market valuation of the company and annual revenue, that one blog post was worth an extra $10 million to the sale price. Not bad for one real-time blog post.

The Time Is Now

As you develop your own real-time mind-set, be on the lookout for ways to engage your marketplace when the time is right. There are many ways to communicate instantly, and the tools and strategies will be different for each situation. Let's take a look at some of the ways you can engage in real time.

Create Advertising Based on Real-Time Events

In a world of boring advertising campaigns, real-time marketing and PR get noticed. During coverage broadcast on NBC of the London Summer Olympics, AT&T ran several near real-time ads involving swimming that astonished me. The ads showed a young person watching the actual footage of a world-record swim from the day before on a mobile phone. You see the NBC clip of the world-record finish and hear the actual commentary. Then you realize the young person is a swimmer and is writing the new world-record time with the word "goal" on a whiteboard at home.

One AT&T ad was Ryan Lochte's world-record 400-meter Individual Medley where he beat Michael Phelps.

A few nights later the AT&T ad was even better because Rebecca Soni had broken the 200-meter breaststroke world record the day before in the semifinals. The near real-time ad ran the next day immediately after the finals, which she won beating her own world record. These commercials related directly to the Olympic event results from the previous day and therefore generated more interest among viewers than the standard TV spot.

Respond to Citizens Right Away

While I was in Kolkata (Calcutta), India, several people told me about the remarkable use of Facebook by the Kolkata Traffic Police. Amazingly, as I write this, more than 200,000 people "like" the Kolkata Traffic Police Facebook page.

In a world where many are skeptical about social media and real-time communications (dismissing tools like Facebook as "for kids"), the Kolkata Traffic Police serve citizens in the way they prefer—via social media and in real time.

The Kolkata Traffic Police Facebook page includes traffic status updates, such as "Traffic along R B Connector & P C Connector are heavy due to water logging" together with detailed reports posted as photos. This one had 119 likes and 46 comments such as: "immensely helpful.:) Thanks a ton KTP" and "This is very proactive. Thank you, Kolkata Traffic Police!" Can you believe that people are fans of the police and are thanking them in public?

In real time, citizens can use the page to lodge complaints and the police will follow up. Many such complaints are about the widespread problem of taxi drivers' refusal of certain fares. With Facebook, a complaint is lodged (people upload photo and video evidence to Facebook) and the police follow up with the result of the inquiry. For example:

> @Akhil Malik. As per your Facebook complaint regarding taxi refusal vide memo No F/B-58 dated – 11.01.13, this is to inform you that the driver of the cabs (WB04D8217 & WB04D5996) have been prosecuted. . . .You may be asked to appear before Ld. Court, if required. Thanks & regards.

This serves as a transparent way for the police to show in real time the work they are doing and also publicly calls out the offender if caught. And over time, as taxi drivers figure out what's going on, the problems should diminish.

Like! I just love this real-time use of social media. So do the citizens of Kolkata. The effort serves as positive PR for the police. Heck, if a police force can use Facebook for real-time communications at work, why are so many organizations still fearful and saying "no"?

Create a Real-Time Application

Hagerty Insurance Agency is a specialty provider of insurance for classic cars. The company created the free smartphone app *Hagerty Insider* to provide valuation tools for classic car enthusiasts. The app helps them easily find their car's value and better understand trends and changing prices in the marketplace.

The real-time component comes as a built-in classic car auction tracker. At the auctions that are a regular and captivating aspect of this hobby community, the app provides updated details of each vehicle offered for sale. The listing includes the current high bid amount and the car's sold or unsold status. This allows people who don't attend the auction in person to follow results as they happen.

For serious classic car collectors, *Hagerty Insider* is especially valuable when the community gathers in Scottsdale, Arizona, each January for a series of major auctions: Barrett-Jackson, Bonhams, Gooding, and RM Sotheby's. Since many of these auctions are held concurrently, people can use *Hagerty Insider* to monitor current prices and make better informed bids.

Offering *Hagerty Insider* free to collectors gets the Hagerty Insurance Agency name in front of buyers at the exact moment when they are doing what they love. The exposure from this and other marketing initiatives inclines collectors to choose Hagerty when they make a new purchase. This strategy has made them the number one classic car insurance company in the United States.

Donate Your Product to Those in Need

It has been estimated that more than a billion people worldwide witnessed part of the live broadcast of the dramatic rescue of the 33 Chilean miners in October 2010. Recall that they had been trapped in the darkness of the underground mine for many weeks.

Thus, many of those billion people also saw the Oakley sunglasses the miners were wearing as they emerged into daylight. That's because Oakley donated the sunglasses, which provided the miners' sensitive eyes with protection from ultraviolet light.

No matter how you choose to measure it, the benefit of such a marketing coup is enormous. According to research done for CNBC by Front Row Analytics, just the worldwide television impact alone generated $41 million in equivalent advertising for Oakley.

To succeed with a real-time product donation like Oakley did, you need to be aware of what's happening in your market category and be prepared to spring into action at a moment's notice.

Tweet Thoughts to Your Market When They Are Watching

As HBO was replaying his 1997 movie *Private Parts*, radio personality Howard Stern popped onto Twitter and offered a real-time running commentary on the movie. It wasn't planned or announced. You had to be there. He tweeted about 100 times with fun insider observations.

Lucky fans who were (1) watching the movie on HBO, (2) simultaneously monitoring Twitter, and (3) following Stern were in the real-time loop.

Many had their questions answered live, as in this reply from @HowardStern: "Giamatti was brilliant. made it all so easy. RT @burtmania How was it working with Giamatti before he was such a well-known actor?"

The buzz generated by Stern prompted many fans to tweet their friends and encourage them to tune in and see what he had to say about the movie.

While very few people have an audience as large as Howard Stern's, we all have opportunities to use Twitter to comment in real time as something is happening in our marketplace. Perhaps you can offer running commentary on a speech at an industry event. Or maybe, like Stern, you can live-tweet comments about a television show as it is broadcast. I'm imagining a clothing designer commenting on the fashion at the Academy Awards or a golf coach offering real-time commentary on an important tournament.

Comment on Regulatory Change in Your Industry

Officials from the U.S. Federal Communications Commission (FCC) were holed up in meetings to discuss the issue of bill shock, the surprise a consumer experiences when receiving a mobile phone bill with much higher charges than expected. While the meeting was taking place, Jeff Barak of Amdocs, a company that provides customer care, billing, and order management systems for telecommunications carriers and Internet services providers, posted: "No need to be (bill) shocked" on the company blog. Barak argued that it's actually in the mobile phone service providers' interest to work with customers to avoid bill shock, because preserving customer loyalty is so important in a highly competitive market.

This clever tactic works because people interested in the potential legislation that might emerge from a meeting of government officials are eagerly looking at the news for any real-time updates. So when a company like Amdocs comments, the information gets picked up by those people's real-time Google Alerts.

Amdocs was rewarded soon after, when Penton Media publication *Connected Planet* devoted an entire blog post to the Amdocs position in a piece called "Not Being Shocked by Bill Shock." Reaching an important industry journalist in real time gets you noticed. Plus, the relationship that's built lasts much longer than just that moment. After the meetings were completed, the FCC published its proposal for new rules requiring companies to notify customers when they are about to exceed plan limits and incur extra charges. Anyone researching the proposal could come upon the Amdocs piece as well.

As we saw in both the Eloqua and Amdocs examples, your blog is a great place to add your take on a story as it is breaking. But don't just write the post and walk away. Alert people to the information by tweeting about it, posting it in your company's online media room, or sending a link to the journalists who might be interested.

Use a News Release to React to Another Company's Announcement

While busy at an industry conference, Richard Harrison, president of email marketing technology company SMTP.com, learned that Amazon.com had just announced that it was entering the email delivery market. Harrison decided to put out an immediate press release with the headline "SMTP, Inc. Welcomes Amazon to the Email Delivery Market."

He received a call from a reporter at online industry trade publication *ClickZ* right away, and soon a story appeared featuring his take on the announcement and looking at how it might affect email service providers (ESPs): "Will Amazon's Commodity E-Mail Service Harm ESPs?"

Harrison's take on the experience? "It's all about momentum," he says. "It's hard to create momentum on your own as the small guy, but if someone else creates it, the sooner you can ride it, the more you can benefit. Like momentum stocks, you don't know how far they will go, but the sooner you buy, the more you make."

* * *

These are just a few examples to get you thinking about the power of real-time communications. As I've studied the phenomenon of instant engagement, I've noticed that speed is typically an advantage that the smaller, nimbler outfits have over the larger ones. If you're an upstart in a competitive industry, real-time marketing and public relations allow you to compete and win. They even permit one person with a computer or mobile phone to start a movement to help thousands of people in time of need, making a huge difference in the world.

Snapchat for Business

Live-streaming and short-form video applications for smartphones have become exciting new ways to share interesting aspects of life and business and gain new followers and customers as a result. The most popular applications include Instagram video, Twitter video, Snapchat Stories, and Facebook Live. You'll learn more about Facebook Live in Chapter 17.

These applications are used to share with the world what you're seeing right at this moment, so others can experience it with you in real time (in the case of the streaming apps) or nearly real time (in the case of short-form video). These apps can turn anyone into a citizen journalist. And for marketers, they open up the possibility of sharing all kinds of information that can serve as marketing content. A live operation at a hospital, a tour of a home for sale, a peek backstage at a rock concert, a coach's pep talk before the big game, or a product design meeting at company headquarters all become shareable in an exciting and intimate way.

Snapchat has exploded in popularity since its launch, surpassing 150 million daily active users. The company went public in March 2017 with a $30 billion valuation. This free iOS and Android mobile app can send video, images, and texts between friends. The Snapchat app offers similar features to Twitter, Instagram, and Facebook, but with a twist: The messages disappear immediately after viewing. Snapchat is a way to chat with people without creating any lasting evidence of the discussion. The Snapchat logo is a ghost because it is ephemeral—now you see it, now you don't.

While the basic Snapchat service is interesting as a real-time communications tool, it doesn't work for marketing and PR because of its one-to-one limitation. However, Snapchat Stories has emerged as a fascinating way to communicate with a market in real time. Snapchat Stories allow you to string video Snaps together to create a narrative, which becomes available either to your choice of Snapchat friends, to a customized group, or to all Snapchatters. The Snaps can be built around photos or short videos. You can choose from a variety of filters to modify the photos, and you can add text or draw in several colors as well.

When you add a Snap to your Story, it "lives" for 24 hours before it disappears, making room for new content. Your ongoing Snapchat Story displays these moments in the order you experienced and shared them, so it essentially becomes your personal feed of things that have happened to you in the past day. You can continually add to your Story, creating a rolling update in which older Snaps disappear after the 24-hour limit is reached. Or you can simply create one-off Stories for special occasions.

Because Snapchat Stories disappear after a day, there is much more of a real-time feel to the service. With video sharing on other services, your videos live on. That means there's no incentive for people to view them right away. Snapchat Stories hark back to the old days of television before VCRs and DVRs. If you didn't watch live, you'd never be able to see the show.

Rebecca Korn is a financial advisor and business strategist with Northwestern Mutual who uses Snapchat to generate new business. On Snapchat she's @Brkorn and goes by the wonderful handle Financial Fashionista. "When I first got started on social networks, I used 'Financial Fashionista' because I wanted to hide behind something just in case I totally messed it up," she says. "But inadvertently I created this personality for people to identify with, and it made finances less intimidating."

Korn makes a point of asking her clients' kids what the popular social networks are and then she gives them a try. That's how she got started with Instagram and Snapchat several years ago. "For a while I just couldn't figure out how to use Snapchat specifically for business because I could see a lot of my friends posting things like pictures of their kids," she says. "But then I started using it to show people that being a financial advisor is not sitting in an office all day and going home at 3 p.m. and that's it. Some nights, I stay here until 10 or 11 at night. I've been here on Saturdays, and my clients follow me on Snapchat and they say, 'Oh my gosh, I had no idea how much dedication it takes to be a financial advisor.'"

Besides showing the behind-the-scenes reality of how a financial advisor works, she also shares valuable information that people can use. "I use little tidbits like 'the three top reasons when you should speak to a financial advisor' and create a Story around that. People's attention spans are very short these days, and I find that creating a short little Story generates interest. Social networking is all about value. I can teach you how to read a financial statement so you can learn about rates of return and what that actually means for you over the next 30 years of investing. If you watch my Snap Story, I revisit that often. It provides extra value. And even if you're not my client, I want to make sure you're okay."

Korn says that she never actually sells from Snapchat. Rather, people who watch her Story sometimes ask her a private question. She always replies, and that sometimes leads to them asking about her services. "I just give them my phone number and we go from there," she says. "One of those was someone I would call an elephant, because he had about $1.5 million in assets that he brought to me after we met on Snapchat, so that's pretty huge. I have clients who are business owners and physicians that also came through Snapchat, which is very surprising. I think that people underestimate Snapchat because they think it's all millennials, but the median age that I'm experiencing is about 42. They have families and many are on Snapchat because of business."

Crowdsourced Support

I followed with interest the terrible flooding situation in and around Brisbane in Queensland, Australia, several years ago. And I also followed the remarkable story of Baked Relief, a crowdsourced support group that emerged to help those affected.

Baked Relief is a movement of thousands of people who bake and cook. They provided home-prepared food to people directly affected by the floods, as well as to volunteers, emergency workers, and the military. The Baked Relief movement was started by Danielle Crismani. "I was just watching the stuff on the news," she says. "I thought, 'Oh gosh, all these people are sandbagging. I wonder what I could do.' I can't go and sandbag, but I wasn't going to sit around." So she tweeted to tell her followers that she was about to take cupcakes to the volunteer sandbaggers working near her home.

The next day, she used the #bakedrelief hashtag on Twitter and was surprised that many others started to use it as well, building on her idea of helping those affected by offering their own support to the volunteers and emergency workers. A real-time movement began, which Crismani then poured all of her energy into. "I got onto Twitter and said, 'Hey, if you're stuck at home and you can't go to work, how about you bake for the SES

[State Emergency Service] and take some stuff down to the people that are sandbagging?' Then I got on Facebook and did the same thing," she says.

Several days later, #bakedrelief was so popular that it was the second-highest-trending hashtag (the second most popular topic discussed at the time on Twitter) in Australia, with #qldfloods (the hashtag used for general information about the floods) in the number one spot.

Things happened quickly, and it soon became apparent that matching thousands of people who were willing to help with those who needed it was too difficult to manage on Twitter alone. "There were a lot of people who wanted to get more involved," Crismani says. "We needed a base to be able to record lots of information every day. So instead of people constantly contacting us through Twitter asking, 'Where do I take my three batches of biscuits?' we needed somewhere to link to and say, 'For this morning, this is where the food needs to go. Come back at midday, and we'll update the blog and this is where the food will need to go then.'"

Once the need was identified, a bakedrelief.org site was developed extremely quickly using a WordPress platform. "Kay, one of the women who worked very closely with us, just did the site up. She called me and said, 'I've got a surprise for you. Have a look in your inbox.' When I got to my inbox, there was the link to the bakedrelief.org [site]. She said it took her like 45 minutes to do it up. We made a few changes over time and added a few things, but we needed something simple." I love that the site was made so quickly. Most people, when considering a new website, imagine months of work, but this took just 45 minutes. The site provides details for those willing to volunteer and those in need. It also accepts cash donations from people (like me) who are far away from the devastation and cannot donate food.

Crismani launched an ".org" site to communicate quickly in this time of crisis. When important news affecting your organization breaks fast, sometimes the best way to connect with customers and the media is to quickly build a new website in real time. An ".org" domain name is an excellent option in this case because it has an inherent reputation of trust, integrity, and credibility.

The key with bakedrelief.org was to get the new site up very quickly, right at the time when people were eager to locate credible information on the breaking issue.

Many people blogged and tweeted to spread the word, and soon Australia's national mainstream media picked up on the movement. Even people outside the area jumped in to help, with some driving for hours to deliver food. One group, Funky Pies, drove up from Sydney (about

1,000 kilometers, a 12-hour drive) to deliver their pies to volunteers, people working at Queensland Police, and an evacuation center.

During this period of time, Crismani was working 20 hours per day on Baked Relief. "I was going to sleep for four hours or so and then waking up and doing it all over again every day," she says. "I hadn't properly eaten with a knife and fork for two weeks."

The Australian government got involved in the movement when Deputy Prime Minister and Federal Treasurer Wayne Swan started talking up Baked Relief. "There was bakedrelief.org on the homepage of his website," Crismani says. "You'd click on it, and it'd give you all the information. And whenever you'd call his office, they would answer the phone with 'Hi, you've reached the office of Treasurer Wayne Swan. If you're phoning about Baked Relief . . .' We had a big laugh. He called me up, and he said, 'How do you like the treasurer working for you?' That was funny."

Soon after, Anna Bligh, the premier of Queensland, used Twitter (her Twitter ID is @theqldpremier) to set up a meeting with Crismani to discuss community recovery and assistance for families of those affected. "The premier wanted me to meet with her team to tell them my ideas," Crismani says. "That meeting happened with the head of the Department of Communities and the premier's director-general, and the concerns of the residents of the Lockyer Valley and in the cyclone areas of Far North Queensland were expressed by me during that meeting. All coordinated via Twitter!"

One person with an Internet connection and a Twitter feed started a movement by communicating in real time. Her efforts helped thousands and were recognized at the national level in Australia. That's power that you have, too. "You can motivate other people; your reach is far broader than you think," Crismani says. "I think it is pretty amazing, and I'm really proud of what's happened. It has taught me the power of social media. I will not be so blasé about it all now!"

This story is a great example of the power of real-time crowdsourcing using social media. No traditional advertising, media relations, or marketing techniques were used. The entire effort was crowdsourced in real time.

Crowdsourcing involves taking a task usually performed by one person or a few people and distributing it among a crowd of people—outsourcing it to a crowd—via online social networks and in real time. There are many ways that organizations are tapping the crowd to perform tasks more quickly or cheaply than by using traditional techniques. During live broadcasts, programs like *American Idol* and *Britain's Got Talent* get audiences to evaluate performers by calling a special phone number or texting their votes. The best example of an enormous crowdsourced project is Wikipedia, the free online encyclopedia that anybody can add to or edit.

Or consider the revolution in Egypt that toppled the Mubarak regime in 2011 after 30 years in power. The protest movement was crowdsourced using a Facebook page called "Kullena Khaled Said"—initially administered anonymously by Wael Ghonim, a Dubai-based Egyptian citizen—to organize people and direct them to the places where demonstrations were to take place. "Kullena Khaled Said" eventually grew to 2.6 million likes, and posts on the page during the early 2011 protests routinely had a million views and thousands of comments. Ghonim's fascinating 2012 memoir *Revolution 2.0: The Power of the People Is Greater Than the People in Power: A Memoir* is well worth checking out if you're interested in learning more about the role of Facebook in the Egyptian revolution. Ghonim, who at the time was employed by Google, was eventually arrested and spent more than a week in prison. His book reads like a spy novel as he describes the ways he hid his identity and had people help him with the Facebook page even when he was unable to administer it.

Just think—if crowdsourcing is powerful enough to bring together tens of thousands of people to help during a natural disaster or even force a government out of power, it has tremendous potential for any business.

Real-time marketing and public relations deliver a decisive competitive advantage to those organizations that engage quickly. It doesn't matter what business you're in; these ideas can work for you, too.

9 Artificial Intelligence and Machine Learning for Marketing and PR

As I write this, I'm using web-based artificial intelligence (AI) transcription software called Trint to help me turn recorded audio interviews into a text transcription. As I researched new ideas for this edition of the book, I conducted interviews either in person or on the phone, recording those conversations on my iPhone. Recording the conversation allows me to focus on what my source is saying, so I can ask better follow-up questions. I'm not distracted by the need to produce accurate notes to pull quotes from later.

I upload these audio files from my iPhone to the app, and then Trint's speech-to-text algorithms quickly generate a quality first-pass transcript of the interview. To ensure that quotes are accurate, I use Trint's built-in editing software to simultaneously listen to the original audio and follow along in the written transcript. I can easily make necessary corrections and then download the final transcript.

Behind the scenes, Trint's digital transcription starts with AI, including automated speech recognition and natural language processing. The software is tuned to interpret the sounds that make up human speech and then match those sounds to the corresponding word in its multi-language dictionary. Since the resulting transcript isn't perfect, users' corrections to first-pass transcripts are used to improve the Trint software and improve future accuracy (hence: "machine learning").

That's just one example of an AI-powered application I use frequently. Artificial intelligence is all around us, helping power many of the tools we use every day. For example, I use my smartphone map application countless times a month. I plug in the address of where I want to go, and the AI-powered algorithms analyze huge sets of data, taking into account the time of day, day of the week, holiday schedule, road construction, accidents, and other factors to compute the optimal route. The app provides an estimated time of arrival, and, if things change while I'm on the road, it will suggest detours or recompute the ETA. A human could never analyze such a massive amount of data.

Artificial intelligence is the umbrella term for the algorithms, technologies, and mathematics that make machines smarter. AI is typically used to perform tasks that have previously been done by humans, and done frequently, but that take lots of time (e.g., audio transcription and route-planning). AI-powered applications require a huge amount of data to do their jobs effectively, so the social networking, online retail, and online entertainment companies that are most invested in AI technologies tend to collect as much as they can get their hands on.

The term *machine learning* (ML) is often used interchangeably with artificial intelligence, although technically ML is just one aspect of AI (the part where computer systems learn from data to make decisions without explicitly being programmed how to make them). An example of an ML program is a system that looks at a huge number of photos and learns to decide which ones depict cats. In this chapter I won't make a distinction between AI and ML.

Here are a few other ways AI is powering my daily routine: The recommendation engines on services like YouTube, Amazon, and Netflix take in the massive amounts of data generated by tens of millions of users to figure out what videos, books, and movies I might like. Similarly, social networks like Facebook and LinkedIn use AI-powered algorithms to figure out what updates to show me—updates I'm likely to engage with and that will keep me coming back to these sites. And when somebody sends me an email, the AI within Gmail will suggest several responses, such as "Sounds good to me!" and "Great!" and "I'm not sure." (An aside: It's interesting to me that most of the suggested Gmail responses end in an explanation point! I wonder why?!)

AI-Powered Marketing and PR ━━━━━━

By now you see that much of our online lives already have AI-powered components. We don't see the actual programs, but they are actively working in the background. The same is increasingly true in the marketing and public relations worlds, because marketing is increasingly a data-driven activity. For example, the ads that appear on many websites are powered by AI engines. Some media companies are even using AI to "read" corporate press releases to create first drafts of stories for reporters to edit.

So, what else is AI good at that can help with your marketing and PR? It can automate routine tasks and let you focus on marketing and PR strategy. AI works best on solving simple problems with help from large amounts of data.

Many worry that AI will take away people's jobs. It's true that certain repetitive jobs, like screening thousands of resumes for a great new marketing hire and testing dozens of web pages to find the one that performs best, probably won't exist in the future. However, many new and exciting opportunities will likely arise as our ability to use this computing power leads to new opportunities for smart people to develop strategy.

As you consider AI in your organization, think about the routine tasks that drive business value and might be possible to automate.

"Machines have no inherent abilities that humans have," says Paul Roetzer, founder of the Marketing Artificial Intelligence Institute. Roetzer's organization educates modern marketers on the potential of AI and connects them with appropriate technologies. "Machines can't see, they can't hear, and they can't understand language. They don't have movement. Artificial intelligence is the science of giving those things to a machine, so it can do things that are more human-like."

Roetzer says well-defined and repetitive processes are the best candidates for AI solutions. "For example, if I write a blog, I want to know what topics I should write about, based on what has the greatest chance of getting seen and shared. I also want to know the best headline to use. From that blog post, I now want to predict what are the best excerpts to pull out of it to share on social media—I'm trying to predict what's the most shareable content. I also want to predict what hashtags to use, what's the best image to use with the post, what's the best time to share it, and which channels are the best to share it on. With every one of those things, I'm trying to make a prediction based largely on instinct and sometimes on analytics. Each of these can be done by a machine. What you want to look for across all marketing and PR categories is what requires prediction, what's repetitive, and what's data-driven."

In Roetzer's blog post example, there is no magical AI platform that a marketer can purchase to instantly do all those things. Rather than look for one overarching solution, it's always best to consider specific, component tasks within the process that a machine can help with.

"We advise making a list of all the things you do in your marketing department in a given week or month, and write out the activities," Roetzer says. "You might write email marketing messages, figure out the subject lines of those emails, decide when in the calendar to send them, and find an image to use with each one. Then you go through and create another column that values intelligently automating each task. On a one to five scale, how valuable would it be to you to automate each of those things? You can consider how much time or money you might save. Then consider artificial intelligence platforms to help with the most important tasks. For example, you can find AI services to tag images and AI services to write email subject lines."

Besides saving time and money, Roetzer also suggests considering how AI can help make certain processes more effective. "Lead scoring is used to predict the likelihood that someone's going to buy," he says. "Historically, most lead scoring is based on a human putting in factors that give points for each attribute that indicates a likelihood to buy. If you do that, you're trying to make the prediction based on your knowledge and experience. But the machine, if it has enough data, can go through and figure out what a great lead looks like and then continually evolve that prediction as new data becomes available."

> Your life is already AI-assisted. Your marketing should be too.

As I was listening to Roetzer, I was thinking about ways I could potentially use AI in my own marketing and public relations efforts. I'd like to be able to use AI to figure out what call-to-action offers would be best for each blog post I write, how to write better emails and headlines based on opt-outs that occur for each email marketing message I've sent, and what kinds of tweets to compose based on the content of blog posts.

Roetzer says the first step is education—understanding what AI actually is (and is *not*) so you're not afraid of it. Roetzer's organization, Marketing Artificial Intelligence Institute, offers free information for beginners who want to learn. It's how I first got educated, and I highly recommend the resources. The Institute also offers a Marketing AI Buyer's Guide, which lists dozens of marketing technology vendors that use artificial intelligence to enhance human knowledge and capabilities.

Some AI-powered tools include the ability to get started building a test application at no cost. For example, IBM's Watson Personality Insights predicts customer needs, values, and personality characteristics based on written text. This service uses linguistic analytics to infer people's interest in different products, as well as people's preferred digital communications channels (email, blogs, tweets, forum posts, etc.).

"You're not going to just flip a switch and become 'all AI, all the time' as a marketing team," Roetzer says. "The key is once you've done the education and you understand the basics of being able to identify opportunities for intelligent automation, then you can go about prioritizing."

Larger enterprises have more opportunity to apply artificial intelligence, simply because they tend to have more data and more resources available to figure out what to do with that data. But that doesn't mean small and mid-size businesses shouldn't be paying very close attention and taking steps to be prepared.

"Right now, you can get a competitive advantage in the market by using a smarter AI solution," Roetzer says. "Simply knowing that you spend 20 hours a month tagging content on your website using a taxonomy, and realizing this task might be a potential use for AI, you can get a massive head start on your peers in the industry. If you're a marketer, don't just sit back and wait. Everything around you will get smarter with AI."

Your Marketing May Already Be AI-Powered

If your marketing includes advertising on search engines using platforms like Google AdWords, or advertising on social networks like Facebook, you're already using AI in your marketing. For example, the Facebook do-it-yourself ad platform has many built-in AI programs to help reach people in order to optimize your advertising spend.

Facebook ads target particular users based on attributes that include their location, demographic data, and other information from their profile (profession, hobbies, etc.). Using an auction system, marketers create an ad, choose the demographic attributes they want to target, set a budget for a particular time frame, and then bid against other marketers for ad clicks or impressions.

Traditionally, it's really difficult to figure out how your ads are performing. Some marketers try to find answers by running many side-by-side A/B tests. But this approach takes time and wastes money. This is a perfect job for AI to tackle. Facebook ad buyers set campaign goals and parameters and then allow Facebook's AI models and algorithms to predict which opportunities are likely to be the most valuable. These decisions are based on real-time incoming data generated as the first ads are being served. The machine makes adjustments needed to help ensure a campaign meets its goals at the best possible price. Besides the AI built into the Facebook ad platform, the company also offers third-party AI plug-ins that optimize particular tasks.

> The AI-powered marketing future may be closer than you think.

The other major social networking platforms and search engines have AI built into their search and discovery systems and advertising networks too.

If you use marketing technology such as customer relationship management (CRM) systems, email marketing platforms, or marketing automation systems, it's possible that AI is powering your marketing right now.

For example, I'm a HubSpot customer: My websites, blog, list management, email marketing, and lead generation are all powered by the HubSpot all-in-one platform. The service includes a number of AI tools built in.

The benefit to me is that massive amounts of data from tens of millions of customer records across more than 70,000 HubSpot customers are anonymously contributing to the AI calculations. One individual customer's HubSpot data, like mine, isn't large enough to predict outcomes using AI. But the entire database of HubSpot customer data offers plenty of analytic insight. This kind of aggregation is the same approach a service like Netflix uses to predict the kinds of films I might like (small data set) from millions of customer viewing records (large data set).

The AI team at HubSpot have launched more than 30 experimental projects to research what's most useful for customers. The AI-powered services that are up and running as I write this include modules in three core areas: anti-abuse, data hygiene, and personalization of content.

The anti-abuse tools look at all HubSpot customers to analyze if the emails people are sending are likely to be flagged as fraud or spam. It predicts if an email list was purchased rather than generated in a legitimate way. It also detects if somebody signing up for a HubSpot product is likely to host malicious content. All customers benefit from the fact that the HubSpot's AI-powered anti-abuse systems flag inappropriate use, proactively defending the email-sending reputation of the platform.

My full name is David Meerman Scott. The problem I have nearly every day is that most online forms don't have a field for middle name. Therefore, sometimes I put my first name as David Meerman and sometimes I put my last name as Meerman Scott. I also use a different email addresses for different purposes. HubSpot uses AI to figure out that people like me, who register in multiple ways, are actually the same person. The system eliminates duplicate data. Another cool AI tool built into HubSpot is a business card reader. You can take a picture of a business card and upload it to the HubSpot system, where the AI pulls the text strings and drops them into database fields such as first name, last name, company, title, telephone number, email address, and so on. It's not perfect and sometimes requires editing. But it will sure save you some time.

My favorite of HubSpot's AI tools is the personalizing of content for different website visitors. This system surfaces articles, blog posts, and other content related to what a user is currently reviewing. These recommendations are based not just on connections between the content but also known attributes of the user. HubSpot customers can create up to five variants of a web page, and then the HubSpot AI kicks in to adjust traffic dynamically, depending on which is performing best. This technique has the wonderful name "multi-armed bandit testing" and is a more sophisticated version of A/B testing that continually serves different offers. Some HubSpot customers have seen as much as 30 percent increases in conversion rates through this AI-powered technique.

Find Ways for AI to Benefit Customers

I was recently poking around a clothing company website, checking out a few items but never buying anything. Soon after, I received an email: "Exclusive 10% off for you," with an image of one of the products I looked at earlier and a coupon to get the special discount. This kind of so-called "retargeting" once felt creepy, but now we're used to the companies we do business with knowing a ton about us and using that information to market to us using AI-powered tools.

In fact, I now hate it when companies *don't* use the information they have about me to make my life easier!

For example, the same week the clothing company cleverly retargeted me, I received an email from my insurance company. The subject line was "Your Bill Is Ready for Payment." Here's what it said:

> Your current bill for your [insurance company name] insurance premium is available and ready for payment online at [insurance company name].com/paymybill. If you are currently enrolled in our automatic payment plan, there is no need to take any further action.
>
> Please note: If a Notice of Cancellation has previously been issued, the payment outstanding shown on that notice must be received by the due date specified on the notice, not by the date shown below, for the policy to remain in effect.

There was more, but they had already lost me. I was super annoyed.

Why the heck doesn't this silly insurance company link the system that sends billing notices to the system that knows if I have automatic billing? And why doesn't the email system know if a Notice of Cancellation is in effect for my account? These are simple math and database problems that can be easily solved by a machine. The communications people who wrote this email need to get with the data scientists and customer representatives to create better targeting. I mean, c'mon—insurance is practically the original "big data" business.

In my view, collecting a ton of personal information from customers means we marketers have an *obligation* to better serve our customers with offers, personalized communications, and more. It's the human thing to do.

And when we *fail* to use data to make our customers' lives better, we're alienating them. Great customer service is fabulous marketing. Poor customer service is an invitation for people to look elsewhere.

Creating an AI Project

"AI is math, not magic," says Christopher Penn, co-founder and chief data scientist at marketing analytics consulting firm Trust Insights. "You need to find a problem that is inherently a math problem."

So far, we've looked at using built-in and off-the-shelf AI tools to automate some particular marketing tasks. However, sometimes the problem you want to tackle doesn't correspond to an existing AI solution. In such cases, you need to build it yourself or hire people who can build it for you.

> The best way to think about AI in your business is to consider automating marketing *tasks*, not automating marketing *jobs*.

No matter what project you decide to take on, you will need a lot of data to analyze. That data also needs to be properly labeled, so a machine can make sense of it. Most marketers don't have internal data sets big enough to run AI programs against, so they have to find the data somewhere else. For example, if you want to determine the best call to action for your blog posts or your email newsletter, it's unlikely you have enough raw data—i.e., tens of thousands (or more) of examples with varying degrees of conversion success.

A good strategy if you don't have enough data from your business processes is to figure out what your competitors are doing and learn from them. Easy-to-use AI-powered competitive intelligence tools like Crayon, Spyfu, and Adbeat analyze your competitors' paid advertising and marketing content and generate reports about what kinds of ads they're running and what kinds of call-to-action and landing page copy they're using, etc.

You can extract these large data sets from the competitive intelligence providers and use them as raw data for an AI project if you don't have other access to a big-enough database. With this data in hand, you can work with an AI algorithm designer to build technology to predict what headlines are best and what calls-to-action might work in your own marketing. You're not copying the competition. You're learning from them and adapting.

"A really good place if you want to use external data would be to look at social media data," Penn says. "For example, you can take Twitter postings that had call-to-action language and then extract hundreds of thousands of these and look at the engagement data for, say, what the top percentage ones with likes and retweets looked like. Then from there you can engineer ideal nouns, verbs, post lengths, readability, use of images, how many hashtags, and other attributes to figure out what's ideal for your own marketing. An AI model could be built that says 'these are the things that high performing posts have in common,' so we can take that knowledge and transfer it to the call to action for our own blog."

Twitter makes it easy to evaluate such data to inform business decisions using its application programming interface (API). If you have an in-house team of developers or plan to use an outside team to build an AI application, Twitter data may be a good substitute if your own database is too small. There are also third-party data companies offering social media data. For example, Talkwalker is a monitoring tool for identifying what's working on social channels and online media in real time.

Penn says the decision to build your custom AI project or bring in a consultant to build it for you comes down to three things: time, money, and strategy. "How much time do I think it's going to take to do the project? If you have time but not the money, you might be able to build it yourself. If you have money but don't have time, you probably want to try and buy it somewhere. And then you need to consider how important the project is. If it's absolutely critical to your marketing and part of your core competency as a marketer, then I would absolutely suggest you want to build that AI process somehow, in house or with help, so you can benefit from it right away."

To sum up: As you consider the problems that AI might solve in your organization, first look around to see if there's an app you can buy to solve the problem. If there isn't, your next consideration is how important that process is. If you want to own the proprietary AI process, then you need to create a custom project. The beauty of this kind of AI model is that once it's deployed at your company, you immediately begin seeding new data and building on successes. Every new decision becomes an experiment that will help your AI help you, promising even better results in the future.

Making AI a Part of Your Marketing

It's a big leap to go from learning about AI in marketing to testing out a few pilot projects to actually deploying AI toward multiple tasks and processes in your organization. Sam Mallikarjunan, chief revenue officer for online collaboration platform Flock, has made each of these leaps in his organization. One of the biggest lessons Mallikarjunan has learned in incorporating AI is to use tools within pay per click (PPC) advertising to test marketing ideas. "One of the super cool things about PPC is that it lets you buy answers quickly," he says. For example, when Flock rolled out a new email tool, Mallikarjunan and the team were unsure of which of the main features would be most compelling to small business owners. "We didn't know which way we wanted to go with our email marketing campaigns and with our blog content. By targeting people on Facebook, we can create what's called a lookalike audience and show them different versions of the ad content to see which one is most effective."

The benefit is that Mallikarjunan can test marketing with huge audiences on Facebook before he creates the next round of website content and other programs. "Back in the day, if you had more than three to five buyer personas you were probably biting off more than you could chew. However, with ad targeting on Facebook you have tens of thousands or hundreds of thousands of micro personas, because the algorithms identify many groups of several thousand people each and learn exactly what motivates those people. It's possible to buy billions of impressions and generate millions of clicks with hundreds of thousands of conversions resulting in tens of thousands of customers." The learning from Facebook advertising programs is then used by the Flock marketing team to market effectively outside of Facebook, including what words and phrases to use on their site, the most effective images, and what might be compelling blog topics to write about.

> The smaller your sample size for training your AI algorithm, the less likely you are to be right about anything.

Another strategic use of AI in Flock's marketing is figuring out who people are as they come to the Flock site and making sure that each lead is tracked throughout the sales process. Many organizations don't dig into their sales leads and therefore don't really know the effectiveness of each marketing channel.

Mallikarjunan shares an example: A person visits the Flock site as a result of a social media post and then fills out a form using a personal email address to download an e-book. Later, the same person is at their work computer, clicks on the e-book link, and ends up on the website to do some more research. If that person then decides to engage with a salesperson by filling out a form with their *work* contact information and then eventually makes a purchase, most companies' lead management systems would count the sale as coming from the website lead. That's when the person first registered with their work details. However, Flock is able to trace that lead source *back to the original social media message.* "Training the algorithm for that was hugely impactful," he says. "It just got me better leads and helped me understand what I really needed to do from the marketing team's perspective."

Flock also uses AI tools to figure out what opportunities are hot in the sales system. Mallikarjunan uses that information to prioritize the kinds of blog posts to write or videos to create, content that will be more likely to generate similarly hot sales leads.

Notice how the learning process is often iterative with AI-based approaches. Experiments yield new approaches through cycles of data analysis, idea generation, deployment, and more analysis. "Be open to trying things," Mallikarjunan says. "With AI you are going to fail more often in the near term than you might otherwise. You need more risk tolerance and a longer expectation for when you expect results. And your effort might totally bomb at first. But then the pace at which your marketing improves will be much better than anything you could have done yourself."

Remaining Human in a World of AI

For decades, marketers have been the experts. We marketing people use our experience and creativity to make decisions. This reality isn't going away! In fact, I think the new world of AI makes our work even more important, because we must always recognize the limitations of machines. AI can't replace human interaction, but it can make the jobs of humans easier, as well give all of us more time for more genuine human interaction.

Yes, for certain tasks, machines can learn to be smarter than people. However, there are many things that machines simply cannot do. Paul Roetzer of the Marketing Artificial Intelligence Institute offers a succinct list of what AI cannot offer: *curiosity, creativity, empathy, emotion, intuition, and maybe most of all, imagination.*

As we begin to roll out AI in marketing, it's essential that we remain vigilant about keeping the human aspects of our marketing intact. As customers become more comfortable and experienced interacting with AI programs, they learn to detect when they are communicating with a machine rather than a human. I predict that in a world of AI, people will continue to crave true and honest connection with actual living and breathing people. Make sure you don't lose personal relationships with your customers!

It goes without saying that there are many potential problems with AI. Yes, the ability for an AI program to detect patterns in massive amounts of data is beyond what a human can do. However, those same AI programs also have the potential to magnify the biases that you unwittingly introduce in your marketing. For example, certain words signal "male" or "female" bias, and particular images might mean different things to different buyer personas. Algorithms trained with data generated or interpreted by homogenous groups have famously failed with more diverse data. Without humans paying attention, AI algorithms may continually skew your marketing such that you miss entire groups of buyers or, worse, become a company that's seen by part of the market as prejudiced or insensitive to diversity.

AI isn't going to solve every marketing problem. But it is certainly an important part of our future. The sooner you learn how to apply it, the bigger head start your organization will have on your competitors.

Always remember that the humanity of what you and your people bring are essential in a world of AI. Machines are not taking over marketing. Rather, an effective "collaboration" between machines and people will be the key to success in the years to come.

Now let's spend some time on the specifics of how you can implement the new rules for your own organization. Part III of this book starts with a discussion of how you build a comprehensive marketing and PR plan to reach your buyers directly with web content. Once armed with your plan, continue to the chapters that follow, which will give you advice for developing thought leadership content and writing for your buyers. In addition, I provide detailed information on how to implement a news release program, build an online media room, create your own blog and podcast, and work with social networking sites. Because I'm convinced of the value of hearing from innovative marketers who have had success with these ideas, I continue to sprinkle case studies throughout the remaining chapters to give you some examples of how others have implemented these ideas and to help you get your own creative juices flowing.

Action Plan for Harnessing the Power of the New Rules

10 You Are What You Publish: Building Your Marketing and PR Plan

Does your company sell great products? Or, if you don't work in a traditional company, does your organization (church, nonprofit, consulting company, school) offer great services? Well, get over it! Marketing is not *only* about your products or services! The most important thing to remember as you develop a marketing and PR plan is to put your products and services to the side for just a little while and focus your complete attention on the *buyers* of your products or services (or those who will donate, subscribe, join, or apply). Devoting attention to buyers and away from products is difficult for many people, but it always pays off in the form of bringing you closer to achieving your goals.

Think Starbucks for a moment. Is the product great? Yeah, I guess the three-dollar cup of coffee I get from Starbucks tastes pretty good. And most marketers, if given the opportunity to market Starbucks, would focus on the coffee itself—the product. But is that really what people are buying at Starbucks, or does Starbucks help solve other buyer problems?

Maybe Starbucks is really selling a place to hang out for a while. Or for that matter, isn't Starbucks a convenient place for people to meet? (I use Starbucks several times a month as a place to connect with people or conduct interviews.) Or do people use Starbucks for the free wireless Internet connections? Maybe Starbucks saves 10 minutes in your day because you don't have to grind beans, pour water into a coffeemaker, wait, and clean up later. For some of us, Starbucks just represents a little splurge because, well, we're worth it.

I'd argue that Starbucks does all those things. Starbucks appeals to many different buyer personas, and it sells lots of things besides just coffee. If you were marketing Starbucks, it would be your job to segment buyers and appeal to them based on their needs, not just talk about coffee.

The approach of thinking about buyers and the problems our organizations solve for them can be difficult for many marketers, since we've constantly been told how important a great product or service is to the marketing mix. In fact, standard marketing education still talks about the four Ps of marketing—product, place, price, and promotion—as being the most important things. That's nonsense. To succeed on the web under the new rules of marketing and PR, you need to consider your organizational goals and then focus on your buyers *first*. Only when you understand buyers should you begin to create compelling web content to reach them. Yes, marketers often argue with me on this. But I strongly believe that the product or service you sell is secondary when you market your organization on the web.

So I will ask you to put aside your products and services as you begin the task for this chapter: building a marketing and PR plan that follows the new rules. While the most important thing to focus on during this process is buyers, we will do that in the context of your organizational goals. Trust me—this will be like no marketing and PR plan you've created before.

What Are Your Organization's Goals?

Marketing and PR people have a collective difficulty getting our departmental goals in sync with the rest of the company. And our management teams go along with this dysfunction. Think about the goals that most marketers have. They usually take the form of an epic to-do list: "Let's see; we should do a few trade shows, buy Google AdWords ads, maybe create a new logo, get press clips, produce some T-shirts, increase website traffic, and, oh yeah, generate some leads for the salespeople." Well, guess what? Those aren't the goals of your company! I've never seen leads or clips or T-shirts on a balance sheet. With typical marketing department goals, we constantly focus on the flare-up du jour and thus focus on the wrong thing. This also gives the marketing profession a bad rap in many companies as a bunch of flaky slackers. No wonder marketing is called the branding police in some organizations and is often the place where failed salespeople end up.

Many marketers and PR people also focus on the wrong measures of success. With websites, people often tell me things like: "We want to have 10,000 unique visitors per month to our site." And PR measurement is often similarly irrelevant: "We want 10 mentions in the trade press and three national magazine hits each month." Unless your site makes money through advertising so that raw traffic adds revenue, traffic is the wrong measure. And simple press clips just don't matter. What matters is leading your site's visitors and your constituent audiences to where they help you reach your real goals, such as building revenue, soliciting donations, and gaining new members.

This lack of clear goals and real measurement reminds me of seven-year-olds playing soccer. If you've ever seen little children on the soccer field, you know that they operate as one huge organism packed together, chasing the ball around the field. On the sidelines are helpful coaches yelling, "Pass!" or "Go to the goal!" Yet as the coaches and parents know, this effort is futile: No matter what the coach says or how many times the kids practice, they still focus on the wrong thing—the ball—instead of the goal.

That's exactly what we marketers and PR people do. We fill our lists with balls and lose sight of the goal. But do you know what's even worse? Our coaches (the management teams at our companies) actually encourage us to focus on balls (like sales leads or press clips or website traffic statistics) instead of real organizational goals such as revenue. The VPs and CEOs of companies happily provide incentives based on leads for the marketing department and on clips for the PR team. And the agencies we contract with—advertising and PR agencies—also focus on the wrong measures.

What we need to do is align marketing and PR objectives with those of the organization. For most corporations, the most important goal is profitable revenue growth. In newer companies and those built around emerging technologies, this usually means generating new customers, but in mature businesses, the management team may need to be more focused on keeping the customers that they already have. Nonprofits have the goal of raising money; politicians, to get out the vote (for them); rock bands, to get people to buy CDs, iTunes downloads, and tickets to live shows; and universities, to get student applications and alumni donations.

So your first step is to meet with the leaders of your organization—your management team or your associates in your church or nonprofit or your spouse if you run a small business—and determine your business goals. If you run a nonprofit, school, church, or political campaign, consider your goals for donations, applications, new members, or votes. Write them down in detail. The important things you write down might be "grow revenue in Europe by 20 percent," "increase new member sign-ups to 100 per month in the fourth quarter," "generate a million dollars in web donations next quarter," or "generate five paid speaking engagements in the upcoming year."

Now that you have the marketing and PR plan focused on the right goals (i.e., those of your organization), the next step is to learn as much as you can about your buyers and to segment them into groups so you can reach them through your web publishing efforts. In the next chapter, we'll go into depth about how your marketing and PR programs drive sales.

Buyer Personas and Your Organization —

Successful online marketing and PR efforts work because they start by identifying one or more buyer personas to target, so you need to make buyer personas a part of your planning process. A buyer persona (which we touched on back in Chapter 3) is essentially a representative of a type of buyer that you have identified as having a specific interest in your organization or product or having a market problem that your product or service solves. Building buyer personas is the first step and probably the single most important thing that you will do in creating your marketing and PR plan.

Consider the market for tricycles. The user of the most common tricycle is a preschool child. Yet a preschooler doesn't buy the tricycle. The most common buyer personas for children's tricycles are parents and grandparents. So what problem does the tricycle solve? Well, for parents, it might be that the child has been asking for one and the purchase quiets the child down. Parents also know that the child is growing quickly and will want a two-wheeler with training wheels soon enough, so a basic trike is typically enough in their eyes. However, grandparents buy tricycles to solve the problem of providing an extravagant gift, so they often buy an expensive model to show their love to the child and his or her parents. When you think about tricycles from the perspective of buyer personas, you can see how the marketing might be different for parents and grandparents.

You, too, need to segment buyer personas so you can then develop marketing programs to reach each one. Let's revisit the college example from Chapter 3 and expand on it. Remember that we identified five different buyer personas for a college website: young alumni who had graduated within the past 10 or 15 years, older alumni, the high school student who is considering college, the parents of the prospective student, and existing customers (current students). That means a well-executed college site might target five distinct buyer personas.

A college might have the marketing and PR goal of generating 500 additional applications for admission from qualified students for the next academic year. Let's also pretend that the college hopes to raise $5 million in donations from alumni who have never contributed in the past. That's great! These are real goals that marketers can build programs around.

The Buyer Persona Profile

After identifying their goals, the marketing people at the college should build a buyer persona profile, essentially a kind of biography, for each group they'll target to achieve those goals. The college might create one buyer persona for prospective students (targeting high school students looking for schools) and another for parents of high school students (who are part of the decision process and often pay the bills). If the school targets a specific type of applicant, say, student athletes, the marketers might build a specific buyer persona profile for the high school student who participates in varsity sports. To effectively target the alumni for donations, the school might decide to build a buyer persona for younger alumni, perhaps those who have graduated within the past 10 years.

For each buyer persona profile, we want to know as much as we can about this group of people. What are their goals and aspirations? What are their problems? What media do they rely on for answers to problems? How can we reach them? We want to know, in detail, the things that are important for each buyer persona. What words and phrases do the buyers use? What sorts of images and multimedia appeal to each? Are short and snappy sentences better than long, verbose ones? I encourage you to write these things down based on your understanding of each buyer persona. You should also read the publications and websites that your buyers read to gain an understanding of the way they think. For example, college marketing people should read the *U.S. News & World Report* issue that ranks America's best colleges as well as the guidebooks that prospective students read. Reading what your buyer personas read will get you thinking like them. By doing some basic research on your buyers, you can learn a great deal, and your marketing will be much more effective.

The best way to learn about buyers and develop buyer persona profiles is to interview people. The marketing person at our hypothetical college must interview people who fit the personas the school identified. The college marketing people might learn a great deal if they turned the traditional in-person college admissions interview around by asking prospective students questions such as the following: When did you first start researching schools? Who influenced your research? How did you learn about this school? How many schools are you applying to? What websites do you read or subscribe to?

Once you know this firsthand information, you should subscribe to, read, and listen to the media that influence your target buyer. When you read what your buyers read, pay attention to the exact words and phrases that are used. If students frequent Facebook or other social networking sites, so should you, and you should pay attention to the lingo students use. By triangulating the information gathered directly from several dozen prospective students plus information from the media that these students pay attention to, you easily build a buyer persona for a high school student ready to apply to a college like yours.

"A buyer persona profile is a short biography of the typical customer, not just a job description but a person description," says Adele Revella, who has been using buyer personas to market technology products for more than 20 years. Revella is the author of *Buyer Personas: How to Gain Insight into Your Customer's Expectations, Align Your Marketing Strategies, and Win More Business*, which is a new release in my New Rules of Social Media books series. "The buyer persona profile gives you a chance to truly empathize with target buyers, to step out of your role as someone who wants to promote a product and see, through your buyers' eyes, the circumstances that drive their decision process. The buyer persona profile includes information on the typical buyer's background, daily activities, and current solutions for their problems. The more experience you have in your market, the more obvious the personas become."

Though it may sound a bit wacky, I think you should go so far as to name your persona. You might even cut out a representative photo from a magazine to help you visualize him or her. This should be an *internal name only* that helps you and your colleagues to develop sympathy with and a deep understanding of the real people to whom you market. Rather than a nameless, faceless prospect, your buyer persona will come to life.

For example, a buyer persona for a male high school student who is a varsity athlete and whom you want to target might be named Sam the Athlete, and his persona might read something like this: "Sam the Athlete began thinking about colleges and the upcoming application process way back when he was a freshman in high school. His coach and parents recognized his athletic talent and suggested that it will help him get into a good college or even secure a scholarship. Sam knows that he's good, but not good enough to play on a Division 1 school team. Sam first started poking around on college websites as a freshman and enjoyed checking out the athletic pages for the colleges in his home state and some nearby ones. He even attended some of these colleges' games when he could. Sam has good grades, but he is not at the top of his class because his sports commitments mean he can't study as much as his peers do. He has close friends and likes to hang out with them on weekends, but he is not heavily into the party scene and avoids alcohol and drugs. Sam frequents Facebook, updates his Facebook at least once a week, and has a group of online friends that he frequently instant messages with on Snapchat. He is hip to online nuance, language, and etiquette. Sam also reads *Sports Illustrated*. Now that he is a junior, he knows it is time to get serious about college applications, and he doesn't really know where to start. But to learn, he's now paying more attention to the application pages than the athletic pages on college websites."

Okay, so you're nodding your head and agreeing with this buyer persona profiling thing. "But," you ask, "how many buyer personas do I need?" You might want to think about your buyer personas based on what factors differentiate them. How can you slice the demographics? For example, some organizations will have a different profile for buyers in North America versus Europe. Or maybe your company sells to buyers both in the automobile industry and in the government sector, and those buyers are different. The important thing is that you will use this buyer persona information to create specific marketing and PR programs to reach each buyer persona, and therefore you need to have the segmentation in fine enough detail that when they encounter your web content, your buyers will say, "Yes, that's me. This organization understands me and my problems and will therefore have products that fit my needs."

Marketers and PR pros are often amazed at the transformation of their materials and programs as a result of buyer persona profiling. "When you really know how your buyers think and what matters to them, you eliminate the agony of guessing about what to say or where and how to communicate with buyers," says Revella. "Marketers tell me that they don't have time to build buyer personas, but these same people are wasting countless hours in meetings debating about whether the message is right. And of course, they're wasting budgets building programs and tools that don't resonate with anyone. It's just so much easier and more effective to listen before you talk."

How Beko Develops Products Global Consumers Are Eager to Buy

Let's step back and look at how buyer persona research is used to develop products that people want to buy. That's the first step in effective marketing. Then, when the resulting product is brought to market, those same buyer insights are used to create compelling web content to educate and inform consumers.

Arcelik, based in Turkey, is one of the largest white goods (refrigerator, washer/dryer, dishwasher) manufacturers in the world. The company sells white goods and other electronics in more than 100 countries under many brand names. The Beko line is the best known around the world.

People from Beko conduct buyer persona research in many of the countries the company sells in and modifies product features based on what the researchers learn from consumers. The key here is that Beko staff develop buyer personas using actual input from interviews. Unlike most companies, which dream up product features in a conference room at headquarters, Beko taps the marketplace to gather intelligence first.

With clothes dryers, Beko marketing people learned through discussions with Chinese consumers that the traditional approach of drying clothing in the sun is an important aspect of Chinese culture. In some parts of China, people believe that clothing is part of an individual's soul. After washing, the clothing must be exposed to sunlight in order to bring the soul back. Thus, Beko realized it might be too much of a leap for consumers to go from hanging clothes outside in sunlight to drying them indoors with a machine.

Seems like an insurmountable problem, doesn't it? Not for Beko! The company developed a dryer that includes a setting to stop the cycle after clothes are about halfway dry. The consumer then hangs the slightly damp clothing outside in the sun to finish the process. These dryers are selling very well in China.

Another insight led to product development in the Beko refrigerator line sold in China. Because rice is a staple of the Chinese diet, rice storage is important for Chinese families. It turns out that rice is best stored at low humidity and at about 10 degrees Celsius. But this is not a good setting for storing most fresh foods. In this case, Beko product engineers created a three-door fridge that has the usual freezer and refrigerator compartments as well as a new compartment for rice storage.

With both the fridge and the dryer, the buyer persona insights are also used to market the product. The actual words and phrases used by Chinese consumers to describe the way they dry clothing and store rice can be used in product descriptions.

At a recent IFA Fair in Berlin, Germany, the world's leading trade show for consumer electronics and home appliances, the Beko refrigerator won a coveted innovation award. But you simply can't make such products up in your conference room. The only way to learn about customer needs in a global marketplace is to spend time speaking with buyers in the countries where you plan to sell.

That's also the only way to tap insights from buyers to create web and social media content that appeals to consumers in your markets.

So whether you're a product developer or a marketer, buyer persona research will give you insights to drive success.

Reaching Senior Executives

Many people ask me about reaching senior executives via the web. That executives do not use the web as much as other people is a commonly held belief, one that I've never bought. Frequently, business-to-business (B2B) marketers use this misperception as an excuse for why they don't have to focus on building buyer personas and marketing materials for senior executives. Based on anecdotal information from meeting with many of them, I have always argued that executives are online in a big way. However, I've never had any solid data to support my hunch until now.

Forbes Insights, in association with Google, released a study called *The Rise of the Digital C-Suite: How Executives Locate and Filter Business Information*. The findings clearly show that executives consider the web to be their most valuable resource for gathering business information, outstripping at-work contacts, personal networks, trade publications, and so on. In a follow-up study, *Video in the C-Suite: Executives Embrace the Non-Text Web*, Forbes Insights found that 75 percent of executives surveyed said they watch work-related videos at least weekly, and 65 percent have visited a vendor's website after watching a video. The social element of online video is strong in the executive suite. More than half of senior executives share videos with colleagues at least weekly and receive work-related videos as often.

"The common perception is that top executives at the largest companies do not use the Internet, but the reality is just the opposite," says Stuart Feil, editorial director of Forbes Insights. "These findings show that C-level executives are more involved online than their counterparts, and younger generations of executives—those whose work careers have coincided with the growth of the PC and the Internet—are bringing profound organizational change to these companies."

The Importance of Buyer Personas in Web Marketing

One of the simplest ways to build an effective website or to create great marketing programs using online content is to target the specific buyer personas that you have created. Yet most websites are big brochures that do not offer specific information for different buyers. Think about it—the typical website is one size fits all, with the content organized by the company's products or services, not by categories corresponding to buyer personas and their associated problems.

The same thing is true about other online marketing programs. Without a focus on the buyer, the typical press release and media relations program are built on what the organization wants to say rather than what the buyer wants to hear. There is a huge difference. Companies that are successful with direct-to-consumer news release strategies write for their buyers. The blogs that are best at reaching an organizational goal are not about companies or products but rather about customers and their problems.

Now that you've set quantifiable organizational goals and identified the buyer personas that you want to reach, your job as you develop your marketing and PR plan is to identify the best ways to reach buyers and develop compelling information that you will use in your web marketing programs. If you've conducted interviews with buyers and developed a buyer persona profile, then you know the buyer problems that your product or service solves, and you know the media that buyers turn to for answers. Do they go first to a search engine? If so, what words and phrases do they enter? Which blogs, chat rooms, forums, and online news sites do they read? Are they open to audio or video? You need to answer these questions before you continue.

In Your Buyers' Own Words

Throughout the book, I often refer to the importance of understanding the words and phrases that buyers use. An effective web marketing plan requires an understanding of the ways your buyers speak and the real words and phrases they use. This is important not only for building a positive online relationship with your buyers but also for planning effective search engine marketing strategies. After all, if you are not using the phrases your buyers search on, how can you possibly reach them?

Let's take a look at the importance of the actual words buyers use, by way of an example. Several years ago, I worked with Shareholder.com to create a web content strategy to reach buyers of the company's new Whistleblower Hotline product and move those buyers into and through the sales cycle. The Shareholder.com product was developed as an outsourced solution for public companies to comply with Rule 301 (the so-called Whistleblower Hotline provision) of the U.S. Sarbanes-Oxley legislation that was passed in the wake of corporate scandals such as Enron. Most important, we interviewed buyers (such as chief financial officers within publicly traded companies) who were required to comply with the legislation. We also read the publications that our buyers read (such as *CFO*, *Directors Monthly*, and the *ACC Docket* of the Association of Corporate Counsel); we actually downloaded and read the massive Sarbanes-Oxley legislation document itself; and we studied the agendas of the many conferences and events that our buyers attended that discussed the importance of Sarbanes-Oxley compliance.

As a result of the buyer persona research, we learned the phrases that buyers used when discussing the Sarbanes-Oxley Whistleblower Hotline rule, so the content that we created for the Shareholder.com website included such important phrases as "SEC mandates," "complete audit trail," "Sarbanes-Oxley rule 301," "confidential and anonymous submission," and "safe and secure employee reporting." An important component of the website we created (based on our buyer persona research) was thought-leadership-based content, including a webinar called "Whistleblower Hotlines: More Than a Mandate" that featured guest speakers Harvey Pitt (former chairman of the U.S. Securities and Exchange Commission) and Lynn Brewer (author of *House of Cards: Confessions of an Enron Executive*). Because this webinar discusses issues of importance to *buyers* (not only Shareholder.com products), and the guest speakers are thought leaders that buyers are interested in learning from, 600 people eagerly watched the presentation live.

"The webinar was very important because when we launched the product we were starting from a position with no market share within this product niche," says Bradley H. Smith, who was director of marketing/communications at Shareholder.com at the time. "Other companies had already entered the market before us. The webinar gave us search engine terms like 'Harvey Pitt' and 'Enron' and offered a celebrity draw. Search engine placement was important because it created our brand as a leader in Whistleblower Hotline technologies even though we were new to this market. Besides prospective clients, the media found us, which resulted in important press including prominent placement in a *Wall Street Journal* article called 'Making It Easier to Complain.'"

Shareholder.com then took the service to the Canadian market, where the legislation was called "Ontario Securities Commission and the Audit Committees Rule of the Canadian Securities Administrators Guidelines Multilateral Instrument 52-110" (quite a mouthful). Smith and his colleagues interviewed buyers in Canada to conduct buyer persona research to determine if there were any differences in the words and phrases used in Canada. There were! Unlike the other U.S. companies attempting to enter the Canadian market for hotline solutions by just using their U.S. marketing materials, Shareholder.com created a separate set of web content for Canadian buyers. In the pages for these buyers were specific phrases that were used by Canadian buyers (but not buyers in the United States), such as "governance hotline," "conducting a forensic accounting investigation," and the exact name of the Canadian legislation.

Because the marketers at Shareholder.com had done extensive buyer persona research and had created web content with the words and phrases used by buyers, the Shareholder.com pages were visited frequently and linked to often, and they became highly ranked by the search engines. In fact, Shareholder.com became number one out of 258,000 hits on Google for the phrase "whistleblower hotline."

As a result of traffic driven from the search engines and great web content for both U.S. and Canadian buyers (such as webinars), the product launch was a success. "In the four months immediately after the webcast, we signed 75 clients," Smith says. "Furthermore, the webcast archive of the event continued to work for us throughout the year, advancing our brand presence, generating sales leads, and contributing to the strongest Shareholder.com stand-alone product launch ever."

After I wrote the original version of this story, the Nasdaq Stock Market, Inc., acquired Shareholder.com.

Figuring out the phrases for your market requires that you buckle down and do some research. Although interviewing buyers about their market problems and listening to the words and phrases they use is best, you can also learn a great deal by reading the publications they read. Check out any blogs in your buyers' marketplace (if you haven't already), and study the agendas and topic descriptions for the conferences and seminars that your buyers frequent. When you have a list of the phrases that are important to your buyers, use those phrases not only to appeal to them specifically but also to make your pages appear in the search engine results when your buyers search for what you have to offer.

What Do You Want Your Buyers to Believe?

Now that you have identified organizational goals, built one or more buyer personas, and researched the words and phrases your buyers use to talk about and search for your product or service, you should think about what you want each of your buyer personas to *believe* about your organization. What are the actual words and phrases that you will use for each buyer persona?

In the 2008 election, Barack Obama focused on his buyer personas and identified as crucially important the concept of "change." Everywhere you saw the Obama campaign, there were nods to this theme: on the podium where the candidate was speaking, on T-shirts and buttons, on posters, and of course on the web. The Obama campaign shrewdly understood that when voters pulled the lever to vote for Obama, they were buying into the idea of the need for change.

The same thing was true with the Donald Trump campaign in 2016. The Trump campaign focused on buyers and clearly articulated a campaign promise to "Make America Great Again." He established the #MAGA hashtag for social media, especially Twitter.

In both of these cases, voters were choosing an idea, not just a man. The Obama and Trump campaign strategists clearly understood, and articulated, what they wanted their buyer personas to believe that the candidate would bring.

You must do the same thing with your buyer personas. What do you want each group to believe about your organization? What messages will you use to reach them on the web? Remember, the best information is not just about your product. What is each buyer persona really buying from you? Is it great customer service? The safe choice? Luxury? For example, Volvo doesn't sell just a car; it sells *safety*.

And don't forget that different buyer personas buy different things from your organization. Think about Gatorade for a moment. For competitive athletes, Gatorade has been the drink of choice for decades. I found some interesting messages on the Gatorade website, including: "If you want to *win*, you've got to replace what you *lose*" and "For some athletes, significant dehydration can occur within the initial 30 minutes of exercise." These are interesting messages, because they target the buyer persona of the competitive athlete and focus on how Gatorade can help those athletes win.

Now, I'm not an expert on Gatorade's buyer personas, but it seems to me that it could further refine its buyer personas based on the sports that athletes play or on whether they are professionals or amateurs. If tennis players see themselves as very different from football players, then Gatorade may need to create buyer persona profiles and messages to target both sports separately. Or maybe women athletes make up a different buyer persona for Gatorade than men.

But there's another buyer persona that I have never seen Gatorade address. I remember back to my early 20s, when I lived in an apartment in New York City and was single and making the rounds in the party circuit and late-night club scene. To be honest, I was partying a little too hard some weeknights, skulking home in the wee hours. I then had to make it down to my Wall Street job by 8 a.m. I discovered that drinking a large bottle of Gatorade on the walk to the subway stop helped me feel a lot better. Now I don't *actually* expect Gatorade to develop messages for young professionals in New York who party and drink too much, but that buyer persona certainly has different problems from those that Gatorade solves for athletes. Imagine advertising for this buyer persona: "Last night's third martini still in your system? Rehydration is not just for athletes. Gatorade."

I told this Gatorade story to a group of people at a seminar I ran for marketing executives, and a woman told the group that her mother had always served Gatorade to her when she had a cold or the flu. How interesting—another buyer persona for Gatorade: parents who are caring for sick children and who want to make sure they are properly hydrated.

The point is that different buyer personas have different problems for your organization to solve. And there's no doubt that your online marketing and PR programs will do better if you develop information specifically for each buyer persona, instead of simply relying on a generic site that uses one set of broad messages for everyone.

Developing Content to Reach Buyers

You must now think like a publisher. You should develop an editorial plan to reach your buyers with focused content in the media they prefer. Your first action might be to create a content-rich website with pages organized by buyer persona. This does not mean you need to redesign the entire existing website, nor does it necessitate a change in the site architecture. You can start by just creating some new individual pages, each with specialized content customized for a particular buyer persona, creating appropriate links to these pages, and leaving the rest of the site alone. For example, our hypothetical college might create content for each of the buyer personas it identified. Sam the Athlete (the high school student who is a varsity athlete and a candidate for admission) should have specific content written for him that describes what it is like to be a student athlete at the college and also gives tips for the admission process. The college could include profiles of current student athletes or even a blog by one of the coaches. In addition, appropriate links on the homepage and the admissions pages should be created for Sam. An appropriate homepage link such as "high school athletes start here" or "special information for student athletes" would attract Sam's attention.

At the same time, the college should develop pages for parents of high school students who are considering applying for admission. The parents have very different problems from those of the students, and the site content designed for parents would deal with things like financial aid and safety on campus.

As you keep your publisher's hat on, consider what other media your organization can publish on the web to reach the buyers you have identified. A technology company might want to consider a white paper detailing solutions to a known buyer problem. Perhaps you have enough information to create an e-book on a subject that would be of interest to one or more of your buyer personas. You may want to develop a series of a dozen videos focusing on issues that you know your buyer is interested in. Or it might be time to start a blog, a podcast, or a Twitter feed to reach your buyers.

Consider creating an editorial plan for each buyer persona. You might do this in the form of a calendar for the upcoming year that includes website content, an e-book or white paper, a blog, and some news releases. Notice as you build an editorial plan and an editorial calendar for the next year that you're now focused on creating the compelling content that your buyers are interested in. Unlike the way you might have done it in the past (and the way your competitors are marketing today), you are not just creating a big brochure about your organization. You're writing for your buyers, not your own ego.

Let's think for a moment about the real estate business. Most Realtors focus on the property itself. In residential markets, they talk about the number of bedrooms and bathrooms, the type of countertops and appliances in the kitchen, and how much land the house sits on. If you're only talking about product *attributes*, you're not marketing to real customer needs effectively.

It's much more important to focus on your buyer's attributes than your product's. Real estate professionals need to step back and understand the people looking for property.

As in many parts of the United States, the countryside around Portland, Maine, has many farmhouses no longer occupied by professional farmers. When the owners of these properties want to sell, the challenge for real estate professionals is to help buyers who aren't professional farmers find and appreciate these homes. (There just aren't that many farmers looking to buy.)

That's where buyer personas come in. Distinct buyer personas relevant to this situation might include the following: newly married couples who want to raise a family in a rural environment; professionals from urban areas seeking a simpler way of life; professionals who live within driving distance of Maine, perhaps in nearby Boston, and want to buy a weekend retreat; people who want a vacation home but can't afford a place on the beach; and people who grew up in a rural area and dream of returning to that life, perhaps becoming hobbyist farmers.

In short, creating content that frames the Maine farmhouse property according to possible lifestyles—rather than as an amalgam of room counts and land acreage—is a subtle but critically important shift. Not for nothing, the associated content on the real estate website, blog, or social media feed will also be a lot more fun to read, and to write.

An effective real estate agent doesn't focus first or even primarily on the farm. They investigate, through interviews and other research, and then cater to the attributes of potential buyers. Then they weave those attributes together to try to understand how people of the desired sales demographics actually think—and speak, and search—about such a property. What words and phrases would they use to describe such a property? How do they feel about the prospects of owning that property?

This information can then be incorporated into online content by an editorial team dedicated to serving each buyer persona with relevant content. It might include YouTube videos, e-books, audio podcasts, photo essays, charts, and interactive tools or calculators. Agents' new knowledge should also inform their participation in real estate forums, social networks, and blogs. It should also inform a search engine optimization strategy, generating relevant and timely information that solves problems for buyers, uses their natural language, and ultimately benefits search rankings. This content also leads buyers down conversion paths where they are more likely to express interest in a property that appeals to them.

The measurable results of countless marketing makeovers I've been privy to demonstrate the benefits of marketing based on detailed understanding of buyer personas.

Clear benefits accrue to marketing based on detailed understanding of buyer personas. In particular, when you stop talking about yourself and your products and services and instead use the web to educate and inform important types of buyers, you will be more successful.

Marketing Strategy Planning Template

Over the past several years, as I've connected with people from around the world who have read earlier editions of this book, I've heard from some readers that they've struggled with getting started. Most of the implementation challenges that people describe involve the shift from focusing on products and services to the more effective approach of focusing on buyer personas and information that helps solve buyers' problems. A secondary challenge people share is the shift in emphasis from offline marketing techniques and programs (such as direct mail, trade shows, and advertising) to reaching buyers on the web.

Taking a suggestion from Toby Jenkins and Adam Franklin of Australian web strategy firm Bluewire Media, I've devised an aid to tackling these challenges: a simple marketing strategy planning template. Jenkins and Franklin had been working on a similar template when we first got connected, so we decided to collaborate. You can download a newly revised and updated full-color and more user-friendly version on my website.

Marketing & PR Strategy : Planning Template

WHO	**BUYER PERSONA**	
	Description Who is this person?	
WHAT	**Problems you solve for this buyer** Why are they buying from you?	
	Actions you'd like them to take Purchase	
	Inquire	
	Connect	
	Download	
WHY	**How are you remarkable?**	
	Proof Guarantees, testimonials, press, etc.	
WHERE	**Where are they?** Google, blogs, Facebook, Twitter, etc.	
	Who do they trust?	
HOW	**Marketing & PR Strategy** What will you publish?	
	Keywords buyers type into Google	
	Marketing & PR Strategy Blog, Twitter, YouTube, email, newsletter, e-books, Facebook, podcasts, etc.	

		SCORECARD		GOAL	RESULT
WHEN	**Things to do this week:** ...this month: ...this quarter: ...this year:		No.of Purchases:		
			No.of Inquiries:		
			No.of Connections:		
			No.of Downloads:		

Marketing & PR Strategy :: Publishing Information for Your Buyers

CONTENT CREATION

- ☒ Blogs
- ☒ News Websites
- ☒ Guest Blog Posts
- ☒ Testimonials
- ☒ Speaker Bios
- ☒ Expert Articles
- ☒ Industry Partners
- ☒ Blog Directories
- ☒ News Releases
- ☒ Affiliates
- ☒ Awards
- ☒ Galleries
- ☒ Infographics
- ☒ Events
- ☒ Reddit
- ☒ **Streaming Video**
- ☒ **Newsjacking**
- ☒ _____
- ☒ _____
- ☒ _____

Google

search

SEO
Organic Searches

SEM
Google Adwords

www.

Mobile & Tablet
Friendly Site

Landing Pages

WEBSITE

Blogs

YouTube

Facebook

Email
Marketing

LinkedIn

Webinars

Content &
Social Networking

Medium

Instagram

Twitter

Pinterest

Apps

Podcasts

Marketing & PR Strategy :: Driving Action

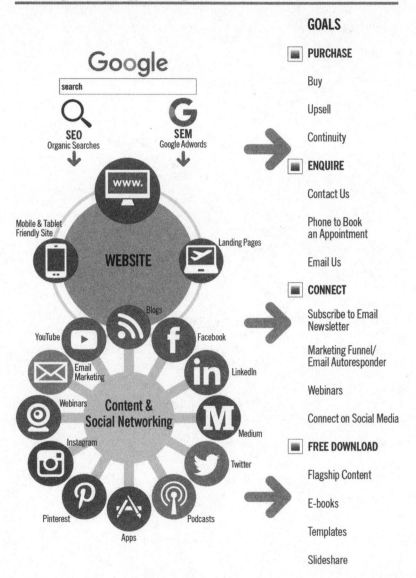

I created the template to help people implement strategies for reaching buyers directly. I believe it's essential to shift out of the marketer's comfort zone of preaching about products and services. For example, if you were to say to me, "I want to start a blog," I would point you to the template and have you start asking the following questions:

- Who are you trying to reach with the blog?
- Is a blog the best tool? Or might another form of content be better?
- What problems can you help solve for your buyers?
- What value do you bring as creator of this content?
- What search terms are people entering to find you? (This will help you name the blog itself and to title individual posts.)
- What sort of person are you, and what is your company's personality? (This is helpful for creating the design.)
- What do you want people to do—buy, donate, subscribe? (It is helpful to create appropriate links to additional content.)

The marketing and PR strategy planning template is built on the same principle I use throughout this book: Understanding buyers and publishing information on the web especially for them drives action. This approach becomes clear on the second and third pages of the strategy template. The second page points out that when you publish valuable information (videos, blogs, Twitter feeds, e-books, and so on), you are creating the sorts of links that search engine algorithms love. Thus, your content surfaces when buyers are looking for help solving their problems! The third page reminds you that the information people find will drive them to action and help you achieve your goals. Moreover, you can monitor your own effectiveness: You can measure how many people follow you on Twitter, sign up for your email newsletter, or download a white paper. You can also measure how your marketing strategies are helping your organization reach its most important goals, such as new sales and revenue growth.

The New Rules of Measurement

Readers of my blog and those who have seen my talks know that I am very critical of the old return on investment (ROI) approach to measuring marketing and public relations success, an approach still popular today. In my days as vice president of marketing and PR for a NASDAQ-traded B2B technology company more than 15 years ago, we measured success in two ways. Our marketing programs were measured via sales leads: the number of people who registered to download a white paper or who tossed a business card into a fishbowl at the trade show. In other words, the only thing that mattered in our approach to marketing was how many people raised their hands by submitting personal information to us. Similarly, our public relations programs were measured via a PR clip book, a collection of all the clippings of magazine and newspaper articles written about the company. The book represented a month's worth of clippings and was usually bound for us by our PR agency. We would then calculate the advertising equivalency value of those press clips—that is, how much we would have had to pay to purchase a similar amount of ad space in that publication. These were the measures my bosses used to gauge my success. And I'm told by tons of marketing and PR people that sales leads and clip books are still the primary metrics used today.

Asking Your Buyer for a Date

To illustrate how the old form of measurement based on sales leads is flawed, I like to appeal to a dating analogy. Imagine that a man goes up to someone he finds attractive at a bar and the first thing out of his mouth is "Give me your phone number."

Imagine that a woman sees someone she finds interesting at the local coffee emporium and starts off the conversation with "How much money do you make?"

If you're a famous celebrity or amazingly hot, this approach might work. However, mere mortals are not likely to get too far in the dating world by acting like this.

Yet this is exactly the way that many companies behave. They apply to the web the old rules they learned for offline marketing. They require the disclosure of personal information before sending an interested party a white paper. They design inane "contact us" forms to fill out before it's possible to speak with a human. How does that make *you* feel? So the next time you have to design a marketing strategy, think about how you would approach it if you were trying to date the buyer.

Measuring the Power of Free

While the dating discussion helps us understand what's at stake for *marketing* measurement, what about for *public relations*? How do we measure the effectiveness of PR?

A reader named Lee put it bluntly: "Wow you really don't like us poor old PR people do you? So—how do you replace the clip books, which you are so scathing of and our bosses and clients still demand? Can you help me understand how to explain to a client exactly what they have paid for on a monthly basis? They want to see results."

Here is a longer version of what I answered back to Lee:

The problem I have with clip book measurement is that it does not reflect the realities of what we can do today to reach our audiences via the web. A clip book implies that all we care about is ink from mainstream media. Measuring success by focusing only on the number of times the mainstream media write or broadcast about you misses the point.

If a blogger is spreading your ideas, that's great.

If a thousand people watch your YouTube video, that's awesome.

If a hundred people email a link to your information out to their networks, tweet about you, or post about you on their Facebook pages, that's amazing.

If a hundred people join your LinkedIn group, go ahead and shout, "Woo-hoo!"

If you come up on the first page of Google results for an important phrase, break out the champagne!

You're reaching people, which was the point of seeking media attention in the first place, right?

The problem is that most PR people measure only traditional media like magazines, newspapers, radio, and TV, and this practice doesn't capture the value of sharing. There's nothing wrong with a clip book, but it's not enough.

What You Should Measure

These days, the web gives everyone—not only B2B companies like the one I worked for but also consumer brands, consultants, nonprofits, schools, and many others—a tremendous opportunity to reach people and engage them in new and different ways. Now we can earn attention by creating and publishing online for free something interesting and valuable: a YouTube video, a blog, a research report, photos, a Twitter stream, an e-book, a Facebook page.

But how *should* we measure the success of this new kind of marketing? The answer is that we need new metrics.

Take another look at the last page of the marketing and PR strategy planning template. Under Goals is a list of many things that you can measure and observe, such as how many people participate in your social networking sites, how many people are reading and downloading your work, and how many are making inquiries about or buying your products and services.

Here are seven things you can measure:

1. How many people are eager to participate in your online efforts? (You can measure how many people like you on Facebook, subscribe to your blog, follow you on Twitter, sign up for your email newsletter, or register for a webinar.)
2. How many people are downloading your stuff? (You can measure how many people are downloading your e-books, presentation slides, videos, podcasts, and other content.)
3. How often are bloggers writing about you and your ideas?
4. (And what are those bloggers saying?)
5. Where are you appearing in search results for important phrases?
6. How many people are engaging with you and choosing to speak to you about your offerings? (You can measure how many people are responding to contact forms and making requests for information.)
7. How are sales looking? Is the company reaching its goals? (Ultimately, the most important form of measurement within management teams is revenue and profit.)

The closer marketers align the way we measure with the real goals of the business, like revenue and profit, the more our marketing programs will help to achieve those goals. And an added benefit of this approach is that you will be more respected by your peers in other parts of your company.

Stop Thinking of Content Creation as a Marketing Expense

I get pushback about the new rules from many entrepreneurs, business owners, and chief marketing officers (CMOs) because they see the investment in "content people" as a barrier. They say things like: "I cannot find money in my budget to spend $5,000 a month (or however much) on content creation."

When I've probed, I've learned the vast majority of these decision makers are looking at content creation in the same way they look at other marketing expenses: advertising, trade show booths, agency retainers, and printing.

Thinking of your online content as just another marketing expense will always lead you to underspend.

For example, if you spent $5,000 in a given month on a Google AdWords advertising campaign, the only thing you bought were the ads appearing in the search results and the resulting clicks on your ads, which appeared against the important phrases people search with to find your business. But as soon as you stop paying, your advertising and clicks completely stop. That is a classic example of a genuine marketing expense. You pay and you get something but when you stop paying it immediately goes away.

However, if you spend $5,000 in a given month to hire a freelance journalist to write a bunch of interesting blog posts, that content will live on beyond that particular month. It will continue to drive people from the search engines to your website for years to come. The content will retain its value many years after it has been paid for.

I started writing my blog in 2004. There are posts that I wrote many years ago that rank highly in the search engines for phrases that people search on today: "brand journalism," "newsjacking," and many others.

My free e-books provide an even more dramatic example. They've been downloaded well over a million times. Every single day, people download my e-books, in some cases years after I have written them. Why? Because they enter search terms like "viral marketing" into a search engine and discover my content created long ago.

Those blog posts and e-books are assets that I own. They're not one-shot marketing expenses. They draw 500 or so search engine users to my website or blog *each day*. For free.

Almost all marketers make this mistake, viewing investment in content as a short-term advertising expense rather than the creation of a long-term asset.

It's time we educated the decision makers that content creation is asset building. I am such a believer in this idea that I think we should start putting our blogs and YouTube channels onto our balance sheets in the same way that many companies value patents, trademarks, or brands.

Allow me to propose a metric for doing so. Let's call it AdWords value equivalency, analogous to the traditional PR metric of advertising value equivalency.

The way to calculate it is to figure out how much you would have to pay for the Google AdWords equivalent of a particular search term for which you rank highly in the natural search results (thanks to that great content you invested in). Then figure out how often that phrase is searched on and clicked to calculate a value for a year (or 10 years, or in perpetuity).

Here's an example. As I write this, my content is currently in the #2 position for the phrase "online media room" on Google. That's from a report titled "Online Media Room Best Practices" I wrote and posted to my site nearly 10 years ago! At the same time, there are companies buying ads against this phrase using Google AdWords, including LVL Studio and Prezly. I would argue that the value of that phrase as a marketing asset to my business is the present value of the maximum AdWords price you have to pay, times the number of searches (or the number of clicks). You could figure it out such that a keyword like that could potentially be worth hundreds of thousands of dollars over, say, 10 years. Maybe millions of dollars.

My point here is simply that a marketing expense is something that you spend money on and, after it's spent, the value is gone. However, a marketing asset like content is a lasting investment and needs to be weighed differently. In many cases, the value far outweighs the initial investment, and benefits accrue for years to come.

Stick to Your Plan

If you've read this far, thank you. If you've developed a marketing and PR plan that uses the new rules of marketing and PR and you're ready to execute, great! The next 13 chapters will give you more specific advice about implementing your plan.

But now I must warn you: Many people who adhere to the old rules will fight you on this strategy. If you are a marketing professional who wants to reach your buyers directly, you are likely to encounter resistance from corporate communications people. PR folks will get resistance from their agencies. They'll say the old rules are still in play. They'll say you have to focus on the four Ps. They'll say you need to talk only about your products. They'll say that using the media is the only way to tell your story and that you can use press releases only to reach journalists, not your buyers directly. They'll say that bloggers are geeks in pajamas who don't matter.

They are wrong. As the dozens of successful marketers profiled in this book say, the old rules are old news. Millions of people are online right now looking for answers to their problems. Will they find your organization? And if so, what will they find?

Remember, on the web, you are what you publish.

11 Growing Your Business: How Marketing and PR Drive Sales

Successful selling no longer follows the playbook that worked even just a few years ago. The rules have changed here, too, yet most organizations and the salespeople they employ haven't made the transition.

Because of the wealth of information on the web, the salesperson no longer controls the relationship between buyer and seller. Now, buyers are in charge. They can see what your CEO is saying on Twitter and LinkedIn. They can check out independent blogs to learn what it's really like to be a customer. Buyers actively go around salespeople, gathering information themselves and engaging a company representative only at the last possible moment. By then, they are armed with tons of information. In the old days, salespeople controlled the information. Now it's the buyers who have the leverage.

It gets worse. As you probably know, salespeople have a bad reputation in the marketplace. Except for salespeople themselves, almost everyone I talk to associates sales with being hustled and taken advantage of. They think of dealing with a salesperson as a purely adversarial relationship. The very word *sales* summons sleazy connotations, so people get defensive immediately to protect themselves.

It's Time for a Sales Transformation

After the first edition of this book was released in 2007, hundreds of people asked me to extend the ideas in this book to the area of sales. I frequently heard from people who had transformed their organizations' marketing and public relations functions and are now ready to do the same with their sales departments. Like anyone following the new rules, I listened. Soon I began research on how the ideas in this book apply to sales. I found incredible examples of how content also influences sales, so I wrote a follow-on book to the one you're reading. Originally released in 2014 and with a newly revised paperback edition in 2016, it's titled *The New Rules of Sales and Service: How to Use Agile Selling, Real-Time Customer Engagement, Big Data, Content, and Storytelling to Grow Your Business.* This chapter explains the basics of how to apply the ideas from the *Sales and Service* book. If you work in a larger organization, you'll learn how to work with your sales colleagues. If you're an entrepreneur, business owner, or employee of a smaller organization, you'll see how to integrate marketing and sales to grow your business.

Before we dig in, let's take a moment to look at how these two disciplines differ. By making certain we understand the difference, we can then close the gap between marketing and sales and grow business faster.

> Marketing generates attention from the many people who make up a buyer persona. Sales content (and salespeople), on the other hand, communicates with one potential customer at a time, putting the buying process into context.

Reaching many people: The job of marketers is to understand buyer personas and communicate with these groups in a one-to-many approach. That's what most of this book is all about. Web content as a marketing asset captures the attention of a group of buyers and drives those people into and through the sales process. The content marketers create—blogs, YouTube videos, infographics, e-books, webinars, and the like—can influence large numbers of people. Done well, with a research-based understanding of buyer personas, this content generates sales leads.

Influencing one person at a time: The role of sales is completely different. The goal of a salesperson is to influence one buyer at a time, typically when the buyer is already close to making a purchase decision. While marketers need to be experts in persuading an audience of many, salespeople excel in persuading the individual buyer. They add context to the company's expertise, products, and services. Through them, the marketers' content fulfills its potential by connecting buyer to salesperson when the buyer is interested.

If, like me, you run a small business, you're probably playing both roles—communicating to your wider marketplace and engaging with one interested buyer at a time.

In this chapter, we're going to build on some of the ideas and concepts I've already introduced. In Chapter 3, we talked about reaching buyers directly with your organization's online content, and Chapter 10 was where we put together a detailed plan to identify and target buyer personas with individualized approaches. But to extend these ideas to sales, we're also going to talk about some new concepts, particularly how content influences individual buyers when they close in on a purchase decision.

Let's start the chapter with some ideas for how you can build a website that walks buyers through the research process as they consider doing business with your organization and moves them toward the place where they are ready to buy (or donate, or join, or subscribe). Remember, that's the goal of all web content! We'll also spend some time discussing how you can work directly with the salespeople in your organization.

How Web Content Influences the Buying Process

As I've said many times in these pages, when people want to buy something, the web is almost always the first stop on their shopping trip. In any market category, potential customers head online to conduct research. The moment of truth is when they reach your site: Will you draw them into your sales process, or allow them to click away?

While many marketers now understand that content drives action, and quite a few have embraced the ideas in this book, the vast majority focus their content effort only at the very top of the sales consideration process. In other words, they create content to attract buyers but none to support the salespeople. That's a big mistake!

> People don't go to the web looking for advertising; they are on a quest for content.

When buyers arrive at your site, you have an opportunity to deliver targeted information at the precise moment when they are looking for what you have to offer. By providing information when they need it, you can begin a long and profitable relationship with them. Editors and publishers obsess over maintaining readership. So should you.

To best leverage the power of content, you first need to help your site's visitors find what they need. When someone arrives for the first time, he or she receives a series of messages—whether you realize it or not. These messages are answering the questions that matter to the visitor.

- Does this organization care about me?
- Does it focus on the problems I face?
- Does it share my perspective or push its own on me?

You need to start with site navigation that is designed and organized with your buyers in mind. Don't simply mimic the way your company or group is organized (e.g., by product, geography, or governmental structure), because the way your audience uses websites rarely coincides with your company's internal priorities. Organizing based on your needs leaves site visitors confused about how to find what they really need.

You should learn as much as possible about your buyers' process, focusing on issues such as how they find your site or how long they consider a purchase. Consider what happens offline in parallel with online interactions. The two should complement each other. For example, if you have an e-commerce site and a printed catalog, coordinate the content so that both efforts support and reinforce the buying process: Include URLs for your online buying guide in the catalog, and use the same product descriptions online, so people don't get confused. In the business-to-business (B2B) world, trade shows should work together with Internet initiatives. For instance, you might collect email addresses at the booth and then send a follow-up email pointing to a show-specific landing page.

For most B2B products and services, as well as higher-priced consumer goods, your buyers will at some point need to reach out to engage with a representative of your company. In that moment, you've gone from marketing to your buyers as a group to selling to your buyer as an individual person. While this process may happen via email, the phone, social networking, or an in-person visit, content still plays a vital role in getting the buyer ready to buy. But you have to understand the process to help shape it.

Tips for Creating a Buyer-Centric Website

The online relationship begins the second a potential customer hits your homepage. The first thing he or she needs to find is a self-reflection. That's why you must organize your site with content for each of your distinct buyer personas. How do your potential customers self-select? Is it based on their job function, on geography, or on the industry they work in? It's important to create a set of appropriate links based on a clear understanding of your buyers, so you can quickly move them from your homepage to pages built specifically for them.

One way many organizations approach navigation is to link to landing pages based on the problems your product or service solves. Start by identifying the situations in which each target audience may find itself. If you are in the supply chain management business, you might have a drop-down menu on the homepage with links that say, "I need to get product to customers faster" or "I want to move products internationally." Each path leads to landing pages built for buyer segments, with content targeted to their problems. Once buyers reach those pages, you have the opportunity to communicate your expertise in solving these problems—building some empathy in the process. Then you can move customers further along the buying cycle, handing them off to a salesperson when appropriate.

As you build a site that focuses on your buyers and their purchasing process, here are some tips to consider.

Develop a Site Personality

It is important to create a distinct, consistent, and memorable site. The tone of voice of the content will contribute to that goal. As visitors interact with the content on your site, they should develop a clear picture of your organization. Is the personality fun and playful? Or is it solid and conservative? For example, when people search on the Google homepage, they can choose to click "I'm Feeling Lucky." That's a fun and playful way for them to be taken directly to the top listing in the search results. That one little phrase, "I'm Feeling Lucky," says a lot about Google.

And there's more where that came from. For example, the collection of more than 100 Google-supported languages goes from Afrikaans to Zulu but also includes the language of Elmer Fudd. If you choose this option, you'll see everything translated into Fudd-speak—"I'm Feewing Wucky," for example. You probably also know about Google's fun tradition of modifying its homepage logo to mark special events. Called Google Doodles, these whimsically altered logos vary around the world to celebrate everything from Australia Day to Cézanne's birthday. This is cool, but it wouldn't work for a more conservative company—it would just seem strange and out of place.

Contrast Google's homepage to Accenture's. At the time of this writing, the Accenture logo appeared just above a tone-creating promise: "High Performance. Delivered." The site features photos with messages such as "We have advised clients on more than 570 merger and acquisition deals in the last 5 years" and "Every year our systems process 300 million airline ticket reservations."

Both of these homepages work because the site personality is compatible with the company personality. Whatever your personality, the way to achieve consistency is to make certain that the written material, as well as the other content on the site, conforms to a defined tone that you've established from the start. A strong focus on site personality and character pays off. As visitors come to rely on the content they find on your site, they will develop an emotional and personal relationship with your organization. A website can evoke a familiar and trusted voice, just like that of a friend on the other end of an email exchange.

For an example of a site with a very distinct personality, check out HOTforSecurity from Bitdefender. Bitdefender is a particularly interesting example because the online security market is very competitive, making product differentiation a challenge. A cornerstone of the company's marketing approach, HOTforSecurity was launched as a stand-alone site focused on key influencers within the information technology (IT) security community. The new site was not a redesign of the existing company site but, rather, an informational supplement to the main Bitdefender product site.

HOTforSecurity is for people who are interested in the latest information on Internet threats. The Bitdefender team clearly understands that the best online initiatives are those that deliver specific information tailored to a particular buyer persona. The HOTforSecurity site was developed to appeal to three different buyer personas:

1. IT security press (both mainstream press and social media).
2. Bitdefender users.
3. A group of "Internet security geeks"—the most important buyer persona for HOTforSecurity.

The HOTforSecurity site appeals directly to the Internet security geek buyer persona. Who else would appreciate dryly incredulous headlines like this one: "Phishing Attacks against Commercial Vessels on the Rise, Alerts US Coast Guard." The design is clearly that of an informational site that might be a media property—in stark contrast to the slew of boring corporate tech sites. It delivers valuable information to everyone interested in Internet security issues, not just Bitdefender users. It is not a sales site, so people trust it. While there are identifiers that the site is an online property of Bitdefender, it is a subtle tie. They don't brag about it, but they don't hide the association, either. HOTforSecurity from Bitdefender is a great example of online content that effectively reaches buyers.

Photos and Images Tell Your Story

Content is not limited to words; smart marketers make use of nontext content—including photos, audio feeds, video clips, cartoons, charts, and graphs—to inform and entertain site visitors. Photographs in particular play an important role for many sites. Photos are powerful content when page visitors see that the images are an integrated component of the website. However, generic stock photographs (happy and good-looking multicultural models in a fake company meeting room) may actually have a negative effect. People will know instantly if you use fake photos. Neither you nor your users are generic.

A technical note: While photos, charts, graphs, and other nontext content make great additions to any site, be wary of very large image sizes and of distracting multimedia content like Flash graphics and animation. Visitors want to access content quickly, they want sites that load fast, and they don't want to be distracted. See Chapter 16 for much more on photos and images.

Include Interactive Content Tools

Anything that gets people involved with the content of a site provides a great way to engage visitors, build their interest, and move them through your sales cycle. Examples of interactive tools include the stock quoting and charting applications found on financial sites and "email your congressman" tools on political advocacy sites. Interactive content provides visitors with a chance to immerse themselves in site content and take action. That makes them more likely to progress through the sales consideration cycle to the point where they are ready to spend money.

Make Feedback Loops Available

Providing a way for users to interact with your organization is a hallmark of a great site. Easy-to-find "contact us" links are a must, and direct feedback mechanisms like "rate this" buttons, online forums, viewer reviews, and opportunities to post comments provide valuable information by and for site visitors.

Provide Ways for Your Customers to Interact with Each Other

A forum or wiki, where customers can share with and help each other, works well for many organizations as a way to show potential customers your vibrant user community. In other words, it's great marketing to get an existing set of customers interacting with each other on your site!

Make Sure Your Site Is Current

Many people are so busy creating new content for their sites that they forget to ensure that existing content is still current. Websites tend to become outdated quickly because of product changes, staff turnover, and other factors. You should make a point of auditing your site regularly, perhaps once per quarter, and revising as appropriate. At a minimum, you must change the copyright date, if you have one, each January 1. I've seen hundreds of pages with copyright dates many years old.

Include Social Media Share Buttons

A great way to extend the potential reach of your content—to people you do not even know yet—is to make it easy for readers to share it with their networks. Share buttons do this best. Your videos, white paper download pages, blog posts, and similar content should definitely have them. Share buttons make it easy for people to point to your content on social networking sites like Facebook, Pinterest, LinkedIn, and Twitter. An example of a share button is the little thumbs-up "Like" button on Facebook. When your fans push that button on your website, the news that they like it is then reported to their Facebook friends. It sounds like such a simple thing, but these buttons are one of the most effective ways to promote content on the web.

Think about Your Buyers' Preferred Media and Learning Styles

Some people prefer to read when researching an organization and its products and services, while others prefer audio or video content. And many, like me, consume all three. We all have different learning styles and media preferences. So on your site, you should have appropriate content designed for your buyers. This does not mean that you need to have every single format, but you should think about augmenting text with photos and maybe some video.

Create Content with Pass-Along Value That Could Go Viral

Web content provides terrific fodder for viral marketing—the phenomenon where people pass on information about your site to their friends and colleagues or link to your content on their blogs. When content proves interesting or useful, visitors tend to tell friends, usually by sending them a link. Creating buzz around a site to encourage people to talk it up for you isn't easy. It's an organic and usually uncertain process. There are a few things you can do to improve your chances, though. When creating site content, think carefully about what content users might want to pass along, and then make that content easy to find and link to. Humor often helps, as does content that is intensely practical. Be sure to make the actual URLs permanent so that no one finds dead links when visiting months (or years) later. To set yourself up for success with viral marketing is to say something interesting and valuable and to make it easy to find and share.

Now let's take a look at how content moves an individual potential buyer from "just looking" to buying. The key is understanding your sales cycle and how buyers interact with your content.

Step 1: Sales Begin with Informational Content

The most successful sites draw buyers directly into the sales cycle. To see how, we need to remember that people considering a purchase go through a fairly predictable thought process. In the case of something simple and low cost (say, a song download from iTunes), the process may take only seconds. But for a major decision such as buying a new car, sending a child to university, or accepting a job offer, the process may take weeks or months. For many B2B sales, the cycle may involve many steps and involvement from representatives of multiple buyer personas (a business buyer and an IT buyer, perhaps). The process may take months or even years to complete.

Effective web marketers take website visitors' buying process into account when writing content and organizing it on the site. The early stages involve gathering basic information about their problems and learning how your organization solves them. Those further along in the process want to compare products and services, so they need detailed information about the benefits of your offerings. And when buyers are ready to whip out their credit cards, they need easy-to-use mechanisms linked directly from the content so they can quickly finish the purchase (or donation, or subscription, or the like).

For an example of a very long sales cycle, consider our university example from earlier chapters. High school students in the United States apply to university in the fall of their final year and typically make a decision in the spring about which school to attend. But having gone through the process with my daughter, I know the sales cycle starts much earlier. Students tend to visit universities in person when they are juniors in high school (third-year secondary school students). And when they first visit university websites, they are probably freshmen or sophomores (first- and second-year high school students). The university website is often the first place that a student comes into contact with the school, and the site must cater to an audience of young teenagers (and their parents) who won't be ready to apply for two or three years. Creating appropriate content to develop a lasting relationship over a long sales cycle is possible only when an organization knows the buyer personas well and understands the sales process in detail. The university must provide high school students with appropriate content so they get a sense of what university life would be like if they were to attend and what the admission process entails.

Based on my years of research, the vast majority of sites are little more than online brochures, vast one-way advertising vehicles. These sites are almost wholly ineffective at shaping and supporting the buying process. To be successful, you must focus on your buyers and understand their buying process.

Step 2: A Friendly Nudge

After you've demonstrated expertise in the market category and knowledge about solving potential customers' problems, you can introduce your product or service. When creating content about your offerings, remain focused on the buyer and the buyer's problems, rather than elaborating on distinctions between products. As people interact with your content at this middle stage in the buying process, it is appropriate to suggest subscriptions to related content—perhaps an email newsletter, webinar (web-based seminar), or podcast. But remember, if you're asking for someone's email address (or other contact details), you must provide something valuable in return.

People want to poke, prod, and test your company to learn what sort of organization you are. They also have questions. That's why well-designed sites include a mechanism for people to inquire about products or services. Be flexible but also consistent; offer them a variety of ways to interact with your company, and make contact information readily available from any page on the site (one click away is best). Also keep in mind that, particularly with expensive products, buyers will test you to see how responsive you are, so you must make responding to these inquiries a priority. Do you respond to email requests in real time? At this stage, you want people to think: "This is an organization I can do business with. They have happy customers, and they are responsive to me and my needs."

As the customer approaches the end of the buying process, you must provide tools that facilitate the decision. Buyers may be unsure which of your products is appropriate for them, so you may need to provide online demonstrations or a tool that allows them to enter specific details about their requirements and then suggests the appropriate product.

Step 3: Closing the Deal

If your product or service is an e-commerce offering, you will need to make it very easy for people to make a purchase when they are ready. Have a "buy now" button on all of the pages at the end of the sales cycle and make sure that the e-commerce engine makes it simple for people to make selections.

For products and services that require interaction with a salesperson, this is the point where you need to have multiple ways for buyers to express interest. You might include a simple "contact us" and "have a salesperson call me" link. But you might also include a way that buyers can preconfigure their order so the salesperson has a great deal of information before the sales call. Auto dealers often have an online tool for buyers to express interest in the make and model of car plus desired features, which serves as a way to show the salesperson that the buyer is ready.

You must respond quickly to any inquiry! When a buyer submits a form, you should respond within minutes. Don't wait until after lunch or the next day.

Now that we've walked through the sales cycle in its totality, and seen how content is vital not just at the beginning but throughout the process, let's look at a few examples of content in action to drive sales.

Triathlon Coach Delivers Content for All Ability Levels

Rebekah Keat enjoyed tremendous success as a professional triathlete. She raced at the elite level for 15 years and is a two-time Junior World Champion, three-time Australian Ironman Distance Champion, and six-time Iron Distance Champion. When a 2016 injury forced her to retire and dried up her sponsorship revenue and prize money, she decided to become a Triathlon coach. She started with just four clients, but that wasn't nearly enough to pay her bills.

Soon after, Keat founded Team Sirius Tri Club to conduct virtual coaching services and began to create content to attract people interested in her sport. Specifically, Keat realized that most other Triathlon clubs focused on elite-level athletes, ignoring the many beginner and weekend warrior triathletes who need basic information. This was an ideal opportunity for Keat to create content, deliver it via social media, and reach the beginner triathlete buyer persona.

Keat worked hard to create a profile for the beginner triathlete. She used that as her guide. For example, her research showed that people new to triathlon had very basic questions about the sport, training, and gear but were often embarrassed to ask. So she started creating content about how to sight in open water so you can swim straight, or how to mount your bike quickly in race conditions.

"I always want my content to add value," Keat says. "I'm not asking people to join my club. Instead I'm just giving away content, and some of them will become interested. Every day I make sure to post at least two times to social media, and it's always adding value, something about training or a workout."

Keat's Team Sirius Tri Club Facebook page has 50,000 likes, her @rebekahkeat Twitter account, over 10,000 followers, and she hosts a members-only group on Facebook. She also shares personal information and snapshots, including her passion for rescuing horses and the beautiful location in Boulder, Colorado, where she trains elite triathletes. This glimpse into Keat's personal life helps people understand more about her and what it might be like to work with her as a coach. (Most people separate business and personal on social media, and I think that's a mistake. A fun aspect of social media is getting to know a bit about the personal lives of those we do business with. You will read more about this idea when I introduce Dr. Jon Marashi in Chapter 23.)

When Keat conducts in-person coaching, she always films the session. "I have a library of thousands of videos now, and I release those on my social channels," she says. "I've learned that a specific workout tends to get much more interest than when I just post a tip. I put [the workouts] out on Twitter or Instagram, and people really like them and learn about me that way."

Once people follow a link to the Team Sirius Tri Club website, they can sign up for a free email newsletter. Keat's email list now includes over 5,000 triathletes and fans. "You have to build a relationship with people first," she says. "Build a following and develop a rapport with your audience, and then you can offer something."

The three club membership levels Keat offers include the Tri Club at $37 per month (a virtual place to interact with Keat and other athletes), Gold level at $199 per month (which includes a personal training plan), and Platinum level at $300 and up per month (which includes personal feedback and customized coaching).

The approach of targeting a specific buyer persona has led to Team Sirius Tri Club growing from those original four clients to 250 members in just three years. The club is now ranked as the #2 Tri Club in the United States, the #5 Tri Club overall, and the #1 female-coached Tri Club out of over 2,000 clubs worldwide. Keat's strategy of using content creation to drive membership is just as responsible for this growth as are her athletic prowess and coaching skill.

The focus on all levels of triathletes has been especially important for driving Keat's business. One club member commented, "Being a rookie to the sport of triathlon I was nervous to join any club, let alone Team Sirius. I had never competed in a single race in my life and the team made me feel like I was a world champion."

Salespeople as Content Curators

When a salesperson is engaged with a potential customer, it's a great time to deliver content and a perfect reason for a salesperson to send an email. A YouTube video, blog post, e-book, or whatever can be precisely what a buyer needs. It's so much more friendly to send a buyer a link to appropriate content than to do the typical "Are you ready to buy now?" email. A focus on understanding the buying process and developing appropriate content that links visitors through the cycle to the point of purchase is essential. And the salespeople, who manage one deal at a time, are the perfect ambassadors to share the content.

Recently I was researching bamboo flooring. It's time to update some of the floors in our home, and I was considering bamboo. When I started my research, I knew absolutely nothing about it. So I began my journey on Google by searching on the phrase "bamboo floors" and checking out the first few pages of results.

There were a number of websites that helped me, but the one I found to be the most valuable was BuildDirect's. The site has excellent product pages for the company's bamboo flooring, and they offer free samples.

The BuildDirect Learning Center offered valuable text-based information: "The Durability of Bamboo Flooring" and "The Sustainability of Bamboo Flooring." The site's YouTube channel included the video "How Hard Is Bamboo Flooring?," which features BuildDirect co-founder Rob Banks. It has been viewed more than 60,000 times.

There were many more videos and reports that I didn't check out. In other words, BuildDirect has a lot of content to share! That's great. All this excellent information led me to request five free samples from BuildDirect. I also ordered samples from two other suppliers.

For many companies, this is the place where marketing's job has finished and sales' job has just begun. But a much better approach is for sales and marketing to work together to provide ideal content to buyers as they continue their journey through the buying process.

After I placed my free sample order with BuildDirect, I received an email confirmation that looked like a basic order form: just the facts. This was a missed opportunity. BuildDirect could have pointed me to some content designed to help at this stage: "How to Evaluate Your Bamboo Floor Samples," or something like that.

> **When sales and marketing work together, business grows more quickly!**

The BuildDirect samples arrived very quickly, and I enjoyed imagining my floors with each of the options. Interestingly, the samples I ordered from the other bamboo flooring suppliers never appeared. A few days after the BuildDirect samples arrived, I got a nice follow-up email from my salesperson at BuildDirect. It was to confirm that the samples had arrived and to offer to answer any questions I had. This was standard sales stuff handled well. But again, there was a missed opportunity to share content that people in my stage of the process might be interested in. Imagine the power of an extra paragraph like this: "By now you've likely compared the samples we sent. At this stage, many of my customers want to learn about installing bamboo flooring, so I am attaching a report that might interest you: 'How to Install a Bamboo Floor.' And here's a link to a video made by our co-founder that explains how bamboo flooring is graded."

BuildDirect had excellent online content, and I liked the samples. But I could have used some nudging to get me to the point where I'd be ready to pull out my credit card. In the end, I purchased my flooring from another supplier.

Your Company's Salesperson-in-Chief

Speaking of salespeople, the person at the top of your organization—your CEO or equivalent—should be your best salesperson. When I speak with CEOs about generating attention for their businesses through real-time marketing and sales, most ask me how to staff for success in their companies. Very few ask the right question: How do they become a social CEO and support the sales cycle?

Richard Branson, Elon Musk, and Arianna Huffington all have something in common. Not only are they CEOs of large organizations, but they are also top executives on social media. In fact, they have a combined 42 million Twitter followers. I have had the social CEO discussion with leaders of smaller organizations. When the best ones do it right, they engage directly with customers whenever possible. And that connection helps drive business.

Another connected CEO is Gerard Vroomen of Open Cycle, whom we met in Chapter 2. Vroomen blogs and tweets and answers emails from interested people, and he has quickly built several businesses based on his open philosophy. Larry Janesky is an inventor with 29 patents and the founder and CEO of Basement Systems and its sister companies. He runs a successful-in-every-way enterprise that is number one in the dry basement industry, with 345 dealers in six countries. But that doesn't keep Janesky from writing a short "Think Daily" blog post for his customers and friends every single day.

> ## What do people find when they go to your CEO's bio page?

An important consideration for the CEO is his or her corporate bio page. That's the place to showcase the content the CEO generates. You can post things like a YouTube video of a recent speech, links to his or her social feeds, and important posts from the CEO blog.

As people consider doing business with your company, they're also evaluating your executive team, especially the CEO. By showing that she is engaged, you help push people along the buying process. Don't let her be reduced to a boring resume of the dusty old degrees she earned decades ago.

For example, when people go to the bio page of HubSpot CEO Brian Halligan, they find valuable information that Brian has generated. How valuable? HubSpot marketers learned that 20 percent of new HubSpot customers in the past three years viewed Brian's bio page on the company website. This is clear evidence that the CEO's bio page is an important aspect in many buyers' journeys, as they evaluate the company and its management. Because HubSpot measures for this phenomenon, the company understands that Brian's bio page is important content to help to drive HubSpot's growth. Your CEO is an important part of your content effort and helps to drive sales—just by being visible and active online.

Educating Your Salespeople about the New Buying Process

Back in the 1990s, there was little love lost between marketing and sales. At many companies, the relationship was downright adversarial. The tension often extended all the way up to senior management. It stemmed from the sales process involving a handoff. Marketing generated leads and then handed them over to sales. Then the sales team owned them until close.

Like a marriage gone bad, the dialogue circa 1995 was an endless tape loop:

Sales said, "Get us some good leads! These leads stink! Our people can't sell."

Marketing responded, "You've got good leads! Your people just stink at closing!"

I've been in the middle of these discussions at several companies. They are so 20 years ago. And if you've made it this far in the chapter, you understand why.

Marketers and salespeople alike need to understand that we're all in this together. We are no longer in a world where marketing hands off to sales. Marketing needs to create content for each step in the process. And salespeople, if they are active in social media, can drive people into the beginning of the sales process just like marketers can.

As a marketer, it is important that you make sure the sales and management teams understand this point—"sales leads" are no longer the primary metric of success. Explain that registration requirements just don't work in an environment where Google delivers the best content. Free content is what drives action today. And the most successful companies are those where salespeople and marketers work together to move people through the sales process.

You want your buyers to consume your content, not be forced to register for it! It's important to measure total exposure to your ideas (e-book downloads, blog post views, and so on) rather than the number of people willing to hand over their private information. But you'll need to make sure that the others in your organization, especially the salespeople, understand this new approach.

Registration or Not? Data from an E-Book Offer

I've looked into the differences in download frequency for content such as e-books when they are made completely free versus when they require registration. My research suggests that you will generate between 10 and 50 times more downloads when you do not require registration. That's right—based on data from companies that have tested offers with and without registration, it's a good guess that if you're getting 100 downloads per month with registration, you might get as many as 5,000 downloads per month without registration.

Think about your own behavior for a moment. When you're interested in a free white paper, do you eagerly give up your email address to get it? Or are you reluctant, and do you sometimes refuse? Now if the paper were completely free, how would you feel? And what's even more interesting, ask yourself if you'd be willing to share a link to the white paper with your followers on Twitter or with your friends and colleagues via email if there were no registration. You'd be much more willing to share, right? Because you'd have nothing to lose. But if there were a registration requirement, would you share the link? The vast majority of people tell me they wouldn't, because they fear that their contacts might get put on a sales list and then receive unwanted emails and phone calls. This is exactly why free e-books with no registration have so many more inbound links and much higher search engine rankings.

I'm always interested in new metrics that help inform this debate. John Mancini, president of the nonprofit Association for Information and Image Management (AIIM), agreed to share his experience. AIIM represents the users and suppliers of document, content, and record management technologies and publishes content on this subject as part of its marketing program.

Mancini released the organization's first e-book, *8 Reasons You Need a Strategy for Managing Information—Before It's Too Late*, as a totally free download, with no registration required. In just the first month, the e-book was downloaded 5,138 times. AIIM also created a presentation version of the book and posted it, also with no registration requirement, on Slide-Share. This version had 3,353 downloads. That makes for a total of 8,491 downloads that month.

"Making the e-book available for free and totally without registration was a new approach for us," Mancini says. "These results for unfettered access are particularly impressive when considered against a couple of more traditional examples (i.e., content requiring a registration on our website)."

As a case in point, Mancini compares the e-book to one of his organization's most popular pieces of content, AIIM Industry Watch research papers. "We require registration for these papers because they are also used as a lead generation program for the sponsors," he says. "During roughly the same period as the e-book, there were [only] 513 actual downloads. I am convinced that open access is best for content like my e-books."

Although it's impossible to know for sure, since we're comparing two different pieces of content, AIIM's data suggest that there is a significant advantage in not requiring registration. Specifically, unlocking content at AIIM seems to have meant more than a 16-fold increase in the number of downloads. Mancini is convinced that the more forward-looking of AIIM's sponsors will start to realize that the future lies in creating as much visibility as possible for their content—rather than viewing this marketing problem solely through the prism of name acquisition and lead generation.

Still not convinced about the power of free? Starting to be, but wanting to hedge your bets? When asked about this debate in my live presentations, I also offer a third option, which is a hybrid. I suggest the first offer be totally free, such as a totally free e-book with no registration requirement. Then, within the e-book, I suggest including a secondary offer that requires a registration that you can use to capture leads. This secondary offer might be access to a webinar or similar premium content. This way, you can spread your ideas yet still collect contact information.

Close the Sale—Continue the Conversation

I talked previously about three steps in the sales process. But there really are four. Once the deal is closed, you must continue the online dialogue with your new customer. Add her to your customer email newsletter or customer-only community site, where she can interact with experts in your organization and other like-minded customers. You should also provide ample opportunities for her to give you feedback on how to make the products (and sales process) better.

The manner in which salespeople engage potential new customers when trying to win new business is often light-years removed from how these same customers are treated by the company only months later.

Focusing a great deal of attention on the buying process and then relegating buyers to poor postsale service means customers are far more likely to leave. This can lead to a churn cycle in which companies add more sales resources to replace the customers who abandoned them, and around and around it goes.

You keep customers happy not by doing something different from how you won them in the first place but by doing exactly the same things that won them in the first place. Shifting strategy doesn't work.

Measure and Improve

There's one more point for you to consider as you attend to every stage of the sales process: Effective marketers constantly measure and improve.

Because it is so easy to modify web content at any time, you should be measuring what people are doing on your site. Benchmarking elements such as the self-select links and testing different landing page content can help. If you have two offers on a landing page (a free white paper and a free demonstration, say), you might measure which one works to get more clicks but also measure how many people who responded to each offer actually bought something. This way you will know not just numbers of clicks, but revenue by offer type, and you can use that in future landing page decisions. Armed with real data, you make valuable modifications. You might want to see what happens if you change the order of the links on the homepage. Sometimes people just click the thing at the top of a list. What happens if something else is at the top? Don't be afraid to experiment—as long as you're committed to acting on what you learn.

Let's close this chapter by meeting someone who has put all the ideas of this chapter to work: built an online content strategy, measured the results, and achieved impressive business growth.

How a Content Strategy Grew Business by 50 Percent in One Year

Sales Benchmark Index is a professional services firm focused exclusively on B2B sales force effectiveness. Before making the switch to a content marketing strategy, the company used classic old-rules marketing to try to reach customers. "We hired telemarketing firms to cold call," says CEO Greg Alexander. "We did batch and blast email. We did interruption-based marketing tactics of all kinds, and for a period of time, that approach met our needs. And our needs are really well defined: We know how many inquiries we need to generate all the way through to paying customers. Then the effectiveness of the outbound channels just stopped. It was like somebody slammed the doors shut."

Alexander thinks that his interruption-based strategies stopped working because his target audience was incredibly busy. "I wasn't competing against other companies," he says. "I was competing for buyers' attention." Alexander did a great deal of research on how his buyer personas solve problems, and that was the starting point for his efforts to reach buyers with online content.

"When our target customer, the head of sales or the head of marketing in a B2B organization, has a problem or needs in their business, the very first thing they do—and we've done a lot of research to support this—is start searching the web and reading and educating themselves," Alexander says. "They typically don't want to engage with a service provider, us or anybody else for that matter, for a long time. Through education on the web, they develop a crisp, well-articulated problem statement. Then they reach out to a small number of people to ask for their assistance in how they might approach solving that problem. It's similar to the way somebody would hire a law firm or a strategy consulting firm or an advertising agency."

Once Alexander and his team understood how their buyers solved problems, the next step was to develop buyer persona profiles. "We wanted to understand the key business objectives of each target audience," Alexander says. "What was standing in the way of them accomplishing those objectives? What were the things that were important to them when they made a decision to hire a service provider? How were they measured? What would the definition of success be? Once we understood that, we mapped the buying process for each persona. We identified when information requests were happening in the buying process, for example, and what those information requests were."

Alexander quickly realized that he had to develop a large number of new content channels, but outside firms couldn't provide writers, editors, and designers who understood well enough what his firm actually does. So he chose to create what he calls an "internal content marketing agency" using his company's smart subject matter experts. To do so, they needed to create an infrastructure to channel their expertise into the creation of blog posts, videos, and longer-form content like e-books.

Alexander's "internal agency" includes three staff members: a full-time editor, who manages an editorial calendar, production schedule, and set of media channels; a search engine optimization (SEO) expert, who increases the likelihood of the content getting found in search; and a copywriter, who works with subject matter experts inside the firm.

"But the actual writers, the contributors of all the content, are the subject matter experts in our company who are working with our clients," Alexander says.

Interestingly, the subject matter experts at Sales Benchmark Index are organized by buyer persona. I always recommend this buyer-centric approach, yet most companies focus on the product lines they offer rather than the personas they sell to. "It was a difficult transition for us," Alexander admits. "We used to be service offering focused. I had to break that. It was a painful transition, and it took us some time to get there."

Another of Alexander's smart strategies that comes straight out of this book is that he named his buyer personas. At Sales Benchmark Index there are nine of them, and there are two people from the firm assigned to work with each persona and to create content for them. "For example, we have a persona called 'Big Company Mark,'" Alexander says. "Big Company Mark is the chief marketing officer or the VP of marketing. We have two individuals in our firm who have been serving the chief marketing officer in the B2B environment for many years, even prior to joining our company. They were the ones who actually constructed the buyer persona, so they understand what their needs and challenges are."

When it came time to start writing, the team started with a blog. They worked with HubSpot to deploy the HubSpot marketing platform for hosting the content. "It started slowly," Alexander says. "Our early blog posts probably weren't our proudest moments. But then we started to build interest and get subscribers. Soon everybody in the company saw the success and wanted to participate, so we began posting to our blog every day."

The team at Sales Benchmark Index also creates long-form content, including a recent e-book targeted to newly promoted VPs of sales. "It was a heavy lift for us to put it together," Alexander says. "But it has created over 4,000 leads for us so far this year."

Alexander knows from his buyer persona research that 75 percent of his potential U.S. clients are on a calendar-based planning cycle. "July through October is when they go through their annual operating plan," he says. This is the time when buyers are most receptive to Sales Benchmark Index services and when the majority of sales take place. "They are trying to figure out things like 'How many salespeople do I need?' 'How should I place the territories?' 'What should the quotas be?' 'How should I pay them?' A lot of their research is centered around those issues, and we can help them with that."

Because most of Alexander's sales happen from July through October, he has a calendar-based approach to content creation. "From November through June, the approach is to give away lots and lots of intellectual property to build up the subscriber base," Alexander says. "We believe that permission to have a conversation with buyers is a valuable asset. Within the blog, we will write about a problem. We'll offer up a tool that we used with one of our clients to solve that specific problem. All we ask is that they click on the link. We put it behind a form, and then they get the tool for free. During this quiet period, we don't bombard them with follow-up marketing activity." This is classic "step 1" stuff.

Alexander's team shifts focus during the selling season, when buyers have a greater need for information because they are planning next year's budgets. "During that time period, we shift the focus of the blog to having subscribers participate in our annual research tour, which we call 'Make the Number: How Your Peers Plan on Allocating People, Money and Time for the Upcoming Year.'"

"Make the Number" gives potential clients access to a personal review of benchmarking data and research. "This is an onsite seminar," Alexander says. "If you want access to all these tools, and you've been a subscriber of ours for months and sometimes years, one of our experts will come and give you a presentation for 90 minutes on a set of best practices heading into the New Year." This is "step 2" content, nudging potential buyers toward the Sales Benchmark Index products.

Alexander has had tremendous success with the calendar-based approach to content creation. "In prior years, we might do between 50 and 100 visits during the July to October period," he says. "But this year, we'll have done over 220 of them. We know that about half of those sites eventually, inside of six quarters, become clients of ours. When people prepare to buy a professional service like ours, the product is intangible. So we use the 'Make the Number' meetings to turn what we do into a tangible. It makes it easier for the buyer to buy."

Alexander's team measures every aspect of his content efforts. After all, this is a company that helps sales and marketing executives be more effective through measurement! In fact, they measure down to the blog-post level. "We grade posts based on things like how closely each is related to the problems of our buyer personas," he says. "We count the number of words in sentences, targeting between six and 14 words per sentence. And we grade the effectiveness of the title. Then there are the hard metrics like the number of comments, social shares, links generated, and view counts."

Alexander also analyzes what he calls "branded versus nonbranded keywords" to understand how many people come to the blog on a monthly basis for each. He tallies a branded keyword hit when somebody arrives at the blog via a term like "sales benchmark index" (which means that person entered the company name into a search engine). A nonbranded word is subject-specific but not company-specific, like "sales territory design."

HubSpot's analytics tools are important in Alexander's efforts. "We're looking at the number of incoming links, and we use the HubSpot Link Grader Search Engine Optimization Tool. This year we've generated 579 new domains linking to us, with 27,780 individual links coming from those domains. The thing that I'm probably the happiest about is that the quality of the links has gone up. HubSpot graded the links earlier in the year at 47 on a scale of 0 to 100. Now the average link rating is 82."

The ultimate measure of success for a business is revenue growth, and the strategies Alexander has implemented have contributed greatly to his company's success. "We're up a little over 50 percent this year," he told me. "That's our revenue number and our head count, which in professional services is a key metric. I can directly attribute much of that gain to content marketing. This is a mental shift to realize that you're really in the publishing business. If you embrace publishing, then the transformation will happen."

Yes, product superiority, advertising, the media, and branding remain important to the marketing mix. But on the web, smart marketers like Greg Alexander understand that an effective content strategy, tightly integrated to the buying process, is critical to success.

12 Strategies for Creating Awesome Content

If you've read this book starting from the beginning, I hope I've been able to convince you that web content sells. (If you've skipped ahead to this chapter, welcome!) An effective online content strategy, artfully executed, drives action. Organizations that use online content well have a clearly defined goal—to sell products, generate leads, secure contributions, or get people to join—and deploy a content strategy that directly contributes to reaching that goal. People often ask me: "How do you recommend that I create an effective _____?" (Fill in the blank with *blog, video, white paper, e-book, email newsletter, webinar,* or other product.) While the technologies for each form of online content are a little different, the one common aspect is that through all of these media, your organization can exercise thought leadership rather than simple advertising and product promotion; a well-crafted white paper, e-book, or webinar contributes to an organization's positive reputation by setting it apart in the marketplace of ideas. This form of content brands a company, a consultant, or a nonprofit as an expert and as a trusted resource.

To create awesome content, the first thing you need to do is put away your company hat for a moment and—you guessed it—think like one of your buyer personas. The content that you create will be a solution to those people's problems and *will not mention your company or products at all!* Imagine for a moment that you are a marketer at an automobile tire manufacturer. Rather than just peddling your tires, you might write an e-book or shoot a video about how to drive safely in the snow, and then promote it on your site and offer it free to other organizations (such as automobile clubs and driver's education schools) to put on their sites. Or imagine that you run a local catering company and you have a blog or a website. You might have a set of web pages or videos available on your site. The topics could include "Plan the Perfect Wedding Reception" and "What You Need to Know for the Ideal Dinner Party for Twelve." A caterer with a video series like this educates visitors about their problems (planning a wedding or a dinner party) but does *not* sell the catering services directly. Instead, the idea here is that people who learn through the caterer's information are more likely to hire that caterer when the time comes.

Mark Howell, a consultant for Lifetogether, is a pastor who works with Christian organizations and uses a thought leadership blog to get his information out. "My primary targets are people who are working in churches or Christian organizations that are trying to figure out better ways to do things," he says. "So I keep my content to things that seem secular but have broad application to churches. For example, I did a post called 'Required Reading: Five Books Every Leader Needs' where I tie broader business trends and marketing strategies to churches."

What makes Howell's blog work is that he's not just promoting his consulting services but instead is providing powerful information with a clear focus, for readers who just might hire him at some point. "My personal bias, and what I write about, is that for a lot of leaders in churches, the personal passion for what they are doing could be enhanced if they just got a taste for what more secular writers, such as Tom Peters, Guy Kawasaki, and Peter Drucker, say," Howell says. "There are so many ideas out there, and if I could just give people a sense of what some of these thinkers are saying, then my hope is that they can see that there is application for church leadership."

Ways to Get Your Information Out There

Here are some of the common forms of content you might consider creating (there may be others in your niche market). We've seen many of these media in earlier chapters, but let's focus now on how they can help your company establish itself as a thought leader.

Important note: You don't have to do all of these! This is just a list to get you thinking.

Blogs

As we've already seen, a blog is a personal website written by someone who is passionate about a subject and wants the world to know about it. The benefits rub off on the company that the blogger works for. Writing a blog is the easiest and simplest way to get your thought leadership ideas out and into the market. See Chapter 15 for information on how to start your blog.

Audio and Video

Podcasts (ongoing series of audio downloads available by subscription) are very popular as thought leadership content in some markets. Some people prefer just audio, and if your buyers do, then a podcast of your own might be the thing for you. Video content, vodcasts, video blogs, and vlogs (lots of names, one medium) are regularly updated videos that offer a powerful opportunity to demonstrate your thought leadership, since most people are familiar with the video medium and are used to the idea of watching a video or television program to learn something. An easy and fun way to create audio and video content is to host an interview show with guests who have something interesting to say. The intelligence of the guests rubs off on you as you interview them. Consider interviewing customers, analysts who cover your marketplace, and authors of books in your field. See Chapter 17 for information on audio and video.

Photos, Images, Graphs, Charts, and Infographics

Don't underestimate the value of an image to tell a story. If your product has visual appeal (sporting goods and real estate come to mind), you can create interesting content based on images. If your expertise lends itself to how-to instruction (example: "Learn How to Surf"), photos can be particularly useful. Expertise that can be depicted as a chart (example: "Real Estate Values in Fairfield County 1976–2020") also stands to be especially useful to your buyers. In fact, any visual representation of information (sometimes called *infographics*) is a potentially valuable form of thought leadership content. I talk much more about the use of images in Chapter 16.

Slide Presentations

Thanks to the success of online slide presentation sites, the humble Power-Point slide show has moved beyond the lecture hall and onto your buyers' desktop computers and smartphones. The best place to host your presentation is SlideShare. Because SlideShare is owned by LinkedIn, it's easy to share your content there. This can help you reach valuable contacts. Slide-Share is a visual medium. Its power comes from users' ability to instantly process and understand your ideas. Great design is essential.

Long-Form Written Content

In an era when micro-sized content (like a tweet at just 140 characters) is so popular, I'm seeing an increase in the number of people publishing much longer text-based information. If you want to write an essay or a report of several thousand pages, the social networking site Medium is a great place to do so. The Medium community is strong, and people comment on and share posts far and wide. A recent story I published on Medium titled "My Personal Experiences with the Medical Marijuana Business and the Opioid Epidemic" was a great way for me to share a recent medical issue. Another place to publish longer articles is using the LinkedIn publishing platform. If you are a member of LinkedIn and you publish your thoughts as long-form content, your original content becomes part of your professional reputation, displayed on the "posts" section of your LinkedIn profile.

Research and Survey Reports

Research and survey reports are used by many companies. By publishing results for free, organizations offer valuable content and get a chance to show off the kind of work they do. This can be an effective approach as long as your research or survey is legitimate and its statistically significant results are interesting to your buyers. (You will read about a survey report created by Steve Johnson when he was at Pragmatic Marketing later in this chapter.)

Email Newsletters

Email newsletters have been around as long as email but still have tremendous value as a way to deliver valuable information in small, regular doses.

However, the vast majority of email newsletters that I see serve mostly as another advertising venue for a company's products and services. You know the type I'm talking about: Each week you get some lame product pitch and a 10-percent-off coupon. Consider using a different type of email newsletter, one that focuses not on your company's products and services, but simply on solving buyers' problems once per month. Let's consider the hypothetical tire manufacturer or caterer that we discussed. Imagine the tire manufacturer doing a monthly newsletter about safe driving or the caterer writing one on party planning. I recommend putting an edition of your email newsletter on your site so people who are not yet subscribers will be able to find the information. This will also be valuable content to drive people to your site from the search engines.

Webinars

Webinars are online seminars that may include audio, video, or graphics (typically in the form of PowerPoint slides) and are often used by companies as a primer about a specific problem that the company's services can solve. However, the best webinars are true thought leadership—like the traditional seminars from which they get their name. Often, webinars feature guests who do not work for the company sponsoring the webinar. For example, I participated as a guest speaker on a webinar series that was part of HubSpot Academy, sponsored by HubSpot. The series featured 10 sessions, each with a different speaker. Nearly 4,000 people attended at least one of the sessions the first time they were offered.

E-Books

Marketers are using e-books more and more as a fun and thoughtful way to get useful information to buyers. As I have mentioned, the book you are reading right now started as an e-book called *The New Rules of PR*, released in January 2006. For the purposes of marketing using web content, I define an e-book as a PDF-formatted document that solves a problem for one of your buyer personas. E-books come with a bit of intrigue—they're like a hip younger sibling to the nerdy white paper. I recommend that e-books be presented in a landscape format, rather than the white paper's portrait format, because the landscape format will fit perfectly onto a computer screen. Well-executed e-books have lots of white space, interesting graphics and images, and copy that is typically written in a lighter style than the denser white paper. In my view, e-books (as marketing tools) should always be free, and I strongly suggest that there be no registration requirement. To get a sense of these elements, check out my free e-book *Agile, Real-Time Customer Service: How to Use the New Rules of Engagement to Grow Your Business.*

E-books are used by all kinds of organizations. Here are a few e-book titles to get your creative juices flowing: *On the Journey to Promoting Loyalty with Prepaid Customers: 5 Strategies That Drive Customers Loyalty with Prepaid Service Offerings* by Rafi Kretchmer of Amdocs Inc.; *Create a Safety Buzz! How Can I Change My Own Behaviors and the Behaviors of Those around Me to Create a True Safety First Culture?* by Dr. James (Skip) Ward; *100 Job Search Tips from Fortune 500 Recruiters* by EMC Corporation; and *Healthy Mouth, Healthy Sex! How Your Oral Health Affects Your Sex Life* by Dr. Helaine Smith.

White Papers

"White papers typically [argue] a specific position or solution to a problem," says Michael A. Stelzner, author of *Writing White Papers*. "Although white papers take their roots in governmental policy, they have become a common tool used to introduce technology innovations and products. A typical search engine query on 'white paper' will return millions of results, with many focused on technology-related issues. White papers are powerful marketing tools used to help key decision makers and influencers justify implementing solutions." The best white papers are *not product brochures*. A good white paper is written for a business audience, defines a problem, and offers a solution, but it does not pitch a particular product or company. White papers are usually free and often have a registration requirement (so the authors can collect the names and contact information of people who download them). Many companies syndicate white papers to business websites through services such as TechTarget.

An App for Anything

There really is an application for anything. For example, the SitOrSquat bathroom finder application for iPhone and other devices indexes, as of this writing, nearly 100,000 public restrooms, all geolocated and rated for cleanliness. Clean bathrooms receive a Sit rating; dirty ones, a Squat. While the application supports adding locations anywhere in the world, at this point most of the potties are located in the United States. If you've got to pee and you are in New York City, you're in luck! However, if you're feeling the urge to tinkle in Helsinki, well, you've got to hold it a bit longer; there are only four loos listed in that city.

The SitOrSquat bathroom finder is sponsored by Charmin, America's most popular toilet paper for more than 25 years. Gotta love that sponsorship! The press release announcing the sponsorship must have been a blast to write: "For nearly a decade, Charmin has been dedicated to giving consumers a great public bathroom experience. This commitment started in 2000 with 'Charminizing' public restrooms at State Fairs, then the mobile unit 'Potty Palooza' from 2003–2005 and finally, with the next evolution, The Charmin Restrooms in Times Square."

Another interesting application is the Live Scoring iPhone and Android applications from the Association of Tennis Professionals (ATP—men's professional tennis) and Women's Tennis Association (WTA). The ATP Live Scoring app delivers real-time point-by-point updates from matches being played on the WTA Tour and the ATP World Tour. The official Live Scoring mobile applications are free and allow fans to follow in real time their favorite professional tennis players, such as Rafael Nadal, Roger Federer, Maria Sharapova, and Serena Williams, as they compete around the globe across 115 events in 43 countries.

"There is a demand for real-time tournament scoring from our hard-core tennis fans," says Philippe Dore, senior director of digital marketing for the ATP World Tour. "If you are not lucky enough to see a match being played in Zagreb or Beijing on TV, this will be the best way to follow it, whether it is on your computer or your iPhone or your Android or on our mobile website. Journalists are using it too, when they are getting ready to write and are on deadline."

I found it interesting that mobile devices are used to gather the data that power the application. "The point-by-point scoring data comes directly from the umpire's chair," Dore says. "So it is the exact official data from the umpire. As the umpire taps a score on his PDA, we get the live scoring to our website and mobile applications. It's being used by both the men's ATP Tour and the women's tour . . . and now we are rolling it out to the lower tournaments, called the challenger circuits." The dedicated fans using the app are also those who buy tickets to see events in person, so the app is driving revenue to the players and tournament sponsors.

How to Create Thoughtful Content

While each technique for getting your information into the marketplace of ideas is different, they share some common considerations:

- Do not write about your company and your products. Content as a marketing asset should be designed to solve buyer problems or answer questions and to show that you and your organization are smart and worth doing business with. This type of marketing and PR technique is *not* a brochure or sales pitch and is *not* advertising.
- Define your organizational goals first (see Chapter 10). Do you want to drive revenue? Get people to donate money to your organization? Encourage people to buy something?
- Based on your goals, decide whether you want to provide the content free and without any registration (you will get many more people to use the content, but you won't know who they are) or you want to include some kind of registration mechanism (*much* lower response rates, but you build a contact list).
- Think like a publisher by understanding your audience. Consider what market problems your buyer personas are faced with, and develop topics that appeal to them.
- Write for your audience. Use examples and stories. Make it interesting.
- Choose a great title that grabs attention. Use subtitles to describe what the content will deliver. The best titles and subtitles include keywords and phrases that your buyers are searching on, using search engines.
- Promote the effort like crazy. Offer the content on your site with easy-to-find links. Add a link to employees' email signatures, and get partners to offer links as well.
- To drive the viral marketing effects, alert appropriate reporters, bloggers, and analysts that the content is available, and send them a download link.

Measure the results, and improve based on what you learn.

How Raytheon Uses Journalists to Create Interesting Content

I'm always fascinated by organizations that embrace brand journalism, the practice of hiring reporters to create content that serves both marketing and public relations purposes. For more than a decade, I've recommended that companies of all kinds avoid their peers' boring old brochure-like approach. I think it's far preferable to aspire to the likes of media outlets like *Forbes*, the BBC, or the *New York Times*. And that means actually hiring reporters and editors, not marketers and copywriters, to produce the content.

One look at the Raytheon homepage shows the company does exactly that. You'll find real-time news features, images, and a top stories section. And Raytheon is a business-to-business (B2B) as well as a business-to-government (B2G) company!

"You can see our homepage is very much a news operation," says Corinne J. Kovalsky, vice president of global public relations at Raytheon. "We've got feature stories and trend stories about cool products."

I've engaged with Kovalsky for several years on social networks. I recently had an opportunity to visit with her and the team at Raytheon headquarters to learn more about their brand journalism approach to marketing and public relations.

"I'm an ex TV producer," Kovalsky says. "I did national news up in Canada for the CTV network for a number of years. I produced the Canadian equivalent of *Meet the Press*, and I have very fond memories of having journalists on staff."

Kovalsky worked with Pam Wickham, Raytheon's vice president of corporate affairs and communications, to implement the brand journalism approach. Wickham recognized the opportunity to establish a more robust footprint in digital and social media for the company, an idea that resonated to the very top of the organization.

Once the pair had buy-in, Kovalsky brought on some very impressive talent. New managing editor Chris Hawley joined Raytheon from the Associated Press (AP), where he had won the 2012 Pulitzer Prize in investigative reporting. His months-long series outlined the New York Police Department's surveillance of minority and particularly Muslim neighborhoods since the 9/11 terror attacks. Now, as a brand journalist, he brings those in-depth reporting skills to Raytheon.

"I'm helping to build a news operation," Hawley says. "We are working at Raytheon just like an AP beat to find interesting stories and tell the world about them in a way that engages. We have bureau chiefs in all of our four divisions. They have certain products that they want to talk about, so we try to find new and interesting ways of exploring those stories. And we refine the story ideas, assign writers, and do a lot of training on editing and getting those stories out."

For example, Raytheon brand journalist John Zaremba, who joined the company from the *Boston Herald* newspaper, was digging through recent patents looking for stories. Zaremba found a patent by a Raytheon employee for a mouse that identifies you by the way you grip and move it. The invention was fascinating, so the team decided to use it as an example of cyber innovation, how Raytheon is constantly coming up with new ways of keeping data safe. The story, written in a journalistic style, appeared on the Raytheon site and inspired reporting by mainstream media, including *Computerworld.*

Hawley has also taken on the role of establishing editorial guidelines for Raytheon and teaching the staff about journalism. "We've tried to codify the writing and editing process," he says. "We've come up with a checklist approach to writing a web story that goes through everything from selecting if it's going to be a hard lead story [begins with "just the facts"] or a soft lead story [begins with an attention-grabbing quote or anecdote], right down to which scientific study I should pay attention to when I'm evaluating background information for an article."

The content that Kovalsky, Hawley, Zaremba, and the others on the team produce serves to educate and entertain existing and potential clients. But it also serves the media, who with increasing regularity use Raytheon content for their own story inspirations. For example, Raytheon's "Tiny Satellites to Give Warfighters a Bird's-Eye View of the Battlefield" led to Gizmodo's "DARPA's SeeMe Satellites Are a Soldier's On-Demand Eye in the Sky."

There is strong evidence that the brand journalism approach is producing results for Raytheon.

"One of our big trade shows is the Association of the United States Army annual conference, which happens each October," Hawley says. "In a recent one, we decided to go for quality content instead of quantity. We did only three stories compared to more than 20 the year before, but we really wrote the heck out of them. They're really well written, and capture trends. And we increased traffic 451 percent over the year before."

Kovalsky points to a story she worked on with Hawley called "Jam Session," published on the Raytheon site. "It tells the story of a significant electronic warfare flight test milestone for a key contract of ours," she says. "Now, electronic warfare or EW can be hard to explain, but in partnership with Chris we were able to tell the story in lay terms, and we were rewarded for it."

Despite its publication late in the year, "Jam Session" rose to become the 11th-most-popular story on the Raytheon website that year. "We used it to drive traffic to our EW capabilities section on the website, which had recently been optimized for mobile," Kovalsky says. The story was the most trafficked URL in Twitter discussions of Raytheon in that quarter, with more than 2,500 tweets referencing the story.

If you're an organization looking to implement a brand journalism approach to content marketing, study what Raytheon does. Kovalsky believes any organization can do it: "A well-merchandised, simply written story with great photos can turn any brand into a successful publisher."

Content Creation in Highly Regulated Industries

On the global speaking circuit, I frequently get pushback from audience members who work in highly regulated industries. They claim that laws like the Health Insurance Portability and Accountability Act (HIPAA) in the United States, which addresses the security and privacy of health data, and regulations like those from the U.S. Securities and Exchange Commission and the U.S. Food and Drug Administration (and equivalent agencies in other countries) forbid them from creating valuable content on the web or engaging in social media.

Nonsense!

This is just a fear-based excuse perpetuated by lawyers in the pharmaceutical, healthcare, and financial services industries who want to avoid risk at all costs. The fear is particularly shortsighted when considering the data on how people make decisions related to their health. I frequently present at healthcare-related events and have had an opportunity to meet many marketers who are happily reaching their audiences with valuable information. They're living in reality, not according to their fears.

According to data presented at a recent National Healthcare Marketing Summit by Tim McGuire from Greenville Hospital System, Bill Moschella of eVariant, and Anne Theis of Salem Health, 80 percent of Internet users look up health information online. More than three out of four people use the web to make healthcare decisions! Yet 64 percent of hospital marketing departments devote less than 25 percent of their marketing budgets to interactive content. Even more telling is how hospital marketers spend their time: 83 percent of hospitals devote less than 30 percent of staff time to interactive media. This is ridiculous.

The fearful lawyers say no to the 80 percent of customers and potential customers who use the web to research health. This fear means that hospital marketers are busy making brochures and TV ads instead of creating thoughtful web content. If you work in a highly regulated industry, can your organization afford such a disconnect?

For an example of someone who ignores what people assume to be legal restrictions and instead creates thoughtful content, consider Chris Boyer, director of digital communications and marketing for Inova Health System, northern Virginia's leading not-for-profit healthcare provider. Inova serves more than one million patients each year.

The company publishes content to reach specific buyer personas. For example, its "Life with Cancer" site contains valuable information for patients and their families. In a world where others are fearful of creating content, Inova publishes videos like "Phil Gilbert's Story—Relief after Hip Replacement."

In the past two years, Boyer has transformed the Inova organization to focus more on creating relevant content. "We take a lot of time understanding who our viewers are and actually write different types of content for different types of users," Boyer says. "Patients are using our patient and visitor information, so they're looking for specifics about how to make their stay easier, and we write with them in mind. Other people view our services and all the different clinical stuff that we provide at Inova. They could either be referring physicians who want to research what we're doing here or consumers who are actually shopping for healthcare. We want to provide them content that's appropriate for them. It is written so that they don't have to read through pages and pages of clinical content to get to the crux of what they're looking for."

Boyer manages the digital marketing and communications team, including a handful of editors and web graphics professionals as well as several part-timers. A full-time social media manager on the team focuses on social media channels, although there's a lot of content interaction and cross-publication efforts; the lines between social media and the website are blurring tremendously at Inova, as at so many other organizations.

"The two main editors for our website are actually former journalists," Boyer says. "So they have experience in terms of writing. Of course, they started in traditional media, but in the last few years they migrated over to focus exclusively on online journalism and communications."

I wanted to know how Boyer has dealt with the whole "fear" thing. Why has he been successful in hiring journalists and creating content when so many other management teams and legal departments refuse?

Boyer says the main concern of Inova's managers was that a shift to content marketing would mean a shift away from what they thought were the key differentiators of Inova Health System. Previously, their efforts had focused on attracting the best physicians. "It took a long time for us to educate that the existing content is not being lost. We're just providing it to each audience in the appropriate places. There will be pages for consumers *and* pages for physicians who are looking to refer or be employed here. It took a while for them to be comfortable with that."

The size of Boyer's team means there are significant resources devoted to the Inova thought leadership effort. Boyer measures effectiveness in three areas:

1. **New patients:** How many people become patients who first connected online either through content on the website or through social networks such as Facebook and Twitter?

2. **Savings:** How much money can be saved by using online tools? For example, the existing Inova nursing communication is a printed newsletter that goes out to all nursing staff and costs $80,000 per year to produce. So converting to a blog means eliminating that expense and increasing readership.

3. **Long-term patient engagement:** How many patients (or potential patients) get involved in wellness programs? For example, Inova offers email content focused on how to have a healthy heart, how to eat well, and so on. It measures the number of people who stay healthy because of the information they consume and how that affects things like readmittance rates.

Boyer has taken a gradual approach in implementing these changes.

"Realize that you don't have to transform your entire organization all at once," he says. "I found a lot of success in focusing on areas where there were some obvious opportunities and used social communications in those areas. Try something and see how it's working. You're gaining valuable expertise and understanding how to use the tools. In most organizations, once you introduce social communications to your portfolio, very quickly you'll start to see how they will augment, if not replace, some of the current ways that you're communicating."

As Boyer shows, content marketing and thought leadership can survive and thrive in highly regulated industries.

Leveraging Thought Leaders outside Your Organization

Some organizations recruit external thought leaders, sometimes referred to as "influencers" that buyers trust, which is an effective technique for showing your buyers that you are plugged in and work with recognized experts. You might have a thought leader from your industry guest-blog for you, be the author of a white paper, participate on a webinar, or speak to your clients at a live event. For example, Cincom Systems, Inc., a software industry pioneer, publishes the *Cincom Expert Access* e-zine that is read by more than 200,000 people in 61 countries. *Cincom Expert Access* delivers information from several dozen business leaders, authors, and analysts such as Al Reis, author of *The Fall of Advertising and the Rise of PR*; Dan Heath, author of *Made to Stick*; and Guy Kawasaki, author of *Reality Check*. *Cincom Expert Access* provides concise, objective information from personalities that Cincom's clients trust, sometimes in an irreverent, humorous manner, to help readers do their jobs better.

Who Wrote That Awesome White Paper?

People often ask me a question that goes something like this: "Should white papers, e-books, and other content have a named author? Or can they simply state a company name or department as author?"

This seemingly small issue has big ramifications.

My strong preference is that content should have an author listed rather than be published without a name. It humanizes your company. It serves as a way for interested people to connect, and it facilitates extending your leaders' expertise to other venues like speaking gigs.

It may be obvious, but the author of the white paper should be, well, its author! I'd rather see the real author of the white paper listed than some senior executive, which is what some organizations do.

If there are several people collaborating on the paper, it can have multiple authors. But you might also choose one lead author. This should be the person who will interact with those who are interested in the topic. The lead author should be good at doing media interviews and should speak at conferences and events on the topic. When these factors align, the author's personal brand and the company's brand align, and both benefit.

A person's bio is a better way of showcasing expertise than a bland company or department description (no author) or some random big shot's name and bio (unless, of course, the CEO actually wrote it).

The author's biography, typically at the end of the white paper or e-book, should have links to the author's social networking feeds, especially Twitter and LinkedIn, so people can follow and connect. It's also important to give an email address for the author, which serves as an invitation to discussion that can lead to a sale.

How Much Money Does Your Buyer Make?

"I'm often asked, 'Steve, how much should we be paying our product managers?'" says Steve Johnson, an industry expert on product management and Vice President of Products for Pragmatic Institute. "I used to just throw out a number that sounded about right. But I realized that my estimated salary figure was based on old data, back from the days when I hired product managers." Because Pragmatic Institute conducts training and coaching for product management and marketing professionals, Johnson wanted to ensure the company stayed up-to-date on all things related to those job functions. This situation created a terrific opportunity for some thought leadership. "We realized that we didn't really know current benchmarks, so we decided to find out." After all, customer compensation is often a key demographic for understanding your buyer persona.

Johnson composed a survey to gather data from the thousands of people in the Pragmatic Institute database plus those who followed Steve on his blog and social media services. "We said, 'If you tell us your salary and other information about your job via the anonymous survey, we will tell you everyone's salary in the form of benchmarks,'" he says. The results were an instant hit with the Pragmatic's buyer persona—product managers.

Johnson started this program in 2001 and it's still running today, nearly twenty years later. Pragmatic's email newsletter goes out to thousands and thousands of people. Pragmatic gets hundreds of responses in just a few days, aggregates the data, and then publishes the results on the web. In a recent year, for example, Pragmatic learned that the average U.S. product management compensation is roughly $122,000 in salary and that 82 percent of product managers get an annual bonus that averages $9,850. But they also learn other information, such as that product managers send and receive almost 100 emails a day and spend roughly two days a week in internal meetings—15 meetings per week. But 55 percent are going to 15 meetings or more each week, and 35 percent attend 20 or more meetings.

Johnson sees tremendous benefits in fact-based thought leadership. "First of all, the data is really useful," he says. "With this information, I command the authority to say something like '93 percent of product managers have completed college and 43 percent have completed a master's program.' But more importantly, the buyers we are trying to reach recognize us as the thought leaders in product management because we have up-to-date information on what's really going on with technology product managers. And the data that sits on our websites is fantastic for search engine marketing. Anyone looking for information about product management and marketing in technology businesses will probably find us."

This is a new world for marketers and corporate communicators. The web offers an easy way for your ideas to spread to a potential audience of millions of people, instantly. Web content in the form of true thought leadership holds the potential to influence many thousands of your buyers in ways that traditional marketing and PR simply cannot.

To embrace the power of the web and the blogosphere requires a different kind of thinking on the part of marketers. We need to learn to give up our command-and-control mentality. It isn't about "the message." It's about being insightful. The new rules of marketing and PR tell us to stop advertising and instead get our ideas out there by understanding buyers and telling them stories that connect with their problems. The new rules are to participate in the discussions going on, not just try to shout your message over everyone else. Done well, web content that delivers authentic thought leadership also brands an organization as one to do business with.

How to Write for Your Buyers

Your buyers (and the media that cover your company) want to know what specific problems your product solves, and they want proof that it works—in plain language. Your marketing and PR are meant to be the beginning of a relationship with buyers and to drive action (such as generating sales leads), which requires a focus on buyer problems. Your buyers want to hear this in *their* own words. Every time you write—yes, even in news releases—you have an opportunity to communicate. At each stage of the sales process, well-written materials will help your buyers understand how you, specifically, will help them.

Whenever you set out to write something (or shoot a video or develop other content), you should be creating specifically for one or more of the buyer personas that you developed as part of your marketing and PR plan (see Chapter 10). You should avoid jargon-laden phrases that are overused in your industry, unless this is the language the persona actually uses. In the technology business, words like *groundbreaking*, *industry-standard*, and *cutting-edge* are what I call gobbledygook. The worst gobbledygook offenders seem to be business-to-business technology companies. For some reason, marketing people at technology companies have a particularly tough time explaining how products solve customer problems. Because these writers don't understand how their products do that, or are too lazy to write for buyers, they cover by explaining myriad nuances of how the product works and pepper this blather with industry jargon that sounds vaguely impressive. What ends up in marketing materials and news releases is a bunch of talk about "industry-leading" solutions that purport to help companies "streamline business process," "achieve business objectives," or "conserve organizational resources." *Huh?*

An Analysis of Gobbledygook

Many of the thousands of websites I've analyzed over the years and the hundreds of news releases and PR pitches I receive each month are laden with meaningless gobbledygook words and phrases. As I'm reading a news release, I'll pause and say to myself, "Oh, jeez, not another flexible, scalable, groundbreaking, industry-standard, cutting-edge product from a market-leading, well-positioned company! I think I'm gonna puke!" Like teenagers overusing catchphrases, these writers use the same words and phrases again and again—so much so that the gobbledygook grates against all our nerves. Well, duh. Like, companies just totally don't communicate very well, you know?

I wanted to see exactly how many of these words are being used, so I created an analysis for doing so. I first analyzed gobbledygook in 2006 and published the findings on my blog and as an e-book called *The Gobbledygook Manifesto*. In 2006, the most overused words and phrases included *next generation, robust, world class, cutting edge, mission critical, market leading, industry standard, groundbreaking*, and *best of breed*.

I then conducted an extensive, revised analysis. For this new round, I first needed to select overused words and phrases, so I turned to the following sources:

- The overused words and phrases from the 2006 analysis, which I had gotten by polling select PR people and journalists.
- Suggestions from readers, who posted comments about the original analysis on my blog.
- Seth Godin's *Encyclopedia of Business Clichés*.
- *This Paperclip Is a Solution*, a survey given to general business and trade publication editors by Dave Schmidt, VP of public relations services at Smith-Winchester, Inc.
- The book *Death Sentences: How Cliches, Weasel Words and Management-Speak Are Strangling Public Language*, by Don Watson.

Then I turned to the Dow Jones Enterprise Media Group for help. The folks at Dow Jones used text-mining tools in their Dow Jones Insight product to analyze all news releases sent in the English language for an entire year. The data we gathered came from all 711,123 press releases distributed through Business Wire, Marketwired, GlobeNewswire, and PR Newswire. Dow Jones Insight identified the number of uses of the 325 gobbledygook phrases in each release.

The results were staggering. The winner for the most overused word or phrase was *innovate*, which was used in 51,390 press releases, followed closely by *unique*, *leading provider*, *new and improved*, *world class*, and *cost-effective*. Each of these terms was used more than 10,000 times in press releases during the year. The problem is that these words are so overused that they have become meaningless. If anything, these terms make the reader feel as if the company is just releasing dozens of copycat communications.

Poor Writing: How Did We Get Here?

When I see words like *flexible*, *scalable*, *groundbreaking*, *industry standard*, or *cutting edge*, my eyes glaze over. What, I ask myself, is this supposed to mean? Just saying your product is "industry standard" means nothing unless some aspect of that standardization is important to your buyers. In the next sentence, I want to know what you mean by industry standard, and I also want you to tell me why that standard matters and give me some proof that what you say is indeed true.

People often say to me, "Everyone in my industry writes this way. Why?" Here's how the usual dysfunctional process works and why these phrases are so overused: Marketers don't understand buyers, the problems buyers face, or how their product helps solve these problems. That's where the gobbledygook happens. First, the marketing person bugs the product managers and others in the organization to provide a set of the product's features. Then the marketing person reverse-engineers the language that the marketer thinks the buyer wants to hear based *not on buyer input* but on what the product does. A favorite trick these ineffective marketers use is to take the language that the product manager provides, go into Microsoft Word's find-and-replace mode, substitute the word *solution* for *product*, and then slather the whole thing with superlative-laden, jargon-sprinkled hype. By just decreeing, through an electronic word substitution, that "our product" is "your solution," these companies effectively deprive themselves of the opportunity to *convince* people that this is the case.

Another major drawback of the generic gobbledygook approach is that it doesn't make your company stand out from the crowd. Here's a test: Take the language that the marketers at your company dreamed up and substitute the name of a competitor and the competitor's product for your own. Does it still make sense to you? Marketing language that can be substituted for another company's isn't effective in explaining to a buyer why *your* company is the right choice.

I'll admit that these gobbledygook phrases are mainly used by technology companies operating in the business-to-business space. If you are writing for a company that sells different kinds of products (shoes, perhaps), then you would probably not be tempted to use many of these phrases. The same thing is true for nonprofits, churches, rock bands, and other organizations—you're also unlikely to use these sorts of phrases. But the lessons are the same. Avoid the insular jargon of your company and your industry. Instead, write for your buyers.

"Hold on," you might say. "The technology industry may be dysfunctional, but I don't write that way." The fact is that there is equivalent nonsense going on in all industries. Here's an example from the world of nonprofits:

> The sustainability group has convened a task force to study the cause of energy inefficiency and to develop a plan to encourage local businesses to apply renewable-energy and energy-efficient technologies which will go a long way toward encouraging community buy-in to potential behavioral changes.

What the heck is that? Or consider this example from the first paragraph of a well-known company's corporate overview page. Can you guess the company?

> The mission of [Company X] is to entertain, inform and inspire people around the globe through the power of unparalleled storytelling, reflecting the iconic brands, creative minds and innovative technologies that make ours the world's premier entertainment company.

Effective Writing for Marketing and PR

Your marketing and PR are meant to be the beginning of a relationship with buyers (and journalists). As the marketing and PR planning process in Chapter 10 showed, this begins when you work at understanding your target audience and figure out how they should be sliced into distinct buying segments or buyer personas. Once this exercise is complete, identify the situations each target audience may find themselves in. What are their problems? Business issues? Needs? Only then are you ready to communicate your expertise to the market. Here's the rule: When you write, start with your buyers, not with your product.

Consider the entertainment company language. The marketing and PR folks at The Walt Disney Company (did you guess it was Disney's corporate overview page I quoted from?) should be thinking about what customers want from an entertainment company, rather than just thinking up fancy words for what they think they already provide. Why not start by defining the problem? "Many television and cinema fans today are frustrated with the state of the global entertainment industry. They believe today's films and shows are too derivative and that entertainment companies don't respect their viewers' intelligence."

Next, successful marketers will use real-world language to convince their customers that they can solve their problem. Be careful to avoid corporate jargon, but you don't want to sound like you're trying too hard, either—that always comes across as phony. Talk to your audience as you might talk to a relative you don't see very often—be friendly and familiar but also respectful: "Like our audience, we care about and enjoy movies and TV shows—that's why we're in this business in the first place. As such, we pledge to always . . ."

Now I have no connection with Disney and don't know about the Disney business. But I have purchased a lot of Disney products: movies, TV shows, videos, and visits to theme parks. It might seem strange to people at Disney to actually write something like I suggest. It might feel strange for the PR and marketing people at Disney to use a phrase like "movies and TV shows" rather than "innovative technologies," but it's absolutely essential to establishing a relationship with customers.

The Power of Writing Feedback (from Your Blog)

I want to pause for a moment to share a story about the power of communications and feedback on the web. When I published the results of this original study on my blog in a post titled "The Gobbledygook Manifesto" (I also sent a news release the next day), there were zero hits on Google for the exact phrase "gobbledygook manifesto." I purposely invented a phrase that I could establish on the web. Within just three weeks, as a result of several dozen bloggers writing about "The Gobbledygook Manifesto" and more than 100 comments on my blog and others, the exact phrase "gobbledygook manifesto" yielded more than 500 hits on Google: zero to 500 in just three weeks. Better yet, readers of my blog and others suggested other overused gobbledygook words and phrases, such as *best practices*, *proactive*, *synergy*, *starting a dialogue*, *thinking outside of the box*, *revolutionary*, *situational fluency*, and *paradigm shift*.

Dave Schmidt, VP of public relations services at Smith-Winchester, Inc., contacted me to share the results of a survey he conducted of general business and trade publication editors. Schmidt asked the editors about the overused words and phrases he's seen and wanted to find out how many editors agreed that each of the phrases was overused in news releases and company-authored articles. He received responses from 80 editors:

- *Leading* (used as an adjective, as in ". . . a leading producer of . . .")— 94 percent of editors feel is overused. Since everyone wants to be the leading something, there are no longer any true leaders.
- *"We're excited about . . ."* (as used in a quote from management)—76 percent of editors feel is overused. Companies also say, "We're pleased . . ." and "We're thrilled . . ." Can you picture an editor running a CEO quote like one of these? You need to quote your spokespeople with words that you would like to see in print.
- *Solutions*—68 percent of editors feel is overused. The word *solutions* has been ruined by overuse in news releases to the point that it is best avoided, even by solutions providers.
- *A wide range of . . .*—64 percent of editors feel is overused. This has become the lazy person's way of avoiding precise writing.
- *Unparalleled*—62 percent of editors feel is overused.
- *Unsurpassed*—53 percent of editors feel is overused.

Thank you to the many people who contacted me with suggestions of overused gobbledygook. I just think it is so cool that you can create something on the web, use it to get thoughtful information into the market quickly and efficiently, and then have people offer suggestions to make the original writing even better.

Most of this chapter has been about what *not* to do. We read a lot of the gobbledygook that so many people use when they create content for their buyers. But there are many organizations with terrific content! I'd like to showcase a couple and lift up their compelling approaches to content creation.

For much more about content creation, check out *Everybody Writes: Your Go-To Guide to Creating Ridiculously Good Content* by Ann Handley. This is the only guide you need to elevate your content to the level of awesomeness. With wisdom and an infective wittiness, Handley shows you how to take your writing from awkward or awful to electric or elegant. She's your favorite teacher, cracking you up while her tough love gets you to do the work to improve. Even though I've written 10 books, I still learned a great deal from her book.

Injecting Humor into Product Descriptions

I recently purchased an IN1 multitool utility case for my iPhone. It's a cool product that stores pens, screwdrivers, scissors, and other small accessories—kind of like a Swiss Army knife for a smartphone.

I wasn't going to buy it, because I thought for sure I couldn't bring it onto an airplane. But the product description sold me. I loved the writing so much that I actually read all the way down to the part about it being TSA compliant. Otherwise I would have missed that it is safe to bring on a plane.

So whilst the IN1 case won't assist you in removing and rebuilding a gearbox from a 1985 GMC [*sic*] Pacer or help you slay, skin and cook a wildebeest, they will help with day to day tasks such as writing notes and cutting open packages. Also by leaving the Cross Bow and Bowie Knife attachment off the IN1 case it has allowed us to make it fully TSA Compliant.

Yes! That's right the IN1 case is also TSA compliant! Which means that you can plan a trip with your new lover without being scared of holding up the queue explaining that it isn't a weapon, it is actually just a phone case (they might still be interested in its fantastic design though).

A pen. An analog writing device on my iPhone case. Brilliant! I can use it to fill out customs forms when I travel. And the screwdrivers and scissors are perfect for small repairs in hotel rooms. It's a great product, and I was able to learn just how great it is because it avoided losing me at hello.

So many product descriptions are practically unreadable. Think about how you can learn from the good people at IN1 and invoke 1985 Pacers or wildebeests or new lovers when describing what your company has to offer. Let's inject some zest into product descriptions!

Brand Journalism at Boeing

When the Boeing Company revamped the website and built a completely new approach to writing for the web, the company shifted dramatically from a dull, technology- and product-focused, gobbledygook-laden site to one focused on interesting stories. The new Boeing site does an excellent job at putting a human (and canine) face on the company.

One of the featured stories I enjoyed is "Rocky Earns His Rest," about a Belgian Malinois who served for 56 "dog years" as a Boeing explosive-detection dog. "Rocky's story is unusual, and we never would have used him on the site before," says Todd Blecher, communications director at Boeing. "Now we show there are real people who work in the company. And we are willing to talk about them—even if they are a dog."

Blecher heads up an editorial team at Boeing, gathering story ideas from all over the company.

"Freezin' in Florida" describes testing the 787 Dreamliner in the largest refrigerated hangar in the world. The hangar simulates temperatures as low as –65 degrees Fahrenheit or as high as 165 degrees Fahrenheit. "Rather than have a standard news release that describes testing, we take you inside the hangar to actually show what people have to do to freeze the airplane," Blecher says. "No airplane comes together without the people who work on it. Now we're talking about our technology from the perspective of the people."

The team also creates videos, such as "Boeing 747-8F Performs Ultimate Rejected Takeoff," in which a fully loaded 747-8 Freighter with worn-out brakes attempts an aborted takeoff on a California runway. The rejected takeoff, or maximum brake energy test, is one of the most dramatic for a new airplane. The video has had 4 million views as of this writing. The video is great brand journalism because it is not a product pitch. Rather, it is branded content that people want to consume and that shows Boeing in a good light. "We publish content that supports business objectives and fosters positive opinions about Boeing," Blecher says. "We're not (directly) selling planes. We're selling Boeing."

Interestingly, many Boeing communicators are former reporters. Blecher himself was formerly a real-time wire service journalist at Bloomberg News (one of his duties is to manage the @Boeing Twitter feed). When a story is posted on the Boeing site, it includes the byline of the person who wrote it. "It provides the same sort of accountability mentality that bylines provide in the regular journalism world," Blecher says. "I know there are some brands that want to be completely brand agnostic, so you don't really know who's behind it. I don't subscribe to that theory. Since most of our creators had been journalists, it was something that was totally natural to them."

Effective brand journalism is about telling stories. "Find yourself some journalists who can work on your staff," Blecher says. "I don't think it's something you can totally outsource. I know some organizations try to hire people to do that. I think that it is going to be counterproductive. Successful brand journalism, at least to us, requires a level of access to our people that only comes from having the journalists who are on staff talking to our subject matter experts all the time, relating to them, building a relationship, so you get the very best kind of story."

Your online and offline marketing content is meant to drive action, which requires a focus on buyer problems. Your buyers want this in their own words, and then they want proof. Every time you write, you have an opportunity to communicate and to *convince*. At each stage of the sales process, well-written materials combined with effective marketing programs will lead your buyers to understand how your company can help them. Good marketing is rare indeed, but a focus on doing it right will most certainly pay off with increased sales, higher retention rates, and more ink and airtime from journalists.

14 Social Networking as Marketing

The popularity of social networking sites such as Facebook, Twitter, and LinkedIn is phenomenal. Social networking sites make it easy for people to create profiles about themselves and use them to form virtual networks combining their offline friends and new online friends. According to Twitter, there are 321 million monthly active users, and people generate an average of half a billion tweets a day. Facebook now reports more than two billion monthly active users, and LinkedIn, the largest professional social network, has more than 500 million members. And it's not just the United States; social networking is extremely popular all over the world. For instance, more than 80 percent of Facebook users are outside the United States. Not all visitors to these sites create their own profiles, but there are millions and millions of people who do—to share their photos, journals, videos, music, and interests with a network of friends.

While these huge numbers are impressive, we can easily lose track of what this means to us as marketers. When we consider the reach of influential people on social networking sites, we should rethink our notions about who can best spread our ideas and tell our stories. Many people tell me that they want to get quoted in important publications like the *Wall Street Journal* or have their products mentioned on television news networks like the BBC or on shows like the *Today* show. These media hits are seen as the holy grail of marketers. But while mainstream media are certainly important (and who wouldn't want to be on BBC news?), is that really the best thing for your business?

As you think about reaching your audience using social networking, consider who really has the power. Is it mainstream media? Or someone else? And how can you reach them?

Television's Eugene Mirman Is Very Nice and Likes Seafood

"There is no middleman between me and an audience," says comedian Eugene Mirman, known for his work in *Flight of the Conchords*; his book of satire, *The Will to Whatevs: A Guide to Modern Life*; and appearances on Comedy Central and late-night television shows. Mirman currently plays Yvgeny Mirminsky on *Delocated* and voices Gene Belcher for the animated comedy *Bob's Burgers*. He writes a blog, has a Facebook page, and is on Twitter. "I want to be entertaining on the web," he says. "That's what's fun for me. While there is a store on my website, the push is to provide things to entertain people, not to sell." And entertain he does. As I write this, Mirman's Twitter bio reads: "I am television's Eugene Mirman. I am very nice and like seafood." Sample tweet: "When it turns out the Black Eyed Peas are hostile aliens spying on earth, humanity will feel silly, since it'll be obvious in hindsight."

Mirman uses Facebook and Twitter as ways to get his information out to multiple audiences very quickly. For example, immediately after he delivered the commencement address at Lexington High School in Massachusetts, he posted the video on YouTube and then pointed to it from his blog, as well as from his Twitter and Facebook profiles. The video got 100,000 views in just one week.

Mirman says that he writes what's interesting to him at the time and doesn't worry about productivity. "I want to do things that are funny and I want a lot of people to see it, but I do what I think is good and funny and then hope that others pass it on," he says. "It's easier for me to do what I like, and if it attracts fans, then that's great. And I'm lucky that it has been effective over the years to do it this way. With social media, you can tell a story. If you have a special interest, like cooking, then you can get an audience."

Think back to my metaphor of the web as a city and social media as a cocktail party, which I discussed in Chapter 4. Cocktail parties are fun. You go because you want to be there. And while the chance of meeting someone who could become a customer is a distinct possibility, that's a by-product of good conversation. Take a tip from Mirman and make sure you bring the right attitude to social media. With that in mind, let's look in detail at several of the most important social networking sites.

How to Use Facebook to Market Your Product or Service

The most important thing to remember about marketing on Facebook (and other social networking sites) is that it is not about generating hype. The best approaches to Facebook marketing are delivering information and ideas to a network of people who are interested in you and your products and services.

Facebook connects members via a friend request process. Until you approve someone as your Facebook friend, your extended profile remains private. I've found Facebook to be a great way to maintain contact with school friends and work colleagues.

A Facebook page is a great first step for getting your organization engaged. Think of a Facebook page as a personal profile, but for a company. For instance, you're likely to use a logo instead of a photo for the image in the upper-left corner (the profile picture). Once your page is complete, you should post interesting information there, like links to blog posts and videos as you create them.

One of the most useful aspects of Facebook is the ability for people to "like" and "tag" the things you do on the site. When users like your page or something you posted on it (they do this by pushing the little thumbs-up "Like" button), the fact that they like it will probably appear on their Facebook profiles for their friends to see. The same thing is true when you tag something. Tagging is when you identify people within a post or a photo on Facebook, such as all of the people appearing in a photo. When you tag people, they get notifications that point them to the tagged content. Isn't that great? When you create something interesting, your friends can spread it for you! But remember what we've discussed previously in these pages: As with other forms of web content, don't use Facebook to overtly sell. Rather, create information that people will want to share.

Steve Broadbelt, managing director at Ocean Frontiers Ltd. in the Cayman Islands, does exactly that. He and his team are constantly posting tagged photos and videos on their Ocean Frontiers Facebook page, photos and videos that people are eager to share. Ocean Frontiers specializes in small-group scuba diving off Grand Cayman's East End. Broadbelt runs a modern scuba-diving operation and dive shop with old-style Caymanian hospitality. Many clients return again and again. He's been active on the web since he first built his Ocean Frontiers site (in 1997), an email newsletter soon after, and more recently a presence in social media, including Facebook and Twitter.

It was the realization that people like to come back year after year that prompted him to create the Green Short Challenge, where scuba divers who visit each of the 55 dive sites within the East End dive zone in Grand Cayman are given special recognition. The prizes include a pair of coveted, limited-edition green shorts (just like the Ocean Frontiers staff wear), a party to celebrate the achievement, a gold medal, a plaque embedded in the dock that leads to the boats, and special recognition on the Ocean Frontiers Facebook page—with photos documenting the achievement. Participants record their visits to each of the 55 dive sites in a custom-designed dive logbook with hand-drawn illustrations. Anybody can download the book for free, with no registration required.

Broadbelt recalls his creation of the award: "I had a customer at a dive show expo in New York who couldn't remember the name of our business, but he remembered that all of our staff wear these green shorts," Broadbelt says. "At the same time, I was frustrated that some of my longest-standing customers, people that have been diving with me for more than 10 years and come back every year, hadn't seen certain dive sites. So that got me on a mission to try to get all my customers to see all of my dive sites, because there's so much variety and diversity to see. So now we get them on this trail where they check off all the sites, and I found out it's quite addictive. So we made the Green Short Challenge and that's how we built our tribe of loyal followers. I never thought it was going to be such a marketing powerhouse and get the reaction that it has. Everybody who touches the Green Short Challenge seems to stick to it."

As I said, Broadbelt uses the Ocean Frontiers Facebook page to recognize the achievement. As I write this, several days after a customer hit the 55-dive-sites milestone, the Facebook post reads: "Congratulations to Michael Piner who completed all 55 dives of the Green Short Challenge. The weather was cooperative and Michael was able to dive The Arch as his last dive. Besides the delicious cake, icy champagne, fancy medal and coveted Green Shorts, Michael will also have a plaque with name engraved on it embedded in the OF walk of fame! Good Job Michael!" There are seven photos of Piner on the Facebook post, including the staff toasting him with champagne and cutting a cake. Plus there's a beaming Piner holding up his new shorts.

"It ties into social media because every time somebody completes the challenge, we have a celebration and they share with their friends on Facebook," Broadbelt says. "It is the scuba diving hall of fame for our customers, as they've reached the ultimate celebrity status with the dive community here. We use Facebook to make everybody aware of the achievement and then people share that with all their friends, and alumni that have already completed the Green Short Challenge comment. There's a lot of warm and fuzzy, feel-good vibes as they're welcomed to the club—and that cements them as a customer for life."

When customers see their achievements recognized on Facebook, they frequently "like" the posts and use tags to identify people in the photos, spreading the love to their own Facebook friends. This is one of the reasons that Ocean Frontiers has nearly 30,000 likes on Facebook. "You couldn't ask for a more loyal and dedicated customer base than what we're building," Broadbelt says. "From whatever social media platform they communicate, if someone wants to go diving in the Caribbean, our customers are going to recommend us. There's a human element that can be brought in with Facebook. You humanize what your business does."

Speaking of humanizing a business, I found out about Ocean Frontiers from Mark Rovner, a communications consultant at Sea Change Strategies, who told me about how he dove all 55 sites and now has his very own pair of Green Shorts. "Steve Broadbelt is a really creative guy and developed a dive logbook with sketches of the dive sites, and little stickers you can put on each dive site," Rovner says. "He gamified it. The Green Short Challenge works in so many different ways. The ceremony gets put on their Facebook page, and then each of us who becomes a Green Short alumnus puts that on our Facebook page. It gives us a story to tell to every diver friend we know. And the one thing that is true of divers, like any other sort of hyperpassionate hobby, is that there's little else that divers want to talk about more than diving."

Increase Engagements with Facebook Groups

A great way for organizations of all kinds to keep interested people informed is to gather them into a Facebook group. All users can create groups, and their membership can be closed (invitation only) or open (anyone may join). There's also a similar place where people can meet called a Facebook page, which is a page of information that anybody can see (compared with groups, where you must register first). Facebook groups are typically for more in-depth communications around a subject (such as a product launch), while Facebook pages are typically for a loose but longer-term presence. Facebook pages are created for a brand or product, an organization, a local business or place, an artist or public figure, or a cause or community. I know this sounds complicated, but it should be further incentive to join some groups and become a fan of a few companies to see what people are doing.

Starting a Facebook group is very straightforward. It takes just a few minutes to set one up, and the process includes a built-in tool for sending invitations to your Facebook friends (and, as appropriate, the friends of your colleagues). You should also mention the group on your organization's regular website or blog. People join Facebook groups because they want to stay informed, and they want to do it on their own time. Just as with blogs, the best way to maintain a Facebook group is simply to make valuable information available. Unlike intrusive email updates, which arrive only when the sender chooses, Facebook groups can be visited at the member's convenience.

I've had some remarkable experiences with Facebook groups, experiences that never would have happened in the absence of social networking tools. One of the most interesting was with Stephen Quigley's New Media and PR class at Boston University. The class uses this book as one of its texts, and for several terms the students have invited me to join their invitation-only Facebook groups. One term's group was called New Media Rocks My PR World (love the name), and another set of students went with Media Socialites (love this one even more). Here is the Media Socialites' description of their group: "Professor Quigley's new batch of student social media sponges, eager to soak up as much information about New Media and PR in a semester as is humanly possible . . . and, in proper social networking fashion, making important connections along the way."

Social networking has given birth to new models for learning. I graduated from Kenyon College in 1983, and in four years I don't recall ever giving textbook authors any thought whatsoever. I certainly never met any of them. But with social media tools like Facebook, smart professors (and students) are now involving textbook authors and other guests, effectively creating virtual classrooms to supplement the physical ones. The students and professors tell me it's transforming their learning process. How about your business? How is social media changing what you do? Take a lesson from these forward-thinking educators and become a part of the discussion.

In short, Facebook is emerging as a primary means for folks to keep in touch with the people and the organizations that are important to them, and it follows that it has become an important marketing tool for many companies. As with other social networking media, success on Facebook comes from being a thought leader and developing information that people *want* to absorb.

Check Out My LinkedIn Profile

Marketing on social networking sites can be tricky, because online communities disdain overt commercial messages. Acceptable marketing and promotion on these sites frequently involves brands or personalities creating pages to build and expand an online following, rather than directly advertising products.

For example, many business-to-business marketing and sales professionals rely on LinkedIn, the world's largest professional social network (more than 500 million users in over 200 countries and territories), to meet business partners. Unlike social networks that people use to keep up friendships, LinkedIn's mission is to connect the world's professionals and make them more productive and successful. LinkedIn is a great way to network with others in your industry and to meet buyers of your products and services.

LinkedIn is used for identifying buyers and potential partners, understanding the competitors, conducting market research, sharing information, and promoting events. Like other social networks, your personal profile is your public face. Given LinkedIn's focus on business, your profile should emphasize the skills you bring to your market niche and the value you add to your community. With your profile up and running, you request to join other people's networks or invite them to join yours—both people must approve the connection. Once you're connected with someone, you can see contacts you share in common and how you might reach someone you want to meet through your connections. One of the fastest-growing aspects of LinkedIn is its company profiles, which deliver an overview of what a company does and for whom, the products and services it offers, and any positions available at the company. When you view a company profile, you can see how many company employees are on LinkedIn and if any are in your network.

"A profile on LinkedIn is not a 'presence' on LinkedIn," says Mark Amtower, director of the government market master's program at Capitol College in Laurel, Maryland, and an active LinkedIn user. "A presence occurs when people start to take serious notice. After you have set up your profile, your outreach begins. Determine who the key players are in your niche and develop a plan to connect with them. Keep in mind, your profile has to be interesting enough to make them want to connect. Short, informative paragraphs and bullet points are more readable than long paragraphs. A great profile can open doors, help you get a job, get you consulting and speaking gigs, and more. A poor profile reverses these actions."

Amtower's goal with LinkedIn is to be among the most connected and most visible people in government contracting. He does this by regularly posting relevant information and starting discussions in groups to raise his visibility and demonstrate value to the community. He has a personal network of more than 7,000 first-degree connections (people he is connected to directly) and manages contractor groups with another 9,000 members.

Amtower says he goes to LinkedIn several times each day and has created a list of his top 10 activities. "None of these activities take very long, and each puts me on the radar, generating leads and social selling," he says. "If you make them part of your LinkedIn routine, you will expand your network, extend your influence, and create more opportunities.

> "1. My profile is never done. I fine-tune it regularly based on ideas I get from reviewing other people's profiles.
> "2. I keep my LinkedIn goals in mind for all my social media activities. LinkedIn is the focal point of my online social networking, and it is important that I present myself in a manner that reflects the real me.
> "3. At least once a day I check the 'Who's viewed my profile' feature on LinkedIn. The results can be quite interesting and lead to some great connections.

"4. I receive many connection requests, but I connect based on my goals. I carefully review the profiles of each person asking to connect. I believe there is an obligation that comes with connecting, to add value to the relationship and not to spam your connections.

"5. When I get an request asking for help from someone in my network, I try to assist. You never know when or how this help will come back. Besides, it feels good to do good deeds.

"6. When I look at a profile of a key influencer in my market, I always look at the 'People also viewed' feature. There are always interesting people there.

"7. When I view other people's profiles, I often take screen shots of the good, the bad, and the ugly. Is there anything there that can help me make my profile better, or a reminder of things I need to avoid?

"8. I try to post in each LinkedIn group I belong to one or two times each month. I make certain that my post is germane to the group where I post it. Groups offer good exposure, and participation is the way to get it.

"9. I review and monitor my groups on a regular basis, especially the groups I manage. There are millions of groups on LinkedIn, and I like to select those that give me the most traction and access to key players in my market.

"10. I post via LinkedIn Pulse, the network's blog feature, frequently, and I monitor the views, likes, and comments. Any time someone comments on one of my posts, I respond.

"For me, LinkedIn has reinforced my position as a leading consultant in the government contracting market," Amtower says. "Through my LinkedIn profile alone, I have landed more than 30 consulting gigs with large, medium, and small government contractors, as well as several speaking engagements. At this point, I would suggest that those without a robust social networking presence will lose market share in direct proportion to their social networking inactivity."

A tactic that some smart nonprofit organizations use is to encourage employees to establish a personal page on Facebook or LinkedIn, with details of the cause they support, as a way to spread the word. Supporters of political candidates (as well as some candidates themselves) create pages on social networking sites, too. As with all good marketing, it is important to create content that is right for the people you want to reach, and that effort starts with the choice of which social networking site (or sites) to post your profile on.

As you consider a strategy to get yourself out there and onto a social networking site for marketing and PR purposes, just remember that authenticity and transparency are critical. Don't try to fool the community into thinking that the page is something that it is not. (You might want to refer to the discussion of ethics in Chapter 15.) Frequent eruptions within these communities happen when members uncover a fraud of some kind, such as an advertising agency creating fake profiles of people applauding products. Yes, you can use social networking sites such as LinkedIn to build a following, but avoid sleazy fake profiles of people who supposedly use your products.

Tweet Your Thoughts to the World

Twitter, sometimes called a "microblogging" service, has become a very popular social network. And popularity is important because of the social nature of Twitter, a service for friends, family, and co-workers to communicate through the exchange of quick, short messages known as tweets (with a maximum of 280 characters).

People use Twitter to keep their followers (people who subscribe to their Twitter feed) updated on their lives. For instance, you might tweet about the conference you're attending or the project you're engrossed in, or you might ask your network a question. Twitter is an excellent way to share links to videos, blog posts, and other content you find interesting. Users can choose to follow the Twitter updates of anyone they want to hear from: family members, colleagues, or perhaps the author of the last book they read.

Because of the constraint on the length of tweets, people use Twitter to post information that is important to update their network about but is much more concise than a blog post and more casual than an email. You can update your Twitter feed from a web browser, a mobile phone, or an instant messaging service, so Twitter is always on. I update my feed a few times a day, tweeting about my travels around the world, whom I'm meeting, and what's going on at the events where I speak. I also frequently send out links to examples of great marketing that people send me, things like e-books, YouTube videos, and blog posts. In this way, Twitter is a way of pointing people to things that I find interesting. As with other forms of social networking, it takes time to build a following. In particular, the best way to get people to pay attention to you is to participate by following others and responding to them.

Every marketing and PR person should be aware of Twitter and understand how people use it. As a first step, you should immediately hightail it over to the Twitter search engine to see what people are saying about you, your organization, your products and services, and perhaps your competitors and the category of product you sell. If you've never done this, please do it right now, because it can be an eye-opening experience to see what (if anything) people are saying. A great way to use Twitter to monitor what people are saying is to use a Twitter client application such as TweetDeck or HootSuite. These free applications allow you to monitor multiple keywords and phrases in real time so you know instantly when something important (such as the name of your CEO or a product your company sells) is mentioned.

When you're ready to set up your own Twitter profile and begin to tweet, the most important aspect from the marketing and PR perspective is—as I say time and again—don't use this service as an advertising channel to talk up your products and services. If that's your intention, you need to be very careful.

With all this online conversation going on, some people think that Facebook, Twitter, and other social networking tools can replace a face-to-face approach to business. I actually think strong social networking ties lead to *stronger* personal relationships because it is easy to facilitate face-to-face meetings that never would have occurred otherwise. For example, before a conference, I might send a tweet saying, "I'll be in San Francisco next Tuesday." I'll frequently get a message right back from someone who is planning to be at the same conference, or someone who lives there, and we end up meeting in person. I'll also create an impromptu meeting of my followers—sometimes called a tweetup—that occurs when people who are connected on Twitter have a face-to-face meeting. I've had between 10 and 50 people show up to connect in cities like New York, Atlanta, and Phoenix, as well as Wellington, New Zealand; Mumbai, India; and Amsterdam.

Social Networking and Personal Branding

I've had many conversations with people who are new to social networking sites such as Twitter, and often they are puzzled at first about what to do. Hey, I've been there, too. We all make mistakes. I recall when I was first getting going with Facebook and my teenage daughter was looking over my shoulder. She rolled her eyes and called me a big dork when I wrote a message on my own Facebook wall (a place for your visitors to write). With my own learning and the experiences with people I've helped over the past few years, I've found that getting a few things right at the start makes the experience more fun (and productive).

Your personal branding shines through when you take care to choose appropriate images and create compelling bios on social networking sites. Many sites, including Twitter, Facebook, and LinkedIn, have similar personal branding elements, so you can apply the ideas here to other sites. While I'll be providing ideas about Twitter here, the basic concepts apply to all social networking sites.

An important thing to consider is how your online actions are a reflection of your personal branding (the image that you project to the world). As you already know, *people* use Twitter to keep others updated on what they find interesting at that moment. Frequently when I am asked about Twitter and its use in personal branding and marketing, people immediately dive into stuff like "How often should I tweet?," "What should I tweet about?," "Is it cool to DM [direct message] people?," and other tweet-related details. Well, that's all fine, but the vast majority of people miss the most basic (and important) personal branding aspect of all.

What does your Twitter page look like?

Most Twitter pages don't say enough, and most have crappy design. While that's all right if you're just communicating with friends, if you care about your personal brand, you need to do better. Much better. And it is so easy! When you first set up your Twitter account, you have choices. And after you've set up the account, you can make these changes to any aspect of your profile at any time (except your Twitter ID) under the Settings tab in Twitter.

Twitter ID: (Mine is @dmscott.) Choose an appropriate ID. Something like @MrSillyGuy is probably not a good idea for most people. However, a silly ID might fit your personal brand, say, if you're a comedian. (Incidentally, the ID @MrSillyGuy has been taken by Niki Dubois @ikiniki from Belgium after he read an early edition of this book.)

Name: (Mine is David Meerman Scott.) Use your real name. Don't just default to your user ID, which so many people seem to do. And don't just use a nickname like Pookie. You can put your nickname in quotes inside your real name if you want to. If you really care about your personal brand, you'll want people to know who you really are.

Location: (Mine is Boston, MA.) Use the town or nearest city that makes sense for you. Saying something cute like Earth or "somewhere in Canada" turns people off who don't know you. Besides, the location is a good way to make local contacts.

Web: (My URL is www.davidmeermanscott.com.) If you have a blog or site, put the URL here. Or maybe your profile on a company website makes sense for you. This should be somewhere people can go to learn more about *you*. If you don't have a blog or site, I recommend that you create an about .me profile and link to that. You can also leave the web link blank if you want, but that says to people that you don't want to be contacted or have people learn more about you.

Bio: As I write this, mine is "Business Growth Strategist, entrepreneur, advisor to emerging companies, bestselling author of 11 books including *Fanocracy* and *New Rules of Marketing & PR*." This is where you say something about yourself. You get only 160 characters. As a component of personal branding, this is a critical section. Don't leave it blank. And don't make a mini-resume from a laundry list of attributes like this: "father, husband, surfer, economics major, world traveler, marketer, and rock star wannabe." (I confess, that would be my list.) I see this sort of thing all the time, and it is not good for personal branding because you don't really focus on your particular expertise. Try to be descriptive. And try to be specific.

Profile photo: Twitter has two places for photos: your profile photo, which will appear anytime you tweet, and your header photo, which is the main image on your Twitter page. Your photos are very important! Don't default to the placeholder egg image that Twitter provides for those with no profile photo. And don't use something clever as a stand-in (like your cat). If you care about your personal brand, you should use a photo of yourself and not a pet or an image of your car. Profile photos appear very tiny on Twitter—like a postage stamp—so use a close-up shot. If you use a full-length view of yourself, then you will appear like a stick figure. Remember that your photo conveys a very important first impression when people see your profile for the first time. Are you wearing a hat? Is it a casual shot of you taken on a vacation with a beer in your hand? Or have you chosen a formal head-and-shoulders shot with business attire taken by a professional photographer? Is your son or daughter in the photo with you? There is no absolute right or wrong, but do keep in mind that each of these choices says a great deal about you.

Header photo: The header photo on your Twitter page is a place where you can really show off. It takes up the entire top of the page, so it is excellent real estate. Many sales and marketing people add an advertising message to this real estate, but I think that's a mistake and recommend resisting this tendency. Adding your messages or heavy-handed branding to the header detracts. Sure, I could have used an image of, say, all my book covers for my banner. Instead I use a great photo of me speaking at an event with more than a thousand people in the background. It's my personal brand on Twitter. Your header photo will show up on your Twitter web page as well as on mobile devices.

These choices are really easy to set up, but they're very important for your personal brand. If you are on Twitter, take the time to make some changes today. Again, the same ideas apply on other social networking sites like Facebook and LinkedIn, so don't forget to carefully consider your personal branding on those sites as well.

The CIA Joins Twitter

Ha! Now you will *know* when they follow you. Well, on Twitter at least.

The @CIA joined Twitter on June 6, 2014. Yes, that CIA. They're also on Facebook. (I never dreamed I'd be writing those words.)

The CIA's first tweet is my favorite single tweet of all time: "We can neither confirm nor deny that this is our first tweet." Love it, right?! So did 300,000+ retweeters.

In less than 24 hours, @CIA amassed more than a quarter million followers, and they are at more than 2.5 million as I write this.

The official CIA press release revealed their plans: "Follow us on Twitter @CIA and on Facebook for the latest CIA updates, #tbt (Throwback Thursday) photos, reflections on intelligence history, and fun facts from the CIA *World Factbook*. You'll also receive updates on CIA career postings and get the latest glimpse into CIA's Museum—the best museum most people never get to see. Our social media expansion will put CIA.gov content right at your fingertips." The CIA Twitter bio reads: "We are the Nation's first line of defense. We accomplish what others cannot accomplish and go where others cannot go."

As advertised, the feed is an excellent collection of historical images and facts, live event streams, quotes, and other interesting information.

I am so glad to see this development.

With this one move, especially that clever first tweet, the CIA did more to humanize its organization than probably anything else in its history. At the same time, it shows organizations of all types that it is okay to open up and it's perfectly acceptable to operate in real time on social networks. The use of humor is icing on the cake. Nicely played, CIA people.

And thanks for making my job easier. Now it's simple what I tell people who are still resistant to the idea of getting active on Twitter and other social networks: If the CIA can do it, so can you.

The Sharing More Than Selling Rule

Social networks are a great place to share content, to interact with others, and to listen in on what's happening, and yes, if approached carefully, social networks can also be a way to get the word out about you and your business. However, as I review individuals' business-related social streams I find way too much selling going on. Too many companies are shouting into the social world.

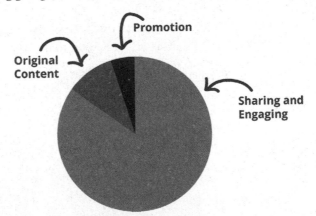

When I speak with people at conferences, many want to know, specifically, how to use social networking feeds such as Twitter, Instagram, LinkedIn, and Facebook to communicate effectively as a marketing and sales tool.

While there is no right or wrong when it comes to content creation and sharing, I'd say that a loose guideline may be helpful as a way to think about the various uses of social networks.

As a way to think about your social activities, I'd suggest you should be doing 85 percent sharing and engaging, 10 percent publishing original content, and only 5 percent or less about what you are trying to promote.

Make 85 Percent Sharing and Engaging

Sharing and engaging include such things as commenting on someone else's blog or Facebook post, quoting a tweet and adding your take, or responding to somebody who has said something that interests you. You can also share an interesting blog post or news report with your network.

Most people, especially those new to a social network, don't share and engage enough. I'd say you should be doing it with at least 85 percent of your social interactions, but it could be much more. Since sharing and engaging are the easiest aspect of social networking, it shouldn't take much for you to do more of it.

Make 10 Percent Original Content

I'd recommend that 1 out of 10 of your social interactions be publishing something original. You can share a photo you shot, write a blog post, compose a tweet about something that interests your marketplace, or publish a video. The more helpful this content is to your buyer personas, the better.

Many people worry about social networks as a tool of business because they think that everything they do has to be new content. But I suggest only 10 percent needs to be!

Make 5 Percent or Less a Promotion about What You Do

One out of 20 interactions (or fewer) can be something that you want to promote to your audience. This is when you can share a new product your company offers, a special discount for social followers, or other content of a promotional nature.

Most people sell way too much and as such their social feeds don't have much interaction. People just don't want to be sold to. However, if you are helpful and engaging and responsive on your social feeds, then you build an audience who will want to hear from you and who will be receptive to learning more about what you and your organization do.

Jay Blakesberg is a perfect example of somebody who interacts with social networks in the way I suggest. Jay is a San Francisco–based music photographer and filmmaker who has shot more than 300 assignments for *Rolling Stone* and has been published in print magazines from *Time* to *Vanity Fair* to *Guitar Player* as well as hundreds of other major magazines.

I first met Jay virtually when he commented on a blog post I wrote about the Grateful Dead some years ago. Jay has photographed the Grateful Dead and the individual band members hundreds of times, so my post was perfect for him to respond to. That simple interaction led me to reach out to Jay, and we've become friends. I've hired Jay for three different projects so far: He supplied the photos for the book I co-authored, *Marketing Lessons from the Grateful Dead*; Jay shot some portraits of me; and I had him photograph me delivering a keynote speech at a major conference. All that work from me is a result of one simple comment Jay left on my blog!

Jay has a very popular Facebook page for his business, with more than 60,000 followers. He posts interesting original photos and, if you're a fan of rock music like I am, the feed is fun to check out. Jay is constantly interacting with his fans and posting his content, for free, for all to enjoy. Jay was the official photographer for the Grateful Dead "Fare Thee Well" final performances in July 2015, and over the several weeks following the shows he posted photos every day for fans to check out. For weeks Jay was share, share, share! But once, Jay sent a rare promotional message to his Facebook fans that read:

> I have a new book out! *Guitars That Jam!*
>
> It features Bob Weir, Jerry Garcia, Phil Lesh, Trey Anastasio, Warren Haynes, Derek Trucks, and so many more! It is the stories about their guitars written by the artists (except Jerry) with my photography!
>
> I know many of you loved my Fare Thee Well photos. . . . Please support your friendly neighborhood Photographer.

This Facebook post generated 578 likes, 38 shares, and 30 comments in just the first 12 hours after it was posted. Imagine that. A promotional message that generated such amazing results.

Because Jay's interactions are mostly sharing, responding, engaging with fans, and publishing his original photographs, he has earned the ability to occasionally talk about his products and services. And because people appreciate Jay's content, they are eager to support him. I've purchased a copy of *Guitars That Jam* for myself and copies for several friends. It is a terrific book.

Social media is about engagement. Sure, it is also a tool for marketing and sales, but you need to engage first.

Connecting with Fans

"Being a touring musician means meeting fans," says Amanda Palmer, an American performer who first rose to prominence as the lead singer, pianist, and lyricist/composer of the duo the Dresden Dolls and is currently with her own act. "I go out and meet fans after every gig. It's important to make contact in real life and not just online in social media like Twitter. If you don't meet fans in real life, too, then you're a fraud. If you're not comfortable getting into the sweat with them and talking with people at shows, then how can you do it successfully online? I love connecting with fans. Speaking to people at the merchandise table after the show is great. I can stay there forever."

This committed attitude has helped make Palmer a personal branding force of nature, using her infectious personality to connect with fans in person and on the web. She has amassed a large online following on her blog, her Facebook fan page (more than 400,000 fans), and her Twitter feed (@AmandaPalmer, more than a million followers).

Palmer is very active on Twitter and uses it as a tool for instant communication with her fans. She frequently answers fans' tweeted questions and comments. Because she truly enjoys her connection with her followers, Twitter comes naturally to her. "It's important to have the makeup that I do," she says. "I love to answer fans' questions, and I love to make people happy. You can't fake being authentic with your fans. It's so easy to see through when other musicians are faking it, such as when some employee of their record labels tweets on behalf of their artists. Fans can see through fake tweets like 'I'm about to play at a rad club. Get tix here.' Fake artists' blogs are the same. Who cares?"

Palmer frequently uses Twitter to bring together groups of fans quickly and spontaneously when she is on the road. She tweeted a secret gig in Los

Angeles one morning, and about 350 people showed up five hours later at a warehouse space where she played the piano. It works great for her because, although she's able to get a large number of people to show up, she is not so popular that she would create a dangerously huge mob. "I'm in the sweet spot of popularity," she says. "I can send out a tweet and get 300 people to show up in a couple of days and do a free gig on the beach. I'll play the ukulele, sing, sign, hug, take pictures, eat cake, and generally hang out and connect. And I'll stay as long as it takes to talk with everyone personally. Trent Reznor of Nine Inch Nails can't do that because he's just too popular."

Palmer does struggle with the amount of time she spends connecting with fans both in person and through the tools of social media like Twitter. "I feel guilty sometimes that I'd often prefer to answer questions from fans and do interviews and meet people than work on new music," she says. Interestingly, she has fans who feel the same way; her prolific online *content* has earned a following of its own. "One person at a record store gig and signing came up to me and said, 'I don't really like your music, but I love your blog.'"

How Amanda Palmer Raised a Million Dollars via Social Networking

After a two-year fight with Roadrunner Records, musician Amanda Palmer freed herself from her record deal. For the seven years prior to her label divorce, anything she wrote and recorded (either solo or with her band, the Dresden Dolls) was technically owned and under the ultimate control of the label.

Palmer knew she could do better on her own, because she enjoys such a terrific relationship with her fans via social networks.

So after much planning, Palmer chose a 30-day Kickstarter to fund her new album by "Amanda Palmer & The Grand Theft Orchestra." Kickstarter is a crowdsourced funding platform for creative projects such as films, games, art, and music. She wrote the following in her Kickstarter pitch: "Since I'm now without a giant label to front the gazillions of dollars that it always takes to manufacture and promote a record this big, I'm coming to you to gather funds so that I have the capital to put it out with a huge bang.

I think Kickstarter and other crowdfunding platforms like this are the BEST way to put out music right now—no label, no rules, no fuss, no muss. Just us, the music, and the art. I'm also making sure EVERY PRODUCT sold through this Kickstarter is unique to this campaign, to reward all of you who KNEW ME WHEN and were willing to support me from Day One."

There were funding packages starting at just $1 (entitling the donor to a digital download of the album, titled *Theatre Is Evil*, once it was released) and ending at $10,000 (good for dinner with Palmer plus all sorts of extras). The package I chose was a pledge of $300; it included tickets to a VIP party and intimate show with Palmer and the band in Boston (there were similar options in other cities).

Through social networking, in just a few days, Palmer raised more money from her fans than she would have gotten from her label. In the one month that the Kickstarter appeal was live, she raised nearly $1.2 million, the largest amount any musician had ever raised on the site. And she retains complete control of the production and the rights to the music.

To succeed at this technique, a musician must build a fan base, one person at a time. Social media is a great way to connect before and after the live gig, but the personal connection is essential.

The point is that social networking is an increasingly important way for people to connect and communicate. Organizations are using it cleverly to benefit their businesses, their followers, and themselves. So should you.

While your work may be completely different from that of a rock star, Palmer has something to teach you. Your product comes first and must be created with passion. And you've got to engage with your customers on a human level. Social networking can help you build this fan base. If you do it well, you can build a great company and a fantastic career.

Which Social Networking Site Is Right for You?

While some people might be tempted to create pages on lots of different social networking sites, this may not be necessary (or even useful), since each one appeals to different users. "While the top social networking sites are typically viewed as directly competing with one another, our analysis demonstrates that each site occupies a slightly different niche," says Jack

Flanagan, executive vice president of comScore. "There is a misconception that social networking is the exclusive domain of teenagers, but [our] analysis confirms that the appeal of social networking sites is far broader." In fact, Facebook says that more than two-thirds of its users are out of college and that the fastest-growing demographic is those 35 years old and older.

So think about the right social networking sites for you and your business. Besides Facebook, LinkedIn, and Twitter, there are many thousands of social networks around the world. Here are a few other popular ones to check out.

Tumblr: People use Tumblr to post multimedia content (photos, video, images) to a sort of mini-blog. Very popular with young people, Tumblr hosts more than 300 million blogs. Within the Tumblr application, you can follow other users' blogs and reblog their posts to your own. Unlike the more traditional blogs that we discuss in Chapters 5 and 15, Tumblr is based on a template approach that makes it very easy to upload a photo, video, or some text—all it takes is a minute or two. If your buyers include teenagers and people in their 20s, you need to understand Tumblr. Just remember to keep it short.

Snapchat: This social network smartphone app originally started so people could share photos and text messages to one friend at a time that would disappear after a few seconds. But with the addition of Snapchat Stories and this feature's ability to broadcast to all of your Snapchat friends at once with content that remains live for 24 hours, users now use Snapchat for marketing purposes.

Medium: This social networking site is optimized for long-form text content. It's a great place to share your thoughts when you're writing more than about 1,000 words. Many people use Medium as an alternative newsfeed to see what's going on in the world, and smart experts add their thoughts to the network to get noticed. It's really easy to get started on Medium because the site has very few formatting options. It's all about what you write.

Local language sites: Keep in mind that many countries have local language social networking sites that may be much more popular than the global sites like Facebook. For example, the Japanese site Mixi is very popular, as is Orkut in both India and Brazil. I lived in Asia for nearly 10 years, most of that time as Asia marketing director for Knight-Ridder. When working in Indonesia, Japan, Singapore, Thailand, Hong Kong, Australia, and the other countries in the Asia-Pacific region, I always had to go local in some way. If you're in the global market, localization is important. Yet many marketers assume that one size fits all.

Shopping and review sites: Okay, I know this is an outlier. Most people don't consider shopping and review sites to be social networking, and they're nothing like the other sites I've mentioned in this chapter. But don't overlook the incredible communities that thrive on sites like Amazon, where customer reviews, profiles of those customer reviewers, and user conversations take place every day. For example, if a new book comes out in your marketplace, why not be the first to review it on Amazon? If you're a real estate agent and you write a thoughtful review of a new book about real estate investing, it may be seen by tens of thousands of people (as well as the author and members of the media). People who then visit your Amazon profile learn about you and your business, and some may contact you. Other review-based sites to check out include TripAdvisor (travel reviews), Rotten Tomatoes (movie reviews), Zagat (restaurant reviews), and Yelp (reviews of local businesses). There are many more such sites covering different products and in languages other than English. Don't forget to create a useful profile for yourself with contact information.

Nextdoor, the Social Network for Local Businesses

Before we continue exploring this metaphor and a related one, it may be helpful to consider a case in which a social media community literally behaves like a little neighborhood.

Local business sectors like real estate, landscaping, healthcare, and fitness pose a particular challenge for social networking. You can only serve people within your geographic area, yet most social networks are global.

If you run a local business in the United States, consider joining Nextdoor, the world's largest social network for neighborhoods. Nextdoor brings together people from more than 200,000 communities and connects them on issues of local importance. The key difference with Nextdoor is that you are required to live within a Nextdoor community to join, and you only see people from your own community on the network.

"We don't advertise our business at all," says Ron Mejia, owner of Miami painting service Royal Environmental Painting. "Most of our business comes from referrals through Nextdoor."

Local homeowners qualify, like Mejia did, to join Nextdoor and be a part of the virtual community of physical neighbors. Then, when questions or requests come in about the sort of business you are in, or looking for a particular recommendation, you can respond on Nextdoor.

You're not actively soliciting business. You're just being neighborly.

It turns out that house painting is a frequent topic of conversation in Mejia's Nextdoor community. When somebody says they are looking for a painter, or has a question about painting, Mejia responds. He doesn't directly pitch his business but rather is seen as a local expert. He also benefits when other Nextdoor members refer people to him through the platform.

"Nextdoor works very well for me because people are more trusting of their neighbors," Mejia says. "I'm somebody from the community and not a stranger. People I interact with on Nextdoor might find me at Publix, which is the local supermarket here, or they might see me in Target. I'm their neighbor. And it works for my business because 90 percent of my new customers come through the referrals and connections I've made on Nextdoor."

You Can't Go to Every Party, So Why Even Try?

Think back to our social-media-as-cocktail-party metaphor for a moment. You can't go to every party thrown in your city. There are literally thousands of social networking sites out there, and it is simply impossible to be active in all of them. And once you choose a few parties to attend, you can't meet and have a conversation with each and every person there. You know there are tons of great conversations going on all around you, and you know that you can't be a part of them all.

What do you do at a party? Some people constantly look over the shoulder of the person they are talking to, always on the lookout for a better conversation. Some flit from one person to another every few minutes all night, having many short, superficial conversations. What I like to do at parties is have a few great conversations and be happy that I'm at a wonderful event. I know I can't be with everyone, so I have fun with the people I'm with. What more could I want?

If you're following my analogy here, you should apply the same thing to your participation in social media. For most people and organizations, it's better to be active in a few social networking sites instead of creating profiles on dozens of them and being too busy to spend much time in any one. In my own case, I have my own blog, I am on LinkedIn, Instagram, and Twitter, I post to Medium and SlideShare, and I'm active on a few forums and chat rooms, but that's about it. There are thousands of other social media and social networking sites that I have chosen not to participate in over the years, such as Nexopia, Bebo, Hi5, Tagged, Xing, Skyrock, Orkut, Xiaonei, Cyworld, and many, many more. Since you can't go to every party, you need to pick and choose. Where do you want to be? Where can you be most helpful? Where are the members of your buyer personas?

Optimizing Social Networking Pages

If you're creating pages on Facebook, LinkedIn, Twitter, and the other social networking sites, and if you've been following the planning process outlined in Chapter 10, then you're creating content that reaches your buyers and helps you achieve your goals. Although social networking sites aren't advertising, you can still use the sites to lead people into your buying process. For example, Amanda Palmer links to her blog from her Twitter profile.

Here are some ideas to get the most out of using social networking sites for marketing:

- **Target a specific audience.** Create a page that reaches an audience important to your organization. It is usually better to target a small niche market (e.g., people who want to do their own car repairs but don't know how to diagnose what's wrong).
- **Create thoughtful content.** Provide valuable and interesting information that people want to check out. As you will remember from Chapter 12, it is better to show your expertise in a market or at solving a buyer's problems than to blather on about your product.
- **Be authentic and transparent.** Don't try to impersonate someone else. It's a sleazy practice, and if you get caught, you can do irreparable

harm to your company's reputation. If your mother would say it's wrong, it probably is.

- **Create lots of links.** Link to your own sites and blog and to those of others in your industry and network. Everybody loves links—they make the web what it is. You should certainly link to your own stuff from a social networking site, but it's important to expand your horizons a bit.
- **Encourage people to contact you.** Make it easy for others to reach you online, and be sure to follow up personally on your fan mail.
- **Participate.** Create groups and participate in online discussions. Become an online leader and organizer.
- **Make it easy to find you.** Tag your page and add it to subject directories.
- **Experiment.** These social networking sites are great because you can try new things. If it isn't working, tweak it. Or abandon the effort and try something new. There is no such thing as an expert in social networking—we're all learning as we go!

Integrate Social Media into an Offline Conference or Event

As you participate in social networking, keep in mind the relationship between the online world of virtual networks and the physical world of in-person networks. There will be many times that one will complement the other.

Consider conferences and other events. Today, the best live events are the ones that integrate social media into the festivities. At conferences all over the world, audience members connect with one another while speakers are up at the podium. These back channels are truly revolutionary, since they allow listeners to discuss content as it is being delivered. What's more, it brings a new virtual audience into the room—sometimes from the opposite end of the earth.

Alan Belniak, director of social media marketing at PTC, a software company producing product life cycle management tools, integrated social media into the PTC/USER World Event. Belniak notes one of the benefits of the conference is integrating the physical event with social networking. "Participants are better off because they can absorb more of the event without being in every session," he says. "They may attend one session, but they can catch a blog of another session or skim the tweet stream of a third. By offering multiple forms of media, it lets people experience more of the event."

Here are some of the ways Belniak used social media at the PTC/USER World Event:

- Developed a single page where all the social media feeds could be found.
- Gave out about a dozen video cameras and had the recipients create videos to upload onto a special YouTube video channel.
- Created a Flickr feed of photos shot at the event.
- Established a common hashtag and later archived its Twitter feed.
- Aggregated 35 different bloggers' posts.

The real-time social networking gave those who could not be present in person a taste of the action. "They can see what they're missing and possibly use these forms of real-time multimedia as justification that they should attend next year," Belniak says. In fact, at least one person didn't wait until the next year. "A local PTC customer wasn't registered for the event but had been following some of the chatter on the website. He was a short drive away, so he told his boss that he should go. And he did."

Build a Passionate Fan Base

During a recent summer, our daughter snapped a photo of me and my wife @YukariWatanabe as we enjoyed a delicious bottle of 2009 Silver Oak Alexander Valley cabernet sauvignon. When I tweeted the photo evidence, @SilverOak responded, "Looks like a beautiful evening! Thank you for sharing with us." Silver Oak engaged with me, unlike many other brands that I tag in a tweet, like, say, the Ritz-Carlton Hotel Company (among many other brands).

When I dug a little deeper by checking out the @SilverOak Twitter and Instagram feeds, the Facebook page, and the YouTube channel, I noticed that the people at Silver Oak aren't just talking up their products. Rather, they authentically engage with people who are current or potential fans of the wine and who are enjoying interesting experiences with a bottle (or two). I also like the way Silver Oak shares beautiful images on social media. There are frequent shots of the vineyard, its buildings, and the people who make the wine. It makes me want to visit the winery in California and try more of its offerings!

"Social is important because it gives us a chance to listen," says Ian Leggat, director of marketing and public relations at Silver Oak. "More than anything else, we look for social signals to get a temperature check on our brand and to understand what our followers are excited about." And people do get excited about Silver Oak, as evidenced by their active online following.

Silver Oak is an expensive bottle, around $100 and up depending on the vintage and where you buy it. What I've noticed about other high-end wines is that the branding plays to snob appeal. Sometimes wineries play hard to get—making wines scarce to increase the perception of value. Silver Oak does the opposite. The wine is widely available when you want it. That attitude seems to extend to interaction with fans.

"The Silver Oak brand is very much linked with special moments, and all we are doing is facilitating people to share the special moments and be excited about them," Leggat says. "Silver Oak is the wine that you drink to celebrate the birth of a child, to celebrate an anniversary. Last fall we were developing our print newsletter, and we reached out on Twitter to get a couple of these 'bottle stories' in 140 characters or less. Some of the things that came back to us were so powerful. We had one where someone had waited out Hurricane Sandy with a bottle of Silver Oak and a flashlight. That's all she had. We had someone who ordered a large-format bottle of Silver Oak in place of a wedding guestbook and just had people sign that bottle of Silver Oak and make this beautiful keepsake in their home. They wanted to take that picture and share with everybody. For us, it's really just maximizing the social capital that we have among the very engaged base."

Some famous people have shared their bottle stories on Twitter and Instagram as well, including LeBron James, Courteney Cox, and Kacey Musgraves.

"We have probably the most passionate fan base of any wine that I'm aware of, and we cultivate evangelists through our social media channels and help celebrate them," Leggat says. "Our strategy has evolved over the years to be less about pushing content out and more about facilitating dialogue in our social channels and reaching out to influencers and pulling them into those conversations. What we really care about is not adding followers as much as the conversations that we have with them, and creating the kind of content that facilitates sharing."

Because Silver Oak has been active on social networks for years and uses the channels to actually engage with customers rather than try to sell products, the company has built a strong presence.

Social Networking and Crisis Communications

The real-time aspects of social networking, and the way it creates opportunities for two-way communication, make the tools of this chapter excellent ways to connect with constituents during a crisis your organization is experiencing. You can be certain that people are talking about you anyway, so getting your voice out during what can be a very tough time for your organization can help you get through the crisis.

Jerry Sandusky, a former Pennsylvania State University assistant football coach, was found guilty on 45 charges of sexual abuse and was sentenced to 60 years in prison. The story was at the forefront of the news cycle from its breaking in November 2011, during the investigation and trial, and through the sentencing in October 2012.

Imagine you are responsible for social media within an organization faced with a major crisis like what happened at Penn State. How would you handle it? How would the senior executives handle it?

The right approach is to be honest and forthright. Communicate the facts quickly and don't hide. Assign a visible spokesperson. Silence and "no comment" are the enemy.

The Penn State story is certainly a tragedy. But the way communication about it was handled by the university administration is worth a look and some reflection. I spoke with Kelly Burns, a Penn State MBA graduate, about that experience. While a student, Burns interned with Penn State Football Marketing & Promotions from May 2009 through April 2012, and for three summers (2009 to 2011) she ran the Penn State Football Facebook and Twitter (@PennStateFball) accounts. "I was very lucky to have the opportunity to assist in developing the Penn State Football Facebook page back when it first launched in summer 2009," Burns says. She posted content (information, photos, videos, and the like) that fans enjoyed. "Having the opportunity to interact with Penn State Football fans was incredible, because Penn State Football has a history rich in tradition and 'Success with Honor,' and its fans literally wear their pride on their sleeves."

The Penn State Football Facebook page, currently with some 700,000 likes, targeted students, recruits to the football program, alumni, and Penn State Football fans in the community. Burns also read each tweet and Facebook comment and responded personally to many. In this role, she frequently put in 40-hour weeks on a voluntary basis.

Then the Sandusky story broke. The grand jury investigation had been initiated in the spring of 2008 but had been kept quiet. In the summer of 2011, Burns was told to remove photos of Sandusky from the Facebook page. On November 4, 2011, Sandusky was indicted, and the next day he was arrested and charged. The story went worldwide instantly. "Our Facebook and Twitter lit up, but that was difficult because initially we were not allowed to post," Burns says. "We were not permitted to post anything about the scandal, nor were any other people working for the university. We were told to wait until Old Main [Penn State's administrative center on campus, which includes the university president's office] made a statement before we could say anything. So we went completely dark."

On November 11, the social media team was permitted to post about the Blue Ribbon Campaign against child abuse, and then on November 16 they were allowed to post some simple messages about football. But still they weren't allowed to say anything about the crisis.

"Penn State Football fans were never permitted to post directly onto the Facebook wall, but during this period fans were engaged on Facebook by commenting on posts that were already there, including the Blue Ribbon post. There were as many as 500 comments on some posts that I moderated. Many people aired their opinions, whether positive or negative."

While the majority of people were thoughtful, some were not. "We patrolled for foul language, rude jokes, and other disturbing comments and removed them," Burns says. Negativity was fine, but with such a sensitive issue, inappropriate language was not allowed. "In several cases we needed to block individuals who insisted on continuing to make fun of Penn State in very inappropriate ways," she says.

A full crisis management discussion is beyond the scope of this book. However, the response typically includes such steps as gathering facts, reporting facts quickly (even if the fact is that nothing is known), giving the name of a spokesperson, acknowledging people's deep emotions, and communicating regularly. Social networks are a great way to communicate in real time during a time of crisis, and in the case of Penn State, the university had a tremendously active Facebook page ready to be used to communicate. However, Penn State Football elected not to take these crisis management steps. Burns says it took days before the board of trustees issued responses and put a face to leadership.

"We should have done a better job providing a way to communicate with the fans," Burns says. "That's not something critical about Penn State Football, because it goes up to Old Main, who decided what was allowed to be said. I think in our day and age of social media, that silence was not the right response. Keeping information private is not the way to go when people are talking 24/7 on social media and need reassurance."

Burns told me how fans of Penn State competitors also used social media and the Penn State Football Facebook page to show their support and understanding for the victims, the Penn State football players, students, alumni, and fans. She shared one of the best examples of a positive fan post from what is usually considered the enemy, Ohio State University. "In this situation, the fan laid aside the on-field rivalry to support a much greater cause (to say the least)," Burns says. Robert Benson, a Buckeye fan, posted in the November 11 comment thread:

> When people are so quick to make sick references to Penn St. I am disgusted. How can anyone label an entire group of people in a negative way and feel good about it? Taking advantage of people who are down, weakened and heartbroken for your own sick pleasure. Does that remind you of someone?
>
> What I see is a community shell-shocked and hurt, trying to find their way through all of this. A horrible situation for them. Surely, among them are kids attending Penn St. who themselves have been victims. Your negative comments about Penn St. must hurt them more than anyone would ever know. They want their university to stand for something better than this.
>
> The whole world is watching Penn St. You will find your way and will come out on the other side to represent something good, and maybe something much bigger and [more] important than before.
>
> Keep your chin up Penn St. When we meet you next week, win or lose, we want you at your best.
>
> —*A Buckeye fan*

When people offer support like this on your social networks, it goes a long way to help mitigate the negative reactions.

If you don't have one already, your organization needs a crisis communications plan in place. As part of the plan, you should secure agreement from executives, public relations professionals, and your legal staff about how you can use social networks like Facebook and Twitter to communicate during a crisis. Don't wait until the bad news comes, because then there is too much happening to make quick decisions.

Why Participating in Social Media Is Like Exercise

One of the most common questions I get at my talks is this: "How do you find the time to do all this social media stuff?" People want the secret to regular participation on Facebook, Twitter, and the other sites that help them create valuable information for their buyers.

I've found that finding the time to participate in social media is just like finding the time for exercise. You have to choose to exercise regularly to stay fit. As far as I know, the only effective way is to make exercise part of your routine. Some people like fitness clubs. Others enjoy running outdoors or dancing or kickboxing. But in all cases, success comes from engaging in the activity regularly.

I enjoy an hour of exercise every morning. I have an elliptical trainer at home, so sometimes I use that. Other days, I go to a nearby health club and swim laps. If I'm near a beach, I enjoy running on sand, and I do yoga and calisthenics when I'm in a hotel room. I get up early, around 4 a.m. most days, and I've been at it for more than a decade. I feel great. I don't even think about finding the time to exercise, because it is a very important part of my life.

It's the same with participating in social networks and creating online content—it becomes part of your life. In my case, I write about 100 blog posts per year and shoot maybe 20 videos. I comment on thousands of blogs. Most years, I write a free e-book. And I'm on forums, chat rooms, Twitter, Instagram, and other social sites.

Many people are surprised when I say that I probably spend about six hours per week on social media, about the same amount of time I spend exercising. I don't even think about it. It's important, so I do it. And I can't really say how I fit it in. Unlike with my exercise routine, I do my social media work mainly in microbursts of a couple of minutes each throughout the day.

I recommend that you don't even try to find the time to create content and participate in social media. You'll fail, just like many of us have in our attempts to find the time to exercise, leading to failure and no small waste of money.

Instead, make social media (and exercise) an important part of your life. A good way to start, in my experience, is to make television a less important part of your life or maybe even eliminate it completely. You will be amazed at how much time you free up.

Make social media both a part of your life and a part of your business, such as the way clever businesses use Twitter to reach out to buyers. I was once in Sofia, Bulgaria, to deliver a New Marketing Masterclass. When I'm in a city for the first time, I always want to poke around a bit. So when the people at Free Sofia Tour (@FreeSofiaTour) tweeted to invite me along (they had heard about my Masterclass), I knew I had to go. Free Sofia Tour relies on volunteer guides and donations from their guests to support the organization.

I love how Free Sofia Tour embraces social media, while the other city tour operators use traditional marketing. I saw the other guys' brochures in the hotel lobby. They have ads at the airport and in the tourist magazines, too. But Free Sofia Tour uses social media, including Facebook, Twitter, and good old-fashioned word of mouth. If you're social, it's easy to find them. They make you feel welcome beforehand, and they follow up via Twitter after the tour.

But you don't have to take my word for it. Free Sofia Tour is ranked the number one activity in Sofia on TripAdvisor, with 645 "excellent" ratings out of 699 as I write this. In a world of commercial approaches (like the big bus tours that operate in many cities), sometimes the personal touch works best. If you ever find yourself in Sofia, now you know who should show you the sights. Just send them a tweet.

This story leads me to one last point about the connecting power of social networks. With all this online conversation going on, social media takes the pervasiveness of the Internet one step further. And while we don't know where they're heading, what is certain is that marketing and PR on the web will continue to evolve—quickly. Success comes from experimentation. With a service like Twitter or an app like Snapchat (or whatever the next new thing is), nobody knows the rules at first. Smart marketers succeed just by trying. JetBlue created a huge following on Twitter because it was an early adopter. The trick to benefiting from any new medium is this: Participate in it; don't just try to take advantage of it. Be a *genuine* part of the action! Whatever is your social networking site of choice, don't hesitate to jump in and see what you can do.

15 Blogging to Reach Your Buyers

Blogs are a mainstream vehicle for organizations to get their ideas out into the marketplace. The readers of blogs view the information shared by smart bloggers as one of the few forms of real, authentic communication. Audiences consume advertising with skepticism and consider pronouncements by CEOs to be out of touch with reality. But a good blog written by someone within a large or small company, a nonprofit, a church, or a political campaign commands attention.

Blogging is a great front door for any individual or organization because it is real estate on the web that you can own. If you use a content tool like HubSpot or WordPress and have your own domain URL, your blog is yours. Search engine traffic goes to you. You can create a blog that showcases your brand. Contrast that with social networks like Twitter, LinkedIn, and Facebook. All are good, but you will never own your real estate there.

At the same time, the term *blog* carries a negative connotation with some people who believe the content contained inside is frivolous. The best marketing and PR strategies must include creating your own content. If you are creating valuable information to market your business, don't let someone's anxiety with the term *blog* hold you back. Or maybe its best to not use the "b-word" at all. For more on this discussion about the term *blog*, please refer back to the section in Chapter 5 called "A Blog (or Not a Blog)."

This chapter sets out the basics of how to establish your own blog. But I recommend that, before you begin to write, you first monitor blogs in your market space, and that you step into the blogosphere by commenting on a few blogs before you write your own. You might want to reread Chapter 5, where I introduced blogs and provided some examples of successful bloggers.

As you begin to comment on other people's blogs, you'll develop your own blogging voice and get a sense of what you like to discuss online. That's great! You're experimenting on someone else's blog real estate. If you're like many people, soon you'll be itching to write your own blog. But if commenting is a painful chore for you, maybe you're not cut out to be a blogger. That's okay—there are many more blog readers than blog writers. This forum isn't for everybody.

It's impossible to tell you everything you need to know about blogging in this one chapter. While the case studies and basic information will certainly get you started, the best thing is to experiment to find your voice. Read other blogs and be aware of what you like and dislike about other bloggers' styles.

What Should You Blog About?

People often struggle to decide what to blog about. This is particularly true for marketing and PR professionals because we have been taught to be slaves to the notion of flogging our products and services with on-message advertising and press releases; but for most organizations, that's exactly the wrong way to blog. The first thing to ask yourself is: "Whom do I want to reach?" For many people, the answer is a combination of buyers, existing customers, and influencers such as analysts and the media. You need to have a topic that you are passionate about. If you aren't excited about the topic or if it feels painful to write about it, you're unlikely to sustain the effort, and if you do manage to keep going, the writing is likely to be forced.

Most first-time bloggers try to cover too much. It is better to start with a narrow subject and leave room to expand. Be authentic. People read blogs because they want to find an honest voice speaking passionately about a subject. You do not have to be harsh or controversial if that is not your style. If you are interesting and provide valuable information, your readership will grow.

Lawrence McGlynn is president of McGlynn, Clinton & Hall Insurance Agencies and maintains the *Massachusetts Family Insurance Blog*. His posts are inspired by his customers' questions. Several weeks prior to the big game, he wrote "Super Bowl, Super Party, Super Liability," in which he talked about the legal issues surrounding hosting a party. "What could go wrong?" he wrote. "I can quickly think of at least three incidents that could happen both on and off your premises. Also, keep in mind that friends can sue friends." Posts like these generate high search engine rankings and brand McGlynn as an expert.

"Most of my posts come from listening to people's questions," he says. "Whether it is in our office or in their office, my clients give me the best ideas." For many people, insurance is an unfamiliar and intimidating topic. When the time comes to learn about auto, home, or life insurance, they don't know where to turn. McGlynn realizes this and creates posts to help. "People use the Internet to search for answers to their insurance questions," McGlynn says. "If I can provide those answers, then people will see me as an expert, and it may lead to them contacting me for both advice and service."

Another blog that delivers interesting information rather than a sales pitch is published by GrabCAD, a community where mechanical engineers share and find project designs and ideas. The multimedia blog features projects that members of the GrabCAD community are working on. One video post, "Volocopter Reinvents Flight," shows how a group of German engineers created a battery-operated machine that lifts off with help from 16 electric-powered rotors. The mechanical engineers in the GrabCAD community love posts like this, and they share the content on their networks.

It has been estimated that there are more than 100 million blogs and that some 100,000 new blogs are created every day, which means that, on average, a new blog is created every second of every day. That's a heck of a lot of competition, and you might ask yourself if it is worth the effort. But remember back to the *long-tail* theory we discussed in Chapter 2. If you write a niche blog (e.g., a blog about Massachusetts family insurance), then you're not competing with 100 million other blogs. You're writing in a space where there are few (if any) other blogs, and you will no doubt find readers who are interested in what you're saying. If you have a small niche, you may interest only a few hundred readers. But you'll reach the *right* readers—those people who are interested in what you and your organization have to say.

Blogging Ethics and Employee Blogging Guidelines

Some organizations such as IBM and the U.S. Air Force have created formal guidelines for employee bloggers and published them online for anyone to access. Your organization should decide for itself whether to create such guidelines, and the decision should be determined based on input from marketing, human resources (HR), and other departments. I think it is much better for an organization to establish a consistent policy about all communications (including verbal communication, email, participation in chat rooms, and the like) rather than focus on just blogs and social media. I feel strongly that a company can and should set specific policies against sexual harassment, disparaging the competition, and revealing company secrets, but there's no reason to have different policies for different media.

Once the policy is set, employees should be permitted to blog away as long as they follow it. No matter what decisions you make about who should blog and what the rules are, it is always better for the blogger not to pass individual posts through a PR department or legal team. However, if your blog posts *must* be reviewed by others in your organization before going live, then have your colleagues focus only on the content, not your actual words. Do not let others in your organization turn your authentic and passionate writing into another form of marketing gobbledygook.

Let's talk about ethics for a moment. All sorts of unethical practices go on in the blogosphere, and you must be certain to hold yourself and your organization accountable for your actions as a blogger. Some organizations have gotten caught using unethical practices on their blogs and have done great harm to their corporate reputations. I've included some of the issues you need to pay attention to, as well as an example of each unethical practice. This is not intended to be a comprehensive list, but rather a starting point for you to think about ethics.

- **Transparency**: You should never pretend to be someone you are not. For example, don't use another name to submit a comment on any blog (your own or somebody else's), and don't create a blog that talks about your company without disclosing that someone from your company is behind it.
- **Privacy**: Unless you've been given permission, don't blog about something that was disclosed to you. For example, don't post material from an email someone sent you unless you have permission.
- **Disclosure**: It is important to disclose anything that people might consider a conflict of interest in a blog post. For example, if I write in my blog about a product from a company that is one of my masterclass

clients or one that I am on the advisory board of, I put a sentence at the end disclosing my relationship with the company.

- **Truthfulness:** Don't lie. For example, never make up a customer story just because it makes good blog content.
- **Credit:** You should give credit to bloggers (and other sources) whose material you have used in your blog. For example, don't read a great post on someone else's blog, take the idea, change a few words, and publish it as your own. Besides being good ethical practice, links to other bloggers whose ideas you have used help to introduce them to your blog, and they may link to you.

Again, this is not a complete list. The Word of Mouth Marketing Association has created an ethics code. I recommend that you read it and follow the guidelines. But you should also follow your gut. If a post feels funny to you for some reason or makes you uncomfortable, it may be unethical. What would your mother say about that post? If she would tell you it is wrong, it probably is, so don't send it. Do the right thing.

Blogging Basics: What You Need to Know to Get Started

Unlike websites, which require design and HTML skills to produce, blogs are quick and easy to set up using off-the-shelf software with easy-to-use features. With just a little basic know-how, you can quickly and easily establish and promote your blog. Here are some specific tips to keep in mind:

- Before you begin, think carefully about the name of your blog, which will be indexed by the search engines. It is very difficult to go back and change this information once you have established it.
- Easy-to-use blogging software is available from TypePad, WordPress, Squarespace, and others. Some of the services are free, and others require a small subscription fee. Research the services, and choose wisely based on your needs, because it is difficult to switch to a different service without losing all the content you have already created. And once your blog has been indexed by search engines, and people have subscribed to your RSS feed or bookmarked your URL, a change to different software is really tough.

- You will need to choose a URL for your blog. The blogging services all offer customizable URLs (such as yourblog.typepad.com). You can also map your blog to your company's domain (www.yourcompany .com/yourblog) or to a custom domain (www.yourblog.com). I recommend that you choose a custom domain because then you can take your blog with you from one blogging platform to another.
- Blogging software makes it easy to choose color, design, and font and to create a simple text-based masthead. You might consider using a custom graphical image as your masthead—these are easy to design and will make your blog more attractive to readers.
- As you begin your blog, tweak your design and tentatively try a few posts. I recommend you use password protection for the first few weeks or so. That way you can share your blog with a few friends and colleagues first and make changes before opening it up to the world.
- The look and feel of the blog could be complementary to your corporate design guidelines, but it should not be identical. For many blogs, it is better to be a bit different from the corporate look to signal to readers that the blog is an independent voice, not corporate-speak.
- Blogging software usually allows you to turn on a comments feature so your visitors can respond to your posts. There are several options for you to consider. Some people prefer their blogs to have no comments from readers at all, and that might be the right choice for you. However, one of the most exciting things about blogging is when your readers comment on what you've written.

Depending on your blogging software, you may opt for open comments (where people can write comments that are not subject to your approval) or for a system where you need to approve each comment before it appears on your blog. Many bloggers use the approval feature to watch for inappropriate comments. But I encourage you to allow comments from people who disagree with you—debate is one of the best indications of a well-read blog.

Unfortunately, the blogosphere is plagued by the problem of comment spam, so to prevent automated comment robots from vandalizing your blog, some comment systems require people to answer a simple question called a *captcha* before their comments go live. (I use this approach, and it works very well.) This will not eliminate comment spam but will greatly reduce it because it requires a human to enter the comment. You will want to review every comment as it comes in and either comment back to your readers or manually delete any obvious comment spam right away.

- Pay close attention to the categories you choose for your blog. Most blogging software platforms include an easy-to-use category feature. Besides helping readers find your posts, search engines use this information to index your content.
- Add social networking sharing tools such as a Facebook "Like" button, LinkedIn "Share" button, Pinterest "Pin it" button, and a Twitter "Tweet this" button to each post. Most blog software packages have these tools as a simple application that makes them easy to implement.
- Rich Site Summary (RSS, often called really simple syndication) is a standard delivery format for many of your readers. Make certain that your new blog has RSS capability. Most blogging software services have RSS feeds as a standard feature.
- Provide an "About" page that includes your photo, biography, affiliations, and information about your blog. Often when people visit a blog for the first time, they want to know about the blogger, so it is important to provide background.
- Encourage people to contact you, make it easy for them to reach you online, and be sure to follow up personally on your fan mail. You'll get a bunch of inquiries, questions, praise, and an occasional detractor if you make it easy for people to contact you. Because of the huge problem with spam, many people don't want to publish email addresses. But the biggest problem is with automated robots that harvest email addresses, so to thwart them, write your email address so humans can read it but the machines cannot. On websites, for example, I list my email address as "david (at) DavidMeermanScott (dot) com."
- Don't write excessively about your company and its products and services. You must resist this urge to blog about what your company offers. Instead, blog about a subject of interest to the people you are trying to reach. What problems do your buyers have that you can write about? How can you create content that informs and educates and entertains?
- Involve other blogs and bloggers by becoming a true participant in the online community. Link to and leave comments on other blogs. Let someone else's post serve as the starting point for a conversation that you continue on your own blog. You'll generate much more interest in what you're doing if you are inclusive.

Bling Out Your Blog

Before my daughter started eighth grade, she spent the entire week blinging out her school binder. All the cool girls do it, transforming standard plastic three-ring binders with photos, stickers, song lyrics, and other bits on the outside. She even had a spot for a quote of the day that she updated each morning. Inside, the binder had page dividers she customized and pocket folders with pens and protractors and whatnot.

I got to thinking that the same is true of good blogs. A blinged out blog shows the blogger's personality. I've blinged out my own blog with lots of cool stuff. On the top is a masthead that I had a friend who is a designer create. In HubSpot (which I use for my blog), you just have someone design an image that is the right number of pixels wide and high and drop it in—the software automatically adds other design elements (such as a border) and replaces the rather plain-looking text masthead with the new design. Other blog software tools also support graphical mastheads, although the specific requirements and implementation methods will be different.

On the right column of my blog, I have my photo and a short bio as well as links to pages on my site and to my other web content. I have easy sign-up links for people who want to view my blog as an RSS subscription, and an email subscription option so people can get each of my blog posts sent to their email inboxes.

One of the downsides of a blog is that the reverse-chronological aspect (most recent post at the top) means that much of your best stuff, which may have been written last month or last year, is hidden away. To offer an alternative navigation, you can also include easy navigation links so people can quickly find the good stuff. For example, you might include "The Best of" with links to a handful of your most popular posts, a scrolling list of recent comments on the blog, and navigation by category of post.

Blinging out your blog is easy. If you devote a few hours to it, you can make a very cool-looking blog that even my daughter would approve of. Sure, the standard templates offered by the blog software providers are great to get started, but once you are fully committed to blogging, it is important to make your blog personality shine through with links, images, a masthead, photos, and other add-ons.

Building an Audience for Your New Blog

When you put up your first few blog posts, you are likely to hear a deafening silence. You'll be waiting for comments, but none will come. You'll check your site statistics and be disappointed by the tiny number of visitors. Don't get discouraged—that's normal! It takes time to build an audience for your blog. When you're just getting started, make sure people know it is there and can find it. Create links to your blog from your homepage, product pages, or online media room. Mention your blog in your email or offline newsletters, and create links to your blog as part of your email signature and those of other people in your organization. Tweet your posts and include links on your social networks.

The good news is that blogs that are regularly updated generate high search engine rankings because the algorithms that are used by Google and the other search engines reward sites (and blogs) that update frequently. It is likely that you will get significant search engine traffic once you've been consistently blogging for a while. I typically post one or two times a week to my blog, and most days my blog generates several hundred visitors via search engines, which is good because these are people who do not know me (yet). To ensure that your new blog is found by your buyers as they search for what you have to offer, be certain to post on topics of interest and to use the important phrases that people are searching on. (See Chapter 10 if you want to review how to identify the words and phrases that your buyers use.) Smart bloggers understand search engines and use their blogs to reach audiences directly.

Commenting on other people's blogs (and including a link to your blog) is a good way to build an audience. If you comment on blogs in the same market category as yours, you might be surprised at how quickly you will get visitors to your new blog. A curious thing about blogging etiquette is that bloggers who are competitive for business offline are usually very cooperative online, with links back and forth from their blogs. It's a bit like all the auto dealers in town congregating on the same street—proximity is good for everyone, so people work together.

Your customers, potential customers, investors, employees, and the media are all reading blogs, and there is no doubt that blogs are a terrific way for marketers to tell authentic stories to their buyers. But building an audience for a blog takes time. Most blog services provide tools for measuring traffic. Use these data to learn which posts are attracting the most attention. You can also learn what sites people are coming from when they visit your blog and what search terms they used to find you. Use this information to continually improve your blog. Once again, think like a publisher.

Tag, and Your Buyer Is It

With the total number of existing blogs now in the hundreds of millions and with the availability of niche blogs on virtually any topic, it is easy to get lost in the blogosphere. The simple truth is that it isn't always easy for people to find a blog post on their subjects of interest. Recently, a colleague of mine needed new tires for his car. Instead of just heading to the local retailer to be at the mercy of a salesperson or poking around tire manufacturer websites, he went to one of the blog search engines to see what people were writing about tires. He entered the keyword *tires*, and sure enough, within a few clicks he reached several blogs that had useful information about purchasing tires. But he also faced a heck of a lot of useless noise with the word *tires* in the results—things like analysis of tires used in a recent NASCAR race, rants about the garbage on the sides of freeways (which includes discarded tires), and even posts about "spare tires" on middle-aged men.

It is precisely this problem—the false hits in word and phrase searches, not middle-aged men's lack of exercise—that led to tagging features in blog software that let bloggers categorize what their posts are about. To use this feature, a blogger simply creates a set of metatags for each blog post. This aids how the search engines find and index your content.

From the blogger's perspective, the benefits of adding tags to create increased precision about the post's content, whereby each post reaches more people, are worth the extra effort. For example, I assign each post that I write to multiple appropriate categories, such as marketing, public relations, and advertising. New visitors reach my blog every day as a result of searching on the tags that I had added to blog posts.

Cities That Blog

While many U.S. cities and towns have dabbled in social media, typically setting up a basic Facebook, YouTube, or Twitter presence, most local government employees and elected officials are averse to blogging. They assume that it's too risky, that it could create legal liability or become a source of primarily negative comments. Contrary to the vast majority of cities, College Station, Texas, has had a blog for years. Jay G. Socol, director of public communications for the City of College Station, maintains the blog, which has been working out very well for his community. According to a message on the homepage, the purpose of the blog is "to be a two-way conversation between College Station residents and their government officials. We hope it allows us to get to know one another a little better in the process, while having genuine and transparent exchanges of ideas."

Socol sometimes tackles difficult topics through the blog. For example, he wrote about how the shooting death of a city law enforcement officer (which generated worldwide attention) brought the community closer together. But he also shows the lighter side of the city, with posts like "Treasure found in a drainage ditch." This story told how city maintenance crews through the years have found objects of value in muddy trenches: jewelry, wallets, purses, car keys, credit cards, and even wads of cash.

"I firmly believe strong, relevant content has helped shift community sentiment toward College Station," Socol says. "It's reduced rumors running rampant and mitigated media-grabbing false stories and angles from anonymous chat forums. Blogging also has driven positive news content and given more texture to some of our biggest public announcements. We don't receive a ton of comments (because we require real names to be used), but the results tell me it's working in the ways we need it to. Sentiment and trust have increased, and those are the main wins for us."

Here's another example of a city using blog content to educate and inform (it also proves that cops can have a sense of humor): On Election Day, 2012, the people of Washington State passed Initiative 502, making it legal for adults over 21 years old to possess up to an ounce of marijuana for personal use (or 16 ounces of solid marijuana-infused product, like cookies, or 72 ounces of infused liquid, like oil). So, Washington residents wondered, what does that actually mean for me? To answer that question, the Seattle Police published on their *SPD Blotter* blog: "Marijwhatnow? A Guide to Legal Marijuana Use in Seattle." The post provides a practical guide for what the Seattle Police Department believes Initiative 502 means.

The "Marijwhatnow?" post uses a Q&A format. Here's one example: "Q: Can I legally carry around an ounce of marijuana? A: According to the recently passed initiative, beginning December 6th, adults over the age of 21 will be able to carry up to an ounce of marijuana for personal use. Please note that the initiative says it 'is unlawful to open a package containing marijuana . . . in view of the general public,' so there's that. Also, you probably shouldn't bring pot with you to the federal courthouse (or any other federal property)."

Many of the Q&A exchanges are quite funny: "Q: What happens if I get pulled over and I'm sober, but an officer or his K9 buddy smells the ounce of Super Skunk I've got in my trunk? A: Under state law, officers have to develop probable cause to search a closed or locked container. Each case stands on its own, but the smell of pot alone will not be reason to search a vehicle. If officers have information that you're trafficking, producing, or delivering marijuana in violation of state law, they can get a warrant to search your vehicle."

I love the fact that the blog provides valuable information about the new law, but in an approachable way.

The *SPD Blotter* began in 2008 and is maintained by the staff of the Seattle Police Department's Public Affairs Office. The "Marijwhatnow?" post was written by Jonah Spangenthal-Lee, a journalist who, as he says in his bio, covered "the always-exciting cops and crime beat at Seattlecrime.com, PubliCola, KIRO Television, and *The Stranger*." Spangenthal-Lee joined the Seattle Police Department in March 2012 to tell those same stories on the department's *SPD Blotter* blog and publish real-time information on breaking news through the SPD's @SeattlePD Twitter feed.

If College Station, Texas, and the Seattle Police Department can blog, so can you.

Blogging outside North America

People often ask me about blogging in other countries. They want to know if the marketing approaches I outline work elsewhere. Specifically, many people ask if blogs are a good way to do marketing and PR in Europe and Asia. While I cannot comment on every single country, I can say that blogging is a global phenomenon in countries with widespread web access and that many bloggers from other countries are active in the global blogging community. I've received links to my blog from bloggers in something like 50 different countries. It's so cool when a comment or a link comes into my blog from someone in, say, Bulgaria or Finland or Thailand.

There is other clear evidence that blogging is alive and well outside of North America. My wife, Yukari Watanabe Scott, a commentator on the

Japanese book business, maintains a blog to reach her readers in Japan. This technique is especially important because her readers there are halfway around the world from where we live, near Boston.

For a true international blogging success story, consider the example of Linas Simonis, a marketing consultant from Lithuania who established one of the first business blogs in that country. The reaction from the Lithuanian business community was almost immediate. "People didn't know what RSS was in Lithuania at that time, so I created an email subscription to my blog," Simonis says. "By the end of the first year, I had 400 subscribers, and you must remember that less than three and a half million people live in Lithuania, so the equivalent would be something like 40,000 subscribers in the United States."

But what's really remarkable about Simonis's story is the new business that he generated via his blog. "Three months after I started the blog, my company stopped needing to make cold calls to solicit new business," he says. "The blog and the company website generated so many requests that we didn't need to actively seek new clients—they come to us. Soon after I started blogging, I was even hired by conference organizers to deliver speeches and seminars, and I had calls from universities to speak to students." Simonis now consults for corporate clients in Lithuania that wish to establish blogs, and he publishes an English-language blog as a forum to write about positioning strategy.

What Are You Waiting For?

Everybody I've spoken with about starting a blog has said the same thing (but in slightly different ways). They were all a bit uncomfortable when they started a blog. They felt a little dorky because they didn't know all the unwritten rules. They were even a little scared to push the button on that first post. We've all been there.

To get comfortable before you take the plunge, remember back to Chapter 5: You should follow a bunch of blogs in your industry first. What things do you like about those blogs? What's annoying? What would you do differently? Then, before you jump into the water by creating your own blog, you can stick your toe in by leaving comments on other people's blogs. Test out your blog voice. Finally, when it feels right, start your own blog. And when you do get going, please send me your URL so I can check it out.

16

An Image Is Worth a Thousand Words

In the past several years, images have become increasingly popular marketing and public relations assets. In particular, we'll look at storytelling through photographs, image-sharing applications (Instagram and Pinterest in particular), and delivering complex data clearly with infographics. As with other forms of content, success in this area comes from a focus on your buyers and creating the images that will be valuable to them as they consider doing business with your organization.

Photographs as Compelling Content Marketing

With all the talk about image-sharing *services* like Pinterest and Instagram, sometimes a basic premise of communication practice is lost. Images are important in all your marketing content. Don't get so excited about the latest tool that you forget about the value of the image itself.

> An original photo is great as a way to communicate with your buyers.

For example, consider Zürsun Idaho Heirloom Beans. The company was the first to offer authentic heirloom beans and unusual legumes to customers worldwide via specialty stores. Dozens of bean, lentil, and pea varieties are available, with colorful names like Dapple Grey, Scarlet Runner, White Emergo, and Tongues of Fire. "The glorious true-to-size pictures, carefully taken in natural light, have done more to promote the beans than any words possibly could," says Allison Boomer, the founder of Eco-Conscious Food Marketing. Boomer worked with Zürsun on website design and content.

It seems so simple, doesn't it? Photos help to tell a story, particularly for a product that comes in unusual shapes and colors. Yet so many marketers rely on boring stock photos that make their organization appear lazy and uncaring and that hide the uniqueness of their products.

You can read about the beans on the site: "Zürsun heirloom beans are grown on small-scale farms in the Snake River Canyon region of south central Idaho known as the Magic Valley Growing Area. The area's arid climate, rich, well-drained loamy soil, moderate temperatures and stable moisture level—internationally recognized as having ideal environmental conditions for bean growing—produce pure, distinctly flavorful beans, superior to common store-bought beans." Sounds yummy, right? Sure, the text Boomer wrote is compelling. But the beautiful photos seal the deal and get buyers to place an order.

"I was careful about writing the content," she says. "However, it turns out the photos resonated so much more with customers than the text. I didn't anticipate this going into designing the site, so I was lucky. Zürsun has reached an awesome tipping point, for which I give much credit to the website and those glorious bean photos. Sales in the last year have doubled. Responding to the many inbound queries through the website has become a daily task for me."

As you're creating the content for your site and blog, learn from the success of Zürsun Idaho Heirloom Beans: Shoot original photographs to tell your story to your buyers. Even organizations without photogenic product offerings can use images. As we will see next, even sellers of commodities and intangible services can still get into the photo game with Instagram and other new photo networking services.

Images of Real People Work Better Than Inane Stock Photos

Several years ago, I helped my mother evaluate senior living centers. My father was suffering from Alzheimer's, so we needed a place that also had a memory care facility onsite.

As I checked out one website after another, I was disheartened that so many used stock photos to depict residents and staff. Ugh. I just don't feel good about a place that doesn't focus on reality. A bunch of photos of generic happy seniors playing cards and riding bikes doesn't inspire me to entrust my parents to this organization.

If you've heard me speak live, you might have seen my riff on stock photography, a subject I wrote about in a blog post titled "Who the Hell ARE These People?" This is one of my most popular posts, so the subject obviously strikes a nerve with other marketers and entrepreneurs as well.

Using models from a stock photography catalog in your content is insulting to your customers and to your employees. It doesn't reflect the reality of your organization. At one facility I checked out, The Greens at Cannondale, the image for spa treatments and salon services was just outrageous! It showed a middle-aged woman with her hair wrapped in a towel. She's gazing knowingly against a Photoshop-perfect blue sky, her arms folded atop a folksy wooden fence. I've been to several senior living facilities in the past several years and this looks like no place I've ever seen. If this woman existed, she'd be living on a ranch outside Santa Fe, not in a seniors community in Wilton, Connecticut. There's no way spa treatments at The Greens at Cannondale look anything like this.

This generic approach doesn't fly at Omaha, Nebraska–based Heritage Communities, a company that runs 14 senior living facilities. There were images and videos of actual residents throughout the site. Since it's so unusual to take this approach, the homepage even points out the fact: "All photographs proudly feature residents of Heritage Communities."

"We hired David Radler, an amazing photographer, to shoot at a handful of our buildings," says Lacy Jungman, director of sales and marketing at Heritage Communities. "Some were staged and some were candid shots. They are of the highest caliber, taken with dignity to show each resident's best attributes—but also to show their humanity. Additionally, since we had such great photos, we are able to share them with family members."

I love the photos. Many tell fun stories of Heritage Communities. There is one I particularly like, showing six residents around a pool table. They're wearing realistic clothes and standing with realistic postures, and you can see out a real window to some trees and another building. There's no set and no props and no models. It's just six men playing pool, guys I'd like to spend some time with. I'm imagining some hysterical conversations as they go at it in the afternoon.

Nate Underwood, chief financial officer of Heritage Communities, shared that the company is doing great. Obviously, website photo policies are a tiny part of the work of this company, but this practice indicates to me that the company cares, goes a little further than the rest, and wants to make a difference. I'm not surprised that attitude has been rewarded with strong financials.

One of the most common excuses I get from marketers is they have trouble getting photo releases from people. But this habit can become a part of an organization's culture.

"Whenever a resident moves in our communities, we ask them to sign a photo release," Lacy Jungman says. "Most sign, but some have declined. After we shot the photos, we made sure each resident had a photo release signed, and those who didn't, we either secured a release at the time or didn't use the photo. We had key associates at each building guiding us to residents who were willing to participate in the photo shoot and also had signed a photo release."

Sometimes people ask me about what to do when an employee no longer works for the company, or after someone is no longer a customer. Do you still use the photo? Tough question, but I generally answer "yes." For Heritage Communities, there's an emotional issue of what to do with photos of a resident who has passed away.

"Some families prefer we do not use an image of their loved one after they pass, because the pain and grief of their loss are still raw," Jungman says. "Seeing that person posted on a website or billboard may stir up too much emotion. Others look at these images as yet another legacy their loved one is leaving, another imprint on the world. Adult children have expressed how honored they are to have their mom or dad remembered in this light—smiling, happy, full of life. When one of our residents passed away, we had his photo framed and matted. We were able to give this gift of love to the family, who were beyond grateful to have such a wonderful reminder of his good days."

Jungman adds, "The stories, feelings, and emotions of our residents are what we wanted to capture. Life isn't flawless like stock photography might want us to believe. Transparency is a big deal to us, and this was an excellent opportunity to showcase what actual people living in our communities are really like."

Photos are important, and people recognize a stock photo instantly. For any product or service, but especially a people-focused one like healthcare, please use real people.

How to Market an Expensive Product with Original Photographs

When Boston-based creative director Doug Eymer was ready to sell his home, he turned to photo-sharing services to get images of the home out to prospective buyers. "We had a unique house in a great spot on the water, and we knew that water is prime real estate," Eymer says. "We also had an incredible view. We felt like that added a significant amount to the price of our house, although it's not something you can really measure. So I started documenting sunrise every morning, and putting the photos together into a collection. What's really cool is how the marsh grasses changed colors and the leaves in the background changed colors. It was an ever-changing view."

Eymer snapped the photo each morning and shared the series *Sunrises at 31 Bow Street* (well over 100 photos) on a wide variety of social networks and photo-sharing sites, including Instagram, Facebook, Twitter, Tumblr, Pinterest, 500px, and Flickr. "On 500px I had sets with all of my photographs, including a set for my sunrise photographs. 500px is great for followers; as soon as you post, you start getting feedback right away. Usually it's like one or two words: 'Love it,' 'Great.' And 500px also gives you a lot of information about the activity on your photos. You can see what people are responding to."

When Eymer listed his home with a Realtor, the photo series became a valuable asset, which the Realtor linked to. "The Realtor that we used was pretty web-savvy," Eymer says. "He was posting information on his blog about the photos, and he mentioned them on Facebook and Pinterest."

Documenting the view from his home as the seasons changed was a subtle but very effective form of marketing. "It brought a lot of attention to our house, especially from people in town, and that's built positive word of mouth," Eymer says. "There were a few people who responded every morning, and I think they looked forward to seeing what photograph I was going to post. When I first started, we had a red canoe that was in the yard, and I always made the red canoe part of the photograph. One day we had some high water, and we moved the canoe so it wouldn't float away. People said, 'What happened to the canoe? Where did it go?' Then someone made the leap of, 'It looks like summer's over. The canoe has been put away.' That was pretty interesting. It was just one little thing, people letting me know that they were actually watching."

Eymer also brought his photo series into the offline world to market his home when buyers were viewing it. In various rooms, he had laptop computers and iPads running a continuous slide show of his photos of the ever-changing view toward the water from 31 Bow Street. "As buyers walked through the house, especially the rooms which overlook the view, we showed how it changed over time. There's summer, the beautiful changing leaves, and photos of wintertime with ice. It gives people another window on what's outside, and gives them an idea of what is there to look at."

Eymer successfully sold his house and credits the photo series he created as an important aspect of his marketing.

Original photos, shared on Instagram and other photo-sharing social networking services, are a powerful way to showcase your offerings. And when you take your photos and integrate them into your online and offline marketing, you set yourself apart from the pack.

Why I Love Instagram

It's rare that I get particularly excited about a new social network, but that's what happened to me when I first joined Instagram. Instagram is a photo-sharing application for iPhone and Android that makes it easy and fun to manipulate a photo; a variety of filters turn a snapshot into instant art. Then, with a few clicks, you can share your photo and caption to your Instagram followers and on other networks. While there are other photo-creation and photo-sharing applications, Instagram has quickly become the most popular, with more than one billion people who use it every month.

I love that Instagram makes it so easy to create and share content. One of the first things people push back on in my conversations with marketers and entrepreneurs is how much time it takes to create content and publish it on the web. Many say they just can't manage to create daily content. But Instagram is so easy! It just takes a minute or two to shoot a photo, manipulate it with the filters, and share it with your network. Other critics tell me they're lousy writers and are therefore hopeless on social sites. But with Instagram, you do almost no writing, so even word-challenged people can create awesome content.

I've taken hundreds of photos as I've traveled the world, and my several thousand Instagram followers can see what I've been up to in just a few seconds. If I want, I can also share the Instagram photo on other social networks like Facebook and Twitter. I love it.

While Instagram started as a photo sharing social network, the service now offers video sharing as well as Instagram stories, a way to curate your life to share with your friends.

Many entrepreneurs use Instagram to capture ideas related to their business. Rachel Brathen, a Swedish native living in Aruba, is an internationally respected yoga instructor. She uses her Instagram feed (@yoga_girl) to share aspects of her life to her two million followers and help her potential clients learn more about her interests. Sure, there are some shots of her doing yoga poses, but she also shares images of beautiful scenery and of her friends.

There are tens of thousands of social networks out there. Many are copycats of existing networks or merely add incremental feature changes. These networks don't succeed. Truly original ideas for social networks are rare—I can count on one hand the number that made me say "wow." YouTube makes video sharing easy. Twitter is for sharing short messages. Facebook is for connecting with friends; and Instagram, for beautiful photos. Instagram is cool because it combines content sharing (photos) with artistic expression. It's addictive, at least for me. When I have a few minutes of downtime, I like to pull out my iPhone and scroll through the photos of the people I follow on Instagram. It's like a stroll through an art gallery.

Okay, so Instagram is a fun way to share photos with your social network. But how can you use it to market your product or service?

Marketing Your Product with Photos on Instagram

Nantucket Island is my favorite surfing spot. When I'm there, I'll frequently take a lesson at Gary Kohner's Nantucket Island Surf School. Kohner grew up on Nantucket and started surfing in 1984. He founded the school in the summer of 1999 to share his love of surfing and the ocean with others. Besides offering lessons for people of all ages and weeklong surf camps for kids, Kohner also rents surfboards, stand-up paddleboards, and wetsuits. He is an avid photographer and shares photos almost daily on his @nantucketsurfing Instagram feed.

Kohner uses simple equipment that anybody can master: a GoPro in the water and an iPhone on land. "I'm a little OCD about certain things I enjoy," Kohner says. "I enjoy taking the pictures. I enjoy playing with the editing tools on Instagram and then putting it out there. It doesn't feel like it's a work thing. It's something I do for fun. I try to keep it fresh and keep it interesting so I figure it gives people something to look at."

Instagram is a great social network to share about any product or service that has a visual component or customers who use the product in interesting ways. It also allows those who don't feel as comfortable creating written content to get their ideas out there.

Kohner shoots a bunch of photos from the water and then looks to find the best ones to post. "If I'm using the GoPro while surfing, I usually have it on an automatic setting. I'll come in sometimes with over 1,000 pictures. I go through them quickly and weed out the ones that are junk, because a lot of those pictures are just not good and you can tell right away," he says. "I will pick out the top 50 or so that look the best, and out of those 50, I usually pick the top three or four that I really like. I'll save them and use them for Instagram. That's why I'm able to post stuff daily. If I go out surfing one day and take a bunch of shots, I can save those up and post them over the next week."

Kohner sometimes posts epic shots of a really good surfer on an awesome wave, but he also posts beginners standing up for the very first time during a lesson. "It's a nice moment to capture," Kohner says. "I wish I had a shot of my first ride when I was a kid. [My account is] an Instagram for the surf school, so it makes sense not just to have surfers inside a tube [a cresting and breaking wave that is challenging to surf], but have it more accessible to everybody."

When Kohner posts shots of people surfing, they often repost on their own Instagram accounts, which extends his reach. "I have a lot of kids who taken lessons with me follow me on Instagram," Kohner says. "I'll ask the parents, especially if they're younger kids, 'Hey, I'm going to take some pictures; if I get a good one, is it cool if I put it on my Instagram?' And the parents almost always agree. I tag the surfer and the kids love it. They say: 'Oh, I'm on Gary's Instagram! I'm on the surf school Instagram! I'm famous!' And they share on their Instagram with their friends. So much of my business here in Nantucket is word of mouth; I'm sure that my Instagram is helping."

I know for a fact Kohner's Instagram is helping market his business. When people who know I love surfing ask how to get started, I just point them to Kohner's wonderful photos. That often leads to them signing up for lessons.

Instagram allows users to comment on each other's photos. Many people pay attention to those who tag them in these comments. If you use Instagram for your business, you should pay attention, too. For example, when I shared a photo of me wearing my Nantucket Surfing T-shirt and hat on Hawaii's North Shore, I included this caption (tagging Kohner's Instagram ID): "Showing my @nantucketsurfing colors at Sunset beach prior to watching the Vans Triple Crown." Kohner responded to me: "I'll be there tomorrow! How long are you going to be around the North Shore?" And I replied: "Hey Gary. I just left. . . . Have fun! It was my first time and loved it." A friendly approach like Gary's is a great way to acknowledge or endorse customers who take the time to talk about you and your product or service.

Kohner's Instagram helps keep his business top of mind with the typical family that visits Nantucket for a few weeks each summer. When the kids follow Kohner's photos all year long and Mom and Dad ask the kids what they want to do while on Nantucket Island, the first thing they're going to say is that they want to go back and take some surfing lessons. "A lot of people are away doing their thing in the winter," Kohner says. "They don't surf year-round, so I remind them of that memory of surfing, the time they spent in Nantucket. If they're coming back, it's going to be 'Let's go surfing!'"

Sharing with Pinterest

Many organizations create original photographs, like Doug Eymer did to market his home. And like Eymer, many share those photos on Pinterest, a pinboard-style social network. Think of Pinterest as the virtual equivalent of a bulletin board where you can "pin" items of interest to come back to later. The marketing aspect is that other people can see your "boards" to follow what you find interesting. In addition, if you create interesting visual content, people will pin it (from your website) or repin it (from Pinterest), driving traffic to your site. Pinterest boasts nearly 300 million users as of this writing and is growing very quickly.

Whole Foods Market, which started with a small store in Austin, Texas, in 1980, is now the world's leader in natural and organic foods. There are more than 300 Whole Foods stores in North America and the United Kingdom. The company uses Pinterest to showcase a wide variety of foods in interesting categories. Like Eymer, Whole Foods uses original photography to display its product offerings. As I write this, Whole Foods has some 450,000 followers and more than 5,000 pins on 44 boards, which include *Who Wants Dinner?!* (144 pins), *Eat Your Veggies* (217 pins), and *Cheese Is the Bee's Knees* (56 pins).

Pinterest is also frequently used to share things you like that aren't your products or services but that get people interacting socially with you. For example, one Whole Foods board showcases photographs of designer kitchens. Whole Foods isn't in the kitchen business, but the food the company sells is, of course, to be prepared in home kitchens. Many of the kitchen photos have hundreds of repins, and many have multiple comments. One commenter wrote, "We live in Maryland now, however, plan to move to Florida by the New Year. I am getting some great ideas for our new/used home."

While creating and sharing content on your own board is a great way to showcase your organization, Pinterest is also extremely valuable as a source for inbound links to your web content, including your blog posts, videos, and images. Many people use Pinterest as a sort of virtual scrapbook, a way to catalog information that is important to them. Others use it as a reminder tool. These people might pin your stuff, which others will then be able to see.

For example, if I'm planning a vacation to a beach resort, I might catalog the locations I'm considering by making a board. It's simple to save the images or videos of the resorts as pins, which point to the web page or blog post where I found the image or video. It takes just seconds. Then I can share my "Dream Holiday" board with family members or friends, and they can help me decide where to stay. Then, after my holiday, I can make another board cataloging the places I visited, restaurants I ate at, and activities I enjoyed. These pins then become recommendations for others.

As I said, it's the social sharing of boards that creates the opportunity for marketing, because others can see my boards, too. Maybe friends or colleagues want to take a similar holiday. All I need to do is point them to my pinboard. Imagine how great that is for the owners of the restaurant I loved—people are sharing my content, introducing that restaurant to an audience of new customers.

To succeed with Pinterest, you need to—you guessed it—publish great content for people to pin. And that content needs to be visual. That means you need to have photographs, videos, and infographics on your blog and site. For example, that restaurant I enjoyed on holiday would be smart to have its current menu available as an image ready to be pinned. The restaurant might also have photos of each dish and the labels of the wines it serves. Interior photos of the tables and exterior shots of the building might make sense, too, particularly if the restaurant has unique design elements. The availability of these images makes it easy for happy diners to pin what they liked.

Whatever your business, you should have content available that people are eager to share. To make it really easy for them to pin your content, you should have a "Pin it" button on each piece of online content. Just like the Facebook "Like" button and the Twitter "Tweet" button, the Pinterest "Pin it" button helps get your content to others via their boards. I have a "Pin it" button at the bottom of each of my blog posts and get many pins of my posts. One recent post was pinned nearly 100 times. Thus, there are 100 new places on the web pointing to that post, and the followers of those 100 people's boards could choose to click through to read it. How great is that?! Pinterest is now an important source of many inbound links for my blog and for the content of all kinds of organizations. It's an exciting way to get your content seen.

The Power of SlideShare for Showcasing Your Ideas

SlideShare has quickly become a valuable sharing platform and can be more powerful than YouTube or a blog if used well. However, most companies don't know about SlideShare as a tool of social sharing. And many that do simply use the platform as a way to pitch products.

Essentially, SlideShare is a place to post slide presentations, those business standbys typically created in Microsoft PowerPoint or Apple Keynote.

Users can scroll through your slides on the SlideShare site and embed them into blogs and social network posts.

As I write this, my own SlideShare *The New Rules of Selling* has been viewed more than 300,000 times and shared more than 2,300 times on LinkedIn. It has also racked up more than 700 Facebook likes and been tweeted over 1,300 times. I'm stunned by this result! The first month of this presentation's life on SlideShare was the fastest sharing of any of my content in more than a decade of sharing free stuff on the web. The SlideShare has spread the word way beyond my own network to reach many people who have never been exposed to my ideas. Here are some lessons I learned. I hope they'll help you achieve similar results for your business.

LESSON 1: Focus on what you are giving away rather than the product you are selling. I created the SlideShare to showcase the ideas in my new book *The New Rules of Sales and Service: How to Use Agile Selling, Real-Time Customer Engagement, Big Data, Content, and Storytelling to Grow Your Business*. The SlideShare release was timed to coincide with the release of the book in September 2014.

Rather than talk about my new book on social networks and in media interviews, I chose instead to promote the SlideShare. This approach differed from the vast majority of book launches, where authors and publishers focus too much on selling books.

The same is true for any type of launch—most marketers focus too much on the product or service. When you focus on offering something of value for free, you generate interest in the products you sell.

LESSON 2: Put your best work out there. I chose not to hold anything back in the SlideShare. I shared my best ideas, for free. Sure, most people will choose to use the free content rather than purchase my book. But many will want to dig into more details and be eager to purchase it. Either way, I benefit from increased name recognition and influence with both groups.

LESSON 3: The social sharing aspect of SlideShare is powerful. There is a heavy graphical element in SlideShare content, and people love to share images. Thus, many will share your content for you, extending your network as a result.

Much of that sharing will take place on LinkedIn, which now owns SlideShare and has made sharing there very simple. This connection offers you a great opportunity to reach senior contacts on a premier business social network.

LESSON 4: People are looking for content to showcase. The fact that so many SlideShare views come from embeds on other sites reminds us that many people are looking for valuable content to share with their readers. If you create something that publishers like, they will help you to reach new audiences. Remember: Success on the web is all about helping other people solve their problems.

LESSON 5: You need a great design, as SlideShare is a visual medium. Its power comes from people's ability to process and understand your ideas quickly. I can create serviceable PowerPoint and Keynote slides, but I'm certainly not a designer. So I hired a designer to help me create my Slide-Share. It cost me some money and took more time, but many people commented on the design. I am sure it helped extend the content's reach.

LESSON 6: One idea per slide. There are 158 slides in my SlideShare. Everyone I spoke with prior to launch said that was way, way too many slides. Many SlideShare presentations consist of only 20 or so slides. But I'm not a fan of cramming a bunch of ideas onto each one. The number of slides doesn't seem to have been a problem.

SlideShare is a powerful tool that can be used to showcase your ideas, too. It doesn't matter if you have a consumer product or are a B2B brand; the easy-to-share visual medium of SlideShare gets your ideas into the marketplace and helps you grow your business.

Infographics

We finish this chapter on marketing using visual images with a discussion of information graphics (or simply "infographics"), which are graphical representations of complex data, information, or knowledge. Infographics take advantage of the human ability to visualize very complex data quickly. For most people, a visual representation is much easier to understand than columns of numbers or percentage representations, which is why I have used several in this book such as those on pages 177 and 178. For example, a map of a train or metropolitan transit system is an infographic, with train lines characteristically appearing as different colors. Frequently, the major stations where you can change trains figure prominently, and sometimes the maps note the neighborhoods each line serves. Can you imagine using the London Underground without the Tube map? It would be nearly impossible!

Increasingly, marketers are delivering complex data to buyers in the form of infographics. Typically offered as an image file or PDF on a website or blog, an infographic that delivers information in a useful way is highly valuable to buyers. It may also be shared via social networks, including Pinterest.

As examples, a few infographics I like are "The World's Biggest Real Estate Bubbles in 2018" and "The Raw Materials that Fuel the Green Revolution." This kind of content is best shown as a graphic rather than as text or numbers. Another, The Sequel Map published by BoxOfficeQuant, a blog about film statistics, graphically compares whether movie sequels are better or worse than their original, based on the consensus opinion of professional film critics from Rotten Tomatoes. In seconds, I can take in the relative sales ratios of movies and their sequels. The graphic is much easier to grasp than a table with star ratings.

To learn about the ins and outs of creating infographics for marketing purposes, I spoke with Marta Kagan, director of brand and buzz for marketing software company HubSpot. "We're extremely dependent on data here: love it, live by it," she says. "Using infographics allows us to cherry-pick the juiciest pieces to draw your eye to what's most relevant in a very appealing way."

Kagan continues: "The other way we use infographics a lot is to explain processes or to tell a story. We do that with our infographic 'The History of Marketing.' With the short attention span people have as a result of all the devices they use and how much information everyone juggles at any given time, an infographic grabs your eye, it gives you a headline, and it includes color in a way that a text blog post can't. You can bookmark it and look at it later, share it, or subscribe. Whenever there's a thirst for information about how to do something, why I need to do it, what's the adoption rate, those types of things, we have a lot of success compiling that as an infographic, because it's a visual and highly shareable format."

Creating a good infographic is more like doing a video than writing a text blog post, because so many elements need to come together. "You're telling a story in a very visual medium," Kagan says. "Buyers' brains are wired to work differently with images, and they notice different things than when they are just reading straight text. So we have to basically lead you down a path of visual cues through how we create the hierarchy of the information. This is different from reading; you read from left to right, from top to bottom."

HubSpot brings employees with varying skills into the process of creating infographics. "Part of our marketing team will focus on brainstorming ideas around what's the topic we want to cover," Kagan explains. "Another group may be the ones that actually pull together the data, either from our own sources or research from external sources. Another few folks will actually then map out the story like you would for a video.

"Is it vertical? Is it horizontal? What's the art direction around it? Is there photography? Is this handwritten? What's the style? What's the tone we're trying to strike? All those questions need to be answered like they would for a video or for another creative piece of media."

HubSpot has a team of in-house graphic designers who create the final artwork. If you don't have your own team, there are a number of options. You can make a simple infographic in PowerPoint. Kagan's team at HubSpot has developed a free resource to make it easy: "The Marketer's Simple Guide to Creating Infographics in PowerPoint." Another option is to use the templates offered by Piktochart, a drag-and-drop infographic editing tool. Or you can outsource the work. A company called Visually (visual.ly) has created a marketplace to tap the expertise of thousands of designers who can make an infographic for you.

Once the infographic is created, post it in appropriate places on your blog and website. You might consider sending links to your customers and the media that cover your industry. And don't forget to put a "Pin it" button on the download page!

Marketing with photos and images is a fast-growing way to tell a story for your buyers. In combination with text-based content and video, images are an important component of any organization's new marketing plan.

17 Video and Podcasting Made Easy

Creating audio and video content for marketing and PR purposes requires the same attention to appropriate topics as other techniques outlined in this book. It requires targeting individual buyer personas with thoughtful information that addresses some aspect of their lives or a problem they face. By doing so, you brand your organization as smart and worthy of doing business with. However, unlike text-based content such as blogs or news releases, audio and video might require a modest investment in additional hardware such as microphones and video cameras, as well as software, and, depending on the level of quality you want to achieve, may also necessitate time-consuming editing of the files. Although the actual procedures for podcasting and video are a bit more convoluted than, say, starting a blog, they are still not all that difficult.

Video and Your Buyers

Organizations that deliver products or services that naturally lend themselves to video have been among the first to actively use the medium to market and deliver information about their offerings. For example, many churches routinely shoot video of weekly services and offer it online for anyone to watch, drawing more people into the congregation. Many amateur and professional sports teams, musicians, and theater groups also use video as a marketing and PR tool.

Video follows both blogs and podcasting on the adoption curve at organizations that don't have a service that naturally lends itself to video.

Companies are certainly experimenting, typically by embedding video (hosted at YouTube or another video site) into their existing blogs and online media rooms. I'm also seeing video snippets of CEO speeches, customer interviews, and quick product demonstrations.

Business-Casual Video

In the United States, there has been a several decade trend toward so-called business-casual clothing in the workplace. My first job, on Wall Street in the 1980s, required me to wear a suit and tie with polished shoes every day. At that time, casual (for men) meant that after 5 p.m. you could loosen your tie. When I lived in Japan in the late 1980s and early 1990s, things were even more formal; you could loosen your tie only while drinking beer late at night.

Casual Fridays started as a parallel to the dot-com boom on both American coasts in the mid-1990s and was partly led by Dockers, a Levi Strauss clothing brand. Casual Friday very quickly became casual every day and spread throughout the United States. These days, except for banking, the law, and a few other professions, business casual is the norm and the trend has spread around the world.

I've noticed in the past five years or so that business video has been going through a similar trend toward the casual. More and more content is created with much less formality. This is a good thing! Both professionals and citizen content creators now reach readers and viewers faster and with less interference from the stuffy conventions associated with content creation.

Perhaps the tremendous rise of social networking tools has helped fuel the desire to consume content that is less formal. At the same time, stiff and structured media like white papers aren't getting as many readers as they did a decade ago.

My friend Cliff Pollan is the one who first brought my attention to what he calls business-casual video. I love the description! The concept is simple: In the beginning, corporate videos were highly produced, like an episode of *60 Minutes*. They tended to cost tens of thousands of dollars and take months to create.

Some classics of the formal online corporate video genre include slickly produced corporate overviews; in-studio, lights-and-makeup customer testimonials; and product managers explaining their amazing new offerings.

Because many executives' experience with video is of this genre, when the subject of online video is discussed at companies, most people immediately think expensive and difficult. It's because they're thinking *formal*.

But if you think about business-casual video, all of a sudden videos can be low-cost or even no-cost and can be completed in a few hours or even a few minutes. The video quality of modern smartphones is stunning! Some people say that quality is essential. While I agree that a video should be appealing, I'm convinced that a lack of a studio, high-wattage lighting, and makeup artists isn't a big deal. If the subject is interesting, people are plenty tolerant of the conditions under which the video was filmed. Of course, you need to stay within reason. I don't advocate poorly shot video, terrible lighting, or bad editing.

I'm convinced that the trend toward casual content means consumers want to get closer to the organizations they do business with. When a company, hospital, educational institution, government agency, or other outfit comes across as friendly and engaging because of the way it communicates with people online, the content will be better received. It's okay if the person in your video doesn't speak like someone with an Ivy League MBA—in fact, it's probably preferable.

Like that transition from wearing formal clothes to putting on a polo shirt, it might feel unprofessional at first. But the increasingly informal nature of business—a willingness to tell it like it is—will make us more efficient and successful. Like the business-casual video that is the result, the equipment you use to create videos for your organization need not be fancy.

Stop Obsessing over Video Release Forms

Part of the trend toward business-casual video is the rise of interviews quickly recorded and used for marketing purposes. However, many people tell me that their companies' legal departments obsess over getting signed release forms from interview participants prior to posting the video online.

In my experience, the mere act of thrusting a legal document in front of potential participants and demanding that they sign causes many of them to rethink the whole thing; some end up choosing not to participate. When this happens, you miss opportunities.

I want to emphasize that I am not a lawyer, and I am not offering legal advice. As always, you should check with an expert before proceeding with an action that may have legal consequences. However, I do want to offer a practical alternative to the formal signed release. It's a simple strategy that I use myself. When I first press "Record" on my iPhone, I simply ask the person I am about to interview if it's okay to post the video on YouTube. I also ask about name spellings and company affiliation and title. I then know how to refer to my interview subjects throughout the video, and I have a record of them giving me permission to record! During the video-editing process, I save the video permissions and post the interview. It works great.

I've interviewed and posted video of rock stars, Fortune 500 CEOs, and top government officials using this method. And it turns out I'm not the only one. I was recently interviewed for a special segment to be aired on MSNBC's *Your Business* program. The first thing the producer did was have me spell my name on camera. There you have it—a technique even the pros use.

Your Smartphone Is All You Need

One development that is helping change the relative formality of corporate marketing video is the ease of use and high quality that you can achieve with today's smartphones. As I write this, I currently use an Apple iPhone X, and the videos it produces are stunning. I love mine and have it with me at all times when I am on the go. You never know where or when a great video interview might present itself, like the one I did with Jim Bridenstine, the Administrator of NASA. Other times, an idea pops up that is best told in video, like the idea in "Social media drove the Egyptian revolution but can it bring back the tourists??," which I filmed at the Pyramids and at Tahrir Square in Egypt a few years ago.

Your smartphone's camera allows you to always be ready to interview customers, employees, and industry analysts and to quickly post the video on your site or blog. It can also help you shoot short clips showing how your products are made or used. No professionals required.

The thing couldn't be easier to use. Even a technology-challenged person like me can use it. I do simple edits like shortening clips, adding graphics, or including B-roll footage (video to show the location that the video is about), such as images of the area around Tahrir Square in my Egypt video mentioned earlier. Or you can upload directly to YouTube, Vimeo, or other video-sharing sites right from your smartphone. Really, it's that easy. In fact, when people push back on the idea of creating a corporate blog or writing an e-book, I always suggest making some simple and short video interviews as an easy way to create valuable content that helps get the word out right away. Hey, did I mention that this is easy?

Facebook Live Is Great for Real-Time Content Marketing

The Facebook Live video application has quickly emerged as a premier live-streaming tool. Facebook Live turns your smartphone into a broadcast television station that people can tune in to live or watch as a replay.

Facebook appears to be giving strong preference to Facebook Live broadcasts. The Facebook algorithm will often give your video priority, showing the feed in real time to your friends and followers at the top of their time lines. Images alone are powerful storytelling tools, but live video pulls your followers right along with you in the moment.

Facebook Live can turn anyone into a citizen journalist. Indeed, news outlets are using Facebook Live too, allowing their reporters to upload live video between their more formal broadcasts or written stories.

And for marketers, live streaming opens up the possibility of sharing all kinds of information that can serve as marketing for you or your company.

A tour of a home for sale, a peek backstage at a rock concert, a manager's pep talk before the big game, or a product design meeting at a company all become shareable in a way that builds excitement and intimacy.

When I delivered a two-hour talk about the ideas in this book at the Tony Robbins Business Mastery seminar in Las Vegas, a 20-minute segment of the talk was filmed by a friend in the Facebook Live app on my iPhone and broadcast in real time.

As followers began to see my live broadcast, many shared it on their own time lines, growing the audience. Tony Robbins also shared it with his nearly four million Facebook followers. Soon there were more than 10,000 people tuned in to my Facebook Live broadcast.

Less than a week later, the recording had been shared by 181 people, liked by 770 people, and viewed some 65,000 times. This turned out to be a wonderful way for me to share information with my existing followers and reach people who didn't know me yet. It can do the same for you.

What I like most about Facebook Live is its simplicity. Simply turn on your smartphone, connect via Facebook, and begin broadcasting. No writing (like for a blog post), no advanced preparation (as in typical video shoots), and no complex uploading process after you shoot your video (as with YouTube).

Unlike almost every other form of content creation, with Facebook Live your media are immediately online and shareable, promoting you or your business right away.

There are many marketing and PR uses for Facebook Live. Politicians, artists, musicians, chefs, authors, teachers, CEOs, and others in the public eye have a great opportunity to create instant video stories about what they are up to. Organizations can showcase how their customers use their wares, especially with highly visual products and services like sporting goods, cars, hotels, restaurants, and hair salons.

In fact, surgery is now being broadcast on Facebook Live. Yes, really! More than half a million people watched as neurosurgeons at Soroka University Medical Center in Israel performed a procedure on a woman suffering from expanded blood vessels in her brain. Medical privacy laws in most countries require a patient's agreement before sharing on social media, something that Dr. Wilberto Cortes, a Houston, Texas, plastic surgeon asks of his patients. When someone agrees to be filmed on Facebook Live, the doctor is giving potential new patients a peek into how he works, which serves as an excellent way to market his practice.

When a news story breaks, Facebook Live can also be an excellent way to do some newsjacking (see Chapter 21), getting your take on the story into the marketplace instantly with the potential to generate media coverage, produce sales leads, and grow business.

Video to Showcase Your Expertise

When Mary McNeight couldn't find anyone in the Seattle area who would help her train her own dog Jasper for service work (dogs that help people manage disabilities and diseases like diabetes), it fell to her to teach her pet to be her service dog. Later, she enrolled in puppy classes to train Liame, her new Labrador retriever puppy. In the process, she became fascinated by dog training—so she made it her business. McNeight spent countless hours learning all aspects of the business, got her accreditation from the Certification Council for Professional Dog Trainers, and is now owner and director of training and behavior at the Service Dog Academy. This business offers private training sessions and small-group adult-and-puppy training classes for both service and pet dog training. It even offers a groundbreaking program for training your own diabetic alert dog.

But credentials, skills, and even passion alone don't bring in customers. Her excellent website (featuring dozens of videos that she shot and edited herself) educates buyers and generates high search engine rankings, driving business her way. "I've gone from barely having any students to getting anywhere from 20 to 40 emails per day requesting my services and advice and verbally praising my work," McNeight says. "If that isn't a story of success, I don't know what is. I have the power to create an audience for any product or service I put my mind to. But I think I will stick with what makes me happiest: helping dogs and the disabled live more productive lives."

In 2010, McNeight started making YouTube videos with an inexpensive video camera and the software that came installed on her Mac notebook computer. "Seeing a need for my students to understand how to make a Kongsicle, I produced my first instructional video," McNeight says. Kongs are natural rubber food-puzzle toys for dogs, and a Kongsicle is a Kong with frozen food inside. The video is titled "Best Dog Food Puzzle: The Kongsicle."

"A couple of months later, I went to the Association of Pet Dog Trainers conference, and I was startled by a young trainer who said, 'You're Mary McNeight, right? You made that video on Kongsicles! I use it as a reference video for my students.' Here was this dog trainer in Florida using my materials for her classes. That was the day I understood the power of YouTube." Since then, McNeight has made many instructional videos, with titles that include "Diabetic Alert Dog Scams," "Puppy Doggie Ants in the Pants," and a multipart series on diabetic alert dog training.

The content on the Service Dog Academy site, including the video series, is created for three buyer personas: pet dog owners, service dog owners, and people who want to train their own diabetic alert dog. After her initial success, McNeight purchased a $400 HD video camera, a $20 microphone, Final Cut Pro software, and, as she describes it, "some funky alien-adjustable-arm-looking lights at Home Depot, since I couldn't afford to light my videos with professional lights. The really cool thing about my content is that it proves that it doesn't have to be shiny, flashy, spiffy, or cost thousands of dollars to produce. People will watch anything as long as it's packed full of useful information."

McNeight's repute and search engine results are aided by her willingness to post content that others in the dog training business are fearful to post because they don't want to give away information for free. "A great success was a video on how to travel with your service dog, something nobody on the entire Internet was teaching people how to do," she says. "I also hosted a webinar that gave an overview of how to train a diabetic alert dog. I placed the webinar capture video on YouTube and was afraid of being banned in the dog-training community. This information was not available [elsewhere] on the web because nobody wanted to share how they trained dogs for tens of thousands of dollars. I started getting emails and phone calls from people all over the world asking me for advice on training their dog or just outright purchasing my online diabetic alert dog training program. I've had dog trainers who want me to fly out to their location and teach a class on diabetic alert dog training for them.

"How cool is it that this now three-person service dog training organization is getting worldwide attention? I never would have gotten that type of exposure printing brochures or running expensive ads on local television. A couple of months ago, I even had a woman tell me the video I made saved her life! It allowed her to get enough information to help her train her own medical alert dog by herself."

You could hardly ask for a more dramatic example of how low-cost videos can expand reach and drive business. And it all started because McNeight identified a problem that no one online was helping people solve.

Getting Started with Video

Whether they're new to the game or have been offering web video for years, organizations get their video content onto the computer screens (and smartphones) of buyers in several different ways:

- **Posting to video-sharing sites:** YouTube is the most popular video-sharing site on the web, although there are others, such as Vimeo. Organizations post video content on YouTube and send people a link to the content (or hope that it goes viral). You can also embed a YouTube video into your site, your blog, or even your news release. Creating a simple video is easy—all you need is a YouTube account and a digital video camera or the video app on your smartphone. There are all sorts of enhancements and editing techniques you can use to make the video more professional. IBM has experimented with mockumentaries, including a hysterical six-part series called *The Art of the Sale*, which is like a cross between *The Office* and a sales training video. And the viral components of these corporate videos clearly work, because here I am sharing them with you.

- **Developing an online video channel**: Companies that take online video programming seriously develop their own channel, often with a unique URL. Examples include Weber Grills' "Grill Skills" videos, which feature instruction on how to grill like "mastering turkey."
- **Attempting stealth insertions to YouTube**: Some companies try to sneak corporate-sponsored video onto YouTube in a way that makes it seem like it was consumer generated. The YouTube community is remarkably skilled at ratting out inauthentic video, so this approach is fraught with danger.
- **Vlogging**: Short for "video blogging," this term refers to video content embedded in a blog. The text part of the blog adds context to each video and aids with search engine marketing.
- **Videocasting**: A videocast is like a podcast but with video—a video series tied to a syndication component with iTunes and RSS feeds.
- **Inviting your customer communities to submit video**: This technique is how some companies try to generate viral marketing interest. These companies sponsor contests where customers submit short videos. The best are usually showcased on the company site, and the winners often get prizes. In some cases, the winning videos are also played on TV as real commercials.

"Video is a remarkably versatile medium," says Dave Jackel, a partner at Shave Media, a Boston-based studio creating video content for corporate clients around the world. "We can use it tell stories, share ideas, and present information at all levels of complexity."

Like me, Jackel is particularly appreciative of how-to furniture assembly videos, which are now mercifully replacing those 12-language illustrated instructions that come folded up along with the screws.

"Video allows you to show it, rather than just say it," Jackel says. "The medium is particularly well suited for conveying emotion, and it can do so in a matter of seconds. As a means of touching the heartstrings, making us laugh, or rousing us to action, video may be the most powerful tool we have. Our clients come to us not to replace the text on their websites, but to tell the stories that can't be told properly through text alone."

Video Created for Buyers Generates Sales Leads

As I've mentioned throughout this book, tailoring content to buyer personas is essential to good marketing. Guess what—it's true for video as well. Rather than creating gobbledygook-laden drivel about products and services, shooting video especially for your buyers makes it important for them.

Attivio, an enterprise software company, uses a buyer-persona-based approach on the company's website. While the different personas might actually all purchase the same product, each one has different problems that can be solved by the company. For instance, marketers at Attivio target what they refer to internally as tech-savvy business champions, people who care about new revenue sources, better customer relationships, regulatory compliance, competitive advantage, and controlling costs. Another buyer persona, information technology professionals, describes the people responsible for getting and keeping the company's systems up and running, so they want to hear about reliability, security, performance, scale, and ease of integration. A third buyer persona is those who work within government and the intelligence agencies. These buyers don't want to hear about improving profitability; instead, they care about sharing information among agencies, which improves their ability to connect the dots and detect threats. Each set of buyer persona pages has video made especially for that buyer, and the goal of the video is to drive buyers to want to learn more by connecting with an Attivio salesperson.

"Video has been a particularly valuable tool in helping us convey the appropriate [information] to each customer segment," says MaryAnne Sinville, senior vice president of marketing at Attivio. "When we do a video shoot, we often ask the same question two or three times, guiding the speaker to frame their answer with a specific audience in mind so we get relevant content to parse out to multiple persona pages."

One of the benefits of this approach is that salespeople know what a buyer is interested in and what persona that buyer represents based on what page the buyer is on when he or she asks to learn more. "When a visitor comes to the site, self-selects a persona path, and then converts to a lead, it's much easier for us to respond with additional information they're likely to find compelling," Sinville says.

Now let's take a look at how to create a podcast. While the general approach of creating valuable information especially for your buyer personas is the same, you do have technology choices to make.

Podcasting 101

A podcast is a piece of audio content tied to a subscription component so people can receive regular updates. The simplest way to think of podcasting is that it's like a radio show except that you listen to each episode at your convenience by downloading or streaming it either to your computer or to a mobile device like an Android phone or iPhone. The equipment you need to start podcasting will range in cost from a few hundred dollars at the low end to a bit over a thousand dollars for professional-level sound. Plus, you'll probably want to host your audio files on an external server requiring a monthly fee.

How do you get started? "I've found that the most important thing is show preparation," says John J. Wall, Partner and Head of Business Development at Trust Insights. He's producer and cohost with Christopher Penn of *Marketing over Coffee*, a 20-minute show covering both new and classic marketing. "Unless you are real comfortable talking extemporaneously, you will want to have a script laid out ahead of time. It just sounds more polished when you do." I don't have my own podcast, but as a frequent guest on radio shows and podcasts, I agree with Wall—the best shows I participate in are those where the interviewer knows the material and keeps things focused.

Beginning with developing a script, following are the steps and technical issues involved with producing a podcast.

- *Show preparation* includes gathering ideas for the show and creating a script. Think about your buyer personas and what you can discuss that interests them. If you plan to interview guests, make sure you know how to pronounce their names (don't laugh—this is a frequent mistake) and you have their titles, affiliations, and other information correct. It's common practice to plug a guest's business, so know ahead of time what URL or product you will mention.

- *Recording when you are near your computer* is done with a microphone (many options to choose from) that delivers the audio into your computer. You'll need audio editing software such as GarageBand, Audacity, Adobe Audition, or ProTools as an interface to create and publish your podcast.
- *Mobile recording gear* is required if you are going to do the roving-reporter thing and interview people at events or perhaps your employees around the world. Mobile recording gear is made by several companies, including Zoom and Tascam.
- *Phone interviews* require a way to record both sides of a conversation. A good way to go is to use Zencastr, Skype, or Google Hangouts on your computer and then record on a digital recorder.
- *Editing your audio files* is optional; you can always just upload the files as you recorded them. If you choose to clean them up, you can edit at the microscale (removing *um*, *uh*, and other audible pauses) or at the macroscale (e.g., removing the last five minutes of an interview). Many podcasters edit segments that they recorded at different times, putting them together to create a show. Audacity and Apple's GarageBand are two software packages that include many of the audio capabilities of a professional radio station and make editing simple.
- *Postproduction editing* sometimes includes running a noise-reduction program (to get rid of that annoying air-conditioner hum in the background) and sound compression (to even out the volume of sections that have been recorded at different times and places). The Levelator is an excellent free tool that does compression and other dynamic adjustments. For less than $100 SoundSoap is another excellent tool to clean up audio.
- *Tagging the audio* is an important step that some people overlook or perform without taking due care. This step involves adding text-based information about the audio to make it easier for people to find. This information is what appears in the search engines and audio distribution sites such as iTunes. Your tags also display on listeners' iPod displays, so don't ignore or gloss over this step. If you are hosting your podcast on a blog, look for a plug-in that allows you to automate this tagging when you post the file.
- *Hosting and distribution* are necessary to ensure that people can easily obtain your podcasts. Services such as Liberated Syndication host the

(sometimes very large) audio files and syndicate them to the distribution networks such as iTunes, Spotify, and Pandora.

- *Promotion* is essential to make sure that people find out about your podcasts. If you do interview shows (which are an easy way to get started, and provide excellent content), make sure that you provide links to the show to all of the guests. Many people will help you promote a show that featured them. You will also want to network with other podcasters in your space, because very short on-air plugs cross-promoting other podcasts are common and a good way for people to build audiences. Don't forget to put links to your podcast on your website, in your email signature, and on or in your offline materials, including business cards and brochures. Also, you should tweet about every show and add a link to your Facebook page as well as send out a news release alerting people to important shows.
- *A companion blog* is a key component used by nearly all podcasters to discuss the content of each show. An important reason for having a companion blog is that its text will be indexed by the search engines, driving more people to sign up for the podcast feed. A blog also allows the show's host to write a few paragraphs about the content of that particular show and to provide links to the blogs and websites of guests (so people can get a sense of a show's content prior to listening). Most organizations that use podcasting as a marketing tool also use the podcast blog as a place to move people into the sales process by providing links to the company site or to demonstrations or trial offers.

As of March 2018, *Marketing over Coffee* serves up an average of 65,000 downloads per month. "Podcasting has been a huge benefit for both Chris and I in earning the trust of our listeners which then gives us credibility for both speaking opportunities and the work we now do at Trust Insights," Wall says. "It's been very satisfying to be in situations where businesses are looking for data science to light up their dark data and do a better job of understanding the flow of leads and customers. They talk with 50-person firms or larger and then say, 'Yes, but we've known you for years through the podcast, we trust you.'"

Wall says you can be up and running with your new podcast in less than a month. "The principles are all quite simple, but it takes a bit of time to figure out the various hardware and software elements," he says. "Be sure to write up accurate show notes, including time codes. Listeners can find the content they want, and you get some extra search engine juice."

Audio and video content on the web is still new for many marketers and communicators. But the potential to deliver information to buyers in fresh and unique ways is greater when you use a new medium. And while your competition is still trying to figure out that blogging thing, you can leverage your existing blog into the new worlds of audio and video and leave the competition way behind.

18

How to Use News Releases to Reach Buyers Directly

Guess what? Press releases have never been exclusively for the press. My first job in the mid-1980s was on a Wall Street trading desk. Every day, I would come to work and watch the Dow Jones Telerate and Reuters screens as they displayed specialized financial data, economic information, and stock prices. The screens also displayed news feeds, and within these news feeds were press releases. For decades, financial market professionals have had access to company press releases distributed through Business Wire, PR Newswire, and other electronic press release distribution services. And they weren't just for publicly traded corporations; any company's release would appear in trading rooms within seconds.

I distinctly remember traders intently watching the newswires for any signs of market-moving events. Often the headline of a press release would cause frenzy: "Did you see? IBM is acquiring a software company!" "It's on the wire; Boeing just got a 20-plane order from Singapore Airlines!" For years, markets often moved and stock prices rose and fell based on the press release content issued directly by companies, *not* on the news stories written minutes or hours later by reporters from newswire outlets like Reuters and Dow Jones (and later Bloomberg).

Press releases have also been available to professionals working within corporations, government agencies, and law firms, all of which have had access to raw press releases through services like those from NewsEdge, Dow Jones, and LexisNexis. These services have been delivering press releases to all kinds of professionals for competitive intelligence, research, discovery, and other purposes for many decades.

315

And since about 1995, the wide availability of the web has meant that press releases have been available for free to anyone with an Internet connection and a web browser.

> Millions of people read press releases directly, unfiltered by the media. You need to be speaking directly to them!

As I tell this story to PR pros, I hear cries of "Hang on! We disagree! The role of public relations and the purpose of the press release as a tool are about communicating with the *media*." For an example of this thinking, look to Steve Rubel, one of the most influential PR bloggers in the world. He responded to my ideas about press releases by writing a post on his blog, titled "Direct to Consumer Press Releases Suck."

Let's take a look at the objections of traditional PR folks. According to the Public Relations Society of America (PRSA), "Public relations is the professional discipline that ethically fosters mutually beneficial relationships among social entities." In 1988, the governing body of the PRSA—its Assembly—formally adopted a definition of public relations that has become the most accepted and widely used: "Public relations helps an organization and its publics adapt mutually to each other." Nowhere does this description mention the media. PR is about reaching your audience!

I think many PR professionals have a fear of the unknown. They don't understand how to communicate directly with consumers and want to live in the past, when there was no choice but to use the media as a mouthpiece. I also think there's a widely held view about the purity of the press release as a tool for the press. PR professionals don't want to know that hundreds of millions of people have the power to read their releases directly. It's easier to imagine a closed audience of a dozen reporters. But this argument is based on fear, not the facts; there is no good reason why organizations shouldn't communicate directly with their audiences, without a media filter, via releases.

Obviously, the first word of the term *press release* throws off some people, particularly PR professionals. On my blog and on other sites, a semantic debate played out. The consensus of the dozens of professional communicators who weighed in was to call releases aimed at consumers *news releases.* This sounds good to me, so from this point on, I'll refer to direct-to-consumer releases as *news releases.*

News Releases in a Web World

The media have been disintermediated. The web has changed the rules. Buyers read your news releases directly, and you need to be speaking their language. Today, savvy marketing and PR professionals use news releases to reach buyers directly. As I mentioned in Chapter 1, this is not to suggest that media relations are no longer important; mainstream media and the trade press must be part of an overall communications strategy. In some markets, mainstream media and the trade press remain *critically* important, and of course the media still derive some content from news releases. But your primary audience is no longer just a handful of journalists. Your audience is millions of people with Internet connections and access to search engines and RSS readers.

The New Rules of News Releases

Here, then, are the rules of this new direct-to-consumer medium.

- Don't send news releases just when big news is happening; find good reasons to send them all the time.
- Instead of targeting a handful of journalists, create news releases that appeal directly to your buyers.
- Write releases that are replete with the keyword-rich language used by your buyers.
- Include offers that compel consumers to respond to your release in some way.
- Place links in releases to deliver potential customers to landing pages on your website.
- Link to related content on your site such as videos, blog posts, or e-books.
- Optimize news release delivery for searching and browsing.
- Point people to your news releases from your social sites like Twitter, Facebook, and LinkedIn.
- Drive people into the sales process with news releases.

You need to fundamentally change the way you use news releases. If you follow these specific strategies for leveraging this once-lowly medium by turning it into one of the most important direct marketing tools at your disposal, you will drive buyers straight to your company's products and services at precisely the time that they are ready to buy.

In the remainder of this chapter, we'll use these rules to develop a news release strategy.

If They Find You, They Will Come

Several years ago, I was preparing a keynote speech called "Shorten Your Sales Cycle: Marketing Programs That Deliver More Revenue Faster" for the Software Marketing Perspectives Conference & Expo. To be honest, I was kind of procrastinating. Facing a blank PowerPoint file, I decided to hit Google in search of inspiration.

I entered the phrase "accelerate sales cycle" to see if there was anything interesting I could use in my presentation. The highest-ranked listings for this phrase were from WebEx, a company that provides online collaboration services. What was most interesting to me was that the links pointed to *news releases* on the WebEx site. That's right; at the top of the Google search results was a news release about a new WebEx product, and right there in the first sentence of the news release was the phrase I was looking for: "accelerate sales cycle."

> WebEx Launches WebEx Sales Center: Leader Expands Suite of Real-Time Collaborative Applications
>
> Enhance Team Selling Process, Engage Prospects throughout Sales Cycle, and Enable Managers to Monitor and Measure Web Sales Operations
>
> *SAN JOSE, Calif.*—WebEx Communications, Inc., the leading provider of on-demand collaborative applications, today launched WebEx Sales Center, a new service that helps companies accelerate sales cycles, increase win rates, and close more deals by leveraging online sales calls. . . .

Then I went over to Google News and checked out the same phrase. Sure enough, WebEx also had the number-one listing on Google's news search with a very recent news release: "Application Integration Industry Leader

Optimizes Marketing and Sales Processes with WebEx Application Suite." The news release, about a WebEx customer, had been sent through PR Newswire and had a direct web link to the WebEx site to provide additional information. WebEx also provided links in some news releases directly to free trial offers of its services. How cool is that?

"That is exactly our strategy," says Colin Smith, director of public relations for WebEx. "Google and news keywords have really transformed the news release as a distribution vehicle. Our thinking is that, especially for companies that have an end-user appeal, news releases are a great channel."

It's certainly no accident that I found WebEx; I was searching on a phrase that Smith had optimized for search. His research had shown that buyers of the communications services that WebEx provides search on the phrase "accelerate sales cycle" (and also many others). So when I searched on that phrase, WebEx was at the top of the listings.

As a result, WebEx provided me with an excellent (and real) example of a company that had optimized the content of news releases to include relevant terms such as the one I was looking for. And WebEx has greatly benefited from its efforts. In addition to the consumers it already reaches online, the company added to its audience by getting the information to someone who tells other people about it (me!). I've used this example in speeches before well over 10,000 marketing and web content professionals and executive audiences, and it was also downloaded more than a million times as part of my *New Rules of PR* e-book. And now you're reading it here, too.

"People are saying that press releases are dead," Smith says. "But that's not true for direct-to-consumer news releases." As Smith has developed his news release strategy to reach buyers directly, he has had to refine his writing and PR skills for this evolving, but very much alive, medium. "I learned the very structured *AP Style Guide* way to write releases," he says. "But that's changed as keywords and phrases have suddenly become important and the scale and reach of the Internet have opened up end users as a channel."

Smith doesn't let keywords dominate how he writes, but he tries to be very aware of keywords and phrases and to insert key phrases, especially, into releases whenever he can. "We don't think that a single keyword works, but phrases are great," he says. "If people are doing a specific search, or one with company names that are in our release, then the goal is that they will find our news release."

Driving Buyers into the Sales Process

Colin Smith is careful to include product information in the end-user-focused news releases he crafts for WebEx. "We try to think about what's important to people," he says. "We put free trial offers in the releases that are about the product." About 80 percent of the releases that WebEx puts out are product or customer related. "WebEx is a great mix of real end-user stories," he says. "People get why you need web meetings, so it is easy to tell the story using news releases."

Because the web meetings story is compelling even for those who don't know the product category, Smith also looks for ways to create a viral marketing buzz. For example, he pays attention to major events in the news where WebEx online collaboration would be useful. "We donated free service for limited use during the time that Boston traffic was snarled as a result of tunnel closures. We did the same thing for the New York City transit strike." Smith knows that people are likely to consider WebEx services during this kind of unusual situation. Offering the service for free often creates loyal future users.

Direct-to-consumer news releases are an important component of the marketing mix at WebEx. "We do track metrics, and we can see how many people are going from the release to the free trial," Smith says. The numbers are significant. But with such success, there's also a danger. "We don't want to abuse the news release channel," Smith says, explaining that the company also has a media relations strategy, of which news releases are a part. "We want the news releases to be interesting for journalists but also to provide consumers with things to do, such as get the free trial."

WebEx is successful in using news releases to appeal to both the journalists who write (and speak) about WebEx products and services, and also the consumers who are searching for what WebEx has to offer. WebEx and thousands of other organizations like it prove that a direct-to-consumer news release strategy can coexist within an organization that cares about media relations.

Since an earlier edition of this book was released, WebEx was acquired by Cisco Systems, a major networking and communications technology company.

Under the old rules, the only way to get published was to have your news release picked up by the media. We've come a long way. The web has turned all kinds of companies, nonprofits, political campaigns, individuals, and even churches and rock bands into just-in-time and just-right publishers. As publishers, these organizations create news releases that deliver useful information directly onto the screens of their buyers—no press involved!

Developing Your News Release Strategy

The most important thing to think about as you begin a news release program is, once again, the need to write for your buyers. You should consider what you learned through the buyer persona research part of your marketing and PR plan (described in Chapter 10) and develop an editorial calendar for news releases based on what buyers need to know. Implementing a news release strategy to reach buyers directly is like publishing an online news service—you are providing your buyers with information they need to find your organization online and then learn more about you.

Part of thinking like a publisher is remembering the critical importance of content. "Everything is content-driven in public relations," says Brian Hennigan, marketing communications manager for dbaDIRECT, a data infrastructure management company. "I like using news releases to reach the market and my potential customers. With news releases, for a hundred bucks you can talk to the world." Hennigan supplements his news releases with longer and more detailed white papers to get dbaDIRECT ideas into the market. "I write the news releases like news stories," he says. "We look at the needs of the market and entrepreneurial trends as interesting, and we write to these trends."

As you make this fundamental change in how you do news releases, you will probably find yourself wondering, at first, what to write about. The rule of thumb is: Big news is great, but don't wait. Write about pretty much anything that your organization is doing.

- Have a new take on an old problem? Write a release.
- Serve a unique marketplace? Write a release.
- Have interesting information to share? Write a release.
- CEO speaking at a conference? Write a release.
- Win an award? Write a release.
- Add a product feature? Write a release.
- Win a new customer? Write a release.
- Publish a white paper? Write a release.
- Get out of bed this morning? Okay, maybe not—but now you're thinking the right way!

Publishing News Releases through a Distribution Service

The best way to publish news releases so they are seen by your buyers is to simultaneously post a release to your own website and send it to one of the news release wires. The benefit of using a news release distribution service is that your release will be sent to the online news services, including Yahoo!, Google, Bing, and many others. Many news release distribution services reach trade and industry websites as well. In fact, you can often reach hundreds of websites with a single news release. The significant benefit of this approach is that your release will be indexed by the news search engines and vertical market sites, and then when somebody does a search for a word or phrase contained in your release, *presto*, that potential customer finds you. As an added bonus, people who have requested alerts about your industry from sites that index news releases will get an alert that something important—your news release—is available.

There are a number of options for wire distribution of news releases. I've included some of the U.S. news release distribution services here. Similar services exist in other countries, such as CanadaNewsWire serving the Canadian market and News2U in Japan. Take a look at the various services and compare them yourself.

A Selection of the Larger U.S. News Release Distribution Services

- Business Wire: businesswire.com
- GlobeNewswire: globenewswire.com
- PR Newswire: prnewswire.com
- PRWeb: prweb.com

To get your news releases to appear on the online news services, including Google News, you just have to purchase a basic news release coverage area offered by a news release distribution service. Coverage is based on geographical distribution of your release to reporters. Because I am located near Boston, Massachusetts, the cheapest distribution with some services for me is the Boston region. The services also have many value-added options for you to consider, such as national distribution. But what is important to know is that most news release distribution services include distribution to online media such as Google News in *any geographical distribution*. So as you make your choice, remember that when your purpose for sending news releases is to reach buyers via search engines and vertical sites, maximizing the newsroom and geographical reach offered by a service is less important than ensuring that your releases are included on major online news sites.

Reach Even More Interested Buyers with RSS Feeds

Many news release distribution services also offer RSS feeds of their news releases, which they make available to other sites, blogs, journalists, and individuals. This means that each time you publish a news release with the service, the news release is seen by potentially thousands of people who have subscribed to the RSS content feeds in your market category (as offered by the distribution service).

So if you tag your release as being important for the automotive industry, your news release will be delivered to anyone (or any site) that has subscribed to the news release distribution service's automotive RSS feed. And online news services such as Google News have RSS feed capability, too, allowing people to receive feeds based on keywords and phrases. Each time your release includes a word or phrase of importance to someone who has saved it as part of his or her alerts, a link to your news releases will appear via email or RSS feed in near real time in the future.

Simultaneously Publish Your News Releases to Your Website

Post your news releases to an appropriate and readily findable section of your website. Many organizations have a media room or press section of their website, which is ideal (see Chapter 19 for details on how to create your online newsroom). You should keep the news release live for as long as the content is appropriate, perhaps for years. This is very important because most of the online news sites do not maintain archives of news for more than a few months. If potential customers look for the content of your news release the week after it is distributed via a service, they will certainly find it on Google News and the others. But they won't find it if they do the search next year unless the release is on your own site as a permanent link so that it is indexed by Google.

The Importance of Links in Your News Releases

Particularly because your releases may be delivered by feeds or on news services and various sites other than your own, creating links from your news releases to content on your website is very important. These links, which might point to a specific offer or to a landing page with more information, allow your buyers to move from the news release to specific content on your website that will then drive them into the sales process, as we saw in the previous chapter.

However, there is another enormous benefit to including links in news releases. Each time your news release is posted on another site, such as an online news site, the inbound link from the online news site to your website helps to increase the search engine ranking of your site, because the search engines use inbound links as one of the important criteria for their page-ranking algorithms. So when your news release has a link to your site and it is indexed somewhere on the web, you actually increase the ranking of the pages on your site! Said another way, when your news release appears on a website somewhere and there is a link in your news release that points to a URL on your site, the search engines will increase the rankings of the page where the URL is pointing. Sending a news release that includes links increases your own website's search engine rankings.

The news release distribution services also provide a way to include social media tags to make the news releases easy to find on services like Twitter, Facebook, and others. Use them! Social media tags make your releases much simpler to locate.

Focus on the Keywords and Phrases Your Buyers Use

As I've suggested before, one thing successful publishers do that web marketers should emulate is to understand the audience first and then set about satisfying their informational needs. A great way to start thinking like a publisher and to create news releases that drive action is to focus on your customers' problems and then create and deliver news releases accordingly. Use the words and phrases that your buyers use. Think about how the people you want to reach are searching, and develop news release content that includes those words and phrases. You can get the information you need to do so by thinking back to your buyer personas. Don't be egotistical and write only about your organization. What are your buyers' problems? What do they want to know? What words and phrases do they use to describe these problems? I know, I've said this already several times—that's because it is very important.

CruiseCompete, cited by *Kiplinger* as one of the 25 best travel sites, helps people secure quotes for cruises from multiple travel agencies, based on the dates and ports specified. CruiseCompete is a great example of a company that uses news releases to reach people based on the phrases that their buyers are searching with. For example, during the lead-up to the holiday season, the company issued a news release via Marketwired with the headline "Cruise Lines Set Sail with Hot Holiday Vacation Prices." Importantly, part of an early sentence in the release, "some seven-night vacations can be booked for well under $1,000 per person, including Thanksgiving cruises, Christmas cruises, and New Year's cruises," included three critical phrases. Not only did this release's mention of "Thanksgiving cruises," "Christmas cruises," and "New Year's cruises" generate traffic from users searching on these common phrases, but it also helped guide searchers into the sales cycle; each of the three phrases in the news release was hyperlinked to a purpose-built landing page on the CruiseCompete site that displayed the holiday cruise deals. Anyone who clicked on the "Christmas cruises" link was taken directly to deals for Christmas cruises.

What makes this case so exciting is that at the time I was writing this, the CruiseCompete holiday cruise news release was at the top of the Google News search results for the phrases "Thanksgiving cruises," "Christmas cruises," and "New Year's cruises." More important, the bump that the links in the news release gave to the three landing pages helped those pages reach the top of the Google web search results lists. For example, the Cruise-Compete landing page for the phrase "Christmas cruises" was ranked in the fourth position among 5,830,000 other hits on Google.

"We know that people have thought about traveling for the holidays," says Heidi M. Allison-Shane, a consultant working with CruiseCompete. "We use the news releases to communicate with consumers that now is the time to book, because there are dynamite prices and they will sell out." Allison-Shane makes sure that CruiseCompete includes the ideal phrases in each news release and that each release has appropriate links to the site. This strategy makes reaching potential customers a matter of "simply understanding what people are likely to be searching on and then linking them to the correct page on the site where we have the content that's relevant," she says. "We try to be useful with the right content and to be focused on what's relevant for our consumers and to provide the links that they need. This stuff is not difficult."

The CruiseCompete news release program produces results by increasing the Google rankings for the site. But the news releases also reach buyers directly as those buyers search on relevant phrases. "Each time we send a targeted news release, we see a spike in the web traffic on the site," Allison-Shane says.

As you craft your own phrases to use in your news releases, don't get trapped by your own jargon; think, speak, and write like your customers do. Though you may have a well-developed lexicon for your products and services, these words don't necessarily mean much to your potential customers. As you write news releases (or any other form of web content), focus on the words and phrases that your buyers use. As a search engine marketing tool, news releases are only as valuable as the keywords and phrases that are contained in them.

If It's Important Enough to Tell the Media, Tell Your Clients and Prospects, Too!

Many companies devote extensive resources to their PR and media relations programs. Often, the results of these efforts are buried in a difficult-to-find news section of the company website. Consider rewriting your news releases in an easy-to-read paragraph or two and making them a section of your email newsletter for clients and prospects. Or establish RSS feeds to deliver your news to anyone who is interested. And don't forget your employees—if they know about your news, they can be your greatest evangelists.

One of the most cost-effective ways to reach buyers is to look for ways to leverage the work you're already doing by repurposing content for other audiences. Too often, organizations spend tons of money on, say, a PR program that targets a handful of journalists but fails to communicate the same information to other constituents. Or a company's advertising program designed to generate new sales may drive people to a website that doesn't match the message of the ads, resulting in lost interest. Sadly, failure to integrate sales, marketing, and communications—both online and offline—will always result in lost opportunities. Happily, the web makes it a relatively simple task to integrate your news release program into your larger online strategy.

Here's one more thing that you may never have considered: Having a regular editorial calendar that includes a series of news releases also means your company is busy. When people go to your online media room and find a lack of news releases, they often assume that you are not moving forward or that you have nothing to contribute to the industry. In the new world of marketing, consistent, high-quality news release content brands a company or a nonprofit as a busy market player, an active expert in the industry, and a trusted resource to turn to.

19

Your Newsroom: A Front Door for Much More Than the Media

The online newsroom (sometimes called a press room, media room, or press page) is the part of your organization's website that you create specifically for the media. In some organizations, this section is simply a list of news releases with contact information for the organization's PR person. But many companies and nonprofits have elaborate newsrooms with a great deal of information available in many different formats: audio, video, photos, news releases, background information, financial data, and much more. A close cousin to the newsroom is the online investor relations (IR) room that many public companies maintain; however, I don't cover IR sites in this book.

Before I give you ideas on how to create a valuable newsroom of your own, I want you to consider something that is vitally important: *All kinds of people visit your newsroom, not just journalists*. Stop and really let that soak in for a moment. Your buyers are snooping around your organization by visiting the media pages on your website. Your current customers, partners, investors, suppliers, and employees all visit those pages. Why is that? Based on casual research I've done (I often speak about visitor statistics with employees who are responsible for their organizations' newsrooms), I'm convinced that when people want to know what's *current* about an organization, they go to a newsroom.

> Your newsroom is for your buyers, not just the media.

Visitors expect that the main pages of a website are basically static (i.e., they are not updated often), but they also expect that the news releases and media-targeted pages on a site will reveal the very latest about a company. For many companies, the news release section is one of the most frequently visited parts of the website. Check out your own website statistics; you may be amazed at how many visitors are already reading your news releases and other media pages online.

So I want you to do something that many traditional PR people think is nuts. I want you to design your newsroom for your *buyers*. By building a media room that targets buyers, you will not only enhance those pages as a powerful marketing tool but also *make a better media site for journalists*. I've reviewed hundreds of newsrooms, and the best ones are built with buyers in mind. This approach may sound a bit radical, but believe me, it works.

Your Newsroom as (Free) Search Engine Optimization

When news releases are posted on your site, search engine crawlers will find the content, index it, and rank it based on words, phrases, and other factors. Because news release pages update more often than any other part of a typical organization's website, search engine algorithms (tuned to pay attention to pages that update frequently) tend to rank news release pages among the highest on your site, driving traffic there first.

"There's no question that a well-organized media room often has higher search results and drives more traffic because of the way the search engines work," says Dee Rambeau, vice president of customer engagement at PR Newswire. "A news release dynamically builds out a new set of content in your newsroom, with each news release generating its own indexable page, which the search engines all capture. Google and the other search engines love fresh content that relates back to similar content on the other pages of the site. Aggressive companies take advantage of this by sending news releases frequently to get high rankings from the search engines. Frequency has a great deal to do with search engine rankings—if you do 10 news releases, that's great; 20 is better, and 100 is better still."

Reaching Reporters and Editors and Telling Your Story

The Kellogg Company—the world's leading producer of cereal and second-largest producer of cookies, crackers, and savory snacks—uses its newsroom for search engine optimization (SEO) purposes and as a tool to reach various audiences, including reporters and editors who cover the company.

"What we found through our research is that, more and more, our newsroom is extending beyond just media to other stakeholders," says Stephanie Slingerland, senior manager of corporate communications at the Kellogg Company. "Anyone coming to the site, be it an investor, an NGO or other partner agency, or even a consumer—the newsroom is inviting for them to get the information which may be relevant."

Slingerland has strong partnerships with people who work in other departments at the company and who also provide information to the public. "Our investor relations team are having conversations and engagements with analysts and investors. So, from our partnership with that team, we know what those stakeholders might be looking for. Or, for example, our government relations team are regularly engaging with government and nongovernmental officials. Again, we have a strong partnership with them. We know what they're looking for and can make sure that they have what they might be looking for on our site. The same with our corporate social responsibility team, who engage with agencies and others as part of our philanthropic activities."

Based on what she learns about the needs of the news media and other stakeholders, Slingerland creates the right content, including news releases, fact sheets, news alerts, and more. "Since we are the folks that regularly engage with the media, we know what we're getting asked for over and over, like the fact sheet section," she says. "And we also know that many people want to know the latest news about the company, but they don't necessarily come to our newsroom every day. So that's why we created our news alerts section, so they opt in to be alerted whenever a new press release hits."

The Kellogg Company has an interesting approach to feeding news to consumers through a consumer-facing site at Kelloggs.com (a different domain than the corporate site at KelloggCompany.com, which houses the newsroom). They use the MediaRoom service from PR Newswire to feed content to both sites. "We post everything for the media on

KelloggCompany.com, knowing that consumers may land on this page but typically go to our Kelloggs.com branded site," Slingerland says. "We have the ability to choose when we issue a press release: If we feel that it would be relevant for our consumer audience, we feed it to our Kelloggs.com site as well." And when all that content hits both sites in real time, it is indexed by the search engines and will rise to the top positions.

A newsroom is an important part of any organization's website and a critical aspect of an effective media relations strategy. When done well, a newsroom will turn journalists who are just browsing into interested writers who will highlight your organization positively in their stories. And more important, a newsroom can move your buyers into and through the sales process, resulting in more business for your organization and contributing to meeting your organization's *real goals* of revenue and customer retention. I've noticed as I've checked out hundreds of newsrooms that most fail to deliver compelling content. Sure, they may look pretty, but often the design and graphics, not the content that journalists (and your buyers) require, are in the forefront. The following sections give you useful tips that will help your newsroom work as effectively as some of the best ones I've seen.

Best Practices for Newsrooms

One important consideration that many marketing and PR people overlook when considering the benefits of a newsroom is that *you control the content*, not your IT department, webmaster, or anyone else. *You* should design your newsroom as a tool to reach buyers and journalists, and you don't need to take into consideration the rules for posting content that the rest of the organization's site may require. If you build this part of your site using a specialized newsroom content-management application, such as the MediaRoom product from PR Newswire, you will control a corner of your organization's website that you can update whenever you like using simple tools, and you won't need to request help from anyone in other departments or locations. So start with your needs and the needs of your buyers and journalists, not the needs of those who own the other parts of your organization's website.

Start with a Needs Analysis

When designing a new newsroom (or planning an extensive redesign), start with a needs analysis. Before you just jump right into site aesthetics and the organization of news releases, take time to analyze how the site fits into your larger marketing, PR, and media relations strategy. Consider the buyer persona profiles you built as part of your marketing and PR plan. Talk with friendly journalists so you can understand what they need. Who are the potential users of the newsroom, and what content will be valuable to them? When you have collected some information, build buyers' and journalists' needs into your newsroom.

As you work toward starting your design, try to think a bit more like a publisher and less like a marketing and PR person. A publisher carefully identifies and defines target audiences and then develops the content required to meet the needs of each distinct demographic. Graphical elements, colors, fonts, and other visual manifestations of the site are also important but should take a backseat during the content needs analysis process.

Optimize Your News Releases for Searching and for Browsing

The best newsrooms are built with the understanding that some people need to search for content and others are browsing. Many people already know what they are looking for—the latest release, perhaps, or the name of the CEO. They need answers to specific questions, and organizations must therefore optimize content so that it can be found, perhaps by including a search engine. The second way that people use content is to be told something that they do not already know and therefore couldn't think to ask. This is why browsability is also important; it allows users to discover useful information they didn't even know they were looking for. While many web-savvy marketers understand the importance of search engine optimization, they often forget that sites must be designed for browsing, too. Failing to do so is particularly unfortunate because the high traffic on news release pages comes partly from the many people who browse these pages as they conduct research.

You should deploy a navigational design in a way that provides valuable information that visitors might not have thought to ask for. Consider including multiple browsing techniques. For instance, you can create different links to targeted releases for different buyer personas (maybe by vertical market or some other demographic factor appropriate to your organization). You might also organize the same releases by product (because some members of the media may be covering just one of your products in a review or story), by geography, or by market served. Most organizations simply list news releases in reverse-chronological order (the newest release is at the top of the page, and ones from last year are hidden away somewhere). While this is fine for the main news release page, you need to have additional navigation links so people can browse the releases. Don't forget that people may also need to print out news releases, so consider providing printer-friendly formats (e.g., PDF format as well as HTML).

Include Links to Your Social Networking Feeds

If you maintain social networks for use with the media, you need to make sure the feeds are easy to access from your newsroom. You'll want your Twitter ID prominently displayed on each page along with other feeds such as your YouTube or Vimeo channel for video, Flickr or Instagram for photos, Pinterest, and so on. If you're creating a newsroom for a smaller organization, it's likely you'll be linking to the corporate social networking feeds. However, in larger organizations you might have a separate Twitter feed for the media relations team like the Kellogg Company does with its @KelloggCompany Twitter feed.

Create Background Information That Helps Journalists Write Stories

You should publish a set of background materials about your organization, sometimes called an online media kit or press kit, in an easy-to-find place in your newsroom. This kit should contain a lot of information, basically anything you think journalists might need to write about you and your products or services. Company history and time line, executive biographies, investor profiles, board of advisors' or board of directors' bios and photos, product and service information, ready-to-use and approved images and logos, information about analysts who cover your company, and links to recent media coverage will help your media kit save journalists time and tedious effort.

Make this content easy to find and to browse with appropriate navigational links. A set of information organized around customers and how they use products and services offered by the company is another key component of a newsroom, and I rarely see it. Case studies in the customers' own words are particularly useful, not only for journalists but also for buyers.

Remember, the easier you make a journalist's job, the more likely she is to write about your organization, particularly when she is on a tight deadline. I recall researching a feature story I was writing for *EContent* magazine called "On Message: The Market for Marketing-Specific Content Management." In the article, I was looking at companies and products that help marketers to organize information, and I knew the top players in the field and interviewed company executives for the article. But to round out the piece, I needed to include some newer niche companies. How did I choose the companies that made it in? You guessed it—the ones that made my job easiest by having an effective newsroom that helped me to instantly understand the company and its products.

Include Multimedia Content

Smart communicators make use of nontext content, such as photos, charts, graphs, audio feeds, and video clips, to inform site visitors and the media. Include executive photos, logo images, product photos, and other content that is ready (and preapproved) to be published or linked to by journalists. You should offer audio and video clips (such as parts of executive speeches or product demonstrations), photos, and logos in such a way that journalists can use them in their written stories, as well as on TV and radio shows. Again, you will find that many people besides journalists will access this, so include appropriate content for your buyer personas as well as for the media.

Include Detailed Product Specs and Other Valuable Data

Communicators who use newsrooms to offer valuable content are more likely to score the positive story. However, organizations often shy away from posting much of their best content because they deem it proprietary. On many sites, even information like detailed product specifications and price lists is available only through a direct connection with a PR contact or a lengthy registration form with approval mechanisms. Yet this is exactly the sort of content that, if freely available, would help convince journalists to write a story.

All communicators and marketing professionals working at corporations, government agencies, or nonprofits struggle to decide what content is appropriate to post on their organizations' sites. However, with well-meaning executives who worry about corporate image, legal departments with a reflexive tendency to say no, and salespeople who think it is easier to sell when they're the sole source of knowledge, it might be difficult to gain the necessary approvals to post proprietary content. But there is no doubt that the more valuable your media room's content looks to reporters and buyers, the more attractive your company will look to them as well.

If Appropriate, Go Global

The web has made reaching the world far easier, so when it is appropriate, the effort to create and offer local content to customers worldwide can help an organization better serve both local and global journalists. Many organizations, particularly those headquartered in the United States, make the mistake of including site content that reflects (and therefore has value for) only the home market. Basic approaches to get your site up to global standards might include offering case studies from customers in various countries or spec sheets describing products with local country standards (such as metric measurements or local regulatory compliance).

Sometimes the little things make a difference. For example, don't forget that the rest of the world uses standard A4 paper instead of the U.S. letter size, so having fact sheets and other materials that print properly on both formats, which have slightly different proportions, is useful to users outside the United States. Providing content in local languages can also help show the global aspect of your business, though this need not mean a wholesale translation of your entire newsroom. A simple web landing page with basic information in the local language, a few news releases, a case study or two, and appropriate local contact information will often suffice.

Provide Content for All Levels of Media Understanding

To be effective, communicators at many organizations specifically design media room content that supports journalists' level of knowledge of the organization. Some journalists may never have written about your company before; they need the basics spelled out in easy-to-understand language. In other cases, a reporter or analyst may have been covering the company for years, enjoy personal relationships with the executives, and know a great deal about what's going on with you, your competitors, and your market. You need content for this person, too; she may want to compare your offerings, and she therefore needs detailed company information, lists of features and benefits, and stories about your customers.

All reporters need easy navigation directly to content so they get what they need quickly. In my experience, the vast majority of newsrooms are little more than online brochures with a bunch of news releases. Don't let the opportunities that the web offers pass your newsroom by. Help journalists along the path to their keyboards by offering content directly linked to their various levels of understanding.

List Executive Appearances, Conferences, and Trade Show Participation

One of the best ways to positively influence journalists is to visit with them in person. Many journalists attend trade shows, conferences, and other events on a regular basis and use that time to meet with representatives of companies that they may consider writing about.

The best way to get your organization on journalists' calendars is to make certain that they know where your executives will be appearing. List all appropriate public speaking appearances, trade show and conference participation, and other events in a separate calendar section in your newsroom. Make certain to list all appropriate future events, and remember to include any international events. Keep the older listings up for at least a few months after the events to show that your executives are in demand as experts in your field, but be sure to keep the list up to date.

Don't forget that even this information is not just for the media. Even if they do not attend industry events, your buyers will see that your company is active and that your executives are in demand as speakers and presenters; this adds to your corporate credibility and your image as an industry leader.

Include Calls to Action for Journalists

It is a great idea to include special offers for the media. Perhaps the simplest thing to offer is an executive interview. But why not include a trial or demonstration offer of some kind, where journalists get to test your offerings, attend your events, or in some way experience what your organization does? You can even create a landing page specifically for journalists with a registration form and special offers. Include this link within news releases and other pages in the newsroom to drive interested journalists to the landing page.

Embrace Bloggers as You Do Traditional Journalists

Bloggers, podcasters, and other nontraditional media who cover your company visit your newsroom. Encourage them by responding to inquiries quickly, by including bloggers in your news release distribution email list, and by granting them interviews with executives upon request. The fact is that bloggers are influential, and they want to be treated with the same respect as traditional journalists. It's to your advantage to do so.

Avoid Jargon, Acronyms, and Industry-Speak

I scan a bunch of news releases in an average week. Some releases are sent directly to me from companies that want me to write about them in a magazine article, an upcoming book, or my blog, and others I find by checking out newsrooms. I visit many newsrooms in an average month and read the other content available as well as news releases.

Unfortunately, most newsrooms are chock-full of jargon, three-letter acronyms that I don't understand, and other egocentric nonsense. I'm interested in what companies are up to, but I'm just too busy to decipher gobbledygook. I normally give a news release 10 seconds to catch my attention, but the surest way to get me to delete a release in frustration is to write in a way that I just can't understand. If your mother doesn't understand your news, a journalist probably won't, either.

The Importance of RSS Feeds in Your Newsroom

To provide alternative content routes, many organizations use digital delivery methods, including email newsletters for journalists and bloggers and RSS feeds, as part of their newsrooms; this pushes content directly to the media and other interested people. Smart organizations are using RSS to easily update prospects, customers, investors, and the media, but too few organizations are using this simple marketing technique for sharing valuable information.

The RSS feeds can (and should) be added to most parts of your website. But because they are essentially subscription mechanisms to regularly updated content, many organizations have the RSS subscription page as part of the newsroom and use it as a primary way to deliver news release content. Companies such as Microsoft, IBM, and Intel syndicate information via RSS feeds to reach specific external audiences such as the media, Wall Street analysts, customers, partners, distributors, and resellers. This is just another example of how the main currency of online marketing is excellent content delivered in the way that people demand.

The Mobile Media Room

Because more and more reporters use their mobile devices while reporting, I'm convinced that the public relations, analyst relations, and investor relations departments of companies need to create applications to reach their editorial, analyst, investor, and other constituents. What we're seeing is the natural evolution of the online newsroom. Companies need a content-rich online media room filled with blog posts, videos, podcasts, e-books, press releases, and background information, and I think those same companies need to think about mobile content delivery to journalists.

In my travels around the world, I've noticed more and more reporters and analysts using mobile devices, especially iPads, to take notes during meetings. I've also seen them with smartphones in constant use while on the go. When a reporter or analyst has an application for the company, or music artist, or nonprofit she covers on her mobile, then she can easily check what's going on, as well as generate alerts for things like press releases—all on her device of choice. An added benefit is that these applications can double as tools to reach employees and partners, as well as existing and potential customers.

Showcase Your Experts

Some of your most important assets for securing interest in the media as well as educating your buyers are the experts who work at your organization. As a part of your newsroom, highlighting your employees is a great way to generate attention. When reporters are looking to quote someone in a story, having a name, photo, bio, and examples of content makes it much more likely they will want to conduct an interview. Similarly, when buyers are exposed to the smart people employed at your company, they will be more likely to trust and want to do business with you. Yet most companies feature only the senior management team on the site, not those with particular and interesting expertise.

The place on your site where you feature your experts should certainly be integrated with your newsroom (which is why I am discussing it in this chapter), but you could also link from other parts of your site. For example, if you have a profile for one of your subject matter experts, you could also link to that person's profile from the appropriate product pages.

Let's look in more depth at an organization putting this last technique to good use.

Ontario University Shines Spotlight on Faculty Researchers

The University of Ontario Institute of Technology (Ontario Tech), a public research university located in Oshawa, just outside Toronto, was founded in 2002. That makes it one of Canada's newest universities. With an enrollment of more than 10,000 students, Ontario Tech offers a range of undergraduate programs, plus graduate programs in science, engineering, health, and information technology.

But because it is such a new institution, the marketers and public affairs people at Ontario Tech have to work extra hard to make sure that potential students, donors, partners, and other constituents know about the school. Unlike other universities, Ontario Tech cannot rely on decades of families that send their children and grandchildren to the institution and support it with financial contributions. So one way the school reaches out to new audiences is by promoting with the media the many faculty experts who teach and do research at Ontario Tech.

"We focus on the experts within the institution," says John MacMillan, director of communications and marketing at Ontario Tech. "We have very few resources, but we have a lot of really interesting people who are focused on very exciting things, like using big data and looking at issues of disability and how it relates to the insurance industry, among other things. We are able to reach the media and people who are organizing conferences or booking speaking engagements."

MacMillan uses the ExpertFile software platform as a way to easily showcase Ontario Tech thought leaders in what's called the Expert Centre. He publishes, promotes, and measures the expert content as a tool to engage business prospects, media, and conference organizers. "We needed to have a way of getting out those important stories that we know are of interest to media, to producers, to editors, but also in many ways to partners, to institutions that might be interested in working with us," MacMillan says.

"And we needed to have a way that did a better job of telling our story to those various groups."

MacMillan started with 26 profiles for faculty in the Expert Centre, and has steadily expanded to 100 faculty profiles. He says that an ideal expert is one who is already comfortable with digital technology. "We're amplifying the presence of each of those faculty members—whether they are involved in multimedia, whether they have their own websites, or whether they have their own followings—and presenting them in a way that gets some response. Part of their success as faculty members lies in establishing their bona fides with granting authorities or with the government or with others. The Expert Centre augments their legitimacy."

With faculty who can speak to a range of topics as diverse as big data, immigration, and crime, the school has seen tens of thousands of digital interactions on its website and more than 500 direct inquiries from media, graduate students, research collaborators, and other interested people. Focusing more on its faculty has helped Ontario Tech garner media attention from a variety of media outlets, including the *New York Times*, *Wired* magazine, CBC TV, and VICE News. Ontario Tech faculty have also received hundreds of inquiries related to everything from new graduate student requests to researcher collaborations and speaking opportunities from organizations in locations as diverse as the University of Michigan, the University of Liverpool, and the U.S. Marine Corps.

As an example of the action that can come from an Expert Centre profile, MacMillan cites Dr. Isabel Pedersen, an associate professor at Ontario Tech and Canada Research Chair in Digital Life, Media, and Culture. "She focuses on a sociological perspective of wearable computing devices," he says. "Her research looks into questions like: 'When we wear gadgets on our body, how will that shift the reality for us? How will it change the way we interact with other people? How will it allow us to participate in digital culture?' She is one of the early profiles that we created because she is one of our Canada Research Chairs, a distinguished researcher who is working on an area of particular national and international importance."

Dr. Pedersen's Expert Centre profile contains her bio and photo, live updates from her Twitter feed, and a list of past speaking engagements, as well as video content, links to her book *Ready to Wear*, and articles she has been quoted in. The profile attracted the attention of a reporter from *IEEE Spectrum* magazine, the publication of the world's largest professional association dedicated to advancing technological innovation and excellence.

"They were working on a story about wearable technology, and they wanted to interview her," MacMillan says. "That's a magazine from the U.S. that has a much broader readership than anything we'd be able to position her for, and it came along as a result of somebody seeing her profile and deciding that they wanted to speak with her. That's an example of where we've been able to use our resources in a very efficient way, in a manner that gets a story out well beyond our own physical boundaries and that tells about the uniqueness of the work that's going on at this university."

A lesson learned from the early days of the Ontario Tech Expert Centre was the importance of having the profiles appear in a consistent voice. "When we started out, our assumption was that the individual faculty members or individual experts would develop their own profiles," MacMillan says. "We realized that would result in a lack of consistency, so we hired a writer, and her job was specifically to interview our experts and to create a story for each of those experts so that when someone does look at this, they're looking at a consistent story, a consistent tone, and a consistent brand for the university. I've learned from creating our Expert Centre that I share some of the same challenges as faculty members: If you don't manage your digital presence actively, someone will do it for you. I like to think that our Expert Centre has helped our faculty to curate their digital content as much as it's helped our university to strengthen its brand."

Your employees are a great resource for generating interest in the media as well as a way to show potential customers and partners that you are doing interesting work. "Experts are a great way to humanize an organization and make it more approachable, yet many marketers struggle with how to best showcase these people online," notes Peter Evans, founder and CEO of ExpertFile. Adding a dedicated section to your media room is an ideal way to showcase them for the world to see.

A Newsroom to Reach Journalists, Customers, and Bloggers

One of the finest examples I've seen of an online newsroom comes from Tourism Whistler, the member-based marketing and sales organization representing Canadian leisure and meeting destination Whistler. The Tourism Whistler newsroom incorporates almost every best practice outlined in this chapter. What struck me about the Tourism Whistler media room is how much it resembles a media site like CNN, the BBC, or the *New York Times*, with text-based content, video, images, and social network links. It turns out that that's no coincidence. Both the organization's manager of corporate communications and CEO come from a media background.

The content on the site is simple to browse and, using the Media Marmot Search Tool, also easy to search based on keywords and phrases. (The Media Marmot was named in honor of the hoary marmot, from which Whistler earned its name due to the whistling sound made by these furry residents.) There's an extensive multimedia library accessible with no registration, including real-time photos and videos. For example, media can access photos of the recent Whistler snowfall. There's also a B-roll video gallery that allows media outlets to preview highlights of Tourism Whistler's significant collection of B-roll footage, which they can then request to use.

One aspect of the newsroom I particularly like is the Whistler Story Starters, which provide journalists with story ideas about Whistler's role in Canadian history, in the 2010 Winter Olympic Games (some events were held in Whistler), and in the area's position as one of the world's top resort destinations.

The Tourism Whistler newsroom is used extensively by the media, including writers, broadcasters, and bloggers. As the Tourism Whistler example shows, providing a great newsroom with lots of content proves useful to journalists. For most organizations, the amount of money spent to create a newsroom will be far less than the quantifiable benefit derived from it.

The newsroom is a place where many people congregate, not just journalists. It is one place on your organization's website that *you can control*, without interference, approval processes, and IT support, so it presents a terrific opportunity for marketing and PR people to get content out into the marketplace. On the web, success equals content. And one of the easiest ways to get content into the market is via a newsroom with RSS feeds.

20 The New Rules for Reaching the Media

As the web has made communicating with reporters and editors extremely easy, breaking through using the online methods everyone else uses has become increasingly difficult. These days, you can find the email addresses of reporters in seconds, either through commercial services that sell subscriptions to their databases of thousands of journalists or simply by using a search engine. Unfortunately, way too many PR people are spamming journalists with unsolicited and unrelenting commercial messages in the form of news releases and untargeted broadcast pitches. I hate to say it, but among the many journalists I speak with, the PR profession has become synonymous with spammers. For years, PR people have been shotgun-blasting news releases and blind pitches to hundreds (or even thousands) of journalists at a time—without giving any thought to what each reporter actually covers—just because the media databases the PR people subscribe to make it so darn simple to do.

> Barraging large groups of journalists with indiscriminate PR materials is not a good strategy to get reporters and editors to pay attention to you.

"Re:," Nontargeted Pitches, and Other Sleazy Tactics

As I've said, I get dozens of news releases, pitches, and announcements from PR agency staffers and corporate communications people every week. Like all journalists, my email address is available in many places: in the articles I write, on my blog, in my books, and in the articles I write for the *HuffPost* and other publications. That easy availability means that my address has also been added to various databases and lists of journalists. Unfortunately, my email address also gets added (without my permission) to many press lists that PR agencies and companies compile and maintain; whenever they have a new announcement, no matter what the subject, I'm part of the broadcast message. *Ugh*. The PR spam approach simply doesn't work. Worse, it brands your organization as one of the bad guys.

Here's a specific example of a PR spam trick that has grown in popularity in recent years: the use of "re:" in subject lines. For years, spam artists have used "re:" in their subject lines to try to trick people into opening the email. The trick is effective because the email now looks to the receiver like a reply to an email he or she originally sent. Many phishing attempts use this tactic.

Here are some examples of this unscrupulous practice, all drawn from my inbox in just the past few days:

- Re: HomeDepot Replacement-Windows-Special
- Re: AUTO-DEALS – Cars-Below Kelly-Blue Book Value
- RE: Your-Energy Bill-was recently-lowered-by 80%
- Re: Automobile Bonanza Sales

It's annoying enough to receive messages like this from spam artists. But it's downright sad to see that many PR agencies and marketing firms are following spammers' lead.

Your approach to PR shouldn't rely on deliberately confusing your reader. Sure, in normal usage, "re:" does mean "in regard to." However, we all know that at the beginning of an email subject line, the only correct use of "re:" is in reply to an email.

Here are a few I've received in the past week or so. Remember, these aren't from petty criminals; they're from PR people:

- Re: What's the "Secret Sauce" to Social Media Marketing?
- RE: Story Idea: 5 Steps to Make Your Ad 'Go Viral'
- RE: Interested in featuring 'The Value of Coupons in Digital Marketing' [Infographic]
- RE: Hope you received my last email
- RE: Mad Men vs. Mad Math: How Data (Not Dimensions) is the Future of Online Advertising
- Re: Update on social media content optimization survey

Don't send spam email to journalists, and don't use sleazy tactics like disguising your message as a reply to something the receiver said.

The New Rules of Media Relations

Okay, that's the depressing news. The good news is that there are effective new rules that work very well to get your messages into the hands (and onto the screens) of reporters so they will be more likely to write about you. Don't forget that reporters are looking for interesting companies, products, and ideas to write about. They want to find you. If you have great content on your website and in your online media room, *reporters will find you* via search engines.

Try to think about reaching journalists with ways that aren't just one-way spam. Pay attention to what individual reporters write about by reading their stories (and, better yet, their blogs), and write specific and targeted pitches crafted especially for them. Or start a real relationship with reporters by commenting on their blogs, interacting with them on Twitter, or sending them information that is not just a blatant pitch for your company. Become part of their network of sources, rather than simply a shill for one company's message. If you or someone in your organization writes a blog in the market category that a reporter covers, let him know about it, because what you blog about may become prime fodder for the reporter's future stories. Don't forget to pitch bloggers. Not only does a mention in a widely read blog reach your buyers, but reporters and editors also read these blogs for story ideas and to understand early market trends.

The web has changed the rules. If you're still following the traditional PR techniques, I'm sure you're finding that they are much less effective. To be more successful, consider and use the new rules of media relations:

- Nontargeted, broadcast pitches are spam.
- News releases sent to reporters in subject areas they do not cover are spam.
- Reporters who don't know you yet are looking for organizations like yours and products like yours—make sure they will find you with search engines such as Google and on industry sites.
- If you blog, reporters who cover the space will find you.
- Pitch bloggers, because being covered in important blogs will get you noticed by mainstream media.
- When was the last news release you sent? Make sure your organization is busy.
- Use newsjacking to get your ideas into the marketplace of ideas when the moment is right.
- Journalists want a great online media room.
- Include video and photos in your online media room.
- Some (but not all) reporters love RSS feeds.
- Personal relationships with reporters are important.
- Don't tell journalists what your product does. Tell them how you solve customer problems.
- Follow journalists on Twitter to learn what interests them.
- Does the reporter have a blog? Read it. Comment on it. Before you pitch, read (or listen to or watch) the publication (or radio program or TV show) you'll be pitching to.
- Once you know what a reporter is interested in, send her an individualized pitch crafted especially for her needs.

Blogs and Media Relations

Getting your organization visible on blogs is an increasingly important way not only to reach your buyers but also to reach the mainstream media that cover your industry, because reporters and editors read blogs for story ideas. Treat influential bloggers exactly as you treat influential reporters: Read their stuff, and send them specifically targeted information that might be useful to them. Offer them interviews with your executives and demonstrations or samples of your products. Offer to take them to lunch.

Pitching influential bloggers as you would pitch mainstream media is an important way to get noticed in the crowded marketplace of ideas. But even more effective is having your own blog so that bloggers and reporters find you. "Blogging gives me a place in the media community to stand out," says John Blossom, president of Shore Communications Inc., a research and analysis company. Blossom has been blogging since 2003 and writes about enterprise publishing and media markets. "In ways that I didn't expect, my blog has allowed me to become a bit of a media personality. I've been picked up by some big bloggers, and that makes me aware that blogging is a terrific way to get exposure, because the rate of pickup and amplification is remarkable. The press reads my blog and reaches out to me for quotes. Sometimes I'm quoted in the media by a reporter who doesn't even speak with me. For example, a reporter from the *Financial Times* recently picked up a quote and used it in a story—based on my blog alone."

How Blog Mentions Drive Mainstream Media Stories

Promoting a valuable, one-of-a-kind object for sale at the best price requires a seller to be clever and utilize both traditional public relations and new media.

This study in extreme cleverness begins with Richard Jurek. Jurek is a marketing and communication professional, as well as a space enthusiast and collector and my co-author on our 2014 book *Marketing the Moon: The Selling of the Apollo Lunar Program*. When he decided to part with a few unique and treasured items from his collection, Jurek put his 20 years of professional experience to work. He knew that one of his items needed special attention.

That item was the unofficial fourth crewmate of Apollo 12.

In a prank of lunar proportions, a vintage November 1969 color calendar photo of *Playboy* Playmate Miss August 1967, DeDe Lind, was stowed away in the Apollo 12 command module *Yankee Clipper* during its November 1969 voyage to the moon.

The photo was affixed to a cardboard cue card and, unbeknownst to the crew, secreted onboard their spacecraft. The iconic piece of 1960s pop culture made the 475,000-mile round-trip to the moon and back and still retains the Velcro strips used to affix it inside the spacecraft for easy viewing.

Jurek acquired the item directly from Apollo 12 astronaut Richard Gordon. "This is an absolutely singular item, unique in the space-collecting world," Jurek says. "But it also has tremendous crossover appeal. I figured that DeDe would appeal not only to space collectors but collectors of 1970s pop culture, because *Playboy* was at its peak in 1970s America. There are also collectors of erotica and collectors of *Playboy* items. So it appeals to a lot of audiences."

Jurek knew that he wanted to sell DeDe through a recognized auction house, and he had narrowed the choice down to a handful. "I selected RRAuction for the sale because the auction house has a phenomenal Internet and social media platform, and they leverage it in their marketing," he says.

Working in the auction business is an incredibly old profession, having been around, well, almost as long as the so-called oldest profession. The idea that you can apply new forms of marketing to an ancient business is fascinating to me, and I wanted to learn more.

I spoke with Bobby Livingston, an auctioneer with a traditional PR background. Livingston is vice president of sales and marketing at RRAuction. He worked with Jurek to write the catalog description for the item and promote the auction itself.

"The Apollo 12 calendar has a great story," Livingston says. "It has a bunch of things going for it: It's Apollo, it's flown, and it's cheesecake, so it's easy to understand and easily translates around the world. It brings back the 1969 time frame. It's just a remarkable piece."

Livingston worked with Mike Graff of the Investor Relations Group in New York City to craft a press release and get it directly to bloggers who write about current events and technology. Graff also made follow-up phone calls. Very quickly, sites like Gawker, Nerdist, and io9 picked up on the story.

"When Gizmodo talked about the auction, suddenly we got 20,000 visitors," Livingston says. "We got 40 new auction registrations. On the best day, we [typically] do seven to 10 registrations. Then we got 30 the next day. Well, this is all coming from viral and new media."

Soon, the international media got news of DeDe from the blogs. Stories appeared in Australia, Brazil, France, China, Japan, and a dozen other countries. Large outlets like BBC, CNN, the Discovery Channel, the *Sun*,

Daily Mail, UPI, *Toronto Star*, and *Time* wrote about the Apollo Playmate stowaway. Even the Playboy Satellite Radio Channel and website got in on the fun.

As Livingston was working the media, Jurek was helping things along by contacting appropriate bloggers via social networking. "Every time I would see an article, I would push it out using appropriate hashtags and try for crossover appeal," Jurek says. The strategy was to target related audiences, so Jurek tagged his tweets with things like #playboy, #photography, #space, #NASA, #auction, #apollo, #moon, #porn, and more. "I wanted to reach not only space collectors but also *Playboy* folks or, hell, even pornography people!"

Jurek says many tweets came from women who run their own webcam businesses and have thousands of followers. "Others were tweeting about space porn and moon porn and so on," he says. "It's hilarious, but I viewed DeDe as perfect for social media and the Internet, because porn is a huge business on the Internet, and so are collectibles, and so is history. It was right in the center of all of that, and people were picking up on it."

The story even made "Weekend Update" on *Saturday Night Live*. I've got to say, I've worked in and around PR for 20 years, and this is the first time I've known anyone who's made "Weekend Update"!

Jurek says he's learned some valuable lessons from this marketing effort. "Content drives marketing," he says. "DeDe, from a content perspective, is perfect. She has appeal not just as a moon-flown artifact for space geeks like me but for collectors of Americana, collectors of erotica, and collectors of unique niche pop culture items. Once you have the content, it is connecting it with the right audience, making sure the pitch is real and right on."

All of these efforts drove large volumes of traffic to the RRAuction site. Visitors were up 350 percent over the previous month and the DeDe Lind item received 30 bids and sold to a high bidder at $17,511.

"DeDe realized phenomenal results," Jurek says. "From a marketing perspective, she also achieved the goal because she drove lots of traffic to the auction. So much so that DeDe, while beating the estimate on where she would sell, also helped many, many other lots realize record results. The knock-off effect of the DeDe media coverage expanded the pool of global bidders and collectors of this material by a dramatic amount, and bidding was healthy across all lots."

Launching Ideas with the U.S. Air Force

The websites of the U.S. Air Force are chock-full of photos, video, and articles written by Air Force Public Affairs officers, all serving to provide the media with information they need to craft a story. These officers don't sit around all day writing press releases and pitching the media with story ideas. Rather, they publish information themselves, information that generates interest from reporters.

"Instead of pushing things out, people are finding us and our information," says Captain Nathan Broshear, director of public affairs at 12th Air Force (Air Forces Southern), the Air Force component to U.S. Southern Command and based at Davis-Monthan Air Force Base in Tucson, Arizona. Broshear is no stranger to working with mainstream media representatives, having previously managed hundreds of Iraq- and Afghanistan-based reporters in that high-pressure war zone environment.

"People are finding our websites to be valuable. For example, many reporters are currently interested in the Predator, Global Hawk, and Reaper systems, our unmanned aerial vehicles. And when they see the pages on our site about Predator and Reaper, then they know whom to contact."

For example, Technical Sergeant Eric Petosky, who works with Broshear in public affairs, wrote a story called "Global Hawk Flying Environmental Mapping Missions in Latin America, Caribbean," which he posted on the site with photos. When a reporter becomes interested in a system like the Global Hawk, he or she can find the information on the site. "The Air Force is a big organization, and if a reporter goes to the Pentagon, it is hard to find the right person. We write stories so reporters can envision what their angle might look like." And together with the stories, photos, and videos is the necessary contact information for getting in touch with the appropriate Air Force Public Affairs staff member.

The published information about unmanned aerial systems proved valuable when *60 Minutes*, the weekly CBS television magazine, became interested in the story. Broshear teamed with Captain Brooke Brander, chief of public affairs at Creech Air Force Base in Nevada (where the pilots of the unmanned systems are based), to help lay the groundwork for the story. They worked with *60 Minutes* producers for more than five months. "Drones: America's New Air Force" aired on *60 Minutes*, with Lara Logan reporting on the increasing use of drones in the battlefield.

Another success story from Broshear's use of online content to help reporters involves Operation New Horizons in Guyana. Operation New Horizons is part of an Air Force program to build infrastructure, partnerships, and relationships in other countries. "The Air Force is building a school and a clinic while providing free medical care for about 100,000 people," Broshear says. "We partner with nongovernmental organizations to make certain the local school, clinics, and doctors have what they need to continue providing services even after U.S. military members depart."

To get the story out to both the local community in Guyana and people back in the United States, Broshear works with those on the ground to create content that reporters can draw from to craft their stories—without the need for constant contact from public affairs staff. "We post photos onto Flickr and have a Facebook page and a blog written by people on the ground. And what's interesting is that the blogs get three times more traffic than our main pages. The newspapers in the local communities are pulling photographs from the sites. After we introduce the projects and key military personalities to the local media the first time through a press release or visit to the construction sites, we don't need to do anything, because the media are pulling information from the blog that we created."

As you know if you've read this far, the importance of creating valuable content (photos, video, news stories) and posting it on your site is the theme of this book. When you create that content, you reach people who are looking for what you have to offer. Broshear reminds us how sometimes those people are members of the mainstream media, and great content can serve as the catalyst to getting the coverage your organization desires. "Here in U.S. Air Force Public Affairs, we're not launching missiles," he says. "We're launching ideas." And those ideas lead to major stories in top-tier media.

How to Pitch the Media

As marketers know, having your company, product, or executive appear in an appropriate publication is great marketing. That's why billions of dollars are spent on PR each year (though much of it's wasted, I'm afraid). When your organization appears in a story, not only do you reach the publication's audience directly, but you also can point your prospects to the piece later, using reprints or web links. Media coverage means legitimacy. As I've said, broadcast spamming of the media doesn't work so well and can actually be harmful to your brand. But sometimes you really want to target a specific publication (your hometown paper, perhaps). So what should you do?

- **Target one reporter at a time.** Taking the time to read a publication and then crafting a unique pitch to a particular journalist can work wonders. Mention a specific article he wrote, and then explain why your company or product would be interesting for the journalist to look at. Reporters are individuals, so find out what they are interested in and writing about, and feed them stories that are not related to you. Make certain to target the subject line of the email to help ensure that it gets opened. For example, I recall getting a perfectly positioned pitch crafted especially for me from a company that provides a web-based sales-lead qualification and management system. The PR person had read my blog and knew what I was interested in, so I emailed back within minutes to set up an interview with the company's CEO.
- **Use the tip line if the media outlet you are targeting has one.** Many news sites maintain tip lines that you should take advantage of when you have important news. For example, the TechCrunch homepage features a prominent tip/pitch invitation. When you click the link, you're taken to a web form: "So you've got the inside scoop on a story or topic that we cover? Please let us know in the form below or email us directly at tips@techcrunch.com. We will respect your anonymity."
- **Help the journalist to understand the big picture.** Often it's difficult to understand how some product or service or organization actually fits into a wider trend. You make a journalist's job much easier if you describe the big picture of why your particular product or service is interesting. Often this helps you get mentioned in the reporter's future articles or columns about trends in your space.
- **Keep it simple.** If you can't explain what you do crisply and intelligently without using three-letter acronyms, few reporters will engage with you. Work on your cocktail party explanation, and don't assume every reporter is an insider.
- **Try newsjacking!** Use current events as hooks to show how people in your organization can comment on breaking news. Newsjacking is

the art and science of injecting your ideas into a breaking news story to generate tons of media coverage. We will cover it in detail in the next chapter.

- **Explain how customers use your product or work with your organization.** Reporters hear hundreds of pitches from company spokespeople about how products work. But it's much more useful to hear about a product in action from someone who actually uses it. If you can set up interviews with customers or provide written case studies of your products or services, it will be much easier for journalists to write about your company.

- **Don't send email attachments unless asked.** These days, it is a rare journalist indeed who opens an unexpected email attachment, even from a recognized company. Yet many PR people still distribute news releases as email attachments. Don't do it. Send plain-text emails instead. If you're asked for other information, you can follow up with attachments, but be sure to clearly reference in the email what you're sending and why, so the journalist will remember asking for it.

- **Follow up promptly with potential contacts.** Recently I agreed to interview a senior executive at a large company. An eager PR person set it up, and we agreed on date and time. But I never got the promised follow-up information via email, which was supposed to include the telephone number to reach the executive. Needless to say, the interview didn't happen. Make certain you follow up as promised.

- **Don't forget, it's a two-way street—journalists need you to pitch them!** The bottom line is that reporters want to know what you have to say. It is unfortunate that the spam problem in PR is as big as it is, because it makes journalists' jobs more difficult.

As an illustration of this last point, a company executive I met at a conference made a comment on a new trend that gave me a brilliant idea for a magazine article I was working on. I was delighted because it made my life easier. Thinking of subjects is hard work, and I need all the help I can get. The executive's company fit in perfectly with the column idea, and I used his product as the example of the trend he told me about. Without the conversation, the story would never have been written—but a straight product pitch wouldn't have worked. We reporters need smart ideas to do our job. Please.

"The single most effective thing PR people do is watch and read my stories and send me personalized, smart pitches for stories that I am actually likely to cover," says Peter J. Howe, business editor for New England Cable News (NECN), a regional channel serving 3.6 million cable homes. Howe was also a business, technology, and political reporter for the *Boston Globe* for 22 years before joining NECN. In both jobs, Howe said, he's preferred to be pitched by email. "'PR pitch for *Boston Globe* reporter Peter Howe' or 'Tuesday story idea for NECN' is actually a very effective way to get my attention. If you're getting literally four or five hundred emails a day like I am, cute subject lines aren't going to work and in fact will likely appear to be spam."

Howe's biggest beef with how PR people operate is that so many have no idea what he writes about before they send him a pitch. "If you simply put 'Peter Howe NECN' into a Google.com/news search and read the first 10 things that pop up, you would have done more work than 98 percent of the PR people who pitch me," he says. "It's maddening how many people in PR have absolutely no sense of what NECN puts on air or the difference between what the *Boston Globe* covers and a trade publication does. And I don't mean to sound like a whining diva; the bigger issue is that if you're not figuring out what I cover and how before you pitch me, you are really wasting your time and your clients' time."

Howe also encourages people to try to think big. "If you have a small thing to pitch, pitch it. But try to also think of the bigger story or roundup package that it can fit into," he says. "That could even wind up meaning your company is mentioned alongside three or four of your competitors, but wouldn't you rather have thousands of people see and hear your company name on TV or read it in a page 1 story?"

There is no doubt that mainstream media are still vital as a channel for your buyers to learn about your products. Besides all the people who will see your company's, product's, or executive's name, a mention in a major publication lends you legitimacy. Reporters have a job to do, and they need the help that PR people can provide to them. But the rules have changed. To get noticed, you need to be smart about how you tell your story on the web—and about how you tell your story to journalists.

21 Newsjacking Your Way into the Media

During the NFL American Football Conference (AFC) Championship game played on January 18, 2015, game officials alleged that the New England Patriots used footballs that were inflated to a pressure below the league standard. Some pundits claim that underinflating an American football makes it easier to grip, throw, and catch, presumably giving the Patriots an unfair advantage over the Indianapolis Colts. Very quickly, the Twitter hashtag #DeflateGate took off on social media, and news outlets adopted the Deflategate moniker in many of the hundreds of stories that were written about the incident in the days that followed.

Soon, brands were tweeting, blogging, and publishing videos using the #DeflateGate hashtag, injecting their ideas into this quickly developing news story. Krispy Kreme Doughnuts tweeted via @KrispyKreme an image of a football shaped like a donut with the line "Ours are fully filled #DeflateGate." (This jab was particularly delicious because Krispy Kreme's rivals, New England–based Dunkin' Donuts, is a sponsor of the Patriots.) The Krispy Kreme image was shared tens of thousands of times on social networks and seen by millions of people. Tire manufacturer Michelin USA tweeted via @MichelinUSA an image of the Michelin Man with a pressure gauge checking a football. It carried the witty line "Inflation Matters #DeflateGate," and it was also widely shared, getting Michelin noticed at no cost.

Newsjacking.

As hundreds of millions of people were learning about the underinflated footballs in news stories and via social media, brands like Michelin USA,

Krispy Kreme, and others seized the moment in real time and injected their brands into the most talked-about news story that week. As a result of these clever tweets, millions of people were exposed to these brands at no cost to the companies. Compare this approach to the traditional route: paying millions of dollars for television commercials during NFL games.

As we'll see in this chapter, newsjacking succeeds when it is very fast to market and tastefully (or at least nonoffensively) ties back to the brand and its ideas.

It's not just consumer brands that newsjack. When Democrat Tim Kaine and Republican Mike Pence faced off in the 2016 vice-presidential debate, then-candidate for president Donald Trump took to his @realDonaldTrump Twitter feed to live tweet during the debate.

For example, when his running mate Pence discussed his views on the police, Trump live tweeted: "I agree Mike – thank you to all of our law enforcement officers! #VPDebate "Police officers are the best of us . . ." @Mike_Pence.

Trump's live tweet during the debate using the hashtag #VPDebate ensured the media would see and comment on his views. I'm convinced that his mastery of real-time communications and newsjacking techniques was an essential strategy in electing Donald Trump the 45th president of the United States.

You can do the same in your marketplace.

Journalists Are Looking for What You Know

The real-time web has opened a tremendous opportunity for anyone to get their brand discussed as part of the news of the day. I've been a marketer for two decades, and I have never seen a technique as powerful. But newsjacking requires speed to market that most organizations reserve only for crisis communications. We'll be covering the basics of newsjacking in this chapter, but if you want to learn even more, you can check out my online course, *Master Newsjacking*.

As journalists scramble to cover breaking news, the basic facts of the story are often easy to find. That's what goes in the first paragraph of any news story. The challenge for reporters is to get background information that rounds out the basic facts, or the details that appear in subsequent paragraphs. If they're lucky, journalists also find unique story angles that competitive media are not yet reporting.

That's what makes newsjacking possible. Reporters are actually looking for additional information for their stories, and they're doing it by searching Google and the other search engines, as well as Twitter and other social networks.

If you have a legitimate tie to a breaking news story and you react in real time—by providing additional content in a blog post, tweet, video, or media alert—journalists may find you while they are researching material for their stories.

Newsjacking opportunities can turn up in unlikely places. But you've got to be quick when the opportunity arises.

Remember the tabloid item about a naked Prince Harry in Las Vegas, first published by TMZ? It was one of the most searched and discussed cell phone photos of all time. Lots of marketers tried to newsjack the stories of the Vegas romp. While most attempts went unnoticed, several were highly successful.

For example, soon after the photos appeared, Unilever-owned Lynx Men's Deodorant responded with a parody of the World War II UK government "Keep Calm and Carry On" posters. Its version used the line "Sorry Harry if it had anything to do with us." Many people talked about the ads in social networks, and the UK media wrote stories—all generating positive buzz for Lynx Men's Deodorant.

Likewise, the scene of the Prince Harry photo incident was the luxurious Encore Wynn Hotel. In what was another very clever newsjack of the story, owner Steve Wynn publicly waived the hotel bill (we're talking tens of thousands of dollars), which got the Encore Wynn into a stunning 3,657 stories by my Google News count. Stories like the one appearing in the United Kingdom's *Daily Mail*, "Living like a king: Prince Harry's £30,000 hotel bill 'waived' by Vegas billionaire," were essentially huge, free advertisements for the hotel. Such stories often came with descriptions and photos of the Encore Wynn and its royal suite.

This is a perfect example of newsjacking success. For the price of waiving a few hotel nights, the Wynn gets mentioned in thousands of stories. How cool is that?

This isn't the first time that representatives from the Wynn hotel organization have successfully newsjacked a story. They also scored thousands of press mentions when they banned infamous party girl Paris Hilton from their properties after she was arrested for alleged cocaine possession. So as the media reported on Hilton's arrest, many also mentioned that she had been banned from the Wynn properties.

Get Your Take on the News into the Marketplace of Ideas

Your goal with newsjacking is to get your take on a breaking news story in front of journalists at the moment they are looking for additional information to put in their stories. There are a number of ways to do that, with the techniques falling into two categories. The first category relies on journalists searching online for interesting story angles. Here, your job is to create the content they will find. The other category is to quickly push your message to the media directly.

Let's look first at the search-based techniques, and then at some techniques that allow you to target individual reporters and media outlets. Here are some of the ways you can make your message stand out.

Blog It and Post It to Your Online Media Room

Google, Bing, and other search engines now index in real time, which means that your blog post or update to your online media room will instantly appear in search results. This capability allows journalists working on a fast-moving story to find your post. The beauty of this technique is that reporters are looking for you by searching for keywords and phrases of the moment as they write their stories. Many journalists also use Google Alerts, which email them whenever certain keywords and phrases appear in blogs or on websites.

To get found in this way, as reporters are looking for experts, you've got to post your take on a story right now. Not tomorrow. Not this afternoon. Now. Make sure to feature appropriate keywords and phrases that journalists are likely to enter, and write your headline so it clearly shows reporters that you have a fresh and compelling take on the story.

Send a Real-Time Media Alert

A media alert is similar to a news release, but designed to provide reporters with specific information as they write about breaking news (see Chapter 18 for more information about creating and publishing news releases). To ensure it gets wide exposure, you'll want to publish your media alert quickly both in your online media room as well as through a press-release distribution service. Services like PR Newswire, Business Wire, and PRWeb are available in many countries and languages.

Use Appropriate Hashtags

When news is trending, frequently members of the media will be looking for the latest information on Twitter and other social networking sites by searching on the hashtag associated with the breaking news.

For example, June 2019 was LGBTQ Pride Month. Many people participated in Pride Month events shared on social media using hashtags including #PrideMonth, #lgbtq, #bornperfect, #equalitymatters, #accelerateacceptance, or #pride2019. As journalists wrote stories about Pride Month activities in their city, they would often turn to the social hashtags to find out what was happening.

Harness the Power of the Podium

If you or the executives in your organization have an opportunity to deliver a speech at a well-timed live event, this can be the perfect opportunity to add your take to breaking news. Politicians who have reporters hanging on their every word do this all the time. By dropping a reference in a speech or mentioning details to reporters afterward, the pols are able to elbow their way into stories that would not otherwise mention them.

Live-Stream It

If your company is in the thick of a story, another great way to get your information out there is to hold a live news conference with reporters and bloggers. News conferences are a time-honored tool for politicians and corporations covered by beat reporters. When a story breaks in real time, you can announce an online news conference to be held at a time a few hours in the future and then live-stream the Q&A session.

It's a good idea to archive the feed so people can watch it later. Live-streaming news feeds are still rare, which surprises me given the increasing ease of this technique on the technology side and the tremendous value of reaching reporters and bloggers in real time.

Comment on Breaking News Stories at Online Publications

Many reporters now blog, and most online publications give readers space to comment on stories. You can comment on breaking stories, pointing out facets of the story they may have overlooked—along with a link to your own blog or website. If your contribution offers real value, the reporter will sometimes follow up.

Use Media Tip Lines

Many media outlets have created simple ways for anybody to contribute to news stories. Sometimes called "tip lines," these entry points can be used when you have important contributions to offer. For example, CNN iReport allows anyone to pitch a story to the global news network.

Tweet to Appropriate Reporters

Twitter is an excellent way to reach journalists directly. If a reporter is on Twitter—and by now most of them are—you can usually find his or her Twitter ID at the beginning or end of a story. If not, use a search engine to find it. Then you can offer a one-sentence take on the reporter's recently filed stories. Better yet, point to your blog post. That way the reporter can see that you've got something to add to the story. You may get lucky and receive a message back to schedule an interview.

How to Find News to Jack

The most important aspect to successfully injecting your ideas into a breaking news story is to follow the new rules of speed. You've got to build that real-time mind-set that I wrote about in Chapter 8. The traditional marketing and PR model—creating "campaigns" with long lead times—just doesn't work when a story breaks quickly. Now doesn't mean tomorrow. It means *now*. Newsjacking is amazingly powerful, but only when executed in real time.

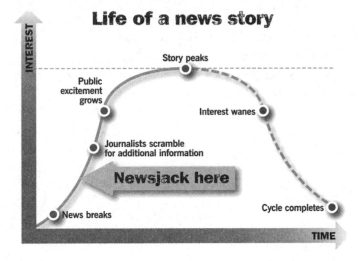

There are three broad areas in which to find stories for newsjacking opportunities:

1. Things you already know—the news that's happening in your market-place, geographical location, or areas of personal interest.
2. Things you didn't think to ask in the wider sphere of breaking national or global news.
3. Widely known current events anticipated in the immediate future to which you can tie a news hook.

The trick is to devise news-monitoring strategies that keep you instantly informed on each of these levels.

To cover the news that's happening right now within your immediate sphere, you will want to monitor media and journalists you may already know, including influential bloggers and the trade publications that cover your marketplace. If you run a local business—a home renovation com-pany, perhaps—then your hometown paper is a perfect place to start. We'll take a look at how to monitor this news first. Then we'll turn our attention to news you don't see coming from outlets you may not yet know, followed by a look at current events such as holidays, elections, and other types of activities that you do know will be occurring.

Tracking People You Know

To find news that you might have something to say about, follow bloggers, analysts, journalists, and others who cover your business and its wider industry. As we discussed in Chapter 5 when we looked at monitoring blogs, start by identifying as many voices as you can. Check the search engines (Google, Yahoo!, Bing, etc.) to help you list relevant keywords and phrases: your company, customers, competitors, prospects, product categories, buzzwords, and whatever else you can think of. Then list all the bloggers and reporters who have discussed issues relating to these keywords.

The next step is to begin monitoring what these people say in real time. You could keep a list of these bloggers and journalists and make a point of checking on their posts and articles a few times a day. Or, to automate the task, you might use RSS feeds, a tool that allows you to harvest content from hundreds of blogs and news feeds without having to visit each one. When you use an RSS reader, you're alerted each time a site changes. I use NewsFire for this task, but there are many others to choose from.

The goal here is to know immediately what people who talk about your industry or marketplace are saying, so you can comment in real time as appropriate.

Monitoring Keywords and Phrases

Besides tracking the journalists and bloggers who write about the subjects you are qualified to comment on, you should also set alerts to notify you instantly when something is said about your industry or marketplace outside the realm of the known bloggers and journalists. Monitoring Twitter and the web for items that mention your important keywords and phrases ensures you are instantly aware of stories you might be able to contribute to.

You can use Google Alerts or another platform for this purpose. Google Alerts allows you to enter many different search terms, so you can create a comprehensive list relevant to your business. Include anything you might want to comment on in an interview or email that could become the second paragraph of a story: industry terms, competitors, customers, prospects, products, and any relevant buzzwords or phrases—every term you can think of. Google Alerts will send you an email each time your search term is used.

Once you start monitoring, you will likely need to modify your search terms, usually because of a flood of false hits (notifications from when your search term is used in stories unrelated to your business). Some services offer advanced features that allow you to refine your searches. For instance, you can make your searches more specific by using the Boolean operators *and*, *or*, and *not*. If you work for an organization that follows many important search terms, you might consider retaining a consultant with a background in information science to help you with search strategies.

Be Open to Serendipity

While monitoring alerts is a great way to find newsjacking opportunities, this technique will surface only stories that are directly tied to the words and phrases you anticipate are important. You also need to be alert for stories that you never saw coming. Let me share two simple approaches that I use to continually open my mind to serendipity, those happy accidents when you see an opportunity to tie a news story to your business.

Every day, no matter where I am in the world, I read a daily print newspaper. It might sound strange that somebody who writes about new media would recommend this practice. The advantage of this form of information consumption is that story choices in print publications give insight into what editors believe is important. This takes some of the pressure off me, and shows me stories I never thought to look for.

I also go to Google News and Twitter Moments when I have short periods of downtime, like in between phone calls or while waiting for a webinar to begin. (And yes, I admit to peeking when I am on a boring conference call. Don't tell!) Twitter Moments is the tab in the Twitter application alongside the "Home," "Notifications," and "Messages" tabs. Clicking the Moments lightning bolt icon takes you to Twitter's curated list of what's important on Twitter at that moment. Unlike Google News, Twitter Moments surfaces stories from more than just mainstream media. The great potential there is finding a popular topic to comment on even before mainstream media figures out the meme.

Tying Your News to Current Events

While the best newsjacking opportunities come at you as a surprise, sometimes a holiday, sporting contest, entertainment release, or other event is a perfect hook on which to hang your news. It's more difficult to get news coverage around these events (many more people will try to newsjack stories they see coming), but you never know what might work.

How to Newsjack

News breaks second by second, 24 hours a day

SPEED

Quickness is essential

SPAM

Always use good judgment

1 Find news to jack

2 Formulate a strategy in real time

3 Instantly get your ideas into the market

Real-Time To-Do List
- Be open to serendipity (happy accidents)
- Monitor keywords, phrases, & trending word clouds
- Track journalists & media outlets
- Follow Twitter hashtags

Strategy Questions
- ? Does your organization have the mind-set to act in real time?
- ? How are you related to the breaking news?
- ? Why should the media care?

Possible Actions
- ✓ Blog your take on the news
- ✓ Tweet using an established hashtag
- ✓ Send a real-time media alert
- ✓ Give a speech
- ✓ Hold a physical or virtual news conference
- ✓ Contact directly a journalist who might be interested

© by David Meerman Scott. Licensed under a Creative Commons Attribution - NoDerivs 3.0 Unported License.

For example, when Justin Bieber released a new single, Charlie Treadwell, director of global social media at technology security company Symantec, thought this seemed like an occasion ripe for newsjacking. "The Biebs was having some personal challenges, and the Grammys were trending," Treadwell says. "I asked my community manager at the time, Allen Kelly, to keep an eye out for a relevant opportunity to create a real-time campaign."

Kelly came up with a very clever idea for a simple tweet sent through the account of Symantec's Norton brand of antivirus software. @NortonOnline sent out an urgent-looking, text-heavy image designed to resemble a security warning. It read, "ALERT: If someone sends you a link to download the latest Bieber single, DON'T DO IT! It's a link to download the latest Bieber single." They also shared the witty image via Facebook and other social networks. So did tens of thousands of people.

"This story not only generated more impressions than we had seen to date, but we had customers running back to us that had been detractors for years," Treadwell says. "We saw comments like, 'I'm on my way to Best Buy right now to purchase your product' or 'I uninstalled your free trial; will you ever forgive me?' Word of mouth leads to loyalty and ultimately sales. We saw an 18 percent spike in online sales for the 48 hours following this tweet."

The goal of newsjacking is to get noticed and let the buzz you create in both social media and traditional outlets drive business. That's exactly what happened to Treadwell, Kelly, and the Symantec team. A simple tweet that cost them nothing took off because of a tie to a news story and drove a measurable increase in sales.

Sometimes you can predict newsworthy events ahead of time and become a part of the story before it breaks. That's what Toyota did to newsjack the story of the newly retired space shuttle *Endeavor* as it made its way from the Los Angeles airport to its permanent home at the California Science Center. The shuttle had to be towed through the streets of Los Angeles, and at one point on the route, it had to cross a bridge that had a weight limit too low for the machines doing the towing. To avoid any issues for that short part of the journey over the bridge, a Toyota Tundra pickup pulled the *Endeavor* instead.

Because marketers at Toyota were able to plan ahead, they built a website for the operation. To get people to talk up the effort, they offered to donate $50 to the California Science Center for every tweet mentioning the #TundraEndeavor event. The total came to just over $200,000 (and yes, I tweeted). That price tag might be a little steep by newsjacking standards, but it did get a lot of people talking about the Tundra.

Twitter Is Your Newsjacking Tool

For dedicated newsjackers, there is no tool more essential than Twitter. It is both a primary source of newsjacking ideas and a powerful channel to get your message out to the media in real time.

Twitter is used by both journalists and media outlets to share links to stories being published. If you follow the Twitter feeds of the reporters and media outlets covering your market, industry, or company, then you'll know about fresh content as it appears. So as you identify key sources, be sure to follow them on Twitter. You can also use a Twitter application like TweetDeck or HootSuite to monitor your key phrases.

Many journalists rely heavily on Twitter to research the stories they're working on. Especially when news breaks, reporters immediately turn to Twitter in search of eyewitness reports or direct comments from people in the know. A vital link between newsjackers and journalists is the Twitter hashtag—a keyword or phrase preceded by the hash mark (#). Hashtags serve as unique identifiers to make it easy to instantly locate references to a particular subject.

For example, Peter Knox's commute was affected by flooding in the New York City area in the aftermath of Hurricane Sandy, which devastated the U.S. East Coast. Knox works in Hoboken, New Jersey, but the PATH rail stop he uses had been closed. Knox (@peterknox) tweeted, "I can't afford the $60 a week ferry anymore. Now attempting the PATH walk from Newport to Hoboken today. pic.twitter.com/8RI9jChu." The attached image was a map of his route. Soon Matt Flegenheimer (@mattfleg) from the *New York Times* tweeted back about a story he was working on. The two used Twitter to agree on a time to speak that day. The resulting story, "In a Hobbled Hoboken, Overbooked Buses, Unfamiliar Ferries and Long Lines," quoted Knox.

When news breaks and you have something to say about it, post your comment as a tweet with the appropriate hashtag. Your idea just might be seen by a journalist eager to fill out a story with additional quotations. Sometimes they'll even quote your tweet directly.

Beware: Newsjacking Can Damage Your Brand

To successfully newsjack a story, it is best if you have a legitimate tie to it. Especially in the case of negative news, such as the death of music legend Prince, a solid connection is essential.

It seems like every few months a well-known brand tries to piggyback off a tragedy. General Mills' tribute to Prince is one such example of newsjacking gone bad.

Like American Apparel (which newsjacked Hurricane Sandy to promote a sale), AT&T (which newsjacked the anniversary of 9/11 to promote its mobile phone plans), General Mills was criticized for its use of a Cheerio as the dot of the "i" of its purple "Rest in peace" graphic.

Many people reacted on Twitter. Stewart O'Brien (@stewN16) had one of the more biting critiques: "Dear Universe. Please return Prince & take the CMO of Cheerios instead. #PrinceRIP"

Yes, Prince is from Minnesota, as is General Mills. But that tie was not strong enough to promote cereal on the back of somebody's untimely death.

The story was widely reported in mainstream media, with the *Wall Street Journal* running a story "Cheerios' Tweet on Prince Is Latest Brand Faux Pas." Fox News also carried the story, saying "Cheerios Tweet saluting Prince angers grieving fans." Soon after the media storm, Mike Siemienas, manager of brand media relations at General Mills, issued a statement: "As a Minnesota brand, Cheerios wanted to acknowledge the loss of a musical legend in our hometown. But we quickly decided that we didn't want the tweet to be misinterpreted, and removed it out of respect for Prince and those mourning." Still, the damage had been done.

This sort of frivolous newsjacking attempt gives the concept of newsjacking (and also marketers in general) a bad name. Ploys like this are blatant attempts to exploit a tragedy, and the insensitivity runs the risk of angering customers and mobilizing the media.

To be successful, attempts at newsjacking must have a legitimate tie to the story, especially when the story is about a disaster, death, or any other negative event.

There were several organizations that legitimately newsjacked the death of Prince. For example, Chevrolet posted a photo of a red Corvette with the caption "Baby, that was much too fast. 1958–2016." Music fans likely know that one of Prince's best-known songs is titled "Little Red Corvette," so this tribute was seen as in good taste. It was shared some 15,000 times on Facebook, and the media noticed and wrote positive stories about Chevrolet.

Newsjacking is indeed powerful. But you must balance the need for quickness with an equal imperative to stay on key. Tone-deaf contributions almost always produce negative feedback.

Newsjacking for Fun and Profit

You can newsjack, too. All it takes is some creativity and the ability to respond very quickly.

Trent Silver, a young Internet entrepreneur, has been building web businesses since he was a 15-year-old high school student. One of his businesses, Cash for Purses, finds new homes for high-quality designer purses and handbags—brands like Gucci, Prada, Hermès, and Chanel. The sales generate cash for the former owners as well as for Silver.

A major challenge for the business is attracting people with used handbags to his site to sell them. That's where newsjacking comes in: Silver monitors the news, looking for breaking stories related to handbags.

For example, Silver enjoyed a barrage of press when he tied his business to financially struggling starlet Lindsay Lohan, who might have been hard up for cash but certainly didn't lack for handbags. Silver recognized that Lohan was sitting on a gold mine and didn't even know it! So he crafted a pitch to celebrity websites that cover Lohan, saying that his company would purchase her extra handbags to help her pay her bills. He even offered to donate his profits to charity.

Silver understands that celebrity sites are always looking for exclusive stories, so he pitched the top sites first. Since Lohan's financial troubles had been in the news, that was his newsjacking hook. *Radar* was the first to run with it: "We'll Buy Your Purses, Lindsay! Company Offers Big Money for Cash-Strapped Lohan's Leftovers."

Once the story was out, other sites started to pick up on the resulting buzz. The *Huffington Post* ran with "Lindsay Lohan Offered Money for Used Handbags by Fundraising Company," and the *Inquisitr* wrote, "Lindsay Lohan's Purses May Be Key to Financial Freedom."

Interestingly, people who read celebrity news sites seem to also be people who want to sell their purses. In the weeks after the story broke, Silver received 8,000 new leads from people who visited Cash for Purses ready to sell their designer bags. "I was able to close 19 percent of the leads," Silver says. "And it brought in almost $250,000 worth of bags. This has also helped me to get to the top page of Google for any searches related to selling purses."

Soon after the online media outlets ran the story, Silver began receiving inquiries from other publishers, resulting in a full-page story in *Essence* magazine and a television mention on Katie Couric's talk show. This publicity led to more people visiting the Cash for Purses site and more business for Silver.

"I use Google News, and I read celebrity news sites, so I'm following the news all day," Silver says. "I've found it helps to have a legitimate position to take when going to the media. I really want Lindsay Lohan to sell me her purses. I really want to donate the same value of all her bags to charity. It's not a publicity stunt; it's a real offer."

Silver is a news junkie, so he enjoys watching for interesting events he can tie his business to. "I read voraciously because I know that I have to get the word out for my businesses in a way that people will understand," he says. "I make sure I am up-to-date on what's going on in the world to see if somehow I can align my businesses in a positive, interesting way. It's definitely an art and a science."

Since Silver runs his own businesses, he has the luxury of being able to put the word out without getting multiple approvals from people in the organization. If you own your own business, too, you should run with his advice.

But if you work at a larger organization, don't use that as an excuse. You can still get buy-in from decision makers when there's good potential to generate interest in your company and its products.

"Don't be afraid to try something different," Silver says. "Different gets noticed. If you don't get noticed, you're not doing your job."

Whenever there is a hot story in the news, there is an opportunity to create and publish original content that the media will find and cover. You can newsjack a story by writing a blog post, shooting a YouTube video, creating an infographic, or even publishing an e-book.

Newsjacking is cool. It's fun. And it gets you ink!

Search Engine Marketing

Search engine marketing is remarkable because, unlike almost every other form of marketing, it does not rely on the interruption technique. Think again for a moment about what I've called old-rules marketing and its interruption-based advertising techniques. As I've discussed in previous chapters, the old rules required you to interrupt TV viewers and hope they weren't already flipping to another channel, interrupt people as they sorted through the mail and hope your message wouldn't go into the junk mail pile, or interrupt magazine readers and hope they would pause at your stinky pull-out perfume sample. These days, ads are everywhere—on signs along the highway, on the sides of supermarket carts, in elevators. These interruptions are not only annoying for consumers (and harmful to a brand if overdone) but also increasingly ineffective.

Now think about how you use search engines. Unlike nontargeted, interruption-based advertising, the information that appears in search engines after you've typed in a phrase is content you actually want to see. You're actually *looking* for it. This should be a marketer's dream come true.

For example, when Shaquille O'Neal was on David Letterman's talk show a few years ago discussing how he had enjoyed his life in Boston since he joined the Boston Celtics, Shaq said he found his multimillion-dollar house on Google! "I live in a small town called Sudbury," he told Letterman. "I signed kind of late, so I really didn't have a chance to find a house. So I went on Google and put 'big house outside of Boston,' and I found this big 10-acre [property with a] farmhouse." A smart real estate mind with just the right information on the web scored big time with that one.

Here's something very important to consider: *This entire book is about search engine marketing.* Please pause to reflect on that. If you followed the new rules of marketing and PR as outlined in these pages, you will have built a fantastic search engine marketing program! You started with your buyer personas, and then you built content especially for these buyers—content that talks about the problems they face in the words and phrases they actually use. Then you delivered the content in the online forms they prefer (podcasts, blogs, e-books, websites, and so on). This terrific content designed especially for your buyers will be indexed by the search engines, and that's it. You already have a terrific search engine marketing program!

But even a great program can benefit from focused enhancements, so in this chapter we'll talk about how to further develop and improve your search engine marketing strategies. Let's start with a few basic definitions:

- *Search engine marketing* means using search engines to reach your buyers directly. Search engines include general search engines such as Google, Bing, and Yahoo!, as well as vertical market search engines that are specific to your industry or to the people you are trying to reach.
- *Search engine optimization (SEO)* is the art and science of ensuring that the words and phrases on your site, blog, and other online content are found by the search engines and that, once found, your site is given the highest ranking possible in the *natural search results* (i.e., what the search engine algorithm deems important for the phrase entered).
- *Search engine advertising* is when a marketer *pays* to have advertising appear in search engine results when a user types in a particular phrase that the marketer has purchased. Usually this advertising comes in the form of small text ads appearing next to the natural search results for a particular search term. Google AdWords and Bing Ads are the two large search engine advertising programs. Marketers bid to have their ads appear based on keywords and phrases, competing against others who want the same phrases. Your ad will appear somewhere in the list of ads for that phrase based on a formula used by the search engine that takes into account two main factors: how much you are willing to bid (in dollars and cents) for each person who clicks the ad, plus your click-through rate (the number of people who click your ad divided by the number of people who see it in the search results).

Making the First Page on Google

Colin Warwick, signal integrity product manager in the Design & Simulation Software Division of Keysight Technologies, is responsible for marketing software to help engineers overcome limitations in high-speed digital connections. As he was working on marketing plans, he came to the realization that traditional business-to-business marketing techniques like trade shows are expensive and increasingly ineffective. He also came to understand the importance of search engines for his business. "Everyone understands Google," he says. "Everybody can instantly see when you enter a phrase into Google if your competitors come up and you don't or vice versa."

The most important search term for Warwick's products is "signal integrity," and Keysight product information was coming up on the fifth page of results—clearly not ideal. So Warwick set out to make Keysight appear at the top of the search results by creating a blog focused on signal integrity. Everything, from the name and URL of the blog to the excellent content, was designed to appeal to the buyer personas interested in this topic and to drive solid search engine rankings. "There are only 50,000 signal integrity engineers in the entire world, and our average sale is about $10,000 with a six-month sales cycle," Warwick says. "While the competitors show their brochures, we have a valuable blog. It helps a great deal to have such valuable information, both for search engine results and in the selling process."

Warwick says that executives at Keysight were very supportive of his starting the blog, but there were some guidelines that he had to work within. "The company said I could blog but that the IT department would not support it," he says. "So I needed to create the blog outside of the company domain. I was required to follow some very commonsense rules: Don't mention the competition, link to the Keysight terms of service and privacy policy, and include a copyright notice. It has been a very good experience. Companies need to trust that employees will do the right thing and let people blog."

The results have been very encouraging. "Many customers say that they like the blog, and our salespeople tell prospects about it," Warwick says. "Having a blog allows me to be spontaneous. For example, I can put diagrams up very quickly and let people know valuable information. If we needed to put content on the corporate site, it would take three days. With the blog I can get into a conversation in just five minutes."

So what about the search results? On Google, Warwick's blog is now on the first page of results for the phrase "signal integrity" (at the number four position when I checked). "Prior to starting the blog, the company products page was ranked number 44 on Google," Warwick says. "That's a huge improvement."

But there are many added benefits to blogging that took Warwick by surprise. "Trade magazine journalists read the blog, and they include links to it in their blogrolls," he says. "And I am making great web connections. For example, I asked an important journalist at *EDN* [a news and information source for electronics design engineers], to moderate a panel for me, and he did because he knows me from the blog."

Search Engine Optimization

In my experience, people often misunderstand search engine marketing because there's a slew of SEO firms that make it all seem so darned complicated. To add to the problem, many (but certainly not all) SEO firms are a bit on the shady side, promising stellar results from simply manipulating keywords on your site. Perhaps you've seen the spam email messages of some of these snake oil salespeople (I've received hundreds of unsolicited email messages with headlines like "Top Search Engine Rankings Guaranteed!"). While many search engine marketing firms are completely reputable and add tremendous value to marketing programs, I am convinced that the single best thing you can do to improve your search engine marketing is to focus on building great content for your buyers. Search engine marketing should not be mysterious and is certainly not trickery.

However, the many intricacies and nuances that can make good search engine marketing great are beyond the scope of this small chapter. Many excellent resources can help you learn even more about the complexities of search engine marketing and especially search engine algorithm factors such as the URL you use, placement of certain words within your content, tags, metadata, inbound links, and other details. These resources also add to our discussion in Chapter 10 of how to identify appropriate keywords and phrases. A great place to start understanding search engine optimization is Search Engine Watch, where you will find resources and active forums to explore. To learn more about search engine advertising, start with the tutorials and frequently asked questions pages of the Google AdWords, Bing Ads, and Yahoo! Search Marketing sites.

Own Your Marketing Assets Instead of Renting Them

In the past several years, many more people than usual have asked me about advertising on the popular online ad networks: Google AdWords, Facebook Advertising, and LinkedIn Ads. While a few people report that they are still having success with these networks, most say this form of advertising isn't working as well anymore. I ask each of these people the same question: "Can you afford to rent your marketing?"

In the old days, advertising on Google AdWords was really successful for a lot of us. In the year or two after Google launched the ad platform, keyword buys were reasonably priced. With a decent landing page, companies could generate sales. In the past several years, the same has been true of newer ad networks from social networking sites. But as word spreads in the entrepreneurial and marketing communities, millions of people jump in. Prices have gone up significantly.

As always, if you're generating success by paying for advertising, that's great! Keep going! I'm not telling you to stop.

But for most of us, the answer is to shift our thinking from advertising (renting our marketing in the form of a monthly ad spend) to owning our marketing by creating original content that gets found by Google and is shared on the networks like Facebook and LinkedIn.

When you rent a house, you have to keep paying your monthly rent. Over time, your rent is likely to increase. And the incentive for your landlord to improve your property goes down once you're all moved in.

Instead you can buy a house and control where you live. Once you've paid for the house, it's yours. And if your home climbs in value, your net worth increases. The same is true of the marketing assets you own. A blog post, e-book, video, or infographic is yours to keep. Forever. The content you created 10 years ago is still indexed by Google today.

Next time you stare at your monthly ad budget and shake your head in disgust, remember that you're just renting your marketing. I'd encourage you to consider putting some of that advertising resource into a content creation initiative that you can own.

The Long Tail of Search

Perhaps you've already tried search engine marketing. Many marketers have. In my experience working with many organizations, I've learned that search engine marketing programs often fail because the marketers optimize on general keywords and phrases that do not produce sufficiently targeted results. For example, someone in the travel business might be tempted to optimize on words like *travel* and *vacation*. I just entered "travel" into Google and got over a billion hits! It is virtually impossible to get to the top of the heap with a generic word or phrase like *travel*, and even if you did, that's not usually how people search. *It is ineffective to try to reach buyers with broad, general search terms.*

You have a choice when you create search engine marketing programs. One method is to optimize on and advertise with a small number of words and phrases that are widely targeted to try to generate huge numbers of clicks. Think of this approach as an oceangoing drag fishing boat being used to harvest one species of fish. Sure, its huge nets capture thousands of fish at a time, but if you throw away all that are not the species you're after, it is a very expensive undertaking.

True success comes from driving buyers directly to the actual content they are looking for. Several years ago, I wanted to take my family on a vacation to Costa Rica, so I went to Google and typed in "Costa Rica adventure travel." I checked out a bunch of sites at the top of the search results (both the natural search results and the advertisements) and chose one that appealed to me. After exchanging several emails to design an itinerary, I booked a trip for several thousand dollars, and a few months later we were checking out howler monkeys in the rain forest. This is how people *really* search (for what they are looking for on the web, not for howler monkeys). If you're in the Costa Rican adventure travel business, don't waste resources optimizing for the generic term *travel*. Instead, run search engine marketing programs for phrases like "Costa Rica ecotourism," "Costa Rica rain forest tour," and so on.

The best approach is to create separate search engine marketing programs for dozens, hundreds, or even tens of thousands of *specific* search terms that people might actually search on. Think of this approach as rigging thousands of individual baited hooks on a long line and exposing them at precisely the right time to catch the species of fish you want. You won't catch a fish on each and every hook. But with so many properly baited hooks, you will certainly catch lots of the fish you are fishing for.

The *Super* Long Tail of Voice Search

With the tremendous rise of voice assistants from the likes of Amazon, Google, and Apple, the percentage of search traffic coming from voice is dramatically increasing. More and more people are using the voice-enabled features of their smartphones to ask questions. They're also installing voice assistants in their homes and cars. TechCrunch estimates that a quarter of U.S. households now have at least one voice-assisted smart speaker.

When people search using a computer or smartphone keyboard, they typically type out a few words, like "Mexican restaurants in Boston." There are likely to be ten or so results on the first page, and consumers will likely scan at least the first few results. Therefore, if you run a Mexican restaurant in Boston, holding the number two or three position in the search results is likely to greatly benefit your business.

It's very different when people search through a voice assistant. Typically, the search is phrased as a question, using a complete sentence. Such searches are likely to be much more specific. For example, a voice search might ask, "What's the best Mexican restaurant nearby that's open now?"

What comes back via the voice assistant is *one result*. If you aren't in the number one position for that search, you get zero people learning about your restaurant from voice assistants.

This new type of search situation means you need to try to understand all of the different ways people are likely to speak when asking about a topic related to your business. Create content accordingly.

A blog can be a great way to generate some of this long-tail content. Use headlines for your posts that correspond to how people might search by voice. Another strategy is to create a detailed Frequently Asked Questions page. Structure your FAQs around what people might ask a voice assistant. For example, the Boston Mexican restaurant might create questions and answers about wait times on a typical day, parking nearby, public transportation options, reservation availability, if alcohol is served, whether children are welcome, and so on.

If you run a local business, make sure you "claim" your My Google Business profile, and ensure that the content is up to date. This Google local listing appears on the right-hand side of the search results (or at the top on mobile!) when somebody enters your business name or closely associated keywords. This profile is where Google picks up details like your business hours, address, and telephone number. This result also features reviews, so encourage your customers to leave positive reviews on Google. This will help when people use words like "best" in their voice search.

Carve Out Your Own Search Engine Real Estate

One rarely discussed but very important aspect of search engine marketing is choosing product and company names so that they will be easy to find on the web via search engines. When you consider the name of a new company, product, book, rock band, or other entity that people want to find on the web, you typically go through a process of thinking up ideas, getting a sense of whether these names sound right, and then perhaps seeing if you can copyright or trademark the ideas. I would suggest adding one more vital step: You should run a web search to see if anything comes up for your proposed name. I urge you to drop the name idea if there are lots of similarly named competitors—even if the competition for the name is in a different industry. Your marketing goal should be that when someone enters the name of your book or band or product, the searcher immediately reaches information about it. For example, before I agree to book titles, I make certain those names are not being used in any other way on the web. It was important for me to own my titles on the search engines; searching on *Eyeball Wars*, *Fanocracy*, *The New Rules of Marketing & PR*, *World Wide Rave*, *Marketing the Moon*, and other titles brings up only my books plus reviews, articles, or discussions about them.

> If you want to be found on the web, you need a unique identity for yourself, your product, and your company to stand out from the crowd and rise to prominence on search engines.

Many people ask me why I use my middle name in my professional endeavors, and I've had people accuse me of being pretentious. Maybe I am a *bit* pretentious, but that's not why I use my middle name—Meerman.

The reason is simple: There are so many other David Scotts out there. One David Scott walked on the moon as commander of Apollo 15. Another is a six-time Iron Man Triathlon champion. Yet another is a U.S. Congressman from Georgia's 13th district. Good company all, but for clarity and search engine optimization purposes, I chose to be unique among my fellow David Scotts by becoming David Meerman Scott.

A side note on creating your own search engine real estate: You should avoid using special characters in your company or product names. Characters such as @, #, %, and so on are not easily indexed by the search engines. While there are exceptions (the C++ software program comes to mind), it is just too difficult to make product names using special characters index properly in search engines.

As you are thinking of names to use for marketing, test them out on the search engines first and try to carve out something that you alone can own.

Web Landing Pages to Drive Action

Although I won't try to cover all the details of search engine marketing, I definitely want to touch on one of the most common mistakes made by search engine marketers. Most people focus a great deal of time on keyword and phrase selection (that's a good thing!), and they also do a good job of ensuring that their organization ranks highly for those phrases by optimizing the site and/or purchasing search engine advertising. But most organizations are terrible at building a landing page—the place people go to after they click on a search hit.

Think back to our last example. As I was planning my family's Costa Rican vacation, many of the sites that were ranked highly for the phrase I entered were a kind of bait and switch. I thought I would be getting targeted information about Costa Rican travel and was instead taken to a generic landing page from a big travel agency, an airline, or a hotel chain. No, thanks, I'm not interested. I wanted information on Costa Rica, not an airline or hotel chain, so I clicked away in a second. Because I wanted information about Costa Rican adventure travel, I chose the landing page that had the best information, one from an outfit called Costa Rica Expeditions. This means that you're likely to need dozens or hundreds of landing pages to implement a great search engine marketing program.

> You need to build landing pages that have specific content to enlighten and inform the people who just clicked over to your site from the search engine.

Marketing with web landing pages is one of the easiest and most cost-effective ways to get your information read by a target market, and it's a terrific tool for moving buyers through the sales cycle. A landing page is simply a place to publish targeted content for a particular buyer persona that you're trying to market to, and landing pages are used not only in search engine marketing but also in other web marketing programs. For example, landing pages are ideal for describing special offers mentioned on your website or calls to action referenced on another content page (such as a blog or e-book). Landing pages also work well for telling an organization's story to a particular target market, promoting a new product offering, or providing more information to people who link from your news releases.

Marketing programs such as search engine optimization are—to borrow an idea from the classic sales cycle definition—designed to attract the prospect's attention. The landing page is where you take the next step; once you've got your audience's attention, you must generate and develop customer interest and conviction, so that your sales team gets a warm lead ready to be worked to a closed sale, or so you can point people to an e-commerce page where they can buy your product right away.

Effective landing page content is written from—you guessed it—the buyers' perspective, not yours. Landing pages should provide additional information to searchers, information based on the offer or keyword they just clicked on. Many successful organizations have hundreds of landing pages, each optimized for a particular set of related search engine marketing terms.

Don't make the mistake so many organizations do by investing tons of money into a search engine advertising program (buying keywords) and then sending all the traffic to the home page. Because the home page needs to serve many audiences, there can never be enough information there for each search term. Instead, keep the following landing page guidelines in mind:

- **Make the landing page content short and the graphics simple**. The landing page is a place to deliver simple information and drive your prospect to respond to your offer. Don't try to do too much.

- **Create the page with your company's look, feel, and tone.** A landing page is an extension of your company's branding, so it must adopt the same voice, tone, and style as the rest of your site.
- **Write from the buyer's point of view.** Think carefully of who will be visiting the landing page, and write for that demographic. You want visitors to feel that the page speaks to their problems and that you have a solution for them.
- **A landing page is communication, not advertising.** Landing pages are where you communicate valuable information. Advertising gets people to click to your landing page, but once a prospect is there, the landing page should focus on communicating the value of your offering to the buyer.
- **Provide a quote from a happy customer.** A simple testimonial on a landing page works brilliantly to show people that others are happy with your product. A sentence (or two) with the customer's name (and affiliation if appropriate) is all you need.
- **Make the landing page a self-contained unit.** The goal of a landing page is to get buyers to respond to your offer so you can sell to them. If you lose traffic from your landing page, you may never get that response. Thus, it is sometimes better to make your landing page a unique place on the web and *not* provide links to your main website.
- **Make the call to action clear and easy to respond to.** Make certain you provide a clear response mechanism for those people who want to go further. Make it easy to sign up, express interest, or buy something.
- **Use multiple calls to action.** You never know what offer will appeal to a specific person, so consider using more than one. In the business-to-business world, you might offer a white paper, a free trial, a return on investment (ROI) calculator, and a price quote all on the same landing page.
- **Ask only for necessary information.** Don't use a sign-up form that requires your buyers to enter lots of data—people will abandon the form. Ask for the absolute minimum you can get away with—name and email address only, if you can, or perhaps even just email. Requiring any additional information will reduce your response rates.
- **Don't forget to follow up!** Okay, you've got a great landing page with an effective call to action, and the leads are coming in. That's great! Don't drop the ball now. Make certain to follow up each response as quickly as possible.

Optimizing the Past

Want to know an SEO secret that almost nobody will tell you? Do not delete old content! Nearly all of your web content should live forever. It's free to save pages on your site, so why delete them? Yet so many people do.

For example, I frequently see this mistake among conference organizers who have a site listing for their annual conference and each year delete the prior year's pages, only displaying the current year's conference. Because media sites, speakers, bloggers, and exhibitors all link to conference content, if the content is deleted soon after the conference ends, those links break. Anyone who tries to visit the site via those links gets an error message. And all SEO benefits from the links are lost.

A well-organized conference site is an important historical artifact that provides valuable information many years later. Who spoke that year? What panel discussions were held? What companies sponsored the event? People want to know that your conference has thrived for over a decade. Rather than using one conference URL, why not choose conference URL/2018 and then next year make it conference URL/2019 and so on? The homepage can then point to the current year's conference.

There are many equivalent mistakes in other markets. For example, many companies delete old product content when the new model is released. Don't do this! There are major SEO benefits from those old links to your site. Your search engine marketing benefits from multiple pages with many inbound links.

Cultivate your content with care, and it will serve as a marketing asset for years to come. I've been writing my blog since 2004, and the vast majority of my traffic from search engines comes from posts that are more than a year old. Other people tell me the same is true with their sites. For example, at HubSpot over 90 percent of leads come from blog posts that are more than a month old, and over 75 percent of HubSpot blog views come from these older posts.

Yet most content managers focus only on the latest blog post. That's the primary content whose stats they measure. I'm guilty of this natural human behavior, too—I want to know how my latest effort is doing. But with so many leads coming from older posts, we can't afford to ignore them. In fact, HubSpot has recently started an internal project dubbed "historical optimization." Its entire focus is to increase traffic to and conversions from older blog posts.

Search Engine Marketing in a Fragmented Business

The market that Scala, Inc., serves is so fragmented, people can't even agree on what the product category is called: Digital signage, digital in-store merchandising, electronic display networks, electronic billboards, and any of a dozen other names are used. And to make the marketing challenge even more difficult, potential customers in this market don't congregate at any one trade show, magazine, or web portal. And that's just the way Gerard Bucas, president and CEO of Scala, Inc., likes it, because he uses search engine marketing to his advantage to reach buyers. "We pioneered the digital signage industry," he says. "Our services are used for retail, corporate communications, factory floor, and many other diverse business applications."

Because Scala serves so many buyers in diverse market segments, there is no clear decision maker. In retail, it's the marketing department. In corporate communications for internal purposes, it is often the CEO or the HR department. And the company serves many verticals such as cruise lines, casinos, and more. "Since we can't possibly advertise in so many different places to reach these people," Bucas explains, "we rely on a great website with a strong focus on search engine marketing."

Bucas says it is critical to use the same terminology as his target market and to include industry terms that lead to an appropriate Scala page. "We continuously monitor the top 30 to 40 search terms that people look for when they search for us on the Net," he says. "When we find new terms, we write content that incorporates those terms, and as the term becomes more important, we expand on the content."

For Bucas, effective search engine marketing means understanding his buyers and creating compelling content using important keywords and phrases, then getting each one indexed by the search engines. "For example, 'digital signage' is one of our search terms," he says. "We want to be at the top of the results. But we also care about similar phrases such as 'digital sign' and 'digital signs.' Each of the terms gives different results. It's amazing to me."

The Scala site includes detailed product content, client case studies, and information on how digital signage is used in different industries. "Regular news releases and case studies are all intended to bring search engines to us," he says. "With case studies and news releases, we're getting some phrases into the market that we don't often use, which cause some long-tail results with the search engines."

Scala has a lead-generation system using search engines to drive buyers to landing pages where traffic converts into leads that are funneled into the company's reseller channel. In this system, the company gathers names through offers (such as a free demo DVD) on each landing page. "Our resellers love us because we're constantly pumping them with new leads," Bucas says. "We effectively help to generate business for them, so they become very loyal to us. Our partners see the value of the lead generation." According to Bucas, the lead system, which manages more than 4,000 open sales leads at any one time, automates communication at particular points in the sales process by sending email to buyers.

The success Scala enjoys shows how a well-executed content strategy on the web will deliver buyers to landing pages who are actually looking for a product. "We are growing very rapidly," Bucas says. "And a large percentage of the business comes from web leads—certainly more than 50 percent of our business comes from the web."

If you're planning on implementing the ideas in this book, you will, by definition, be doing search engine marketing. You will understand your buyers and create great, indexable web content especially for them. The best search engine marketing comes from paying attention to and understanding your buyers, not from manipulating or tricking them. Still, once you've executed a great content strategy, adding effective landing pages and focusing on the long tail of search terms will give you an even more powerful marketing asset that will generate results for months and years to come.

23 Make It Happen

Thanks for hanging in there with me and for reading this far! When I speak to audiences and run seminars on the new rules of marketing and PR, this is the point at which many people are stimulated to get out there and make it happen. They want to start a blog right away, shoot a video to embed in their site, do some newsjacking, or begin buyer persona research in preparation for writing a marketing and PR plan that will guide them to create a content-rich website. If that describes you, great!

But in the audiences of my seminars and speeches, there is always another group of people who tend to feel a bit overwhelmed. There is just too much information, they say, or too many new and unfamiliar ideas. If you are in this category, you might be thinking that the people profiled in the book were able to figure out things that are just too complex and time-consuming for you to tackle, especially given your already hectic schedule. Hey, we all have stuff on our plates, and for most of us, implementing the ideas in the book will represent an addition to our workload.

But here's one of the greatest things about the new rules of marketing and PR: You can implement these ideas in bits and pieces! In fact, I don't expect anybody to implement *all* the ideas here. I don't do *that* many of them myself (okay, I admitted it—don't tell). Yes, I have a blog, and it is very important to me. I'm on Twitter, and I create some original videos. But I don't have a podcast, and I'm not active on Snapchat. I just do what I can and what works for me. And so should you.

Unlike a linear, offline marketing campaign where you must take a methodical, step-by-step approach leading up to a big release day, the web is, well, a *web*. You can add to the web at any time because it is iterative, not linear. Think about the last print advertisement you or others in your organization did. Everything had to be perfect, requiring thorough proof-reading, tons of approvals from your colleagues (or your spouse), lengthy consultation with a bunch of third parties such as advertising agencies and printers, and—above all—lots of money. Your neck was on the line if there was a screw-up, so you obsessed over the details.

Contrast that with a web content initiative that you can implement quickly, get people to check out live, and make changes to on the fly. It really is much less stressful to create an online program. If you create a web page that doesn't work for you, you can just delete it. You can't do that with a print ad or direct-mail campaign. So I would urge you to think about how you might *selectively* experiment with the ideas in these pages rather than fret about coordinating them all and trying to get everything right on the first go.

Many organizations I've worked with have found that an excellent approach is first to do some buyer persona research. By reading the publi-cations that your buyers read, perhaps attending a webinar that they attend, reading a few of the blogs in the space, and maybe interviewing a few buy-ers, you can narrow down the book's large list of techniques to determine the most appropriate web-based marketing and PR initiatives for you and work on them first.

Others have found that the best way to get started is to add a few pages of targeted content for an important buyer persona to an existing website (perhaps with links from the homepage). What's great about this approach is that you don't have to redesign your site; all you are doing is *adding* some valuable content to what you already have. That's easy, right?

Still another first step might be to read the blogs in your market and begin to comment on them in order to coax your blogging voice out of its shell. Once you feel comfortable, you can take the plunge by creating your own blog and Twitter feed. But the good news is that you don't need to show the world right away—you can password-protect your fledgling blog and share it with only a few colleagues at first. Then, with some feedback, you can tweak your approach and finally remove the password protection, and you're off and running. The important thing is to just get out there. Remember, on the web, you are what you publish.

Your Mind-Set

To make the new rules of marketing and PR part of your personal world, you may have to change your mind-set. You'll need to understand your buyers, rather than just talk about your products and services. You'll need to be aware of what's going on in the real-time news and on social networks. You'll need to create content and publish it on the web, and sometimes you'll need to do it urgently to be successful. On social networks, two-way communication is required, not just the typical broadcast approach that most marketers are used to. These habits and techniques do not come naturally to entrepreneurs, business owners, or marketing and PR professionals steeped in more traditional ways.

I've talked with people all over the world who are struggling to adapt to these new rules. The process often starts with your coming to understand just how severely conventional methods can handicap your business and your career. But since you've read this far in the book, you know that already. So let me first introduce you to a chief marketing officer (CMO) who has made the transition, and then share a few ideas for how you too can make the mind-set shift I'm describing. It will take some time, but I've seen thousands of people come to thrive in the always-on world of instant communication—and you will, too.

The Journey from a Traditional Marketing Executive to a Modern CMO

With an MBA from Wharton, a bunch of high-profile marketing gigs on his resume, and a bit of gray hair to show he's got experience, Brian Kardon is what people think of as a typical chief marketing officer. He's been there and done that. But he realized one day that everything he had learned in school and from the early part of his career in the publishing business had become obsolete.

"I cared about arts and crafts," he says. "I cared about brochures and direct mail. I cared about the color on the website. And what's happened is the world has gone digital. It's gone social. It's gone mobile. And we have to learn a completely new language of conversion rates and pay per click and search engine optimization and authoritative inbound links. It's a whole new world."

Today Kardon is chief marketing officer at InVision, a digital product design platform.

There was a moment that caused Kardon to realize he was turning into a marketing dinosaur and heading toward extinction. "Within my second month being CMO at Eloqua, I read a book called *Inbound Marketing* and didn't put it down," Kardon says. "I read it in two and a half hours, and I said to myself, 'I have to give this book to everyone in my team, because the world of outbound marketing is being disrupted. Everyone is time-shifting. You can pause, and you don't have to watch commercials. Spam filters are out there. Messages aren't going through.'"

Kardon realized that there was a new way to do marketing, and the tools and techniques that were described in the book were things he didn't understand. He realized he needed to learn.

"I didn't really understand what metatags, alt tags, and title tags were," he says. "I didn't understand about blog platforms and how WordPress worked. I didn't understand about pay per click. I didn't understand all of these things. I was the CMO. Could I have just skated along and had all my team members understand those things? I think I could have, but you can't outrun the ball. For a certain amount of time you can, but you'll get to a point where someone asks a technical question or something with a little more depth, and if you haven't done it, you're not going to be successful."

Kardon then did something that many executives are unwilling to do. He asked his team for help. Often. He freely admitted his ignorance but also showed he was willing to learn. And he proved he was willing to jump in and actually do real work rather than just direct from the sidelines.

"I decided just to roll up my sleeves and ask people on my team, 'How did you do that?' I had a bunch of people in their 20s, and I would just sit next to them and say, 'Tell me how you did that. How did you push that out there?' or 'What are those social sharing links? How did you put that on there?' I asked how HTML works and what JavaScript is."

Today, Kardon's 17,000+ followers on Twitter (@bkardon) show that he's in the thick of the action and making it happen. And his work at InVision wouldn't be possible without his willingness to get down into the weeds to understand data and the technologies of digital communications.

I asked Kardon to offer advice to other senior marketers making the transition: "You've got to tell yourself you're a child again, and you have to relearn what you're doing." Kardon managed his fear of making the transition, and you must do the same if you want to achieve similar success.

Manage Your Fear

Every day, I encounter fear in the people I work with. Many company executives and public relations people trace their worries about the new rules of marketing and PR to their concern that "people will say bad things about our company" via social media.

This fear leads them to ignore blogs and online forums and to prohibit employees from participating in social media. And, yet, in every discussion that I've had with employees who freely participate in social media, I've confirmed that this fear is significantly overblown. Let me repeat: Everyone who has experience tells me this fear is overblown.

Sure, an occasional outlier might vent frustrations online, and now and then a dissatisfied customer will complain (unless you're in the airline industry, and then it might be more than a few).

But the benefit of this kind of communication is that you can monitor in real time what's being said and then respond appropriately. Employees, customers, and other stakeholders are talking about your organization offline anyway, so unless you are participating online, you'll never know what's being said at all.

The beauty of the web is that you benefit from instant access to conversations you could never have participated in before. And frequently you can turn around impressions by commenting on a negative post. So not only is this fear overblown—it's often dead wrong. Participating in social media gives you the chance to make sure *fewer* bad things are being said about your company.

Mixing Business with Your Personal Life on Social Networks

Speaking of fear, many people tell me they are reluctant to talk about their personal lives on social networks like Facebook, Twitter, and Instagram. Most make a point to separate business from the personal. When they use social networking for business, they present themselves as one dimensional. They're all work and no play.

I think that's a mistake. Social networks are, well, social. Think about the best business relationships you have: Don't you enjoy getting to know the people you work with? Do you look forward to certain business meetings simply because you enjoy having a conversation with that person?

Like a cocktail party, social media offers an opportunity for you to share a bit about yourself: your family, your hobbies, your passions, your love of a favorite sports team. A fun aspect of social media is getting to know a bit about the personal lives of those we do business with.

I'm not suggesting you share everything. It's fine to leave out that shot of you relaxing on the beach while you're on holiday. Some people aren't comfortable posting photos of family members. And it should go without saying to avoid posts that don't reflect well on you or that describe or depict activities you would, um, never do in public.

But don't underestimate the power of opening yourself up. Your passions say a lot about you—even what you might be like to do business with. Humanize yourself.

For example, Dr. Jon Marashi is a cosmetic dentist in southern California, and he's got more than 13,000 Instagram followers (@drjonmarashi). His Instagram is responsible for 30 percent growth in his business, and I believe he's successful because he not only posts about his work and his clients but also about his passions. By doing so, he differentiates himself from the thousands of other dentists in southern California.

"I had a lot of reservations with social media at first," Marashi says. "I'm 45 years old, and I thought of myself as old school. I didn't want to share what I eat all day long. And because of the nature of my business, I felt like I needed to be careful and not say too much. But what I realized is that the world has changed around me, and social media sharing is okay and that, in fact, there could be a way to do it strategically that . . . could be tasteful and on brand for me—and even fun."

If you walk around Marashi's office, you'll see that the two most important things in his life besides his business are skateboarding and his family. "I've got skateboards all over the walls, and I have pictures of my family," he says. "I thought about what I talk to my patients about during the day and what they find interesting about me, and it was those two things. You know, a dentist who skateboards is just kind of a weird thing to begin with! So I decided to post on Instagram about skateboarding and my family."

Marashi's website calls him "The dentist behind the world's most famous smiles." He lists patients including actor Ben Affleck, TV and radio host Ryan Seacrest, and actress Catherine Bell. "Because of the good quality of cosmetic dentistry that I'm doing, I've been able to attract some of the most famous people in the world," he says. "Initially, I was afraid of sharing my relationship with them on social media because I had never done that before, and I'm concerned about patient privacy. But I learned that many celebrities have built their brand on social media, and when I started to make a humble ask if they would be willing to do a photo with me to share, they said, 'Of course, I would love to!' That was the overwhelming response."

He makes sure to check first if the celebrity is active on social networks and asks only those who are. As I check his Instagram feed, I recognize Marashi posing with Tom Hanks, Cher, Justin Timberlake, Renée Zellweger, and Pink.

Overcoming his fear of social media, being open to posting about his personal life, and asking patients if they would shoot a shareable photo with him have all been instrumental in building Marashi's business. For the past year, when new patients first come into the practice, staff ask how they found out about him. He says 30 percent of new patients come as a result of finding him on social media. "And that doesn't even take into account people that were referred in by friends," he says. "We know when people are referred to me, they go online and research us. While I can't measure that, I believe that when somebody refers their friend and then they look me up and see my social media, that is the last little nudge that got them to book an appointment."

Getting the Help You Need (and Rejecting What You Don't)

As you develop a strategy to get started implementing the new rules of marketing and PR, you may find occasions to call on others for help. Many people tell me that they occasionally need the services of an agency to provide them with some extra people to help execute a big project. But I constantly hear that they have difficulty finding people skilled in using the ideas that we've been discussing in this book.

Still others report that well-meaning colleagues and meddlesome bosses have an annoying tendency to look over shoulders and second-guess them as they start a blog, get going on Twitter, or begin filming YouTube videos. Add to that mix the fact that, in many larger organizations, the legal department tends to muck things up with nitpicky rules about what can and cannot be said.

If these sound like some of the problems that you're encountering, fear not! Here are some things you can do to get the help you need, while rejecting what you don't.

The One Question to Ask a Prospective Agency

An increasingly large cadre of self-proclaimed new marketing gurus claim to be really good at generating attention using the new rules of marketing and PR. In addition, I've noticed that in the past several years established agencies of all kinds are adding departments devoted to social media. Traditional advertising agencies that have focused on television commercials for decades all of a sudden claim to be experts on blogging. Public relations agencies skilled in relating to the media somehow become instant experts on Facebook and Twitter. So how do you navigate all these potential partners if you really do need some help implementing the ideas in this book?

Many people ask me if I can recommend an agency that understands social media or help them evaluate agencies that claim to be good at this kind of work. My answer to the challenge of finding good people is simple: Ask the prospective agency to show you its social media presence. Ask about such things as blogs, Twitter feeds, YouTube videos, e-books, websites, Facebook profiles, and any other stuff the agency has. Make it an open-ended question.

This is not to say that an agency needs to be active in every medium, but if it is worthy of taking your money to advise you on the use of these tools, then it should certainly be out there using them. My theory is that if an agency can't blog or tweet or create interesting content such as videos for itself with any success, then it's going to come up short for clients as well.

The answers can be fascinating! All of a sudden many of these self-styled experts clam up and don't say much. This vetting tool eliminates ninety-five percent of agencies that just plain stink at understanding social media.

When Lawyers Get in the Way

At many larger organizations, the legal department is heavily involved in all marketing and communications initiatives, frequently requiring every blog post and press release to be vetted by a lawyer. In some extremes, corporate legal eagles even forbid employees from starting a blog or participating on Twitter and Facebook at work. I've found that the restrictions come down to two factors: *ignorance of social media* and *a lack of trust in employees*.

Since legal people don't usually understand social media themselves (and don't use social media for business in their jobs), they naturally respond by just slapping on controls. After all, their job is to reduce risks within a company, so it's temptingly simple to just say no. This is especially true in companies that mistrust their employees. However, if a company trusts its employees and understands that social media can be a powerful way to do business, then it is the lawyers' job to create an environment where you can do what you know is right.

My recommendation is to work with your managers and your organization's legal team (and perhaps the human resources department as well) to create guidelines that you can operate under. Your company's guidelines should include advice about how to communicate in any medium, including face-to-face conversations, presentations at events, email, social media, online forums and chat rooms, and other forms of communication.

Rather than putting restrictions on social media (that is, the technology), it's better to focus on guiding the way people behave. The corporate guidelines should include statements that employees can't reveal company secrets, can't use inside information to trade stock or influence prices, and must be transparent and provide their real name and affiliation when communicating.

You might take a look at how IBM, a company on the forefront of embracing employee use of social media, has handled this issue. IBM has developed a set of social computing guidelines for employees' use of blogs, wikis, social networks, virtual worlds, and social media. You may have to take the lead on creating the guidelines at your organization, but the effort will be worth it.

Bring a Journalist onto Your Team

A remarkable convergence is upon us right now, creating a perfect opportunity for you to hire someone with the skills that you need. Sadly, many mainstream media outlets are reducing their pools of staff journalists. Newspapers, magazines, radio stations, and television outlets face tough economic challenges, and unfortunately that means that many talented reporters and editors have been (or will be) laid off. I've had a chance to speak with several dozen journalists recently, and many are downcast about career prospects.

> Hire a journalist to help you create amazing content. Journalists know how to tell a story.

At the same time, people like you in many different organizations—corporations, nonprofits, government agencies, and educational institutions—understand the value of the ideas we've explored in this book. One of the best ways to create great web content is to actually hire a journalist, either full-time or part-time, to create it. Journalists, both print and broadcast, are great at understanding an audience and creating content that buyers want to consume—it's the bread and butter of their skill set.

I'm not talking about PR and media relations here. This isn't about hiring a journalist to write press releases and try to get his or her former colleagues to write or broadcast about you. Instead, I'm talking about having journalists create stories just as they are doing now—but for a corporation, a government agency, a nonprofit, or an educational institution instead of a media outlet.

Editors are in demand by companies that create terrific online media rooms, like the one at Raytheon that we looked at in Chapter 12. What better background than journalism could there be for the person running your online media efforts? For much smaller organizations, maybe it makes sense to hire a freelance print journalist to help you with that e-book. Again, what better way to create valuable information than to hire someone who has done it for years? Sure, web marketing represents a dramatically different job description from, say, beat reporter. Yet times (including the *New York Times*) are changing. And that gives smart marketers an amazing opportunity to hire people with the skills we need.

Managing Your Colleagues and Bosses

If I may be so bold as to boil down into one word thousands of conversations I've had over the past several decades, as well as my more than 10 years' worth of blogging and the entire contents of this book, it would be this: *attention*. Entrepreneurs, CEOs, and business owners want people to pay attention to their company. Marketers, PR pros, advertisers, and salespeople are on the payroll to generate attention. Hopefully, this book opened your eyes to a new approach to this classic problem.

I've identified four main ways to generate attention in today's marketing landscape. We've discussed them throughout these pages, so this list is not really new, but seeing them all collected together will give us some fresh perspective for dealing with people who might be skeptical or meddlesome.

1. *You can buy attention with advertising* such as television commercials, magazine and newspaper ads, the yellow pages, billboards, trade show floor space, direct-mail lists, and the like.
2. *You can get attention from the editorial gatekeepers* at radio and TV stations, magazines, newspapers, and trade journals.
3. *You can have a team of salespeople generate attention one person at a time* by knocking on doors, calling people on the telephone, sending personal emails, or waiting for individuals to walk into your showroom.
4. *You can earn attention online by using the ideas in this book*, creating something interesting, and publishing it online for free: a YouTube video, blog, research report, series of photos, Twitter stream, e-book, Facebook fan page, or other piece of web content.

To understand the motivations of your colleagues and bosses as they offer advice and give you unwanted criticism, I recommend that you know and understand these four means of generating attention. And you should understand the point of view of the person you are talking to about attention, especially when the inevitable pushback about earning it in new ways surfaces.

You see, most organizations have a corporate culture centered on one of these approaches. As examples, Procter & Gamble primarily generates attention through advertising, Apple via PR, Oracle via sales, and Zappos via the new rules of marketing and PR. Often the defining organizational culture springs from the founder's or CEO's strong point of view. So if the CEO came up through the sales track, all attention problems are likely to become sales problems. Chances are that your colleagues and bosses did not come up via the social media track or read this book.

The point is, you'll have to *convince* your boss to invest in social media, because it's likely he or she doesn't consider it the most important way of gaining attention. Most organizations overspend on advertising and sales and underinvest in social media, but nearly all organizations should be doing some combination of these. If you can help your bosses and colleagues understand this trend, they'll probably lighten up a little.

Bringing It All Together: Brand Journalism at Cleveland Metropolitan School District

Recently I had an opportunity to meet with Roseann Canfora, chief communications officer for the Cleveland Metropolitan School District (CMSD). I spent a day with her entire team. It was incredibly interesting to hear how CMSD deploys journalism techniques to communicate with students, parents, the media, and the wider Cleveland community. Canfora's team focuses on reaching not only the families of the district's 40,000 students but also those who attend other schools and might consider CMSD.

This excellent example should be useful for any individual or organization making the transition from traditional marketing and PR to the new forms of communication I've outlined in these pages. It's also instructive for those facing resistance from parts of the organization.

Canfora operates what's effectively a full-time news operation—including a television studio—in support of CMSD and the wider Cleveland community. She leads a team of 12 people divided into two teams: news and information, and marketing and advertising. The CMSD staff includes a multimedia journalist who came to the district from television and a station manager who taught television production for many years. The news director was a reporter for nearly 25 years with the *Cleveland Plain Dealer*, including three years as a beat reporter. Everybody on the entire news team, including Canfora, comes from a journalism background.

"It's our responsibility to let families know about the choices they have in Cleveland," Canfora says. "Unfortunately, we don't have much of an identity but that of a struggling, inner-city school district if the people telling our stories are the local media. The daily stories that big-city journalists are drawn to include gang fights, low test scores, truancy, and weapons finding their way past metal detectors. These stories fall short of what I learned in journalism school was our social responsibility to tell the deeper stories, the root causes of these things, the incredible stories of triumph over those challenges that take place in schools every single day. Those are the types of stories we now tell ourselves."

When she started at CMSD, Canfora inherited a virtually inert communications operation that was producing print materials to be taken home by students. Each school in the district also did its own communications, further diluting the CSMD brand.

"The buy-in took years, because it meant disturbing the comfort level of thousands of people, people who felt very territorial. 'Well, that's my event. Why are you doing that?' 'That's my task. We do the mailers. Why are you doing that?' Even prying from them their love of ClipArt and WordArt and telling them to throw out their hot pink paper [was difficult]. The pushback I was experiencing was coming school-by-school and department-by-department. But I had the buy-in from the top for a clearly defined brand framework. I set the boundaries regarding what stories are told, how they are told, and more importantly by whom."

It was clear to Canfora that CMSD was not effectively reaching families until the district approached marketing and advertising as a much bigger stream of content. "It meant creating a team of writers. It meant finding a multimedia journalist to go out with a camera and convey these stories in depth," she says. "It meant having social media specialists in every part of our team to not only write for our brand but also create content that will be interesting for the media. We're looking for interesting stories, unique angles, and beating the local media to the punch by telling it better so that they see us as a thought partner and even a thought leader."

A major challenge for Canfora was finding journalists who were eager to move over to CMSD and become a brand journalist. Many reporters are reluctant to join what they call the "dark side" of communications—working outside of a media company. On the other hand, there are many people with a marketing and PR background who are not qualified for the roles Canfora had available.

"I can clearly see the difference between a story and a story with credibility, one with facts, stats, and all the elements of good journalism," Canfora says. "That is probably the greatest challenge in going the brand journalism route. We're telling our own stories, as journalists, and that's different from a PR writer writing a bio about a new person, introducing a new product or a new way of doing things. Readers see through it quickly if your content marketing reads more like selling and less like telling. Hiring trained journalists is key to establishing credibility in our news bureau, but having good reporters who love to tell good stories is what is making it work."

To further complicate the hiring process, Canfora tries to bring journalists onto the team who know the Cleveland market and who have covered the news there. "What sold me on my multimedia journalist was her work as a news reporter at WKYC Channel 3 here in Cleveland and also as a news anchor in Michigan where the stories she always wanted to tell and the ones that were her favorites were taking place in schools. Our youngest and newest member of the news bureau was a crime reporter at the *Plain Dealer*. These are people who know our city. They know our families. They know our challenges. They know the poverty in this district, which has the highest number of children of poverty in the nation. If you don't know these people, you can't really write about what's happening in their lives with any kind of meaning or with any kind of accuracy."

Now CMSD delivers constantly across multiple channels to multiple audiences every single day. "This is the first year I can actually say we are a mobile, digital, multiplatform operation where brand journalism, which was always my goal, works," Canfora says.

Poking around on the CMSD news site offers some fun stories produced by the television team. For example, they produced a news story about how students at Design Lab Early College High School have set an example for makers across the country. The school had a special visit from Adam Savage, former cohost of the hit Discovery Channel TV series *Mythbusters*.

There's a written story, "New School to Have Space at MetroHealth," that tells how CMSD's new Lincoln-West School of Science and Health is being based partly at the MetroHealth System's main campus. District and hospital leaders believe the school, which opened July 25, 2016, with ninth and tenth graders, may be the only one in the country located within a hospital.

Canfora is currently working to hire an individual who understands the metrics associated with the site and social channels. "Incorporating analytics into the brand journalism strategy is the only way to know if we are truly engaged," she says.

It's exciting to see what's possible for any organization willing to do the work.

Great for Any Organization

There's no doubt that your organization will benefit from your getting out there and creating web content in whatever form you're most comfortable with. But I'm also convinced that no matter who you are or what you do, your professional and personal life will improve, too. If you are an innovator using the ideas in this book, it may lead to greater recognition in the office. And if you're like many bloggers and podcasters I know, you will derive a therapeutic benefit as well.

> It's fun to blog and tweet, and it makes you feel good to get your ideas out into the world.

If you're like me, you will prefer to write rather than create audio or video content. But I know plenty of people who hate to write and have created terrific photo, video, and audio content to reach buyers. And it works for all kinds of organizations: corporations, nonprofits, rock bands, and politicians. People often say to me: "But I'm just a _____ [fill in the blank with *pastor, painter, lawyer, consultant, sales representative, auto dealer*, or *real estate agent*, for example]; why should I blog or create a podcast?" My answer is that not only will you reach your buyers directly with targeted content, but you'll also have fun, too—web content is for everyone, not just big companies.

In fact, one of my all-time favorite examples of success with the new rules of marketing and PR comes from an unlikely marketer: the pastor of a church in Washington, D.C. But his isn't a typical church, because he doesn't actually have a church building. Instead he uses video technology, blogs, podcasts, and the web to tell stories and build a spiritual community both online and offline.

"The church should be using technology to reach people; that's what Gutenberg did in the fifteenth century with the printing press," says Mark Batterson, lead pastor of National Community Church (also known as the Theater Church), a multisite church that conducts many services per week in six nontraditional locations. "Most churches have a church building, but we feel that a building can be an obstacle to some people, so we do church in theaters and have built the largest coffeehouse in the Washington, D.C., area."

What distinguishes National Community Church is Batterson's approach of embracing technology and web marketing and applying it to church. The vehicles include a content-rich website, podcasts of the weekly services, a motivational webcast series, video, an email newsletter, Batterson's extremely popular "evotional" blog (tagline: "Spirit Fuel"), and his Twitter feed (@MarkBatterson) with well over 100,000 followers. "The greatest message deserves the greatest marketing," Batterson says. "I am challenged that Madison Avenue and Hollywood are so smart at delivering messages. But I believe that we need to be just as smart about how we deliver our messages."

Attendance at National Community Church includes several thousand adults in an average weekend; 70 percent of them are single people in their 20s. "I think we attract 20-somethings because our personality as a church lends itself to 20-somethings," Batterson says. "Our two key values are authenticity and creativity. That plays itself out in the way we do church. I think that church should be the most creative place on the planet. The medieval church had stained glass to tell the gospel story to the churchgoers, who were mostly illiterate. We use the movie studio to tell the story to people. We use video to add color and to add flavor to what we do. If Jesus had video in his day, it wouldn't surprise me if he made short films."

Batterson's focus on the website, podcasts, and online video (as well as video at the services) means that National Community Church staff members have some unique job titles, including media pastor, digital pastor, and buzz coordinator. "We want to use technology for really good purposes," Batterson says. "Our website and my blog are our front door to National Community Church. The site is a virtual location in a sense. We have a lot more people who listen to the podcast and watch the webcast than who go to the services, so it is a great test drive for people. They can get a sense of the church before they arrive physically."

Batterson has gained online fame well beyond the Washington, D.C., area—his blog is followed by tens of thousands of readers all over the world, and the podcast is one of the fastest-growing church podcasts in the United States. He has also written several books, including *In a Pit with a Lion on a Snowy Day: How to Survive and Thrive When Opportunity Roars*. "Blogging cuts six degrees of separation into three," he says. "I write knowing that my audience is another pastor in Australia, a housewife in Indiana, my friends, and people in Washington, D.C. Marketing through my blog is powerful. For example, last week I did a blog post about my book and asked my blogging friends to also post about it. We went up to number 44 on the Amazon bestseller list, and Amazon sold out of the book that day. They just ordered another thousand copies."

Batterson's enthusiasm for how churches can use the web has caught the attention of thousands of other church leaders who follow his blog. "The two most powerful forms of marketing are word of mouth and what I call word of mouse. A guy named John Wesley, who founded the Methodist Church, traveled 250,000 miles on horseback and preached something like 40,000 sermons. With one click of the mouse, I preach that many sermons with my podcast—that's word of mouse. It is about leveraging the unique vehicles on the web. The message has not changed, but the medium has changed. We need to continually find new vehicles to get the messages out."

Now It's Your Turn

Isn't the power of web content and the new rules of marketing and PR something? Here's a guy who's a church leader *without* a church building, and through innovative use of a blog, a podcast, and some video, he has become a leader in his field. He's got bestselling books and tens of thousands of devoted online followers. Whether you're religious or not, you've got to be impressed with Batterson's business savvy and with the way the new rules have helped him reach his buyers.

You can do it, too. It doesn't matter what line of work you're in or what group of buyers you're trying to reach. You can harness the power of the web to reach your target audience directly.

If you're like many of my readers, those who see me speak at conferences, and the people who attend my masterclasses, you have colleagues who will argue with you about the new rules. They will say that the old rules still apply. They will tell you that you need to spend big bucks on advertising. They will tell you that the only way to do PR is to get the media to write about you. By now you know that they are wrong. If I haven't convinced you myself, surely the 50 or so successful people profiled in these pages must have. Go on. Be like the people you met in this book—get out there and make it happen!

Acknowledgments for the Seventh Edition

First, a disclosure: Because I do advisory work, run seminars, and do paid speaking gigs in the world that I write about, there are inevitable conflicts. I have friends in some of the organizations that I discuss in this book, as well as on my blog and on the speaking circuit, and I have run seminars for or advised several of the companies mentioned in the book.

At John Wiley & Sons, my publisher Matt Holt and my editor Shannon Vargo have steered me through the publishing business with wit and wisdom. We've now done seven books together! Also at Wiley, thanks to Peter Knox, Sally Baker, and Deborah Schindlar for their help and support.

Kyle Matthew Oliver read every word of each draft of this book, and his sound advice and practical suggestions made it much better.

I work with awesome people who make me look good, especially my daughter Allison, who works with me on my Master Newsjacking and New Marketing Mastery online learning programs; Doug Eymer, who designs web and print materials for me; Bob Ruffolo and the team from IMPACT Branding & Design, who create magic on my websites; Shana Bethune and Dave Jackel, who help me create videos; and Colin Warwick, who helps with words. Thank you all.

I have some wonderful partners, including Juanito Pascual, whom I work with in our sonic branding agency Signature Tones. I am particularly grateful to Tony Robbins for bringing me into the Business Mastery community, where I present several times a year and deliver my New Marketing Mastery program. Thank you, Tony, and the entire team at Robbins Research International.

I would also like to thank the thousands of bloggers who added to the conversations around *The New Rules of Marketing & PR* by writing on their blogs or by leaving intelligent and useful comments on my blog.

A particular thank-you goes to Tony D'Amelio, who manages my speaking activities. Tony together with his colleagues Matt Anderson, Carin Kalt, Meg Joray, Kirsten Riemer, and Jenny Taylor play critically important roles in making sure that I am speaking in front of the best audiences around the world.

And especially, thank you to my wife, Yukari, for supporting my work and understanding when I am under deadline or away from home speaking in some far-flung part of the world.

About the Author

Our always-on, web-driven world has new rules for competing and growing business. Advance planning is out—agile response is IN! Those who embrace new ways will be far more successful than those who get stuck and are afraid to change. No one knows more than David Meerman Scott about using new real-time tools and strategies to spread ideas, influence minds, and build business. It's his specialty.

Photo credit: Bruce Rogovin, rogovin.com

David is an internationally acclaimed business growth strategist whose books and blog are must-reads for professionals seeking to generate attention in ways that grow their businesses. His advice and insights help people, products, and organizations stand out, get noticed, and capture hearts and minds. He is author or co-author of 11 books, including four international bestsellers.

The New Rules of Marketing & PR, now in its seventh edition, has been translated into 29 languages from Albanian to Vietnamese and is used as a text in hundreds of universities and business schools worldwide. It has become a modern business classic, with over 400,000 copies sold to date. Scott is also the author of *Real-Time Marketing & PR*, a *Wall Street Journal* bestseller, and *The New Rules of Sales and Service*. He co-authored *Marketing the Moon* (the inspiration for a PBS American Experience miniseries titled *Chasing the Moon*) and *Marketing Lessons from the Grateful Dead*. David's newest book *Fanocracy: How to Turn Fans into Customers and Customers into Fans*, a *Wall Street Journal* bestseller, was co-written with his daughter.

For most of his career, David worked in the online news business. He was vice president of marketing at NewsEdge Corporation (sold to Thomson Reuters) and held executive positions in an electronic information division of Knight-Ridder, at the time one of the world's largest newspaper companies.

David has worked on a Wall Street bond trading desk and was a male model. He collects artifacts from the Apollo space program and has a lunar module descent engine in his home museum. He has acted in TV commercials and the movies *Chappaquiddick* and *American Hustle*, and he even appeared in an opera production of La Scala.

He is a partner in the sonic branding studio Signature Tones, and a go-to-market LP in Stage 2 Capital, a venture capital fund that invests in and helps companies scale sustainable revenue. He serves as an advisor to HubSpot, Geoversity, Mynd, InstaViser, YayPay, SlapFive, and ExpertFile.

A graduate of Kenyon College, David has lived in New York, Tokyo, Boston, and Hong Kong.

Check out his blog at www.davidmeermanscott.com and follow him on Twitter @dmscott.

INDEX

MASTER Newsjacking

THE ONLINE COURSE

With Newsjacking pioneer David Meerman Scott

LEARN HOW TO:

 Generate sales leads and add new customers. For free!

! Get media attention. With little effort!

✓ Grow your business. Faster than ever!

"After David taught me his breakthrough concept of Newsjacking, I was able to grow my CashForPurses.com business from literally 0 to over 8,000 customers in a little over 6 weeks. This resulted in 6-figure revenue in a very short time, as well as major media and venture capital attention."
Trent Silver, CEO
CashForPurses.com

Register now at www.newsjacking.com

Have David Meerman Scott Speak at Your Next Event!

Photo of David Meerman Scott speaking at Tony Robbins Business Mastery by Rajiv Sankarlall.

David Meerman Scott's high-energy presentations are a treat for the senses. He's informative, entertaining, and inspiring. David has spoken on all seven continents and in more than 40 countries. The prestigious list of firms, organizations, and associations underscores the value he brings to audiences.

David's keynotes and masterclasses serve as an urgent call to action. Scale and media buying power are no longer decisive advantages; what counts today is speed and agility. The real-time mind-set is the way of the future—and content rules! David's tailored presentations delve deep, offering strategies and tactics that help audiences seize the initiative, open new channels, and grow their brands. Don't just slap social media onto dusty old strategies—reinvent the way business engages the marketplace. Audiences walk away knowing how to use blogs, YouTube, Facebook, Twitter, AI, and the newest tools like newsjacking to engage the media, increase sales, exert influence, disseminate ideas, build awareness, and command premium prices by using speed as a strategic ally.

Top firms and organizations have engaged David to present at conferences, expos, and meetings. They include Cisco Systems, HP Enterprise, LinkedIn, PricewaterhouseCoopers, GenRe, SAP, Google, Microsoft, McCormick, Nestlé Purina, Amdocs, Konica Minolta, Red Hat, Comcast, Jackson Healthcare, Ford Motor Company, Century 21, the New York Islanders, Self Storage Association, Vocus, Mosaic, Direct Marketing Association, South by Southwest, National Healthcare Marketing Summit, Kronos, Public Relations Society of America, National Geographic, Ingram Micro, Abbott Medical Devices, NASDAQ Stock Market, the Government of Ontario, McKesson, U.S. Air Force, U.S. Marine Corps, Digital River, Hill & Knowlton, Dow Jones, SAS, National Investor Relations Institute, Milken Institute, Entrepreneurs Organization, International Health Forum, Credit Union National Association, and many more.

All of David's presentations are a combination of three things: education, entertainment, and motivation. With his expertise and your business poised for growth, that promises to be a recipe for success.

Visit www.davidmeermanscott.com for information on booking David to speak at your event.

PROFITS FROM PENNY STOCKS

An Investor's Guide to Low Cost Stocks and Company Start-ups

by Robert Irwin

 FRANKLIN WATTS
New York   1986   Toronto

Schaumburg Township District Library
130 South Roselle Road
Schaumburg, IL 60193

This publication contains the author's opinion on the subject.
It must be noted that neither the publisher nor the author is
engaged in rendering investment, legal, tax, accounting, or
similar professional services. While investment, legal, tax
and accounting issues in this book have been checked
with sources believed to be reliable, some material may be
affected by changes in the laws or in the interpretations of
such laws since the manuscript for this book was completed.
Therefore, the accuracy and completeness of such information and the opinions based thereon are not and cannot be
guaranteed. In addition, state or local tax laws or procedural
rules may have a material impact on the recommendations
made by the author, and the strategies outlined in this book
may not necessarily be suitable in every case. If legal, accounting, tax, investment, or other expert advice is required,
one should obtain the services of a competent practitioner.
The publisher and author hereby specifically disclaim any
personal liability for loss or risk incurred as a consequence
of the advice or information presented in this book.

Library of Congress Cataloging-in-Publication Data

Irwin, Robert, 1941–
Profits from penny stocks.

Includes index.
1. Stocks. 2. Speculation. I. Title. II. Title:
Penny stocks : an investor's guide to low cost stocks and
company start-ups.
HG6041.I79 1986   332.63'22   86-10968
ISBN 0-531-15513-7

Copyright © 1986 by Robert Irwin
All rights reserved
Printed in the United States of America
6 5 4 3 2

7/87
Bot

CONTENTS
■

332.6322
IRWIN, R

3 1257 00522 6765

PROFITS
FROM
PENNY
STOCKS

■

INTRODUCTION
TO PENNY STOCKS
■

How would you like to buy a stock that costs just one cent? That's right, the full price per share is just a penny. Think of it—for a hundred dollars you could own ten thousand shares. For five hundred dollars you could own fifty thousand shares. And for a thousand-dollar investment, you could own a hundred thousand shares!

Of course, you may be thinking, "So what if it's cheap? So are bottle caps—the usual reason is that they aren't worth anything. If that's the case, what am I going to do with thousands of shares, paper my bathroom walls?!"

But wait; what if within a few months that penny-a-share stock you purchased was now selling for three cents a share—a 300 percent increase? Your hundred-dollar investment was now worth three hundred dollars. Your five-hundred-dollar investment was worth fifteen hundred dollars and your thousand-dollar investment was now up to three thousand dollars. Hardly the sort of thing that you'd use to paper walls.

Sure, you may be saying. Once in a great while a stock might go up 300 percent. But how realistic is that? After all, what we're talking about here is a threefold increase. That's like having IBM go from a hundred dollars (or wherever it currently happens to be) to three hundred dollars. It happens, but the chances are probably so remote as to be minuscule.

Don't bet on it. Let's go back to that one-cent stock. As it turns out, there are plenty of low-priced stocks that go up 300 percent in a short time. In 1985, for example— which in general was a bad year for low-priced stocks— scores of them did it. They had names like *Seburg Phonograph* or *Midas Gold* or *Metcom* or *NTN Communications* or a dozen others. The names can go on and on.

What's really interesting, however, is that the stock I was thinking of when I wrote the first few paragraphs of this introduction wasn't any of these. Rather, it was a controversion stock called *Nastech Pharmaceuticals*.

Nastech came out in April of 1984 at a cent a share. Within a few months it was up to three cents a share. By the end of 1985, it was at $1.25 a share.

That's right, $1.25! It only went up $1.24 in price, but that amounted to an increase of 125,000 percent!

If you had bought just $100 of Nastech when it came out, by the end of 1985 your stock would have been valued at $12,500. If you had purchased $500, your stock would have been valued at $62,500, and if you had stuck in the less than enormous sum of $1,000, you would have had a bundle valued at $125,000!

Certainly, for a stock to go up by that much doesn't happen every day. But it does happen, and Nastech isn't the first or the last low-priced stock to have it happen. (Prices can also go down. Nastech had plummeted back below fifty cents a share by the time this was written!)

In the world of penny stocks, big changes in value are commonplace. For example, let's take those stocks I mentioned earlier besides Nastech. Here's what their increases were during 1985:

STOCK	TIME FRAME	INCREASE	ORIGINAL COST
Seburg Phonograph	11 months	500%	$.25
Midas Gold	12 months	550%	$.20
Metcom	6 months	2,200%	$.01
NTN Communications	11 months	4,000%	$.20

Remember, these are just a fraction of the stocks that showed such increases. There are dozens that have also done as well. And probably thousands that have at least gone up somewhat in price. In fact, the penny stock market is loaded with success stocks. (It's also loaded with failed stocks. We'll see ways to avoid these in future chapters.)

BIG PROFITS—LITTLE PUBLICITY

This, of course, is the big reason that people invest in penny stocks—the chance to make a fortune. It's hard to find an individual who would turn down the opportunity to double, quadruple, or more his or her money in a short time. (Of course, that's not to say this market is without risk. As we'll see, both the rewards and the risks can be substantial.)

Yet, if you call up the average broker (one who handles stocks in general, not one who specializes in this field) and ask him or her about penny stocks, the chances are probably nine out of ten that the broker will suggest (perhaps insist) that you stay away from the pennies. I've heard brokers say, "It's a place where you can get hurt," or "The market is manipulated," or "You'll just lose all the money you put in."

The criticism of this field can also come from high places.

Louis Rukeyser, the host of the *Wall Street Week* television show and perhaps the most listened-to authority in stocks, suggests, "Don't buy a stock just because it's cheap. . . . Playing with low-priced stocks is a dangerous game that requires extra-strong information about the company and its prospects. It's not a safe game for beginners, who are all too apt to buy junk in the mistaken belief that its price makes it a bargain." (From *How to Make Money in Wall Street,* Doubleday Dolphin, 1976 edition.) By the way, the book is *must* reading for any beginner in stocks.

If Mr. Rukeyser and others of experience and reputation say low-priced stocks are bad, must not they be?

To these criticisms I would reply, yes, there's some truth in each of them. Yet, people still invest, and many of those investors do reap fortunes—as in any other field, from high-priced stocks to real estate to commodities. There are those who win and those who lose.

I personally think it is possible to profit in pennies, if you avoid the risks and the pitfalls. However, at the onset it's important to understand that this is not a field for the faint of heart or those who don't relish a challenge. There's money to be made here, but you do have to educate yourself and be willing to take a chance. (We'll have more to say about the psychology of the investor!) However, you don't need a lot of money to get started. In fact, that's another of the big appeals of this field.

THE REASON PEOPLE INVEST IN PENNIES

1. The Chances Are Greater for a Big Jump in Price in Low-Priced Stocks.

This should be obvious. If you have a hundred dollars to spend and you have a choice between buying a stock that sells for a hundred dollars a share or one that sells for ten cents a share, which is more likely to take a *big* price increase?

Most people will opt for a lower-priced stock. Here's why. Let's say that both stocks go up ten cents in value. With the high-priced stock you now have one share worth $100.10. You've made one thin dime. With the lower-priced stock you now have a thousand shares worth twenty cents apiece, or $200. You've made $100. The mathematics make it appealing.

Ah, but that comparison's not fair, I hear a Big Board (New York Stock Exchange) broker saying. It's easy as pie for a hundred-dollar stock to go up ten cents; after all, we're only talking about a .10 percent increase. But it's very hard for a ten-cent stock to go up ten cents. That's a doubling, or a 100 percent increase. In the long run, so this reasoning goes, you'll still make out better with the higher-priced stock.

Maybe, but to my way of thinking, it's a lot easier for *any* stock to go up ten cents a share (doubling the lower-priced stock) than it is for any stock to go up a hundred dollars a share (doubling the higher-priced stock). It's simply because a hundred dollars is so much more money than ten cents.

2. It's More Psychologically Appealing to Buy a Low-Priced Stock.

Everyone knows this, including the major corporations. People simply prefer stocks that are lower in price. That's why whenever a corporation's stock gets high, the company orders a "split." They issue two shares for one, or some such fraction, in order to get the price down to where investors will feel comfortable buying it.

After all, if this weren't really the case, then some stocks would be up there at a thousand dollars a share or higher.

(IBM or Xerox without splitting would be good examples.) Yet, except for some privately held companies, this almost never happens.

For a stock to be marketable, it must be low enough in price to appeal to investors. After all, only the largest institutional investors today can afford 1,000 shares of a stock costing over $100 a share. At $20, many more investors can own 1,000 shares. And at twenty cents, almost anyone can.

It's all a matter of how low is low. Is $20 the threshold of investor psychological appeal? Or $10? Or ten cents?

It's in the psychology of it. Would you rather own two or three shares of a high-priced stock or two or three hundred shares of a low-priced one? If you're the sort who would opt for the two or three shares of high-priced stock, then perhaps you'd best reconsider investing the time reading this book. On the other hand, if owning a lot of shares in what is undoubtedly a riskier company, but one with the potential to double or more in value, appeals to you, read on!

3. "It's One Gamble I Can Afford to Lose!"

A great many low-priced stock investors have no illusions about the market. They know it's a gamble and they know that the odds may be against them.

Nevertheless, they also know that even if they don't happen to hit it big, they won't get hurt too bad. They make sure that they don't invest more money than they can afford to lose. (Of course, as in any investment, the sky's the limit as to what you can put in.) Maybe it's only a few hundred dollars. Perhaps it's a thousand. But these investors know they can get into the market without a lot of cash. And they restrict their investment to just the amount they know won't hurt them in case things don't work out.

If they don't hit the long shot, well then, they'll sustain the loss and try again some other time. It's not like playing the Big Board, where you may need five thousand dollars just to get a round lot order (a hundred shares), or commodities, where the minimum margin may be three to five thousand dollars, or even real estate, where just a 10 percent down payment (which is what's realistic in today's market) can be ten thousand dollars.

Here you can put up less and lose less. Remember, at ten cents a share, investing a hundred dollars gives you a thousand shares. How bad can a person who owns a thousand shares for a hundred dollars get hurt? If the stock goes to zero, you're still only out a hundred bucks.

4. "It's a Long Shot That Could Make My Fortune!"

As those who play the pennies know, when dealing with stock that costs under a dollar a share, we're dealing with companies that are high risk. In most cases the chances of failure are far greater than the chances of success.

Nevertheless, a good many of these companies do succeed against the odds. And when they do, if you're holding their stock, you reap the benefits. You might lose on two, three, or more penny stocks before you hit it big. But if you do hit it, you could make your fortune on one stock. That's the long shot that holds the allure for this field.

IT'S UP TO YOU

What would you rather do? Go into your stockbroker's office and consider a stock that, if it does very well, might go up 25 percent? Or consider a stock that, if it does very well, might go up 10,000 percent! If you'd consider the latter, then you may be ready to try a fling at the pennies.

ARE YOU READY FOR PENNY STOCKS?

■

There was a time when the way to win in stocks, almost guaranteed, was to buy the "blue chips."

Blue-chip stocks, so called probably as a reference to the highest-priced blue chips at a poker table, were those that might not necessarily grow the fastest, but that would indeed continue to pay a strong dividend year after year.

Twenty years ago, in the 1960s, the bluest of the blue were the utility stocks. Everyone needed electricity. The country's growth was a certainty and the utilities would grow with it. Moody's (the rating service) maintains a utility stock average. In 1965 it hit a top of 120. Most people felt this was only the beginning.

Brokers in those days were urging "widows' and orphans' funds" (the euphemism for money you can't afford to gamble with and must preserve) to go into utilities. They offered "guaranteed" high dividends and "guaranteed" growth.

Many investors seeking security and reward opted for the utility stocks. They bought public power all over the country. Then they put their stocks in their safe-deposit boxes and forgot about them, confident they had made a wise and safe investment.

Of course, as anyone who really has invested in utilities knows, things didn't quite work out as planned. By the mid-1970s the utility average was down under fifty. Recently, after much struggling, it has only been able to get close to the nineties. As of this writing, it still isn't at the peak it achieved over twenty years ago.

What happened? Ask the investors in companies such as Washington Public Power Supply System. The utilities (many of them) invested in the future—nuclear power. Only, the costs of nuclear power were grossly underestimated and the productivity of that source of energy widely overrated. The utilities lost money.

Today many brokers consider utilities to be high-risk speculative issues. Yes, some still pay high dividends, right up until the day they default, like WHPSS. Utilities are hardly in the class of blue-chip stocks.

Of course, the utilities aren't the only casualties. There's the classic case of U.S. Steel, once considered the solid rock of blue-chip stocks. Beset by high costs and foreign competition, it turned out to be a true paper tiger.

Even high-tech blue chips have not worked out as many anticipated. Just a few years ago Apple Computer was considered one of the newest, brightest high-tech stocks—a new blue chip. Then it ran into that brick wall called IBM and its stock plummeted.

Of course, there is always IBM. But with the inroads in computers that the Japanese are making, can we still be sure?

I hope the picture is clear. Today most people realize that there is no such thing as a sure bet in stocks. The days of the blue chips are long gone. *All* stock investing today is inherently risky.

WHAT SHOULD YOU RISK?

My goal is *not* to convince you to take "widows' and or-phans' '' money and stick it in penny stocks. My recommendation is that you *do not* risk even 10 percent of your total investment money in pennies. What I do suggest, however, is that you do give this field a chance. Compare it with other investments. You may be surprised.

Of course, you should only make an investment after consulting with your own personal financial adviser. Even then you should only invest money that you are fully prepared to lose.

Just remember, we aren't necessarily talking big bucks here. This is a field where a hundred dollars can buy as much as 10,000 shares of stock.

ARE YOU THE RIGHT
PSYCHOLOGICAL TYPE?

A final word needs to be said here about psychology and the market. When people talk about "gaining experience" and "learning the market," what do they really mean?

What they are talking about is not "book learning" or the gathering of information on stocks. Rather, what they are in truth speaking of is learning about themselves.

I've tried a wide variety of investments, including real estate, stocks, precious metals, and others. Along the way I've learned a few things about myself.

MY OWN EXPERIENCE

For example, I can still vividly remember the first time I invested in commodities. I bought a contract (just one) for gold. In commodities an individual can buy "long," betting the price will go up, or "short," betting it will go down. I bought long, anticipating the price would go up.

I only put up $3,500 as margin. However, at the time gold was $520 an ounce and my contract was for $52,000. For every dollar an ounce gold went up, I would make $100. For every dollar an ounce gold went down, I would lose $100. While the sky was the limit as to what I could make, if the price of gold plummeted by some horrible twist of fate all the way to zero and I couldn't get out of the market (which occasionally happens), I potentially could lose as much as $52,000!

Since I was convinced gold would go up in price, I wasn't worried . . . until that night.

Suddenly, from a deep sleep I sat bolt upright. I looked at my clock. It was 3 A.M. "My God," I asked myself, "what if I lose $52,000?!"

Never mind that the chance of losing that full amount was so remote as to be virtually impossible. It was the thought that held my mind. And I couldn't get back to sleep.

First thing the next morning, I called my broker. Gold had slipped $5.00 an ounce. I had lost $500. "Sell!" I shouted into the phone.

He unfortunately followed my instructions. I took my loss. However, within days the price had jumped $50 an ounce. If I had held, I would have made a $4,500 profit.

"KNOW THYSELF IN LOVE, WAR, AND IN MONEY"

I had lost at the market, but I had learned about myself. At that time in my life, I simply didn't have the temperament to risk more money than I put up. I left commodities (to return some years and a lot of experience later) and tried penny stocks.

Here the potential rewards were as great if not greater than with commodities. *But I only stood to lose what I initially invested.* If it put up $500 (assuming no margin), that's the most I could lose.

When I bought pennies, even though in some cases I might lose all the money I invested, I could still sleep peacefully at night.

WHAT IS YOUR COMFORT LEVEL?

How about you?

What is your comfort level in an investment? Is it similar to mine? Does knowing that you can't lose more than you have invested allow you to sleep at night? It might not.

There are some people I know who can't stand to lose any money at all. I have a friend, Jim, who is like this.

When Jim makes an investment, he wants to see a profit from the very first moment. If he buys a stock at $1.00 a share, he expects it to go to $1.10 the next day. If he buys real estate, he expects price appreciation immediately. If for any reason the price drops below his initial investment (the stock goes to ninety-nine cents or the real estate fails to appreciate), he gets apprehensive and nervous. He begins to think he's made a bad move. So he sells.

Needless to say, Jim doesn't get involved in many investments. In fact, right now he's got all his money tied up in certificates of deposit at banks. With a CD you start making money the moment you put your money in and it continues making money as long as it's deposited, often guaranteed (for what that's worth) by the U.S. government. Jim feels it's a no-lose situation.

Of course, he's only making 6.5 percent interest as of this writing. So it's not much of a win situation, either.

The point is, Jim has found an investment that fits his comfort level. He should never invest in penny stocks (where he might lose all the money he puts up) and certainly not in commodities (where he could lose more than his initial investment).

IT'S BETTER TO SLEEP AT NIGHT

What's your comfort level?

Are you a big risk taker?

Are you willing to lose a buck to make a buck or more?

Or do you like to hold your cash in your hand, where you can see and feel it all the time?

You really need to know. Finding out isn't a frivolous exercise. To succeed in penny stocks, you have to be willing to risk losing some money. If you're the sort who isn't comfortable doing that, then this chapter has more than just paid for the cost of this book. It's just saved you countless sleepless nights. Forget about penny stocks and run (don't walk) with your cash down to the bank and get a CD. You'll sleep easier, be healthier, and—even if you never get rich—probably live longer.

On the other hand, if you can take the heat, read on. Your fortune's waiting to be made.

WHERE PENNIES AREN'T
(A LOOK AT THE
TRADITIONAL MARKETS)
■

W
here do we buy penny stocks?

That's a question I'm frequently asked, and if you're a traditional stock investor who hasn't bought pennies before, I'm sure you're also interested to know. Where are these elusive low-priced penny stock bargains to be found? After all, when we ask a traditional stockbroker about pennies, he or she usually gives us a scratch of the head and says, "There just aren't many out there worth considering."

Nonsense! There are hundreds, thousands out there. However, to find them we have to be willing to move beyond what most investors (particularly neophytes) consider the "traditional markets." This can be quite confusing, especially if you're new to penny stocks. So in this chapter we are going to set the stage. We're going to examine the traditional markets such as the New York Stock Exchange and the American Stock Exchange (called AMEX). Then, once we have firmly grasped what these are and how they operate, we'll move on to the exciting world of pennies.

First, let's define what a penny stock is.

WHAT IS A PENNY STOCK?

In the marketplace a penny stock is normally considered to be any stock selling for under $5 a share.

Of course, that's not a rule carved in granite. It's arbitrary, but it's widely accepted, so we might just as well go along with it. By this definition a stock that sells for $4.90 a share is just as much a penny stock as one that sells for ten cents a share.

Stocks for under $5 a share can be found in virtually any market. There are some (very few) on the New York Stock Exchange, the much smaller American Stock Exchange, and the various other smaller exchanges around the country. But most frequently we will find stocks for under five dollars in the "over-the-counter" or OTC market. It is here that we will primarily be looking.

Before getting to the OTC market, let's be sure we understand why we won't be looking for low-priced stocks on the Big Board and its various cousins.

THE NEW YORK
STOCK EXCHANGE

The New York Stock Exchange is the largest and, without a doubt, most prestigious exchange in the world. It traces its origin back to the very founding of the country. It has the top companies listed (more than 2,000 of them).

It's important to understand at the outset that the Big

Board, as it is affectionately called, is not itself a buyer or seller of stocks. Rather, it is a marketplace where those who buy and sell come to conduct their business.

Those who buy and sell are said to have "seats" on the board. These individuals are usually officers or board members of large stockbrokerage firms, and they buy and sell stocks on an "auction" basis.

STOCK AUCTIONS

One of the more confusing things that newcomers to low-priced stocks get involved with is how the stocks are traded. Since the Big Board uses auctions, many neophytes believe that this is how all stocks not only are, but *should be*, traded. To avoid this problem, let's take a look at how an auction works so that when we get to the OTC market, we'll know the difference and be ready for it.

The vital thing to understand about auctions is that they are handled by *brokers*. Brokers representing various stock houses are on the floor executing their clients' orders. When you or I want to buy a Big Board stock, we go to our local stockbroker and explain what we want. Our request is phoned in to the floor man for the firm who, acting for us, finds another broker acting for a seller. A sale is then made.

It's not quite that simple, but the principle holds true. In an auction, stocks are continuously being exchanged, and their price is determined by supply and demand in an open market environment.

Of course, there has to be a little grease to keep the wheels of the market moving along smoothly, and this is provided in several ways. One way is by "odd lot dealers," who will buy orders for under a hundred shares. (A hundred shares, or a "lot," is the minimum order many brokers will handle.) These odd lot dealers essentially buy for themselves and then resell at a markup, thus explaining why there is sometimes a markup on less than a hundred shares. (Today, many large brokerage firms handle odd lot sales internally as a convenience for their clients.)

But the largest part of the lubricant that keeps the Big Board going is the "specialist." Specialists are located at various places on the floor of the exchange, and they "make a market" in a particular stock. It's important to understand that a specialist is a *dealer*. He buys and sells stocks for himself. He is dealing in the stock.

THE SPECIALIST

The specialist is needed because at any given time, there might not be enough buyers and sellers of a stock to keep an open auction going . . . or the buy prices and the sell prices might be so far apart that the market in a stock could come to a grinding halt.

Because he is committed to making a market in a given stock, at such times the specialist steps in and buys or sells so that there is always an open market for an issue. That is why he is called a "market maker." In theory, he buys when most others want to sell and sells when most others want to buy.

There have been countless articles and books written on how specialists may or may not manipulate the market. That's not really our concern here since we're only dealing with the Big Board in passing. However, it's important to note these concerns because when we get to the OTC market, we'll see a striking similarity between specialists and OTC dealers.

LISTED STOCKS

In the past the goal of many a board chairman was to get his or her stock "listed" on the Big Board. Besides prestige, it meant an entrée to the capital markets of the world. (This is changing today as many companies opt for other markets.)

Getting listed on the Big Board, however, is rather difficult. The New York Stock Exchange has strict requirements, such as insisting that the company show strong earning power (in the millions of dollars annually, going back several years), that it have enough shares to provide an open trading arena (usually a million or more), and that the total value of the company as measured by the value of the shares of stock outstanding be substantial (usually in the tens of millions).

Obviously, relatively few companies are going to have the qualifications to be listed here. And those that are listed are going to be quite substantial, meaning the value of their shares will probably be high, usually higher than $5 a share. (Finding stocks that are listed is an easy matter. Just check the financial section of any major newspaper, or if that fails, the *Wall Street Journal*. All Big Board stocks and their recent prices are given there.)

This, then, is the first reason we are not going to be looking for low-priced stocks on the New York Stock Exchange. There simply are not many there.

DOWN-AND-OUT

There are, however, occasionally some stocks listed on the Big Board that do indeed sell for under five dollars a share. In most cases we are going to be very skeptical of these.

My experience has been that low-priced stocks on the Big Board are from companies that are on the rocks. Usually stocks will come onto the Big Board at a price of at least $10 a share. Thus, if they are under $5, too often they are down from earlier levels and they may be on their way out. In other words, they are the losers.

For one reason or another, I have found that often a low-priced stock on the Big Board signals a company that is floundering. Of course, it could make a comeback, in which case buying the low-priced Big Board stock would be smart. (Good examples of just this are Wickes Co., which dropped to around $4 during its reorganization, then bounced back, and Sharon Steel, which dropped to fifty cents.) Most of the time, however, it hasn't worked that way for me. Too often, these companies just hang around for a while until they are "delisted."

DELISTING

When a company drops below the minimum requirements for listing on the Big Board, it is in danger of being delisted. The Exchange may warn the company and tell it to get its house in order. But if there is no significant improvement after a time, the stock may be removed, or delisted, from the board. This is roughly the equivalent of a one-way ticket to oblivion.

Thus, the second reason for not buying low-priced stocks on the Big Board is that too often they represent a company that is on its way out.

OTHER EXCHANGES

Besides the New York Stock Exchange, there are many other exchanges. The most well known is the American

Stock Exchange. Between 1980 and 1985, the total number of shares traded on the New York Stock Exchange virtually doubled. That of AMEX, however, remained relatively unchanged. As of this writing, AMEX ranks roughly sixth in dollar volume of exchanges worldwide. (NASDAQ, as we'll see, is technically not an auction exchange.)

DOLLAR VOLUME OF EXCHANGES
1. New York Stock Exchange
2. Tokyo Stock Exchange
3. NASDAQ
4. London Stock Exchange
5. Zurich Stock Exchange
6. German Republic Stock Exchange
7. AMEX

AMEX is the little sister of the New York Stock Exchange. Its listing requirements are not as stringent and the average price per share is not as high. However, to my way of thinking, much of what was said about the Big Board applies here as well. It is still not an appropriate arena for low-priced stocks. We are not going to search much on AMEX, either.

In addition, there are numerous smaller regional exchanges, which provide an auction market across the country.

These include the following:

Midwest Stock Exchange
Pacific Coast Stock Exchange
Philadelphia Stock Exchange (PBW)
Cincinnati Stock Exchange
Boston Stock Exchange
Spokane Stock Exchange
Salt Lake City Stock Exchange

Most of these exchanges actually trade stocks that are also listed on the Big Board, although they do encourage regional stocks.

In later chapters we will look at several of these exchanges with regard to low-priced stocks. In addition, we will also pay particular attention to the Vancouver, British Columbia (Canada) Stock Exchange, which is a true penny stock exchange.

WHERE THE PENNIES AREN'T

These, then, are the major *auction* exchanges. However, as we've noted, in most cases a low-priced stock that we might find appealing probably won't be listed here (with certain exceptions).

We've looked at these exchanges not to find out where the pennies are, but instead to get a perspective, to set the stage. We've seen the traditional investment markets for investors.

Now, let's move on to something that may not be quite so traditional (although it certainly has a long history). Let's move on to the markets where the pennies are. In the next chapters we'll discuss the OTC markets and their opportunities.

FINDING THE PENNIES— THE OTC MARKET

■

When a new investor begins searching for penny stocks, he or she may ask a broker, "I can't find the penny stocks—where's the list?"

Most brokers may try to dissuade the investors from journeying down that "treacherous" path to the pennies. But if the investor is insistent, the broker may dump a telephone-book-size stack of stock lists on his or her lap and say, "You're on your own!"

In other words, the traditional broker (one who day in and day out makes a living trading the Big Board) probably isn't going to be encouraging or helpful with regard to pennies. If you're an investor who wants to get started in the field, therefore, you're going to find that, at least at first, you're pretty much out on your own.

But don't fret. In this chapter we're going to take a look at where we need to go to find the penny stocks.

Most penny stocks can be found on the over-the-counter market. However, unlike the auction exchanges we were looking at in the last chapter, where the action, so to speak, takes place on the floor of a central building, in the OTC market (to paraphrase Gertrude Stein), "There's no there, there."

The OTC market doesn't have an "auction floor" where sales take place. There is no continuous auction going on where brokers for buyers and brokers for sellers compete in a supply/demand situation to determine the price of a stock. A perfect example of this is the Denver market. An enormous amount of OTC oil and gas stock used to be handled in Denver during the days of the oil boom, and a great many penny stocks still change hands there. Yet, there is no official floor for a Denver exchange in the sense that there is one for the New York Stock Exchange. Instead there is the Denver OTC market.

This is a quieter market in a sense. It's conceivable that some time may pass between OTC stock transactions. Depending on the stock and demand for it, it might be hours, days, or even weeks between transactions. Or sales might be hot and heavy for a stock that's in particular demand. Sales take place only when someone wants to buy or sell a particular stock. No buyers or sellers, no market.

While at first glance this might seem like a small market, it is in reality the largest stock market of all. It accounts for *all* those other stocks that aren't listed on the New York Stock Exchange and its relatives. It's the unseen giant where as many as 30,000 different companies in this country alone have their stocks.

A DEALER/TRADER MARKET

The OTC market works because the participants are not only brokers, but are also dealers. The participants don't just act for investors, they also buy and sell stock for their own account.

It's important to see this difference between the OTC market and the auction market. In an auction market, when we want to buy a stock, we call up a broker. She gets hold of her firm's floor person and, acting on our account, tries to buy. This means going to a specialist or another broker who represents someone who wants to sell. When your broker representing you finds another broker representing a seller, a sale is made.

In the OTC market it's a bit different. We call up our broker and want to buy an over-the-counter stock. But remember, there is no exchange floor where brokers representing sellers are waiting to sell. Our broker instead must now locate someone who is willing to sell that stock to us.

Think of how hard it would be for our broker to find an individual investor who happened to want to sell that stock just when we wanted to buy. We might have to wait a very long time for such a person to show up. Without an auction floor, the chances of running into a seller for that stock would be remote.

Were it necessary for our broker to find an individual stock investor who wanted to sell just when we wanted to buy without having an exchange, there would be virtually no market. We wouldn't be able to buy and sellers wouldn't be able to sell stock.

However, do you remember that in the Big Board there were the specialists who dealt in specific stocks and made markets? They acted as a lubricant to keep the market flowing smoothly.

In the OTC market there are dealers who not only are the lubricant, but who virtually are the market itself. These are firms that have agreed to be market makers in particular stocks. They acquire an inventory of the stock themselves and then offer to sell it at any time to anyone who wants to buy. Or offer to buy at any time from anyone who wants to sell. They "deal" in the stock. To carry our

SCHAUMBURG TWP. PUBLIC LIBRARY

analogy to an extreme, this is a market where the grease becomes the motor.

Because there are market makers for specific stocks (frequently more than one market maker per stock), when we tell our broker to buy an OTC stock for us, we've actually given her a fairly easy task.

Our broker now only has to find the market maker who deals in the stock we want. (We'll see how she does this in a moment.) Once she finds out the name of the firm that is making a market in the particular stock we want, she calls up that firm and begins to negotiate.

PRICE IN OTC STOCKS

Because there is no auction where supply and demand are continuously setting the price, in the OTC market, what we'll pay for the stock is a matter of negotiation. Our broker and the dealer negotiate back and forth for a while over the phone (or computer), our broker trying to get the best price for us, the dealer trying to get the best price for the market maker. Eventually a deal is struck and the sale made.

Notice that here our broker dealt with a *dealer*. She dealt with a firm that probably owned the stock we were buying, not with a broker for another investor who was selling. In this case the brokerage house probably was acting as a principal. It was selling *its own stock* to us.

DIFFERENCES BETWEEN AN AUCTION AND A TRADE

There are a number of important differences between an OTC trade and an auction, as we've seen, and we should be aware of them. Here are three:

1.   An auction takes place on the floor of an exchange. An OTC trade often takes place over the phone between two brokers, one of whom may be acting as a dealer.

2.   In an auction the price is constantly set by the forces of supply and demand on a moment-to-moment basis. In an OTC trade the price is set by negotiation with the market maker/dealer, who presumably is also affected by supply and demand for the stock.

3.   In an auction, there is a single price for a stock determined by the auction process. In an OTC trade there is a price "range." The range is the difference between the price the market maker will pay you to buy the stock and the price he asks from you when he sells the stock.

AN INTRODUCTION
TO BID/ASK

This price range for OTC stock can be confusing to those new to the field. Since it's critical to low-priced stock investment, however, it's vital that it be thoroughly understood. Let's compare it again with an auction price.

We'll say we want to buy IBM on the Big Board; the price may be $120 a share. We buy 100 shares at $120 apiece (plus commission). A few minutes later we have a change of heart and decide to sell. It just happens that the price hasn't changed, so we sell at $120 (plus commission). We essentially bought and sold at the same price and our only actual costs were the commissions.

In an OTC trade there is no single price. Rather, there is a "bid/ask" range. The "bid" will represent the price at which the market maker will buy the stock from us or any other investor. The "ask" is the price at which he will sell to us or any other investor. For example, the bid may be twenty cents a share, while the ask may be twenty-five cents. If we buy the stock, it costs us twenty-five cents.

But if the next minute we want to sell, we can only sell (to this market maker) for twenty cents, or an immediate loss of a nickel a share for us.

That nickel a share represents the market maker's cost of doing business and a profit. (A commission may be tacked on top of this.)

As should be obvious, an OTC trade is quite different from an auction. It tends to be much more a matter of negotiation, which is another reason why the investor needs to plan investments carefully.

FINDING THE MARKET

We'll return to bid/ask in a few pages to see how it influences our investment strategy, but first let's consider how our broker found that market maker to begin with. (This, after all, is the heart of our interest—where are the penny stocks!)

There are over four thousand registered OTC brokerage companies and many times that number of brokers selling OTC stocks. How did our broker find a firm that was making a market in the one stock we wanted to buy?

The SEC, or Securities and Exchange Commission, oversees all stock trading. However, with regard to OTC stock, it has in effect delegated much of the regulating to the National Association of Securities Dealers (NASD). (NASD membership is an absolute minimum for any broker you are dealing with.)

PINK SHEETS

The NASD oversees trading in about thirty thousand different over-the-counter stocks. (As noted, this is why the

OTC market is considered the largest in the world.) Virtually *all* of these stocks are listed daily in the "pink sheets."

The pink sheets are published by the National Quotation Bureau, Inc. They are indeed pink, are about half a foot wide and nearly two feet long. They come in a stack about as thick as a major city phone book.

The pink sheets are vital to a penny stock buyer because they list the market makers for each stock. If you want to find out what stocks are available and who's making a market in them, you will need to know about the "pinks."

While it is possible to subscribe to the pink sheets, the cost is prohibitive for most investors. It costs $42 a month plus $16 a month for timely delivery. All brokerage houses subscribe, however. Therefore, what you need to do is to make friends with a broker. Since they normally throw out the pink sheets at the end of each day, they should be willing to let you have them. Getting a copy will introduce you to the world of penny stocks.

NASDAQ

Of course, having to check the pinks for market makers, then having to call the makers for their current quotes, is really a rather primitive approach to handling stocks in our modern day. The NASD wrestled with this very problem: how to quickly and efficiently find the market maker and quote for a given stock.

Their solution, begun in 1971, was NASDAQ, which stands for National Association of Securities Dealers Automated Quotations system. This is an enormous computer network that is piped into each of the NASD's member firms.

NASDAQ lists *only the biggest and most active of the*

OTC stocks, about five thousand of them. If we want to find the market maker of a stock listed on NASDAQ, we just go to a member firm's office and have the broker call up the stock on the computer. In an instant we will have on-screen the name of each market maker as well as his or her retail bid/ask for the stock. Not only that, but since most stocks listed by NASDAQ have many market makers (the average is eleven), the computer will show the high bid and the low ask among the market makers.

Today NASDAQ is the third largest stock trading market in the world (after only the New York and Tokyo Stock Exchanges). In dollar volume in 1984 it did roughly seven times the volume of AMEX, the next biggest American trading market. (Remember, of course, that both the Big Board and AMEX are auction markets with a trading floor. NASDAQ doesn't have any "there, there." It exists only on computer screens and over the phone lines of NASD member firms.)

NASDAQ, by bringing computers to the world of OTC stock, revolutionized the industry and created the second largest functioning stock market in the country.

THE KINDS OF COMPANIES ON NASDAQ

NASDAQ, like the Big Board, Amex, and other trading markets, has strict requirements for listing. In general they require that a company have a minimum number of shares, market value, and net worth or net income for the company. *In some cases they also require a minimum bid price of $3.*

When a company is getting started, there are many things it needs, usually including visibility, market share, and investors. Investors not only provide capital, but they also support the company.

One way to get all three of the above and more is to be listed on a major exchange. However, as we've seen, getting listed on the Big Board can be difficult.

Getting listed on NASDAQ, however, is somewhat less difficult. The company doesn't have to be as old and established. And once listed, the company's stock now has a major market in which to trade.

Another way of looking at it is that it's all symbolic, literally. When a company gets listed on NASDAQ, it's given a symbol. This symbol is usually the first few letters of its name. For example, Apple Computers is listed as *Apple C.*

This NASDAQ symbol can mean success or failure to many companies. When a company has a symbol, any NASD broker can punch the symbol into the computer and call up the stock. This means that it can easily be traded. In other words, the NASD symbol is an entrée into the world of investors.

To put it yet another way, few people will buy a product until it gets to market. The NASDAQ symbol is a sort of ticket to the marketplace.

Additionally, because of the requirements for being listed on NASDAQ, many investors are inclined to look with favor on listed companies.

BREAKING INTO PRINT

This all comes to roost in publicity. When we buy a stock, generally we want to be able to follow its course on a regular basis. We want to be able, for example, to look in the paper to see how that stock is doing.

If the stock is with NASDAQ, that's often possible. NASDAQ releases to the media two "recommended" lists, which are then published in major newspapers in this country and even worldwide.

The first list is called the OTC "national list" and is the one most commonly printed. The second list is called the "additional list," which appears in some of the larger papers. These lists give the company symbol, the recent volume, and bid and ask for the stock. Inclusion on the lists is determined on the basis of the size of the company and the volume of shares traded. (If you really want to see how good your local paper is, check to see if it has both lists, one, or neither list. Of course, they are all available in the *Wall Street Journal*.)

While not all NASDAQ companies are listed, many are. If you own a company and you need shareholders to provide capital and support, having your stock symbol listed in the paper as part of a major trading market means that investors are more inclined to trust your company, invest in it, and support it. In other words, it may mean the difference between success and failure.

PINKS VS. NASDAQ

Because NASDAQ is such a powerful influence on the market, a common error those new to stocks make is to think that *all* OTC stocks are listed on NASDAQ—in other words, that the terms NASDAQ and OTC are synonymous. Nothing could be further from the truth.

OTC STANDS FOR *ANY* OVER-THE-COUNTER STOCK (about 30,000 different stocks in this country alone.)

NASDAQ STANDS FOR WHAT ARE USUALLY THE *TOP* OTC STOCKS (about 5,000 of them).

That means that there are twenty-five thousand OTC

stocks that are *not* listed on NASDAQ (but which can provide excellent buying opportunities for the penny stock investor). These stocks have *no* NASDAQ symbol and never appear on the NASDAQ lists.

Another difference between a NASDAQ listing and an OTC pink sheet listing is that typically the NASDAQ listing in a newspaper will show the stock's symbol, its volume (if available), it's week's high and low bid, and the change from the previous week. On the other hand, a non-NASDAQ stock listed on the pinks will often just show its market maker(s). To find a quote, you'll have to call the market maker.

WHAT TO DO ONCE YOU'VE LOCATED THE PENNIES

In this chapter we've covered the basics of the OTC market. We've seen where the pennies are listed and we've delved into the differences between the NASDAQ list and the pinks.

But once we've gotten hold of the pinks and the NASDAQ list, what do we do next? How do we determine which stocks to buy?

There are at least three more steps we need to take, and they all can be done simultaneously:

1. Check with investment advisories that give information about penny stocks.
2. Find out how the market really works and get a winning strategy.
3. Locate a good broker.

In the next chapter we'll begin by looking at the investment advisories.

INVESTMENT
ADVISORIES
■

I f you've read through this
book thus far, I'm sure
you've come to realize that
in penny stocks, knowledge
is vital. The problem, of
course, is that accurate information in the field tends to
be difficult to come by.

Because we are dealing with small companies, the regular news channels don't maintain very good coverage. In addition, sometimes the companies as well as the underwriters will "leak" information that may exaggerate the potential of a company. Finally, there is always the temptation on the part of those reporting to themselves invest in a company and then promote its stock through carefully placed "news" items.

For the investor, particularly one new to the field, finding accurate information, therefore, can be a real problem. It's hard to know where to start looking.

Well, this is the place to start in terms of getting informed. In this chapter I've listed many of the different investment advisories and news publications. I've also put down my own comments regarding them. Even if you're not ready to start investing, subscribing to one or more is an excellent way to become familiar with the market.

NOTE: I am neither recommending nor endorsing any of these publications. While most endeavor to provide accurate news information, the author specifically disclaims any liability for loss caused by relying on any information or recommendations contained in any of these publications.

(Also note that costs quoted may be different by the time you read this information.)

The National OTC Stock Journal
Weekly (Under $80 per year)
1780 S. Bellaire St., Suite 400
Denver, CO 80222
This is one of the most widely read journals in penny stocks. Although it states it covers stocks "under ten dollars," it's coverage of what's happening in pennies has been both comprehensive and credible. For anyone who wants to invest in pennies, this is a "must."

COVERAGE: News Affecting Low-Priced Stocks
                People in the News
                NASDAQ Volume Leaders
                Columns:
                      Press Releases
                      Market Talk
                      Editorial Opinion
                      Corporate Comments
                      Corporate Reports
                      Spotlight (featuring newsletters)
                Pulse of the Market
                      (featuring multiple indices)

New Issue Summaries
Quotes (OTC market)
New Issue Aftermarket Quotes
New Issues in Registration
Rule 144 (insider) Proposed Stock Sales
Paid Advertising

PennyStock News
Weekly ($50 per year)
8930 J Oakland Center
Columbia, MD 21045

This is a highly readable tabloid, which contains information on the penny stock field. It contains many columns of special interest. However, it was the subject of an SEC investigation in 1984 involving alleged improprieties.

COVERAGE: News Affecting Penny Stocks
PSN Index
Volume Watch
Company Profiles
New Issues Update
Market Digest
Insider Trading
New Issues Ratings
New Issues in Registration
New Issues Market Performance
Updates
PSB Recommendations
Quotations (OTC)
Warrant Watch
Columns:
Investor Notebook
Ahead of the Pack

People in Business
New Issues Update
Corporate Corner
Paid Advertising

Penny Stock Preview and *Low-Priced Stock Digest*
Monthly (*Preview*—$48, *Digest*—$68 per year)
Idea Publishing Corporation
55 East Afton Ave.
Yardley, PA 19067

The *Low-Priced Stock Digest* is a newsletter that is a summary of other newsletters. The editor claims to read more than a hundred other newsletters a month and then pick the best of what's been said for this publication. I have found it to be extremely informative.

The *Penny Stock Preview* is a newsletter that features new issues. It gives brief descriptions of new stocks and has a "Sneak Preview" section, which gives stocks, underwriters, and prices of recent issues. Also helpful are an "Underwriter's Box Score," in which it rates the success of underwriters in bringing new issues to market, and "Top 10 Percentage Gainers," in which it rates the best new issues of the past year.

The Cheap Investor
Published by Bill Mathews
Monthly ($78 per year)
36 King Arthur Court
Suite 10
Northlake, IL 60164

This is a newsletter that makes buy and sell recommendations. It specializes in stocks under ten dollars. It also features a "Blue Cheap Index" on its favored stocks. It includes analyses of companies and explanations of why they may do better or worse in the future.

The Prospector
Published by The Penny Mining Prospector, Inc.,
Darrell Brookstein
1096 "D" Coast Village Rd.
Santa Barbara, CA 93108
This newsletter "prospects" for good mining stocks. The publisher makes no bones about stating up front that he is a "registered representative and major shareholder of First Georgetown Securities, Inc. . . ." which is "the only stockbroker he recommends for the execution of trades."

The newsletter contains its own index of penny mining stocks as well as buy and sell recommendations.

Uptrend
Published by Continental, Carlisle, Douglas; editor:
Henry Huber
Published every three weeks ($55 for six issues, $220 for twenty-four issues)
Investment Services, Ltd.
P.O. Box 49333
Four Bentall Centre
Vancouver, B. S. V7X 1L4
This is a Canadian stock newsletter. The editor analyzes a great many stocks and provides a rating system for grading them. He also provides information about trading in the Vancouver market. If you're interested in Vancouver, then this is a "must" newsletter.

The Silver Baron
Edited by Elliott Pearson
About every three weeks ($125 per year)
350 S. Center St.
Reno, NV 89501
This newsletter tries to predict those inexpensive mining stocks that are likely to do well in the future. It main-

tains updates on previous recommendations as well as conducting in-depth analyses of current recommendations.

WHERE TO FIND OUT ABOUT
OTHER NEWSLETTERS

The *OTC Stock Journal* publishes a "Special Report," which lists some of the publications noted above as well as a great many others. This report sells for ten dollars. (Write directly to the *OTC Stock Journal* at the address noted previously.)

WAYS TO WIN
IN PENNIES

■

In one sense penny stocks are an easy investment to figure out. There are really only three ways to win. (There are countless ways to lose, but that's the subject of a later chapter.) These three ways can quickly be listed:

1. Go for long-term growth.
2. Play a stock.
3. Buy new issues.

Of course, if you're new to penny stocks, just having this list isn't going to be all that helpful. You have to know what the three methods mean and how to use them successfully. That's what we'll get started on in this chapter.

NOTE: Before starting this chapter, it's important to understand that it is only part of a whole. Here we're going to look at how to win. In a later chapter we're going to look at how to avoid losing. *Don't just read this chapter and think you've got it all. Be sure to at least read Chapter 10, "Pitfalls in Pennies," as well.*

THE SEARCH FOR LOW-PRICED GROWTH STOCKS

In our search for low-priced stocks in which we might invest, we have covered three tiers. The first tier was represented by the Big Board, AMEX, and similar exchanges. I noted that it was unlikely we would find stocks there that would be appealing because in many cases, those that had a low enough price were from companies on their way down-and-out.

The second tier is the NASDAQ stocks. Are we likely to find good low-priced stocks here?

The answer is yes. In my opinion one of the best places to find low-priced *growth* stocks is on NASDAQ. (Although we shouldn't be under the illusion that NASDAQ is filled with stocks under five dollars. Even here they are the exception, rather than the rule.)

WHAT IS A GROWTH STOCK?

Since the first category for winning with pennies is to buy growth stocks, let's take a few paragraphs to define them. We'll use the old tried-and-true Wall Street definition here. A growth stock is one in which the earnings of the company are plowed back into the company so that it grows bigger and bigger and becomes worth more and more.

Companies that have made it to NASDAQ have often overcome that first hurdle that weeds out the weak, the unlikely to succeed, the "no-chance" companies. They have survived their first years and have shown they can make an income (not necessarily a profit, but an income).

Some of these companies are going to be the IBMs and the Xeroxes and even the General Motors of tomorrow. Unlike the Big Board, where a low price for a stock often indicates trouble, on NASDAQ a low price may indicate a fledgling company just getting off the ground.

It all becomes a matter of direction. Think of low price on the Big Board with an arrow pointed downward. Think of low price on NASDAQ with an arrow pointed upward. (Unfortunately, sometimes the arrow goes the other way for NASDAQ companies as well.)

Of course, this certainly is not true for all NASDAQ stocks. It may not even be true for most of them. But if we can identify those stocks that indeed represent companies that are growing, and indeed have the arrow pointed upward, we are going to be successful.

Find a good growth stock, stick with it, and we can grow rich beyond our wildest dreams. Their growth can become our growth. We can watch them move from a few dollars a share to ultimately hundreds of dollars. It's the old story of hitching our wagon to a shooting star. If we pick a star among the NASDAQ stocks, we, too, can shoot across the sky.

Of course, the eternal question is, "Which stock?" We'll have much more to say about picking winners from the national list later. Suffice it to say here that the first place we are likely to find winning stocks is the second tier of stock investment—those stocks that have NASDAQ symbols.

THE SEARCH FOR
PLAYING STOCKS

I define a stock for "playing" as one in which we really don't worry about growth. For a variety of reasons (explained in a later chapter) we think the stock is going to make a big jump. We want to get in quick and then get out quick. Where are we likely to find stocks for playing?

The answer is the third tier, the pink sheets. We are going to find thousands of start-up companies on the pink sheets, some of which will blossom in just a few weeks. If we're careful, do our homework, and have a pinch of luck, we'll be able to do very well playing winners from the pinks.

We'll discuss how to play a stock in great detail in Chapter 8. For now, however, let's just remember that it's the second way to win.

BUYING NEW ISSUES

The final way of making a profit in penny stocks that we'll discuss is to buy new issues.

A new issue is new stock issued by a company. It could be a company already in business that already has public stock and is now coming out with more of it. Such a company could be on the Big Board, or AMEX, or on NASDAQ.

But what we are more likely to be concerned with is a company that's been private and is just now going public. This is its first public offering. This is the kind of new issue that penny stock investors scramble to get.

Why?

Because when the penny stock market is hot, there is no place where money can be made faster than in new issues. Everybody wants them; investors don't even care what the company is, who manages it, what its product may be. If it's a new issue, *Buy!*

Of course, such investing is foolhardy, and the old saying about a fool and his money soon being parted certainly holds true here. We'll devote an entire chapter (Chapter 9) to the ins and outs of new issues. But for now, let's just see where and why the money is made here.

THE STORY BEHIND
NEW ISSUES

BESTNEWPRODUCT company consists of six engineers. At one time they all worked for a major computer firm. But they got laid off in the computer downturn of 1984-85. So they decided to go to work for themselves. Opening up a "laboratory" in one of their garages, they have invented a computer that talks to the user.

They feel it's a remarkable invention. Instead of a keyboard, when you want to write a letter, you simply dictate it. The computer understands the words and produces a written page, every sentence in correct context, every word properly spelled.

Now they want to produce the product. . . . Only, that takes money. They decide to raise the money by going public. They already have a corporation. Now the corporation will issue stock.

The first thing they do is get a brokerage house to handle the sale, or "underwrite" it. Typically, an underwriter is the same company we were just introduced to as a market maker. As an underwriter, the brokerage company helps get the stock to market. Once it's on the market (called the "after market"), they handle it as the market maker.

The issue comes out at twenty cents a share. There are going to be five million shares, which if sold out will raise $1 million. The company will get $750,000 of this, paying the underwriter $250,000 for its efforts. (In a new issue the company pays the commission, not you, the buyer.)

A SUCCESS STORY

However, as soon as investors hear what the company has to offer, they go wild. A talking computer! It's sensational. The five million shares are gobbled up, with plenty of people waiting.

The stock is issued at twenty cents a share. Because there's so much demand for the company, it quickly rises. Within weeks it's at fifty cents a share.

Let's pause in our description of the company to note the position of the investor who bought the new issue. If he or she was lucky enough to get it at the twenty-cent price before it hit after market, this investor has made a neat profit of thirty cents *on each share*. The investor now can decide to keep the stock hoping for a much higher return, or sell.

In this case, our investor decides to sell. Which turns out to be a wise move. A short time later the BESTNEW-PRODUCT company comes out with it's first product. Oh, the computer talks, all right, but it only speaks in guttural Hindustani. The market for it is severely limited and the stock price plunges to one cent a share. A few months later the company disappears from view.

A QUICK RIDE

Does this really happen? Yes, all the time. New companies filled with promise are continually coming out. A few do indeed have products that become successful. But the vast majority, whether in pharmaceuticals, high tech, mining, or whatever, will fail.

Nevertheless, for a few breathless weeks or months they may ride high, and it is on this *anticipation* that investors buy. You see, many investors in new issues *don't really care* if the company is going to ultimately succeed or not. As long as it has "sizzle," as long as it has "sex appeal," they'll buy the stock hoping that the public will clamber aboard. Then these shrewd investors will bail out before the crash.

Of course, it doesn't always happen that way. Many times new issues won't go up in price, but will instead go straight down. Other times the company will have a truly revolutionary product and the stock will seem to never stop climbing, causing those "shrewd" investors who sold early to pull out their hairs.

Nevertheless, the new issues market is a place where profits—very quick profits—are made in penny stocks. Of course, there are substantial pitfalls, as we'll see. However, for the person who wants to become an investor in pennies, new issues is an arena that cannot be ignored.

THE MECHANICS OF BUYING AND SELLING PENNY (OTC) STOCKS

We briefly summarized the three ways to win at penny stocks. We'll devote the next three chapters to covering each in detail. But now, let's get down to brass tacks with the market. Let's see how it really operates.

When we buy a penny stock, the transaction is handled much the same as it is for any other OTC stock. We talk to our broker and decide to make a purchase. The broker fills out a ticket and takes it to the trading desk.

This desk is occupied by a person who specializes in locating the market maker and handling the transaction. The trader locates the stock we want, haggles trying to get the best price, and finally a sale is made. We are told we have the stock and the price we paid. Eventually we receive a confirmation slip (called a "confirm" in the trade), which indeed confirms what we already know.

COMMISSIONS

When we play a stock, that is, buy it in the anticipation of selling after it goes up quickly, we need to buy as low as possible. After all, this is strictly a matter of buying low and selling high. If we do it the other way around, the results will not in the least please us.

With true penny stocks, those in the under-a-dollar range, the commission can become a significant factor. It can, in fact, be the difference between making a profit or losing money. Therefore, if we're going to play with stocks, it's vital that we understand how the commission structure works.

The amount of the commission can vary enormously. This is something to straighten out with your broker before you buy. It is worth noting that there is no "set" or "required" fee schedule. The National Association of Securities Dealers requires that its members charge fees that are both fair and reasonable. However, the interpretation of "reasonable and fair" can vary quite a bit, depending on your perspective. In addition, some brokers have a "minimum fee" regardless of the amount of the transaction. If the minimum fee happens to be $35 and your total stock cost is $100, then the fee is close to 35 percent of the cost of the transaction!

Note: The reason for the minimum fee is that many brokerage houses use an accounting system that allocates a percentage of overhead to every transaction. Thus, regardless of the amount of the transaction, the house's accounting system may determine that there is an automatic expense of between $20 and $30 involved. Hence, we have the minimum fee. (The minimum fee may not even make a profit for the house!)

LOCATING THE FEE

In addition to the amount of the fee, there is also the problem of determining what it actually was. This can be a bit more difficult than it first seems.

If the broker we deal with goes to a market maker to find the stock for us, then his commission should dutifully be noted on the confirm slip. We'll see just what he charged.

On the other hand, if we buy directly from the market maker (as some brokers advise), then we probably won't see a commission tacked onto the confirm. That doesn't, of course, mean that no commission was charged. It just means that the commission was added into the spread.

BUYING DIRECT FROM
THE MARKET MAKER

You'll recall that with OTC stock there is a spread between the bid price and the ask price. For example, a market maker could have a bid of fifteen cents and an ask of twenty cents. Bid fifteen/ask twenty (or fifteen at twenty as it is sometimes called) means that if you want to buy, you must pay twenty cents. If you want to sell, you will get fifteen cents.

This is generally referred to as the "retail" price or the "advertised" price. When our broker calls up, however, he negotiates a price. Perhaps instead of twenty, he determines that the market maker is desperate to sell and so gets us a price of eighteen cents. When we get our confirm, we see a price of eighteen cents plus whatever the broker's commission happened to be.

On the other hand, let's say we go directly to the market maker. We are probably going to end up paying the retail price. In this case, it might be twenty or twenty-one cents. (The price might have mysteriously gone up a cent or two just before our order came in.)

When we get back our confirm from the market maker, it would show only that we had paid, for example, twenty-one cents a share for the stock. There would be no commission.

However, we did, in effect, pay a commission. The stock was just "marked up" (its price increased) to account for it. If the price turned out to be twenty-one cents, well then, the commission was just that much higher. The point is that the piper must be paid. There is a commission one way or the other. This is the reason some other brokers suggest you *never* buy direct from a market maker.

Note: in some cases the broker we go to will handle the sale directly as a principal. In other words, the broker's firm may have the stock on hand in its own account. It will then sell it to us. This is essentially the same as buying from a market maker. The confirm may not show a commission, but you can be sure it's there in a markup on the stock.

MARKDOWNS ON SELLING

This commission process works in a similar way when it's time to sell. If we go through a broker who then buys from a market maker, we may get a slightly better than retail bid price plus a commission tacked on.

On the other hand, if we're dealing directly with the market maker or with a broker/principal, we may find that the bid price is *lower* than we anticipated. The stock was "marked down" (we got less for our stock than we anticipated). The lower price paid to us means that the spread was increased. This, in effect, amounts to a tacked-on commission.

CALCULATING OUR COSTS

What's important here is not to get alarmed by either the size of the commission (unless it's unreasonable—we'll have more to say about that later) or the method of it's being assessed. We must understand that the commission is part of doing business in penny stocks. It's a volatile, sometimes thin market. The market makers and the brokers have to make their share in order to stay in business. After all, without them, there wouldn't be any penny market at all.

The point is that if we are going to play a stock, to win, we have to win fairly big. For example, if the spread is indeed five cents, as it was in our preceding example, then the stock is going to have to go up five cents in price *before* we break even. It's going to have to go a lot higher for us to make a profit.

Of course, many do, and that's why people play the field. In a field as highly speculative as this, however, more stocks don't succeed than do. For example, the stock we bought at twenty cents may dip down to an ask of ten cents. Even though the stock has only gone down five cents in price, if we sell, we will lose half our investment (bought at twenty cents, sold at ten cents) because of the spread.

All of which leads us to the first rule of playing a stock. You have to hit a winner to succeed. Just buying and selling stocks, even if they don't move in price, will eventually use up all your investment money.

Some people start with $500 and either aren't careful or aren't lucky, and don't hit a winner. It's easy to see how very soon they end up with nothing. If they are new to the field, they may begin thinking they were cheated or that the broker churned their funds. ("Churned" means buying and selling stocks in our account simply to generate commissions for the broker.)

While both those possibilities could have occurred, more likely they simply lost their money to the spread. They just didn't realize that without hitting a winner, they would quickly use up their capital and be out of the market.

But that's just the way it is when you play the pennies. You're risking your money on hitting it big. If you're going to worry about losing your investment, then you don't belong here.

WINNING AT PENNIES

As I noted at the beginning of this chapter, the three ways of winning at pennies are not hard to define. They are:

1. Buy for growth.
2. Play a stock.
3. Buy new issues.

To these we should also add at least two commonsense rules that we've touched on in various places. They are:

DON'T BUY JUST ONE STOCK: We should try to get at least four or five stocks rather than just one. In most cases this increases our chances of hitting at least one winner. And in this field, one winner can quickly offset half a dozen losers.

START WITH A MINIMUM INVESTMENT: We should come in with a minimum investment, say $500. We should be able to invest this money and not fear that the world will end if we lose it.

To win at pennies, you have to know how to play the game. In this chapter we've outlined the game as it stands. We've briefly looked at the mechanics—in a sense, we've been given the basic rules of play. In the next chapters we'll delve deeper and look at some of the winning "tricks of the trade" to see where the money is to be made.

PICKING GROWTH STOCKS
■

I recently had occasion to talk with two unrelated people who invested in low-priced stocks, one successfully and the other with little success. One had spent a great deal of time carefully analyzing the market and several dozen stocks. The other had literally taken a long list of stocks, pinned it to a wall, and thrown a felt-tip pen at it. (He couldn't find a dart, so he used the next best thing.)

Which one of these two investors do you think was the successful one, and which was not?

Interestingly enough, the one who threw the pen had picked a stock that had nearly tripled in value! The other investor had picked three stocks to buy. One had gone down drastically in price while the other two had shown little to no movement.

Does this mean, therefore, that throwing darts (or pens) at a list of stocks is the way to pick winners?

NO ANALYSIS IS PERFECT

Well, the method certainly does have its advocates, and the preceding example does go to show the fallibility of analysis. There's no doubt that you can spend a lot of time investigating stocks only to come up dry. I know of one individual who spent at least two years carefully analyzing the market only to come up with loser after loser. (He subsequently picked a number of winners and walked off with $150,000 in profit.)

Nevertheless, I don't pick stocks by the dart/pen method and I suspect you won't want to, either. Most of us would prefer an educated guess to a wild guess. And that's what analyzing the market to pick winners actually comes down to—educated guessing.

KNOW WHAT YOU'RE LOOKING FOR

The first step in making an educated guess is to narrow the field. What are you looking for in a stock? From the last chapter we should recall that there are at least three ways to win:

1. Buy a stock for growth.
2. Play a stock.
3. Buy new issues.

One might think that the way to begin is to examine the market and then see which of the three methods offers the most immediate opportunity. That, however, is actually a dead-end course. At any given time there's plenty of opportunity available in all three areas.

Rather, the way to proceed is to pick one of the three and then try to find the best stock to fit that category. In this chapter we'll consider the first, buying a stock for growth. In the next chapters we'll look at what's involved in playing a stock and new issues.

FUNDAMENTAL VS. TECHNICAL ANALYSIS

What all stock analysis comes down to are two perspectives—fundamental and technical. A fundamental analysis looks at causes. What might cause a stock to go up (or down) in price? It considers such things as the economy, the health of the company, its earnings, and a host of other indicators.

A technical analysis, on the other hand, is quite different. It looks for patterns in the market. Technical analysts are heavily into charts and use such terms as "rising bottoms" or "falling tops," referring to the sawtooth pattern a stock's price makes on those charts. The underlying goal of a true technician is to identify the pattern (trend) of a stock in the past and project that into the future.

Both fundamental and technical analyses have their advocates. In penny stocks, however, there are some who say that there is no room for technical analysis. Dr. Bob Kirk, a long-time investor and broker, points out that "technical analysis on penny stocks has no basis. Technical analysis assumes the market has equal access to information on the company and this is discounted. With pennies, timely and accurate information is difficult to obtain and verify."

Lest we proceed further without you, the reader, understanding my bias, let me say that I'm a dyed-in-the-wool fundamentalist. I personally believe the way to find winners is through careful analysis of the items likely to cause a stock to move and that technical analysis is just so much hokum.

On the other hand, that does not mean that I would dare to ignore technical analysis. As we'll see shortly, it can be useful in selecting winners when we're playing stocks, but not for the reasons technicians give. For now, on to the fundamentals.

FUNDAMENTALS AND GROWTH STOCK

When we're looking for a growth stock, we're looking for a company whose earnings will multiply and whose stock price will steadily go up. In that case what we are really talking about is long term. We don't buy such a stock today to sell it tomorrow. We buy it to hang on to for years.

When we're buying a stock for long-term growth, we can tend to ignore the moment-to-moment fluctuations of the market. True, we will want to buy on a dip. But dips and small rises tend to even out over time, and if we're in for the long haul, it's more important that we pay attention to the potential for steady growth.

The ideal kind of analysis to use to find this kind of a stock is the fundamental approach. If we discover the reasons that a stock should go up, and if our analysis is correct, then eventually, in spite of passing fads and market ups and downs, that stock should appreciate in price.

Of course, such analysis requires a bit of a track record. A company that's brand new with no track record leaves us little to go on. Therefore, we're going to pick established companies, those that have been around for a while, at least eighteen months at a minimum. And we will probably be searching principally for those companies that have a NASDAQ symbol. That doesn't mean we will automatically eliminate others. It's just that NASDAQ will probably be our basic hunting grounds. (Remember, we're just looking for a *growth* stock here. When we begin looking for a stock to play, we'll have different rules.)

GETTING STARTED

So, how do we get started?

Ideally we will have a list of stocks to consider. Once we have that list, we will take the time to analyze each from a fundamental perspective.

Here are seven different ways to analyze a stock from a fundamental perspective. Look through these seven tests and then, the next time you want to buy a growth stock, apply each of them. If the stock passes all or most of them, it has to be considered a potential winner.

1. Is There Strong Earnings Potential?

Earnings are what a company makes for it's efforts in business. And every investor with any smarts at all looks first at earnings.

This is true in any business. Let's say we're going to buy a racehorse. We have a choice between "Old Blue" and "In The Money." Old Blue has a nice disposition, but during the past year she hasn't won a race and has come in second only twice. She has earned only $7,500. In The Money, on the other hand, has won three of her last five races. Her earnings have come to $80,000.

Now, which horse would you buy?

Obviously, in the harsh business world, a nice disposition holds no candle to hard cash. Old Blue is out and In The Money is going to be our pick.

But why? Just because In The Money had higher earnings than Old Blue in the past doesn't mean it's going to continue in the future.

No, of course it doesn't. In The Money could break a leg tomorrow. But past performance still is one of the best indications of future performance. If In The Money earned $80,000 last year, maybe she'll earn $100,000 this year.

The same reasoning applies to companies. Investors look at past earnings to give them some idea of future earnings. The better past earnings were, the more likely they are to want to buy the company's stock. Many penny stock companies, however, have a history of little to no past earnings.

Investors buy the future

It's important to see, therefore, that investors don't buy *past* earnings. They buy *future* earnings.

In other words, if a company called "HitItBig" has strong earnings, investors will buy because they hope for even stronger earnings in the future. It's those future earnings they are looking at when they buy. The past earnings are the indicator, but future earnings are the motivator.

Beware of dividends

Earnings are not dividends. Dividends are what a company pays to stockholders. They come out of earnings. If a company earns a dollar a share, it can decide to pay that whole dollar to its stockholders. Or it can decide to pay only fifty cents. Or it can opt to pay nothing.

Smart investors look for companies with earnings and little to no dividends. The reason is that when earnings aren't paid out, they are plowed back into the company.

Money reinvested in the company means even higher earnings in the future. It means stronger growth.

Of course, one must be careful, particularly with smaller companies. Earnings plowed back into research and development that proves futile, or other nonproductive schemes, aren't going to eventually translate into profits.

2. Does the Stock Have a Low P/E Ratio?

This is the big indicator that most stock analysts always are on the watch for. Many investors feel this indicates whether or not the stock is ripe for buying or is overpriced.

Of course, the problem with many penny stocks is that many have no earnings history at all. We cover that possibility in a few paragraphs. But first, let's consider the company with both price *and* earnings.

The "price per earnings" (P/E) ratio is quite easy to calculate. We simply need to know the earnings per share of a company's stock and it's price per share. (To find the earnings per share—if you know the total earnings, simply divide by the number of shares.)

To find the P/E ratio, divide the earnings into the price (remember, the denominator goes into the numerator). This gives us a ratio. For example, if the stock is selling for $4 a share and the earnings are fifty cents a share, we end up with a ratio of eight:

$$\$4.00 \div .50 = 8$$

Now, for a test of what we know. Suppose we have three stocks and their P/Es are four, eight, and twelve. *Without knowing anything else,* which stock is the best buy?

Without knowing anything else, we would have to go for the first stock, stock A in the following table. To see why, suppose that each stock has the same earnings, fifty cents. Here's what they would cost to buy.

STOCK A	STOCK B	STOCK C
Earnings $ .50	$ .50	$ .50
Ratio 4	8	12
Price $2.00	$4.00	$6.00

Since each stock has the same earnings, the one that costs us the least to buy (stock A) is obviously the best deal.

The problem with a low P/E ratio

I have seen brokers advise clients to look *only* for those low-priced stocks with low P/Es for just the reasons cited above. Frequently the advice takes the form of, "Only buy stocks with ratios below eight (or below ten or whatever)." This advice is simpleminded in the extreme.

Remember, our example had as its constraint, "without knowing anything else." In reality, we always know something else, often quite a bit more.

Maybe stock C's ratio is so high because it's growing superfast and everyone wants to get it. Perhaps it's a company that's come out with a proven cancer test that's currently being marketed in Europe. Investors feel that within a few years, when it finally gets FDA approval for sales here in the United States, that fifty-cent dividend might be $2 or $3. Hence the high ratio.

On the other hand, maybe stock A has such a low ratio because people feel the company is stagnant. It's earned that same fifty cents a share for the past three years and it's not going anywhere. (The company makes clothes hangers and it's not going to improve its market share or its earnings.) Stock A might simply be a no-growth company.

It's for this reason that the much vaunted P/E ratio has to be taken with a grain of salt . . . and with a lot of other investigating. It's a great indicator, but it should not be the *only* indicator you use.

(NOTE: The price per share of a stock is given in any newspaper that lists that stock. The earnings per share shows up in a variety of places, such as the *Wall Street Journal, Barrons,* or any of the stock rating services such as Standard & Poor. Or you can always ask your broker, who should be able to provide the information.)

When there are no earnings

Some penny stocks have a history of no earnings at all, ever. Yet, the stock is priced at a certain level, say fifty cents a share. With no earnings history at all, how is that price level determined?

It's a good question. I see two possible answers. The first is that the buyers see some potential down the road and the stock's price reflects that enthusiasm. The second is that there really is no justification for the price and that it is being artificially held up (see Chapter 10, "Pitfalls in Pennies").

3. Is the Stock in a Growth Industry?

The next fundamental is an industry analysis. The simple truth is that some industries are better than others. And those that are better change.

Consider computers. Back in the early 1980s, the computer industry was the darling of stock investors. When Apple stock came out, people swarmed to it. It was a good time to buy computer stock . . . of almost any company.

However, sometime during 1984 the public decided that, unlike a can opener and a TV, there might not be a place in every house for a computer (at least not until somebody found out what the average homemaker could do with it). Hence, an industry that had been a "golden boy" suddenly turned sour. When KayPro went public about this time and tried to sell its stock, it encountered difficulty.

The same holds true for all the small-computer-related companies. When the industry as a whole was booming, so, too, were their stocks, *even the stocks of the "also-rans" and "never-will-bes."* On the other hand, once the word got out that the industry was "in a slump," even the substantial computer companies (including IBM for a time) found their stocks depressed.

When you're looking for a low-priced growth stock, keep abreast of what's happening in various industries. Find out which ones are showing overall strong earnings and go there. But be careful that the shine they exhibit today isn't going to tarnish tomorrow.

Look at market share

To those "in the know," this is possibly the single most important indicator of a company's potential. What share of the market does the company now have and what is its potential?

A classic success story here has to be Xerox. When it started out, it had a copier. But it was virtually the only company with a copier that operated well. Consequently, it had almost all of the market.

McDonald's is another. When it started, it was selling hamburgers for fifteen cents apiece. (I know, I bought some of them!) It had virtually the whole low-end fast-food hamburger market to itself. And as the market grew, it grew with it, maintaining a strong market share.

What new company today is in a similar position? Perhaps it's making a new kind of dog leash that won't tangle in the feet of the person walking the dog. It's a small company and its product is just getting to market. But it's got 100 percent of that market because nobody else is making that kind of leash. As pet owners realize the advantage of this product, and as it becomes an accepted household name, it has an excellent chance of maintaining its dominance over that market.

The drawback comes from competition. Could a large Fortune 500 company suddenly move into the field, reposition the product, and take over the market? Does the management have the skill and wits to anticipate and counter such a move?

Can you relate to the product?

This is the personal test. You find a low-priced stock of a company that's manufacturing soundproof earmuffs. It's marketed them in the Northeast so far with good results. It's got virtually the entire market for this kind of product. It's about to move its operation into the West and South. All the earnings tests indicate "go."

But you live in Los Angeles and you say to yourself, "Soundproof earmuffs? They've got to be kidding! Who on earth would buy such a ridiculous thing?"

Do you ignore your own instincts and buy the stock? Or do you reconsider?

I'd trust my instincts. Certainly, I could be wrong. But I figure I'm an average person with average likes and dislikes. If I don't like the product, there are a lot of other people who won't like it, either. There are so many stocks and so many companies out there to choose from that at the very least I should like the product my company manufactures.

4. Is the Stock's Price Low Enough?

We are, after all, looking for low-priced stock. Is this stock that we are considering low enough in price for us?

This is first a personal consideration. Yes, perhaps we'll consider any stock under $5. But what we really want is any stock under fifty cents. We may have found what appears to be the perfect stock from the viewpoint of earnings and market at $3.50 a share, but something is holding us back. Could it be that the price is just not appealing to us?

How does the current price relate to previous prices?

This is the nonpersonal part of our analysis. The stock is selling today for a bid of forty-four cents, ask fifty cents. If that's all we know, then we should *not* buy. In order to buy, we need to know much more.

How much was the stock selling for yesterday, a week ago, a month ago, six months ago, a year ago, eighteen months ago, and two years ago? We need to know the answers to all of these questions before we buy.

It may turn out that two years ago this stock was selling for bid $1.80, ask $2. It's steadily progressed downward until today. If you have this information, would you now buy this stock? (While at first glance the answer is undoubtedly no, it might turn out that the stock was oversold or undervalued at the higher amount and now the price is realistic—it takes investigation.)

On the other hand, maybe the stock started at two cents and has moved steadily upward until it's near fifty cents today. Now would you feel better about buying it? (Maybe you shouldn't. A stock with this kind of a surge may indicate price manipulation—see Chapter 10, on pitfalls.)

Or in yet another case, over the past two years it's had a fifty-two-week high bid of $2 and a fifty-two-week low

bid of two cents, and it's been bouncing around in between for the past six months. That paints yet a different
picture.

The past performance with regard to highs and lows for
the past year should be readily available in your local paper, if the stock is listed. More detailed information on
price history should be available from your broker. If worst
comes to worst and you want to buy but can't find out
this price background, call the company. Somebody there
surely knows and can tell you.

What is the book value relative to price?

This is for those who like to see what they are getting.
Book value relates to a company's tangible assets. (It's also
sometimes called liquidation value.) It's found by going
through the balance sheet and performing the following
calculations:

START WITH	All tangible assets
DEDUCT	All debts
DEDUCT	*All liabilities*
THE RESULT IS	Liquidation value
DIVIDED BY	*Number of shares*
EQUALS	Book value

The book value, in essence, is what each share of stock
would be worth if the company were to be sold and the
resulting money given to the shareholders.

If the market price (what the stock is selling for on the
market) is *higher* than the book value, the stock is in an
overpriced position *at the current time*. If the market price
is *lower* than the book value, the stock is in an underpriced position *at the current time*. If both prices are about
the same, then the stock is currently priced about right.

At first glance this may seem like a foolproof way to determine what a stock should be selling for. However, remember, investors buy on anticipation of future earnings (and stock values). This book value figure only tells what the stock should be worth today. If its market value is considerably higher, that doesn't mean it's necessarily a bad buy. It may only mean that investors see this as a strong growth stock and are buying in anticipation of future earnings.

Book value is a useful tool only when used in conjunction with what we've already said about earnings. For example, if earnings have been steadily increasing, and other signs are go, and the stock's market price is still below book value, then this may be a great opportunity. On the other hand, if earnings are increasing but the stock is way over book price, it may indicate an inflated value, setting the stock up for a potential price drop in the not-too-distant future.

5. Is the Company Healthy?

In an individual, health is sometimes defined as a lack of illness. If we aren't sick with some disease, then we're healthy. This can also be a useful way of assessing the health of a company.

If we're looking to buy the low-priced stock of a company for growth, we want to be sure that the company doesn't have some illness that will cause it to flounder, or worse, to fail. It's important to realize that some companies, like people, can give the impression of health, all the while concealing a serious problem.

With companies there are usually three illnesses that we want to particularly watch out for. They are "overindebtedness," "liabilitiespressure," and "managementitis." Let's consider them one at a time.

Overindebtedness

This is perhaps the most serious problem that can afflict a company in times of high interest rates. Many companies borrow to buy materials for products, to advertise their lines, to meet current obligations. There is nothing wrong with borrowing . . . as long as the company can afford it. When a company can't afford the borrowing, then the creditors come pounding on the doors and sometimes bankruptcy is not far off.

How do we know if a company is borrowing too much? One way is to check the most recent income statement. Information on larger companies can also be found in "Moody's Investor's Fact Sheets" and the "Stock Reports" issued by Standard & Poor.

The thing to look for is long-term debt. How big is it in relationship to the size of the company?

One way to judge is to divide long-term debt into the equity of the shareholders. (We find shareholders' equity by multiplying book value—described above—by the total number of shares.) In a sense, what we are trying to find out is what percentage of the company has been put into hock.

If we find that 100 percent or more is in hock, then it's an automatic warning signal. The investors have essentially no equity and the company is sure to be having trouble paying interest payments from current income.

A more reasonable ratio is 50 percent. (In other than low-priced stocks, a ratio of about 35 percent is advised, but small start-up companies often have higher costs.)

Liabilitiespressure

This is a quick test to determine solvency. To use it, however, we need the most up-to-the-minute information. We need to know *current* liabilities and *current* assets.

Assets have to be greater than liabilities. If not, the company can't pay its bills tomorrow without borrowing. Sometimes companies will run cash short and have to undertake short-term borrowing to cover problems. If, however, the company already has a large long-term debt (see the previous discussion), this could be a critical problem.

Generally speaking, the greater current assets than current liabilities, the healthier the company.

Managementitis

This is the hardest of all problems to diagnose. Everyone knows that a company with bad management is ultimately not going to succeed. What no one knows is how to tell bad management from good.

I have seen advisers insist that potential investors thoroughly investigate a company's management. How does one do this? Can you trust the findings of brokers or consultants who claim to have investigated the management? (My experience has been you can't trust outside opinion on this subject further than you can throw it.) Have you the time to call the managers and talk with them? And if you do, what will you learn?

For myself I have developed three little tests for management's abilities. It really has nothing to do with examining what management has done in the past. (After all, how can we judge if a success or failure was due to management or some other cause?) This information can often be found out from a call to a broker (if he or she has done his or her homework) or by a call to a manager at the company.

TEST 1—What's the turnover rate in management? If top or middle managers are turning over in less than eighteen months, there could be a problem. If it's less than six months, there *definitely* are suggestions of a problem. On the other hand, if the same team has been around for four or five years or more, what's wrong with them? Why aren't they moving up to bigger and better companies? You want management that's in the middle, that's been around for a while, but not too long.

TEST 2—How old is the management team? I mean two things. How old are they chronologically? If they are very young (fresh out of college), then chances are they are learning at the company. If they are very old, then maybe the company is their nest until they retire. We want someone who is still active, but not wet behind the ears.

Second, how long have they been in management? Five years? Ten years? Or six months? The more experience, the better.

TEST 3—Has management put its money where its mouth is? How much stock did the managers themselves buy? They undoubtedly received insider (Rule 144) stock. How much actual cash out-of-pocket was paid for it?

There are other health problems that can affect a company. But the most serious have been noted. Passing the health test should be a minimum requirement for any stock you are considering purchasing for its long-term growth.

6. Is the Economy Favorable?

There is an old wive's tale that goes something like, "The pennies are the first and the last to run."

What this means is that when the economy is coming out of a recession and starting to boom, the first to make a big move up are the pennies. Similarly, just as the economy is starting to take a downturn, the last stocks to make advances are the pennies.

The reason I call it an old wives' tale is that sometimes it just doesn't work. On the other hand, it works enough times not to be ignored. When it works, I think it works for these reasons. Coming out of a recession, many investors remain unsure. Are we really coming out? Or is it a false start? The serious money isn't yet willing to invest. Yet, many are willing to gamble small amounts. So the pennies get heavy attention.

Similarly, once the economy has expanded for a time, the serious money will get the jitters and stop investing, anticipating a downturn. At that time there will be many investors who don't believe it, who think the expansion will continue. They're willing to take a gamble on small amounts of money, so once again low-priced stocks move.

Of course, since there are numerous false turns during recessions and expansions, there are many runs for penny stocks. And, of course, sometimes the rule doesn't apply.

Nevertheless, it would be foolish not to see that there is sometimes a link and that it's important to track the economy.

Tracking the economy

This can be harder than it first appears to be. We are barraged on all sides with economic opinions, some good, some not quite so good, and some just plain terrible. If you're economically savvy, then you should be able to sort it out. If you're not, then here are three clues to help:

1. Watch interest rates. Stocks love low interest rates, hate high rates. (Watch the *trend* in rates, whether up or down, more than the current rate.)

2. Watch employment. Stocks love high employment, disdain low (although in recent years high stock prices have been sustained with historically high unemployment).

3. Watch the money supply. It's reported every Thursday. Big jumps today often portend higher inflation down the road. Stocks like low inflation, dislike high.

7. Is the Market Moving Up
or Moving Down?

I really get tickled listening to the market reports on TV at the end of the day. Perhaps like me you've heard reporters say something like, "The market sold off today in response to fighting in Lebanon." Or perhaps the reporter said, "There was a big surge in buying, reacting to the release of money supply figures." Or, "Failure in Congress to pass the tax reform bill pushed the market down."

Now really, did that reporter talk to the "market" to get those conclusions? On an average day there might have been sixty to a hundred million shares traded on the New York Stock Exchange alone, let alone AMEX, NASDAQ, and other OTC stock. Does the reporter mean that in each of those trades, the determining element was a world crisis, the economy, or politics? How does he or she know?

The truth of the matter is, no one knows why the market is doing this or doing that, ever. The best we can hope to do is follow along and see trends long after they've developed.

This doesn't mean, of course, that we can ignore the market. If we recognize that the market is bearish (trending lower), then perhaps we ought to wait before buying (for lower prices), or sell now (to take advantage of what might be currently higher prices). Similarly, if the market is bullish (trending higher), then perhaps we ought to reverse our decisions.

The point is that we must spend some effort following the market. For the Big Board we might follow the Dow Jones Averages or the S&P 500. There are also separate indices for utilities and other types of stocks.

Of course, the logical question is, "How does the Dow or other Big Board index relate to the pennies?" The answer is that there is no direct relation. However, many investors and brokers do tend to look for a "trickle-down" effect, which takes about two to three months. In other words, what we see on the Dow today may be reflected in the pennies two to three months from today. (Again, this is just a rule of thumb. It's not set in granite.)

For low-priced stocks, we might also want to follow the indices listed in various publications. For example, shown opposite is the index for the past three years—as listed by the *OTC Stock Journal.*

Indices such as these should neither be ignored nor followed religiously. They should be watched and the information they provide factored in with other information and judgments.

One last point: I've frequently heard people say that "the market's always right." Usually what they mean is that marketplace determines price. It's not what you or I think the price should be, it's what the market says it is that counts.

That's all well and good as long as it's taken no further. But some new investors see it as saying that the market is a kind of guru that points to proper pricing. We'll say more about this in the next section on technical analysis. But suffice it to say that that market isn't right or wrong in this sense, it's just the market. At any moment it expresses the anticipations of all buyers and sellers as evidenced by their willingness to trade. That's it, nothing more. There's nothing mystical about it.

The market isn't smart or stupid. If you find seventeen reasons why it must do one thing, all I can guarantee is that the chances are at least fifty-fifty it will do the opposite. It doesn't think, it doesn't care. The less we think of it as being a personality, the better off we are.

Listen to advice, but don't rely on it

This is the last comment I have to make regarding the market and picking stocks. It's important to get the advice

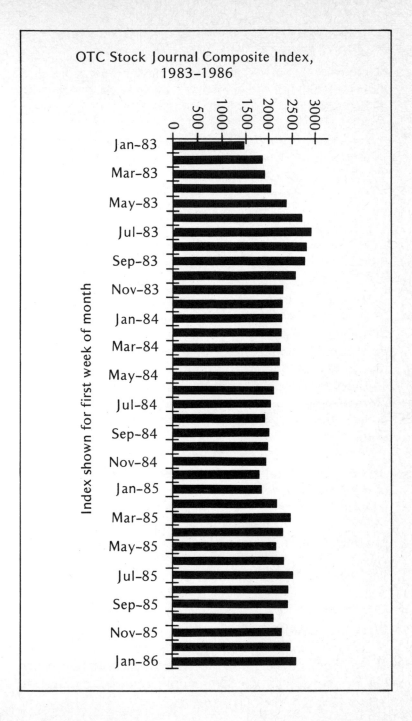

OTC Stock Journal Composite Index, 1983–1986

of others, particularly those who have spent more time than we studying the market or a particular stock. This advice generally comes from four sources:

1. *Brokers (including their firms' research departments).* This can be good or bad, as we'll see in Chapter 11, "Finding a Good Broker."
2. *Rating Services.* These rate different stocks. Unfortunately, many of the companies we'll consider aren't regularly rated; hence, it's of limited value.
3. *Financial Advisories.* These are newsletters put out by different individuals around the country. At last count there were over a hundred of them devoted to stocks alone. (See the last chapter for more information on them.)

These can provide useful and timely information. Unfortunately, they tend to be slanted toward the views of the publisher. Sometimes, however, those publishers also may have vested interests in the stocks they are touting.

4. *Newspapers, tabloids, and magazines.* These provide general information of a sort to help us in a general way. (Again, see the last chapter for more information.)

Now, why should you read these but not rely on their advice? The answer is that they really don't know, they may be prejudiced, they may have their hand in the till.

The input from these sources should be only one part of your overall fundamental analysis of a stock. It should give you clues and helpful hints, but don't let it make your decisions.

WHY FUNDAMENTALS?

These, then, are the seven different fundamentals to watch out for. As you can see, some apply in the form of tests to stock. Others (such as economic trends) are items you need to be ever aware of.

As you go through your investment life looking for growth stocks, try to remember these fundamentals. When a stock comes along that is sizzling hot with all kinds of appeal, try to step aside, count to ten, and consider. If you're really buying the stock for growth, how does it stack up fundamentally? If it doesn't cut it fundamentally, then you probably should look elsewhere.

HOW TO PLAY A STOCK

■

In advertising, it's common to look at two elements of any product with an eye toward marketing it. The first element involves the actual benefits the product offers: If it's a drug, what will it cure? If it's a candy, how sweet is it? If it's a car, is it reliable and comfortable? . . . and so forth. This is, so to speak, looking at the "meat" of it.

The other element in marketing, oftentimes considered even more important, is the "sizzle." How much "sex appeal" does the product have? Is it trendy? Does it catch the eye?

Sometimes virtually worthless products, such as common rocks or plastic hoops or simple dolls, can be marketed almost entirely on their sizzle. People want them, indeed fight to pay inflated sums of money to get them, because they are perceived as having great intangible value.

In penny stocks a similar situation prevails. In the last chapter we looked at the traditional method of finding winning stock—looking for growth. We approached stocks in a fundamental way—what was the P/E ratio, the book value, the price history, and so on? In essence, we were analyzing the "steak."

In this chapter, however, we're going to look at stock a different way. We are going to analyze the sizzle. We are going to see the effect popularity has on a stock.

Remember, here we're not concerned with fundamental analysis, which tries to determine true value. Instead we're concerned with perceived value.

PERCEIVED VALUE

This is a trickier notion to deal with than most people realize. Almost all of us would be in agreement as to value as determined in the previous chapter by a fundamental analysis. But what about value when there is no "steak?"

For example, consider high fashion. A dress in Penney's might cost fifty dollars. On the other hand, a dress by *Halston* might cost five thousand dollars. Fundamentally, this makes no sense. The material used in the five-thousand-dollar dress may not be much more valuable than the material used in the fifty-dollar dress. In addition, fashions change quickly. That dress for five thousand dollars today might be worthless by next season.

Yet, there is a market for the high-priced dress. In fact, buyers may be standing in line to get it. The reason is that the higher-priced dress is perceived to have fashion value, and for those who worship fashion, price is no object.

Something similar happens in penny stocks. Some stocks are perceived as having great value. They sizzle. They are fashionable, they catch the eye, they have sex appeal.

However they are described, the value of these stocks comes not from a fundamental analysis, but rather from a perception of value on the part of the buyers. (Of course, if the stocks have fundamental strength, then all the better, but that's last chapter's story.)

AN EXAMPLE OF SIZZLE

For example, as this is being written, there are at least half a dozen low-priced stock companies in the United States that are coming out with medical products that purport to either cure, treat, or test for the disease AIDS (Acquired Immune Deficiency Syndrome).

This is good timing because also as of this writing, there is great concern and even downright fear among the general population regarding this disease, and any product that promises relief is welcomed. (Of course, by the time you read this, the disease may have vanished or may be an epidemic. But the point here is with regard to its effect on stock, not on health.)

In almost every case the stock of those companies with AIDS-related products is doing very well. The question we need to ask is, why?

Well, obviously if these companies do indeed have beneficial products, those products will be extremely valuable and the stock will be in great demand. This is the fundamental approach.

However, I would be willing to wager that ninety-nine out of a hundred investors who bought stock in these companies did *no* fundamental analysis of any kind. In fact, without knowing anything about those companies and just given the history of small pharmaceutical companies in general that purport to have miracle drugs, I would be surprised if any of them ever came to market with a product, let alone actually came up with something successful.

In other words, the *idea* of an AIDS-related product is what counts, not necessarily the product itself. The concept has sizzle, it has investment sex appeal, it catches the eye, it's fashionable. Hence, the concept has perceived value; many investors will buy the stock and, at least temporarily, this may boost the stock's price.

INVESTOR SAVVY

Does this suggest that these investors are somehow fools or ignoramuses? Hardly, they are probably being very shrewd. They see an opportunity and they are playing it. They have bought a popular stock, gambling that its popularity will increase and that they will be able to sell before it peaks. They may hold it a few days, weeks, or months until it has run its course. Along the way, they hope, speculation will have forced the price up until they can sell at a handsome profit.

This is what I mean by playing a stock.

The investors here are not interested in looking for growth. They are only interested in speculating on price. The smart player will determine which stocks have the best perceived value and ride with those as long as they are winners.

WHEN THE CRASH COMES

Of course, these speculative bubbles don't last forever. Sometimes they only last a few days. Other times they last for as long as six months. But eventually they burst.

Perhaps the company is forced to make an announcement that initial testing of its product was "inconclusive."

In other words, it doesn't work. Or maybe there is the positive announcement by another company of a true cure. Or maybe the illness itself suddenly disappears and the need for the product vanishes.

For whatever the reason, the sizzle suddenly goes away. And without sizzle, there is no support for these stocks, so they plummet in price. Of course, the smart investor has long since moved on.

It's important to note that I'm not suggesting that all companies whose products have sizzle have no fundamental value. Ideally a stock will have *both* steak *and* sizzle. However, in the penny stock market, even if it's mostly just sizzle, the smart investor can still profit.

LOOKING FOR THE SIZZLE

With regard to penny stocks, finding stocks with sizzle requires technical analysis. (The term "technical analysis" here has a slightly different meaning than with regard to higher-priced stocks, as we'll see shortly.)

For low-priced stock a technical analysis means determining which stock is going to make a big move for other than fundamental reasons.

No field is exempt from these speculative bubbles. In the recent past we saw it happen in low-priced oil stocks (exploration as well as development) in the seventies, in gold and silver mining stocks in the early eighties, and in many start-up pharmaceuticals involved with genetic engineering in the mid-eighties. Along the way we had excitement in robotics and in computers (both widely considered "dead" as of this writing).

Hundreds of companies, some no more than shells, got involved in these fields at the height of the excitement. In many cases their stocks soared, at least temporarily. And those investors who bought wisely and sold timely did indeed do very well.

HOW TO PLAY A STOCK

In general, I've found that those who did succeed in playing stocks followed at least these three rules:

   1.   They picked companies on the basis of the sex appeal (sizzle) of their products.
   2.   They bought at the beginning of the popularity curve and sold immediately at the sign of any drop in price.
   3.   They sold when the stock reached a predetermined level (for example, twice, three times, or whatever the original price).

Of course, a fourth rule was that they adhered strictly to the first three. We'll discuss picking a stock in a few paragraphs, but first a few words about rules 2 and 3.

SELLING

When playing a stock, it's important to keep focused on what you're doing. *You are speculating.* Nothing more, nothing less. That means you're not looking for long-term growth, you're not going to get personally attached to the stock. The only time you can win when playing a stock (we'll talk about selling short, another way of winning, in a later chapter) is by dumping the losers.

Determining a loser on a stock *play* is easy. If it goes down in value, it's a loser. Usually a drop of 10 percent in value is a sufficient indication.

A player who hangs on to a "played" stock that drops is going to be a big loser. Remember, these stocks were bought for sizzle, not for steak. They probably don't have the fundamental strength to rebound from a loss. Once they start down, it's a sure sign that they've run out of sizzle. Now it's only a quick trip to the bottom and out for most of them.

Sell, sell, sell—the three most important words to remember when playing a stock that goes down in price.

On the other hand, you want to hang on to your winners. You've got a stock that's got plenty of sizzle, you got in at the right time, and it's moving up fast. How long do you hold it?

Obviously, you hold it as long as it's going up. But that's hard to judge. A speculative penny stock can peak and plummet in value in a day, in hours—much faster, in general, than most nonprofessional investors can react.

Therefore, shrewd investors have arbitrary limits they establish. The exact nature of these limits isn't critical. What is critical is that you have them.

THE LIMITS FOR
A TYPICAL PLAY

Here are the rules by which one investor I know limits her stock plays:

"When the stock doubles, I will sell half. I will then have my original investment out and still have half the stock I purchased.

"I will then hold this until the stock doubles again and again sell half. I will continue to do this as long as the stock goes up.

"In any event, as soon as it drops ten percent from its previous high, I will immediately sell all shares I own."

These limits don't guarantee she'll win. But they at least give her a fighting chance at not losing.

PICKING THE STOCKS
TO PLAY

This is certainly the most difficult part of playing a stock. The reason is that even within a hot field, some stocks will do well while others fare poorly. We want to get the former. There are five suggestions I have:

1. Be Sure the Field Has Sizzle.
This is the prerequisite for playing a stock. I don't care whether it's robotics, frozen yogurt, drugs, or hair growth. The field has to have sex appeal.

This isn't hard to judge. Look around you. What do people want? What are they afraid of? Who is offering solutions? Answer these three questions and you have the sizzle field for the moment.

Of course, there's always confirmation. Check with any low-priced stockbroker. He or she will instantly be able to confirm which field is hot.

CAUTION: Fields lose their sizzle very quickly. One big mistake in playing stocks that many new investors make is going into yesterday's field. To win here, you've got to get in at the beginning.

2. Find the Stock That the
Technicians Recommend.
Technical analysts love charts. These charts invariably show the months, days, or weeks along the bottom axis and the price of a stock (or group of stocks) along the vertical axis. The price is a sawtooth moving up and down in the market.

Technicians draw lines on these charts frequently, connecting the price tops or price bottoms. By doing this they identify such things as "resistance levels" (a price through which a stock will have trouble passing either up or down) or "breakout points" (a price figure that, if attained by a stock, means it will continue to move some distance in whatever direction it has been going).

If you're into astrology, you'll love technicians. They can come up with a prediction for anything. What's more, frequently they're right!

Just as myths and legends are frequently the remnants of the dead science and religion of former civilizations lingering on in the present, so, too, is technical analysis the lingering judgment connected with former market events. Technicians look at the past and try to predict the future.

Beware the "science" of technical analysis

Regardless of how much chartists may disagree, there *is no science of technical analysis.* Rather, it is only subjective interpretation, much as reading entrails was for the ancient Greeks and Romans.

But, just as voodoo and witch doctoring sometimes work, so, too, does technical analysis sometimes work, and for that reason it cannot be ignored. As is said about witch doctors and voodoo, that they work because some believe in them, so it may be true of technical analysis.

A technician says a stock must do this or that, and perhaps it happens *because* the technician said it would. Maybe it's a self-fulfilling prophecy.

It makes no difference. When playing a stock, listen to the technical analysis. Get a readout on the field (to be sure it's beginning, not ending, and does have sizzle) and the stock (to be sure it's a leader in the field).

Finding technical analysis

Where do you get technical analysis? Start with your stockbroker. In my experience, while they *all* profess to carefully evaluate the fundamentals of a stock, nine out of ten don't make their decisions based on fundamentals.

Talk to brokers, ask them why they think this or that, and when you start hearing terms such as "tops" and "bottoms" and "rising lines" and "resistance" and "breakout," you know you're getting technical analysis.

Be polite and ask them their sources and check it out. There's no better way to find a sizzling stock than to follow a technician to it.

On the other hand, the broker may simply be following the company line and have no idea what technical theory is. If that's the case, then your next bet is to find a broker or an underwriter who does know the theory and go with him or her.

3. Pick a Company That Has a No-Fail Product.

You know the kind. The world is crazy for dolls. This company has just come out with a doll that is the central character of a hit movie of the same name. The doll has been test-marketed in three major malls in different cities and kids waited an average of one and a half hours just to get it. In addition, it is being endorsed by a Saturday morning cartoon idol. How can it lose?

It probably can't, as long as the field has sizzle. Even if the doll is a dud, the strength of the field itself should carry it along for some profits. The product is "no-fail."

4. Look for Management with Sizzle.

Look for stars, names that ring bells. Ideally you want someone who has been a winner before.

There are some classic cases here, not always limited

to penny stocks. Consider Lee A. Iacocca and Chrysler. Or a low-priced stock example, PaperBack Software, led by Adam Osborne, whose reputation remained untarnished even after his Osborne Computer company failed. His name alone was sufficient to initially promote the stock.

5. Always Look for a Little Steak.

Playing a stock is like getting a fever. If it's a mining stock, it's "gold fever." If it's a computer stock, it's "high-tech fever." It's contagious, and once you get it, it's hard to lose. Getting a fever for gold stocks can make you feverish for high tech, for pharmaceuticals, for the whole spectrum. It can cloud overall judgment.

The best way to avoid these fevers is, once you've picked a group of stocks you're considering playing (say a dozen), to try a fundamental analysis of each. All other things being equal, go with the stock that has the best fundamentals. It's the way to put a little sanity into what is admittedly a wild and sometimes wicked field.

BOTTOM LINE

Remember, when you play a stock, you are speculating, gambling. It's risky and you won't always win. You're shooting for the moon and you hope to retire on your winnings, so don't complain if you get shot down quite a few times before you have any success.

WINNING WITH NEW ISSUES

■

When some investors speak of penny stocks, what they are really talking about are new issues. New issues are undoubtedly the fastest way to make (or lose) money in penny stocks. Prices here shoot up or tumble, often in days. If you're on the winning side, you can make a fortune. Or, if your timing is bad, you could lose a great deal.

WHAT IS A NEW ISSUE?

A new issue is *new* stock issued by a company. Although it could be an addition to existing public stock already offered by the company, in most cases with low-priced stock, what we're speaking of is the first issue. In other words, we have a private company. Now it's going public, and in the process it is issuing stock.

Regardless of what you may already know about new issues, there are at least three important facts that must be remembered when we are dealing with low-priced stock:

1.   Typically the *total value* of the new issue is low. Under two million dollars is common. A million to half a million is not unusual. This means we are dealing with a *thin* market. While there may be a great many shares because of the low cost (a few cents per share), the total money raised is not great, meaning that any one wealthy individual or company theoretically can corner and influence the stock (see the next chapter).

2.   Virtually all new issue stock must have Securities and Exchange Commission approval. BUT THIS APPROVAL IS NOT A RECOMMENDATION—IN MOST CASES THERE IS NO GOVERNMENT DETERMINATION OF MERIT ON NEW ISSUES. There are exceptions, of course, as in the case where in addition to the SEC, a stock is issued in a state that makes a merit determination. But in most cases, no official body has said this is a good company and the offering is a good investment. In terms of quality, it's strictly a case of caveat emptor, let the buyer beware.

3.   Most of the money made on new issues is made on the first *day* or within the first few weeks of issue. This means that the shrewd investors try to buy the new issues, then try to get out as quickly as possible after the stock starts trading.

Finally, it's fair to say that although the new issues market is risky, it is also potentially quite profitable. Having said that, let's see how it works and where the money can be made.

WHY ARE THERE NEW ISSUES?

You are a chemist working for a large photographic company. In your garage in your spare time you work on new ways to create emulsions. One day you stumble on a process for creating a "fast" (highly receptive) photographic film *that does not use silver* as part of the process.

Chemists have been working unsuccessfully for eighty years trying to develop this process, but you think you have stumbled onto the key to it. What you need is time to conduct some more experiments.

So you contact several friends—one is a lawyer, another an accountant, yet a third is in manufacturing. You explain what you've found and they are enthusiastic. You look around and see that each partner is an expert in an area vital to success if the product is ever to reach market. "Hmm," you think, "this could be the start of something big!"

Each of you puts up $10,000 and you form a corporation. You quit your job at the photographic company and use the money to live on while you work full-time in your garage.

After six months the money is gone. You're convinced the process will work, as soon as you get a few glitches out of it. But that will take time and more money. So you get a second mortgage on your house and come up with $25,000. One way or another, each of your partners does likewise. Now you open a small research and development office in a local industrial park.

It goes slowly, but eight months later, just as the money is about gone, you make it work! Of course, you've only done it in a few experimental situations. Now you need the money to rent a large plant and start making film on a mass scale. Once you do this, you can either market the film yourself or sell out for what will probably be hundreds of millions to a big photographic company.

But you need a million dollars, cash, to get off the ground. Where are you going to get it?

You and your partners have exhausted your cash and

all your other personal reserves. The bank won't touch your scheme since you have no collateral. Venture capitalists will consider it, but only if you give them 90 percent ownership.

What do you do?

You decide to go public and issue stock.

You call every stockbroker you know and eventually one firm agrees to handle, or underwrite, your offering, and you're on your way. (We'll get into the actual process of underwriting new stock in a few pages.)

WHERE THE PROFIT IS

What we've been seeing is the great American way of raising capital to start a new business. It's been done over and over since this country was founded, and many of the largest corporations got their start in this fashion. It's stretching to grasp a dream.

Let's continue the scenario. When your *company's* stock finally gets to market, investors will analyze it. The underwriter who is promoting it will add hype such as, "A revolutionary product," "It could be a new Kodak or Xerox," "A chance to get in on the ground floor of tomorrow's Fortune 500 company." This is the sizzle we were talking about.

In this case investors are probably going to be very excited. You have experiments to show that the product actually works. The potential is enormous. Word spreads and investors start calling asking for stock. The offering is quickly gobbled up (all the shares offered are sold).

After all the new issues are sold, the stock starts trading. Note: Up until now there has been no trading of the stock. Instead, there have been a set number of shares offered for sale through the underwriter and his associates.

Once the stock is actually issued, however, a trading market begins (the after market). Those who bought the new issues may want to sell. Those who didn't get in on the ground floor may now want to buy.

Demand is heavy for the stock on the first day of trading. It opens at ten cents a share and quickly moves to twenty cents. Within three days it is up to thirty cents.

Now let's stop the scenario. Who's made money so far and where?

WHERE THE MONEY IS

1. The investors who bought the new issue (for ten cents a share) before it began trading have tripled their money, if they sell immediately.

2. The underwriter who issued the stock was paid a commission by the company and probably has made a substantial profit in addition on the trading.

3. Investors who bought on the first day at a low price and have ridden the stock up have made a considerable profit if they now sell.

These three groups have made money. But then, on the fourth day of trading, the photographic company where you, the inventor, formerly worked brings suit against you. It says you developed your revolutionary process while working for it, hence technically the process belongs to it.

You say the suit is without merit and demand to know why your lawyer partner didn't foresee this. He says he's a real estate lawyer; how should he know about patent suits?

The suit seeks to tie up all your funds from the stock issue, so you can't begin manufacturing the product further until the court settles the dispute. Your funds are wide open in easily accessed accounts. You ask your accountant partner why he didn't foresee this and shield the funds.

He says he's just an accountant who prepares 1040 tax returns in April. How could he know this was going to happen?

You turn to your partner whose expertise is in manufacturing and he shrugs his shoulders. He says he can tell someone how to operate a lathe, but what does he know about this high finance?

That day your stock drops to five cents a share. Within a month it's down to a penny. Two months later you file for Chapter 11 bankruptcy and no broker will handle your stock anymore.

Now, once again, who's made money?

WHERE THE MONEY'S GONE
1. The investors who bought the issue *and sold* almost immediately in the after market.
2. The underwriter (provided he didn't get stuck with a lot of your stock).
3. The investors who bought immediately and then quickly *resold* in the after market.

In other words, anyone who bought early and sold quickly made money, perhaps a great deal of money. Who lost money? Anyone who bought your company's stock and held it for future growth.

IN THE REAL WORLD

The preceding example (which is probably much closer to real life than many brokers would care to admit) illustrates where profits are made in new issues. The company has a dream. That dream is hyped by the underwriter. And investors buy in.

In many cases what investors are buying is 90 percent or more sizzle. When that's the case, the way to win is to get in as early and as low as possible and then get out as quickly as possible after the stock has moved up. (This strategy has a down side, of course. If you get out too early, you chance losing out if the stock turns out to be a real long-term winner, a stock that happens to have some steak as well as sizzle. To compensate, some investors will always keep a portion of each winning new issue for the long term, just in case.)

Of course, things don't usually happen quite as fast as in our example. A new company may have a trial period of six months or more in which to succeed or fail. The underwriter may support the stock for a variety of reasons for quite some time. (See the chapter on underwriter pitfalls.) Nevertheless, from the investor's viewpoint, speed is of the essence here. *Most* new companies fail. Once investors smell failure, it's usually too late to dump the stock.

WHEN THE MARKET SIZZLES

When there's a lot of interest in the penny stock market, almost any new issue has a good chance of going up in value the first few days on the after market, particularly if it has a strong underwriter. Therefore, investors scramble to get these issues as early and as low as possible. (It's a different story in a cold market—there, particularly if there are too many new issues coming out, many may open down the first few days.)

A sizzling market presents some problems for investors. Frequently in such a market, it is hard to get new issues. Everyone wants them; hence, there aren't enough to go around. What you need here is a good broker. (See Chapter 11 for how to find one.)

Additionally, in a sizzling market, scoundrels have a tendency to come in and start up hopeless companies just to profit from issuing virtually worthless new stock. (Remember, the SEC requires *full disclosure*. It normally doesn't comment on merit.)

And underwriters—who are well aware that investors often don't care a hoot if the company has a chance or not for success, but just want in and out quick—are sometimes tempted to promote less than promising companies and then to undertake devious if not downright illegal methods to support the stock in the after market. A hot market breeds all kinds of problems. We'll cover pitfalls in the next chapter.

The important thing to remember is speed. In most cases when the market's got everyone talking, new issue profits are made by getting in early and selling quick. Also, remember the exception to this rule. I bought new issue stock years ago that I am still holding to this day. It turned out to be that rare breed of a fundamentally good company. Always keep a watchful eye out for the company that has both sizzle and steak.

HOW TO FIND OUT
ABOUT NEW ISSUES

There are essentially three sources. The first is the broker. A good broker will keep you informed of what's coming out.

Second, there are the advisories. We noted these in Chapter 5. Many of them list *all* new stock issues in registration. Some of them are devoted exclusively to picking the best of the new issues.

Finally, there is word of mouth. As you get more familiar with the field and as those in the field get to know you, you'll begin getting phone calls telling you about this new issue or that.

HOW TO SELECT THE BEST NEW ISSUES

Obviously, some companies are better than others. Not all will have troubles such as those seen in our previous example. Some will go forward and may eventually become the IBMs of tomorrow. As elsewhere, therefore, if buying new issues is your cup of tea, it's important that you aim for the best quality stock you can get.

When buying new issues, I have found that there are three rules that are particularly helpful:

1. Don't waste time chasing unavailable stock.
2. Get a reliable broker who does his homework.
3. Know the process.

With regard to the first rule, it's simply the case that on any given day there are probably upwards of twenty new issues available. The biggest mistake is to focus in on only one and desperately try to get that stock. If you can't get one new issue, aim for another. There are always plenty out there. Waiting for that impossible dream means you'll probably lose out.

The second rule is also vital. It's the broker who's going to get you the new issues. If the broker you're using can't get good new issues for you, you need a new broker. We'll cover this in greater detail in Chapter 11.

Finally, there's the matter of understanding the process of issuing new stocks.

KNOW WHAT'S HAPPENING

If you're already an experienced low-priced stock investor, you may want to skip to the next section. But if you're new to the field, you should find some valuable information here.

The process of coming out with new issue stock is really not that complex, although it is fairly rigid. There are some things that must be done and others that must be avoided. And there are a number of factors that end up affecting you, the future buyer.

Probably the best way to learn is to follow a new stock to market. Here are the steps involved:

1. The Company Decides
It Needs New Capital.

In our earlier example of a photo company, the capital was to go for setting up manufacturing. This is typical. Most often companies that go public have already done the research and development. Now they need funds to get their product ready for market.

2. The Company May Try
a "Private Placement."

This means selling stock to individuals or companies that specialize in taking risks on new ventures. If this works, they may still go public later if they need more money.

3. The Company Decides to Go
Public and Looks for an Underwriter.

An underwriter is an entity that will undertake to help move the offering through the various legal steps to market, then offer the stock to the public, and then (usually) handle the stock in the after market as a market maker. Most brokerage houses that specialize in penny stocks also underwrite new issues.

The importance of the underwriter

The first critical step for the *company*, therefore, is getting a good underwriter. As it turns out, this is also a critical step for the investor. Some underwriters over the long haul have brought out one excellent offering after another. Other houses have brought out one piece of junk stock after another.

In choosing an underwriter, the *company* usually has as its goal finding a brokerage house that has a track record of offering successful new issues. Since investors sometimes shop underwriters before companies (for reasons that should be evident from the previous paragraphs), this is the surest way to get a successful offering. The *company* owners will now begin knocking on doors trying to get the best underwriter.

From the underwriter's viewpoint, this is a time-consuming and often bothersome process. In a sizzling market, top underwriters say they get proposals from a hundred companies for each one they seriously consider. And they only accept one out of each twenty they consider.

The odds, therefore, of getting a strong underwriter do not favor the *company*. Nevertheless, if the *company* is strong and it and/or its product has sizzle, underwriters will pay attention.

Eventually an underwriter agrees to work with the *company*. From its perspective, the underwriter, in making the decision to handle a stock, is expected to protect investors by thoroughly investigating the *company* to make sure that it is a good and safe investment. This "due diligence" investigation should be such that the underwriter is convinced that the *company* is good enough for the underwriter itself to buy the stock.

(Unfortunately, my experience has been that while some underwriters are indeed extremely diligent, others are not. While some try to bring only public companies that have the best chance to succeed, others seem more involved in companies that offer the highest profit to the underwriter. Also, unfortunately, this problem appears not to reside only with the small underwriters, nor only with those that just occasionally put out successful issues.)

Of course, it all comes down to the investors. Experienced investors know a good underwriter is probably more responsible for pushing a company's stock than the company. An underwriter that has a track record of six successful new issues is going to be much in demand by investors. (To find such underwriters, check into Chapter 5, "Investment Advisories.")

4. The Underwriter Lines Up the Sales Team.

The underwriter might handle the entire sale of the stock itself, if it is strong enough. In many cases, however, the underwriter puts together a syndicate that includes other brokerage houses that will act as market makers and brokers, which may also handle sale of the new issue.

5. A Proposal Is Presented to the SEC.

This proposal, prepared by the *company,* usually with the underwriter's help, is in the form of a registration statement. It describes the *company,* its officers, the business of the *company,* the plan for offering the new issues, the potential risks involved, and many other important facts. The SEC will examine this material to make sure that all facts, good and bad, have been disclosed. As noted, the SEC does not judge the merit of the offering, only whether or not proper procedure has been followed and whether there is outright fraud involved in the stock sale.

6. State Registration Is Sought.

The team also submits registration proposals to the states in which the new issue stock will be sold. It's important to understand that in addition to SEC registration, new issues must be registered in every state in which they are sold.

This can be a far more complex and difficult process than getting SEC registration. The reason is that the laws for registration differ state by state. In addition, many states not only pass judgment on whether all items are disclosed, but they also render merit judgments on whether or not the stock is a sound investment. In merit states, getting approval can be a very long and difficult process.

Almost always, therefore, new issues are not registered in all states in the country, but rather only in those that have short and nonmerit registration processes. This is called "blue-skying" the stock.

As of this writing, those states in which new issues are most commonly registered include:

Colorado
Connecticut
Delaware
Florida
Illinois
Maryland
Nevada
New Jersey
New York
Washington, D.C.

Blue-sky states

It's important to understand that *an underwriter or a broker cannot legitimately sell you a new issue stock unless you are a resident of a state in which the stock is registered.*

Of course, people are always finding ways to buy new issues out-of-state. Frequently people maintain an address in a registered state in order to be able to get stock. Some individuals buy stock through relatives or friends residing in a registered state.

In any event, getting clearance by the states is necessary before stock can be sold.

7. A Prospectus Is Issued.

This essentially reveals everything that was submitted to the SEC. It describes the *company* and the principal officers. It indicates the product or service the *company* is going to offer and it outlines the risks involved.

The initial prospectus will have stamped in red on its cover a notice that SEC approval for issue of the stock has not yet been given. These are sometimes called "red herring" prospectuses. (We'll have a more detailed explanation of the prospectus later in the chapter.)

8. A "Quiet Period" Occurs.

From the time registration starts until ninety days after the stock has been cleared for sale by the SEC, no one involved in the sale may make any statements other than those contained in the prospectus. If anyone involved with the stock issue should make contradictory statements or add information other than that contained in the prospectus, it might be deemed misleading and the SEC could halt the sale.

Should there be some significant changes affecting the *company* that must be publicized, then these must be attached by "stickering" (adding them on a sticker) to each prospectus.

9. Stock Sales Start.

Within three days after the SEC gives approval for sale of the stock, the underwriter, brokers, and the sales team may start selling it. They normally have a maximum period of ninety days in which to sell out the issue.

10. Terms of Sale.

The new issue can be sold in one of two ways. The first way is termed "all or nothing." It is fairly self-descriptive. During the sales period all of the stock offered must be sold. If it is not sold, then all of the investors' money must be returned and there is no new issue.

The second way a stock can be sold is "minimum/maximum." In a mini/maxi there is a minimum amount of stock that must be sold before the issue can go forth. If this minimum isn't reached, then investors' money is returned. On the other hand, if interest is great, there is a maximum number of shares that may be sold in the sale period. No more than this number may be sold.

In addition, the sale itself can be handled in two ways. The most common method is for the underwriter to make a "best efforts" attempt at selling the stock. The underwriter will contact all brokers and associates possible in an attempt to get the widest possible distribution for the stock. In other words, the underwriter will use its best efforts to get a new issue sold out. However, if those efforts happen not to be enough, then the new stock doesn't get to market.

On the other hand, in some cases the underwriter may make a guarantee. This guarantee takes the form of the underwriter agreeing to buy up all the shares of the new issue. The underwriter in turn will then resell them. In a firm commitment a sellout is assured.

11. Syndication.

As noted earlier, in many cases more than one brokerage house will underwrite and sell the stock. Usually this is the case when there is a very large new issue or the underwriter doesn't have that much retail muscle. The term "syndicate" usually just means all those involved in the sale of the new issue.

Another reason for syndication is to bring more market makers in on the deal. This spreads the stock out and tends to heighten interest in it. Also, sometimes houses may "scratch each other's backs." They may carry an "average" new issue for the chance to be in on the action of a "hot" new issue.

12. Warrants and Units.

Many companies offering new issues will do so in "units." This consists of both stock and "warrants." A "warrant" is the right but not the obligation to buy additional stock at a set price until a set future date.

There are really two separate reasons a company might try to sell units instead of simply stock. The first is sales appeal. With stock alone, the buyer simply gets the certificates he purchases and that's it. With a unit, he gets the stock plus a warrant allowing him to buy additional stock up to a future date.

To see why this is appealing to investors, let's say the *company* offers units at fifty cents, which include two shares of stock and one warrant to buy an additional share of stock for fifty cents within six months of the offering.

If an investor buys a thousand units for five hundred dollars, he now has two thousand shares of stock plus warrants for an additional thousand. Further, let's say the stock does very well out of the starting gate and within a month is up to seventy-five cents a share.

If the investor were to buy more stock on the market, it would cost seventy-five cents a share. But he can exercise the warrant and buy it for fifty cents. There's a neat profit to be turned by simply selling the warrant. That's why investors like them.

Companies like units (stocks plus warrants) because it means they get capital initially when the stock is first issued and then again a second time if the stock's price goes up.

Warrants can be bought and sold on the market just like stocks. Their price is really a function of three separate factors:

1. *Time.* How much time to their expiration date? The more time until that date, the greater the opportunity for the price of the stock to move up and the more valuable the warrant.

2. *Intrinsic Value.* This is the difference between the price of the warrant and the price of the stock. In the preceding example, the intrinsic value was twenty-five cents. Of course, should the stock have gone down, then there could be a negative intrinsic value.

3. *Volatility.* This is the perception by the buying public of how volatile the stock is. If investors perceive that the stock behind the warrant is heading for the moon, then the warrant's price is going to be higher. If, on the other hand, they think it's getting ready to crash, the warrant's price will be affected adversely.

Finally, it is worth noting that sometimes companies will use units in an attempt to sell unpopular stock. The company says in effect, "We know you don't like our stock. So we're offering a bargain. Not only do you get our stock, but we'll throw in warrants as well."

The rejoinder should be, "If I don't like your stock, why should I like it better if you offer me more of it via warrants?" Besides, sometimes the price of units is jacked up over what the new issue would be if plain stock were offered.

13. The Prospectus.

Finally we come to the prospectus. Except for the actual sale, the biggest step in the process of bringing the stock to market for the *company* (although often the first step for the investor) is presenting the prospectus. If you're considering buying a new issue, your broker will hand over a booklet to you and suggest that you look it over carefully. He or she may even add something such as, "It contains everything you should know about the company."

Indeed, however, it's frequently written in six-point type and it may be a hundred or more pages long. The prospectus may very well be the key to separating the winning stocks from the losers. But it's a key that's hard to use.

We are put on our guard right from the beginning by the standard disclaimer written in very large type: THIS MATERIAL HAS NEITHER BEEN APPROVED NOR DISAPPROVED BY THE SEC NOR HAS THE COMMISSION PASSED UPON THE ACCURACY OR ADEQUACY OF THE PROSPECTUS.

Remember, the SEC doesn't judge merits. It is basically concerned with disclosure.

READING THE PROSPECTUS

Well then, having discovered that what's easiest to read in the prospectus is the disclaimer, what are the important things to read? What should we concentrate on?

An honest answer is, "Everything."

However, there are some things I look at before others. Before beginning the following list, please understand that it is neither complete nor comprehensive. There are many other vital items to consider besides those noted here. I'm only indicating my preference for the order in which I consider items. My order of preference is as follows:

1. Management.
The prospectus should list the main officers of the company. It should give their background and experience. It

should state how and why they are fit to handle the particular position they hold.

I look for age (Are they mature enough to handle the job?), past experience (Have they *successfully* done it before?), and background. This last can be fascinating. When the penny stock market was sizzling about a year ago, I came across a number of prospectuses that had the most interesting management. In each case several of the top positions were filled by people who had previously been in jail. It makes you stop and wonder.

2. Dilution.

This tells you what you are actually getting for your money. Novice investors sometimes make an erroneous assumption regarding new issues. They assume, for example, that if two million new shares are being issued at a dollar a share, then each share they buy represents one two-millionth interest in the company. Or, to put it another way, after the stock is sold, the total value of the company is the total value of the stock—$2 million. Nothing could be further from the truth.

What's being forgotten is the interest in the company that the founders have. They may be giving up some interest when they sell new issues, but they surely aren't giving it all up. In fact, often they may be giving up less than half. The total value of the new issues may be less than half of the total shares outstanding. For me, this becomes the primary issue with regard to dilution.

To see how this works, let's take an example. The *company* decides to make a public offering. The *company* currently has ten insiders, officers, and board of directors members who have ownership. Between them they have three million shares, for which they originally put up a total of $250,000.

The *company* has decided to issue two million new

shares at fifty cents apiece. The total raised will be $1 million, of which the company will receive $750,000 after paying the commissions for the sale of the new stock.

All of this information is revealed in the prospectus. Now, there are at least three questions the prospective investor must ask with respect to dilution:

What is the dilution?

This is actually a question that relates to the book value of the stock. I don't think it's that critical, especially since there are other questions of more importance, which we'll consider next. However, for those who do think book value is vital, here's how it's calculated:

We find the dilution of book value by adding the total old book value to the new capital (proceeds) from the sale, and dividing the sum by the total number of shares available after the sale. The equation looks like this:

$$\text{NEW BOOK VALUE} = \frac{\text{TOTAL BOOK VALUE} + \text{NEW CAPITAL}}{\text{TOTAL SHARES}}$$

For the *company* we'll assume that total old book value was $100,000. (Remember, total book value is found by taking tangible assets and subtracting all liabilities and debts.) Since we know the new capital and total shares, we can proceed right to the equation:

$$\$.17 = \frac{\$100,000 + \$750,000 \; (= \$850,000)}{5,000,000 \text{ shares}}$$

In other words, in this particular new issue the investor is putting up fifty cents to get a share of stock with a book value of seventeen cents. In terms of book value, this amounts to an immediate loss of 66 percent. For those readers who like to buy according to the book value, look elsewhere!

Of course, we need to be realistic. Most of the book value is the new capital. If it's used wisely, it can very quickly turn into earnings and new assets, which can jump the book value of the company. If it's used poorly, it can be dissipated and the book value can drop to zero.

New issues are a risk and this is where it is. But we knew there was risk coming in, so we shouldn't be too shocked when we see dilution.

How many total shares outstanding are there, and what is the relationship of new shares to old?

In this case, after the sale of the new issue, there will be five million shares outstanding, of which *all* the new investors will own two million while the original ten insiders will own three million. The old shareholders will control the company with 60 percent of the stock.

Who has voting rights? Who will control the company? In this case it's going to be the original ten investors. If *all* the new investors got together in a voting block, they still wouldn't outnumber (in terms of shares) the original investors. Am I comfortable with this?

Who has what at risk?

I had an old English professor who once told me, "If you want to analyze a play, look to motive. See why the characters are doing what they do." Much of the same holds true here.

What the new investors have at risk is obvious, the $1 million put up to buy the new issue. But what do the original investors, the insiders, have at risk?

In this case, they have invested $250,000. Having already risked that amount of money, what are they now inclined to do with a new infusion of $750,000? If the company is solid and there is a marketable product on the way, they may be inclined to use it to develop the company. On the other hand, they could take it and run. (To put it nicely, pay themselves high salaries until it's all gone.)

In this example, since the new investors are putting up much more cash than the original investors, it would be wise to now turn to that part of the prospectus that details where the new money is to go.

3. Use for Proceeds.

We would expect the prospectus to outline what the money raised is to be used for. I like to pay attention to specifics here. How much is going to salaries? Big salaries take funds away from the product.

Is there a specific plan for putting out a product? Is there a timetable? Are specific sums of money to be spent at specific times to implement the plan?

I like to see a company with a reasonable plan and with a timetable.

On the other hand, I have seen prospectuses that baldly state that there is no product envisioned, no timetable for developing one, and the money is to go as salary to the officers of the company while they dream up something to produce! Incredible, but it's there in black and white in the prospectus, if we read it.

I also like to pay particular attention to existing debts. How much of the proceeds is going to pay them off?

4. Is the Company Overburdened by Debts?

I have seen companies get into trouble by borrowing too much. They may have a terrific product, but bad management. They tried to bring it to market themselves, borrowed to do it, and failed. Now they are having a public offering to try to get themselves bailed out.

However, most of the new capital is going to pay off the old debt (or pay interest on it). If that's the case, the *company* isn't bailing out—it's sinking even deeper. For investors it amounts to throwing good money after bad. Watch out for companies with big, old debts.

5. Is There a Market for the Product?
Most prospectuses will give some indication of the market potential for the product. I use common sense here. I look to see if I personally would find the product useful. Then I look at market share. Is this the only company in the field? Or is it bucking big competition?

6. Finally, I Look to Risks.
I put risks last because they are so hard to evaluate in a prospectus. Remember, the nature of a prospectus is to divulge information. Therefore, as part of the disclosure process, almost every company will list every possible risk that could happen.

The list is frequently very long and very scary. And because everything imaginable that could happen is put in, it's hard to judge which risks are realistic and which are unlikely.

Quite frankly, when we get to the risk portion of the prospectus, I feel it's time for professional help. Unless I'm an expert in the field, there's no way I can evaluate the true business risks. It's at this point that a good underwriter and broker can step in and provide both cautions and assurances where needed.

THE BOTTOM LINE

This, then, is the order in which I read a prospectus. But please note that my list of items to examine is neither comprehensive nor complete. There are literally dozens of other items to carefully consider. As you develop your own techniques for reading a prospectus, undoubtedly there will be different clues that you will look for.

The only unswervable advice I can give is to DEFI-NITELY READ THE WHOLE PROSPECTUS. In many cases it is your first line of defense against a bogus offering. Just as it can be a confirmation of a really sizzling deal.

PITFALLS IN PENNIES

■

I f you've come here looking for horror stories, you're going to be disappointed.

This chapter isn't aimed at scaring you away from penny stocks by telling you what terrible things were done to poor, innocent investors. It's been my experience in life and business that most of us get what we deserve. Or to put it as W. C. Fields used to, "You can't cheat an honest man."

If you go looking for bargains and ways to connive an advantage where none exists, be prepared to get your fingers burned. I'm here reminded of an investor I ran into who lost a great deal of money by buying gold bullion marked down 40 percent to wholesale prices. "Why," I told him, "there's no such thing as wholesale gold any more than there are wholesale dollar bills."

"I know," he nodded sorrowfully, "I know."

If you're over twelve years old, you should know that there are no real guarantees in life or business. You pay your money and you take your chance. In penny stocks the rewards tend to be greater, but so, too, tend to be the risks.

MINE FIELDS

Having thus noted that the greatest danger of all lies within, let's move on to point out that there are plenty of mine fields out there in penny stocks. The unwary investor can indeed get caught in a whole plethora of problems that he or she may never have suspected exist.

Most of these problems occur because this field is so speculative. Anytime there's the opportunity to make a huge profit, there are going to be those who try to siphon off part or all of that profit for themselves. Greed is always a great motivator.

Nevertheless, what we're going to be discussing should not be taken as true of the majority of the industry. Most brokers, houses, and dealers try to be reputable. However, in any field there are always going to be a few bad apples, a few who try to take advantage of investors. What we're concerned with here is to point out the pitfalls of dealing with the latter group.

NOTE: THE EXAMPLES IN THIS CHAPTER ARE NOT REFLECTIVE OF ANY PARTICULAR PERSON OR COMPANY. RATHER, THEY ARE GIVEN TO ILLUSTRATE PROBLEMS THAT HAVE EXISTED IN THIS FIELD AT ONE TIME OR ANOTHER. THE READER SHOULD BE AWARE THAT NO ATTEMPT IS MADE HERE TO BE COMPLETE OR COMPREHENSIVE. AS THIS IS BEING WRITTEN, NEW PITFALLS MAY BE ARISING. NO ASSURANCE IS GIVEN THAT BY AVOIDING THE PROBLEMS LISTED HERE, YOU WILL BE SUCCESSFUL IN A PENNY STOCK INVESTMENT.

THE BROKER WHO
REFUSES TO SELL

Perhaps this should come under the chapter on brokers; however, I have listened to so many people complain about this that it must surely be considered a pitfall, and a prime one.

As you should know by now, having read the previous chapters, timeliness is critical in this field. Frequently making a profit depends on getting in early and then getting out before the stock stops sizzling.

But what if you can't get out when you want to? What if your broker refuses to sell your stock? It could mean a loss for you.

Would a broker really refuse to sell a stock (and reap a commission?)

Remember, we're dealing with low-priced stocks in a thin market. Frequently the brokerage house is responsible for keeping up the market for the stock. If many investors want to sell, then the stock will tend to drift down in price. That could mean a loss for the brokerage house.

Although it is illegal for a brokerage house to tell its brokers not to allow investors to sell a stock in order to artificially keep the price up, it is possible for houses to make it plain to their brokers that they will be unhappy about such sales. There are many ways they can do this. For example, instead of honoring the sell order, the house can tell the broker to "cross stocks."

The Broker Who Tries to Cross Stocks.

"Crossing stock" means finding an investor who wants to buy a seller's stock within a house instead of going to the house for the sale. Mr. Jones wants to sell; Ms. Smith wants to buy. They both are trading with the same brokerage house, so an exchange is made. This can save each of them as much as 10 percent on commissions.

In an active market, there's nothing wrong with this as buyers and sellers are going to be constantly in the market within a brokerage house. But sometimes the market is inactive; the stock is so thinly traded that there are no buyers, only sellers, so no crossing of stock can take place. Consequently your broker sits on your order, waiting. And your stock doesn't get sold.

The broker is under pressure from two sides. You want to sell, the house doesn't want to buy. Often the investor offers the least pressure. (After all, if the broker doesn't produce the way the house wants, he or she will soon be looking for a new job.)

Thus, when you go to sell, the broker may repeatedly find "reasons" (excuses) why it would be better for you to hang on to the stock. When you bring up the subject of selling, the broker may note that the company is about to make a new announcement that will favorably affect the stock's price. Or that he or she has heard something from reliable sources indicating that the price is about to take off.

If this happens again and again every time you bring up the subject of selling over a period of a month or more, you should begin to suspect that the broker has other motives for wanting you to hang on to the stock. If that's the case and you can't sell, you've just lost your leverage (your liquidity) in the market and you are in grave jeopardy of losing your investment.

What should you do? Of course, this usually only happens to beginning investors. An experienced investor who suspects such finagling will immediately order the broker to sell and give a time limit of a few hours. If the sale isn't completed, the investor will threaten to take the matter to

NASD and/or the SEC. Such action usually produces the desired response—a sale.

Of course, you may have ruined your rapport with your broker and may need to shop around for another one. But then, you'd probably be better off without the one you had, anyway.

THE UNCONSCIONABLE SPREAD

As we know, the spread is the difference between the ask, or what the house wants to sell a stock for, and the bid, which is what the house is willing to buy a stock for. For example, if the ask is fifteen cents and the bid is twelve cents, the spread is three cents.

But who determines the spread?

In penny stocks it is the market maker, the house. The house determines just how much of a spread it needs in order to cover its risk of stocking inventory.

Typically a brokerage house will want a large spread because low-priced stock is so thinly traded. With the value of total shares outstanding often less than $1 million, the house needs to protect itself against a sudden drop in price caused by a few large investors deciding to sell.

But how large a spread is justifiable? I have seen spreads where the ask is eleven cents and the bid is six cents. The spread is five cents, or almost 50 percent of the ask! If you buy the stock at eleven cents, it has to go up a nickel in price (almost 50 percent) before you could sell back and just break even. Is this justifiable? Is it conscionable?

Probably not. The house does have its risks, but sometimes it exaggerates them in order to make a killing on the spread. Sometimes houses may prefer to handle low-priced stocks mainly because they can get so much higher a spread (percentagewise) than they can with higher-priced stocks.

What to do? Here's a rule of thumb to follow that a broker friend, Dr. Bob Kirk, suggests:

When the stock is between zero and twenty-five cents, the spread should be three cents or less. If the spread is any higher, then the market may be too thin for you to consider.

When the stock is between twenty-five cents and a dollar, the spread should be six cents or less.

BE CAREFUL WHEN YOU BUY
STOCKS ON THE PINKS

Remember, stocks that are not on NASDAQ are usually quoted on the pink sheets. However, the market here can be treacherous. When a stock is on NASDAQ, there usually is a retail price to which the market maker commits itself.

However, when a stock is on the pink sheets, the market maker is dealing with a very thin market and frequently can adjust the price without notice. For example, the pink might have one bid/ask quoted. However, if you want to sell a big order of stock, you may suddenly find that the bid drops 25 percent!

How come? The market maker didn't want to risk acquiring a larger inventory in such a thin market, so is decreasing its exposure. You, on the other hand, may find that you suddenly can't sell for the profit you anticipated.

There's nothing wrong with this, as long as you understand the risk. Be careful when you buy stocks on the pinks. A good thing to look for when buying stocks on the pinks is a narrow spread. A narrow spread tends to indicate an active and large market, one in which you have a better chance of selling without this problem occuring.

BEWARE THE COMPANY
LINE WHEN BUYING

It's important that you, as an investor, understand the relationship your broker has with the brokerage house for which he or she works. Your broker is a "producer" in the eyes of the house. Your broker's job is to find investors who will buy stock, thus generating commissions for the broker and the house. Indirectly your broker's job also is to promote the stock the company is selling.

Thus, when you have a private, confidential conversation with your broker and he or she suggests you buy this or that stock, who's really talking? Is it the broker's best judgment in looking out for you, the client? Or is the company speaking?

In the past a few houses ran broker mills. They would hire new brokers, indoctrinate them with the company line, offer high commissions, and then send them out to find investors. These brokers would use high pressure tactics to get investors to put up funds.

When it worked out and the investors made money, everyone was happy. But too often things didn't work out. For a few months the new brokers might make big, *big* commissions, but then the hens came home to roost. Their investors were losing money, so they dropped the broker and, unfortunately, also the field. Suddenly these brokers couldn't find more investors. Their production went down and the house didn't need or want them anymore. They left and a new set of brokers was hired to repeat the process. Along the way, it was the investor who got hurt.

What to do? Find a good broker. He or she may not always belong to the largest firm. But be sure that your broker has done his or her homework. When a stock is touted, be sure it's the broker speaking, not the house. (We'll see how in the next chapter.)

CHURNING

This is the oldest trick in the book and the most obvious. Yet, since it still happens, it's worth mentioning.

A broker is supposed to look out for the interests of his or her clients. But just how the broker does the job is open to wide interpretation.

For example, I have a doctor friend who invested $50,000 in low-priced stocks this year. Thus far he has been involved in over 100 trades and has lost in excess of $26,000. His broker, however, has made a fortune on commissions.

My doctor friend told the broker something like, put me in the market, buy and sell as needed, and let's make some money. The broker interpreted this to mean something like, I'll move this guy in and out of the market as often as I can to make commissions.

The broker churned the account. The doctor is very unhappy. But if you asked the broker, she would probably respond, "It's just the risks of the market."

Since frequent buying and selling is typical of the low-priced stock market, it would be hard to prove the broker wrong.

How to avoid churning? That's simple. Number one, get a scrupulously honest broker, one who is interested in earning a living by making money for the clients, not by living off the client's money.

Number two, take an interest in what's happening. Like it or not, if you don't personally get involved in the penny stock market, you stand an excellent chance of getting burned. This is not an absentee field. You need to devote your time and energy to it in order to succeed.

WATCH OUT FOR PACKAGING

Thus far we've been concerned with broker and house problems. Now let's move on to other areas. This pitfall relates to new issues. It comes about because new issues can be hard to get, particularly when everyone wants them.

When the market for new issues is tight, some brokers may offer "packages." Yes, they can get you the stock you want, *but only* if you buy another stock they are selling as well. In other words, you need to buy a package. No, it's not legitimate, but it sometimes happens.

Many investors are so determined to get a new issue that they will go along. They reason, "So what if I buy a second stock. At least I'll get the new issue I want, which I'm sure will be a winner, and it will make up for any loss I might have on the second stock."

Such reasoning is simply fallacious. Not all new issues are winners. Even if a new issue is a winner, it may not be able to make up for losses on a big loser that was packaged with it. When you buy a package, almost always you significantly decrease your chance of success.

What to do? Experienced investors simply won't buy packages. They know that if they can't get one new issue, they'll be able to get another. There are *always* more coming out.

SHELL GAMES

A "shell" is a phony company that only looks like it's viable. The outside looks great, the inside is hollow.

A shell is made, not born. It occurs something like this. A company is formed with a dream. However, for one reason or another the product turns out to be unsuccessful. The company is a failure. Eventually there are a lot of shareholders, but very few assets. The company is not yet in bankruptcy, but it's getting close.

Promoters look for just such companies. They pick up the company for next to nothing. Now they own it.

Next the promoters go looking for a second company. This one has some sizzle—perhaps it's in mining or robotics or whatever happens to be catching investors' interests at the time.

The promoters buy the second company and merge the stock from the newly failed company with it. Now we have a shell, a company that superficially looks good because of the sizzle. But there's already a lot of existing stock out there free-floating.

Now we, as investors, come along and, because of hype and promotion by the promoters, are encouraged to buy the company's stock. On the surface, the purchase may look good.

However, we are actually buying stock at a high price that the promoters got for virtually nothing. (Remember, when they took over that nearly failed company for a song, they got a lot of stock for almost nothing.) In effect, we are buying "insider's" stock.

(Insider's stock is stock held by officers and directors of a company. Also called "Rule 144" stock, to protect outside investors it normally cannot be sold for at least two years.)

Eventually, when the promoters have sold all of the stock they can, the company has a "sudden" reversal. The promoters abandon it, it goes bankrupt, and we, as outside investors, have lost all our money.

How do we avoid shells?

There are a variety of things to watch out for. First of all, investigate all companies *before* you buy. If you discover through your investigation that the company was *recently reorganized,* be wary. If it was *recently reorganized with new management,* be doubly wary. There may be nothing wrong here, but it could be a shell game.

In addition, scrutinize the annual and quarterly reports. You can frequently tell a shell because it has little to no asset base. The book value of the stock is virtually zero.

Finally, if it has no NASDAQ listing, question why. If it's because there aren't enough stockholders to qualify for listing (remember, the promoters bought up the stock), it may be a shell.

The shell game seems to be played primarily out of the West. But it could occur anywhere, anytime. In this case watchfulness is what could save you from a fall.

THE RULES ARE DIFFERENT
IN VANCOUVER

We mentioned the Vancouver market earlier. It specializes in gold mining stocks. There are some excellent opportunities up there. Unfortunately, there are also some rip-off deals.

If you're interested in playing the Vancouver market, you must realize at the outset that the rules are different. The SEC does *not* clear Canadian stock. There are other important differences as well.

For example, in Canada insiders are allowed to sell their shares much sooner than they are in the United States. Sometimes this leads to situations where they sell on opening day. Because this tends to be a thin market, this can skew a stock's price wildly up or down, misleading investors into thinking there's a lot of activity.

Also, in Vancouver a great many of the mining stocks can be only claims, not actual *producing* mines.

Finally, in Vancouver the investors are allowed to "short" their stocks, or sell stock before they buy it. (There's a more detailed explanation of shorting later in this chapter.) This adds a great deal of volatility to the market.

It's the old story of, "When in Rome, do as the Romans do." When you're playing the Canadian market, spend the time to learn the rules there. Or don't get involved.

DON'T OVERLOOK
THE ADVISORIES

No one, not even full-time stockbrokers, has the energy or the time to check out all the stock opportunities. Most don't have the time to check out even 10 percent of them. Many don't have the time to check out 1 percent.

If this is true, then there may be a lot of bargains out there that we all could be missing.

To find these choice deals, I suggest you do not overlook the advisories (see Chapter 5). The advisories are not a panacea. Too often the adviser might be touting a stock that he or she owns. However, they are an excellent starting point for investigation.

WATCH OUT FOR
"STALE" ISSUES

As we've noted, there is a certain time limit, usually ninety days, during which the underwriter must sell new issue stock. If a minimum number of shares haven't been sold by that time, no stock can be issued.

One way to judge the popularity of a new issue is to ask how much time is left before the end of the sales period. If there's very little time left, a week or two, and the broker is desperately trying to get you to buy the stock, that tells you that for one reason or another, the sale isn't going well. There really isn't a whole lot of demand for the stock. All of which suggests it might not do well in the after market.

On the other hand, if there are still several months to run in the sales period and your broker is having all kinds of trouble getting it for you (assuming you have a competent broker), it suggests the stock is sizzling and may do very well in the after market.

The rule here is to beware of stale issues.

NEW ISSUE UNDERWRITER PROBLEMS

For the remainder of this chapter we'll concentrate on a specific group of pitfalls, namely those that have to do with the underwriters of new issues. Remember, we're not talking about most underwriters here, just those few who are out to take advantage of the investor.

We've already touched on some of these. However, now we'll expand and dig deeper.

1. Underwriting Mills.

Some brokerage houses have discovered a quick way to make easy money. Come out with new issues as often as possible.

When the market is sizzling, investors scramble to get

those new issues, so these brokerage houses feel they are just serving a need. However, a question of quality and service arises.

A house is expected to thoroughly investigate a company and only underwrite new issues of quality. But if the house is bringing out new issues almost every other week, just how much investigation can it possibly have done?

Additionally, the house is expected to service the new issue, that is, to not only promote it, but to support it through its first year. If the house is grinding out the new issues, does it have the ability to support all of them? Or will it be stretched too thin?

Be alert for brokerage houses that in reality are just underwriting mills. When a house comes out with new issues every few weeks, insist on seeing a track record going back several years. See how well the house supported stocks it brought out twelve months and eighteen months ago—not just the stocks that happened to do well, but *all* of them.

You may find a graveyard of failed companies.

2. Weak Muscles.

Be sure the underwriter isn't biting off more than it can chew. Every brokerage house wants to be an underwriter. Some can handle it, some can't.

Critical things to look for are how many offices the house has, how many brokers it has working for it, how much of the deal it is syndicating with others (and how much muscle they have).

However, perhaps the best way to judge the muscle of an underwriter is to look at the levels at which its previous three underwritings were stabilized. Remember, it's up to the underwriter to support the stock in the after market. How well the underwriter did in this capacity in the past is a good indicator of how well it will do in the future. If its last three issues quickly dropped off in price, is there much hope for the next?

3. Strong Muscles.

This is just the opposite sort of problem. Here we're dealing with an underwriter that is very strong. The underwriter has a lot of capital behind it. It may come out with a new issue and keep it entirely in-house. The idea is that the underwriter will use its muscle to retail the issue, at the same time controlling the supply. However, in such a case, how does the investor really know what the stock is worth?

After all, in such a thin market the price of the stock may not really be determined by investor demand, but instead by the underwriter. Since the house controls the supply (having bought up all the outstanding shares), it is in effect supporting the stock's price. It may be bid thirty cents/ask thirty-six. But the quote might be artificial, held up entirely by the underwriter's muscle. Since no other houses have it, it shouldn't be that hard to support the price.

Maybe the underwriter will support the stock for six months or so. But if it doesn't take off on its own, the underwriter's patience may diminish (particularly when income from commissions and sales diminishes) and it may let it go. Since the stock was probably overpriced to begin with, when the house stops supporting it, it tends to drop right off in value. The stock could suddenly plummet.

How do we avoid getting muscled by a house? The thing to do is to be alert for new issues that have these three things in common:

1. *Small amounts,* particularly in the $500,000 range and under. (The smaller the issue, the easier for the house to control the supply.)

2. Strong house.

3. No syndication—the only market maker from whom you can buy the stock is the house.

Of course, just because a stock has these three characteristics doesn't mean it's being muscled. But it's something to consider, particularly if in the past the house handled stock similarly and it went up dramatically in price, perhaps by factors of three and four, and then, after a few months, came down just as quickly.

4. Syndication Troubles.

The fact that a stock is syndicated is no guarantee of its success. Yes, syndication does spread the stock around to other brokers and other houses. But will they promote it? Is the original underwriter big enough and respected enough to command their support?

Be careful when you are asked to buy a stock and are assured of its doing well mainly because it is in syndication. This fact alone does not mean things will work out well in the end.

5. The Greedy House.

This refers to a sort of cycle that sometimes occurs in the market. Often there is every intention of doing a good job. It's just a matter of trying to get too big too fast.

Sometimes an underwriter will have particularly good luck with one or two issues. Investors will note what's happened and will come swarming in. The house will put on more brokers and business will be booming.

But to keep things going, the house needs more stock. So it comes out with several new issues. However, for one reason or another, these new issues aren't as attractive as the previous ones. The house suddenly finds that it has to support a lot more stock than it anticipated.

The house gets spread too thin. It can't support the stock and prices begin to fall. Its brokers get disgusted and they begin to leave. Investors are disenchanted and sell orders pour in. Ultimately the house can't meet its capitalization requirements and it has to close its doors.

Be careful when dealing with houses that are in the process of expanding. It's a critical period. Yes, they might do very well. Or things might just go wrong for them . . . and for you.

6. Stepping Up an Issue.

This is a tricky concept, but an important one to understand. Here we have an underwriter that increases the price of a stock and makes a profit for its investors. It seems to be a good idea on the surface, but if you buy late, watch out.

Let's suppose the new issue is sold for ten cents a share and the house brings out the stock in the after market at a bid of twelve and an ask of nineteen. Note that this is an enormous spread, seven cents a share on a very low-priced stock.

Those who bought the new issue obviously bought in at ten cents. The house brokers are encouraged to get these individuals to sell; after all, they will be making a two-cent profit (before commission, which may absorb most of their profit) on their sales.

At the same time, the brokers are encouraged to sell the stock to new investors at nineteen. The house uses its PR muscle and sales force to move the stock. It also sells at less than the stated ask price to those who buy bigger blocks.

The intention is to sell everybody out of the market who bought originally at ten cents. Eventually all the holders of the stock will have bought in at a stepped-up level, say fifteen or sixteen cents. Now the price of the stock can be moved up to, say, a bid of sixteen cents and an ask of twenty-three cents.

The idea here is that since no investors are into the stock for less than about sixteen cents, there's no downside risk to the underwriter. No one will want to sell and they won't have to take in any inventory.

On the other hand, the stock appears to be performing well. It's moved up substantially from its new issue price. And there are lots of happy investors along the way.

If it turns out that the stock has a little steak along with the sizzle, the underwriter may try stepping it up a second time, or a third.

However, eventually reality has a way of popping holes in the bubble. Sooner or later the stock has to prove itself. If it can, then of course the sky is the limit. But too often what we're dealing with is hot air, nothing but sizzle.

When disenchantment sets in

For one reason or another (usually no upward price momentum), after two or three months investors begin becoming disenchanted with the stock. One day there is "net selling" (more sales than purchases). Now it's up to the underwriter to support the stock.

However, the underwriter may be satisfied with the large commissions and profits it has already made. It may simply let the stock find its own level. It may allow demand to lower the bid price.

Lowering the bid price may alarm some investors, who will want to get out before a crash. They will want to sell before the price drops down below what they paid. In a very short time the stock could plummet to below the original ten-cent offering.

Timing is everything

As I noted, if you get in and out early, you can actually make some money on stock that is stepped-up. On the other hand, if you're the last one on the list, you could take a beating.

My guess is that no underwriter would admit to stepping up a stock, and the vast majority don't do it. However, occasionally it may happen.

The tip-off that a stock is being stepped up can be a huge differential between the bid and ask prices. Of course, this could also simply indicate a prudent underwriter protecting itself. Ultimately, probably the best way to avoid such a situation goes back to checking the track record of the underwriter. What's happened to *all* the stocks the company has come out with in the past six months to a year? Have some produced the pattern described here? If so, be careful.

7. Shorting Your Own Issue.

This is never supposed to happen. However, in any business there are always a few unscrupulous people. It goes like this.

The house is also a dealer. It maintains its own internal account. It can buy and sell stock for itself. But it has one big advantage over investors, particularly when it is stepping up a stock or muscling it or doing something similar. It knows when it's going to stop supporting the issue. It knows when the price is going to fall.

The underwriter can benefit from this knowledge by shorting the stock. Shorting, as indicated earlier in this chapter, is simply reversing the time order of a transaction. In normal time we buy first and sell later. When shorting, we sell first and buy later. Normally we want the price to go up; we buy low and then sell high. When shorting, we want the price to go down. We sell high and then buy low.

The actual mechanics of shorting involve making a commitment to sell and borrowing the stock from someone who already owns it. For example, the house "borrows" the stock from other houses, brokers, or investors and sells it at twenty-five cents a share.

The sale is really made to actual investors like you or me who are hoping it will go up in price. Now the house watches the stock drift down in price. When it reaches ten cents a share, it buys it (from investors such as us) and gives back the shares it originally borrowed. Along the way it's made itself a neat fifteen-cents-a-share profit (which we have lost).

Investors can short stock, too. There's nothing wrong with that. However, investors can only short those stocks on the "approved margin list." And this rarely includes penny stocks.

When the house shorts stock that it's underwriting, we have a definite no-no. (Note: some people understand shorting and others don't. If you're one of those who doesn't, simply believe that it does happen and watch out when the house does it.)

Detecting this is probably impossible for the average investor. Probably the only thing to do is to be careful with whom you do business.

THE BOTTOM LINE

We've discussed many things to watch out for, but I want to emphasize one particularly—track record. Before you become involved with any house or broker, ask for, insist, demand to be shown the *full* track record. Don't be satisfied to see just those issues that did well. See everything, every issue an underwriter has brought out. (If they don't want to show you, that tells you something, too.)

Remember, if you go back six months, a year, eighteen months, you may find a graveyard of failed companies. If you do, then the stock you are buying today may have a terminal illness.

Once again, I want to emphasize that what we are talking about here does not happen in the majority of cases. It's just a matter of a few bad apples in the barrel. You just want to be sure that you don't end up dealing with one of them.

FINDING A GOOD BROKER

■

inding a good stockbroker, some have commented, is like Diogenes, the ancient Greek philosopher who reportedly walked the streets of his city with a lantern searching for an honest citizen.

I don't subscribe to quite such a cynical viewpoint. However, it is unquestionably true that it can be difficult to find just the right broker. After all, a stockbroker tends to combine aspects of an adviser, confessor, and confidant. It may take quite some searching before we turn up a person who can play these roles and with whom we can still feel comfortable. Adding to the difficulty are the problems that inherently are involved in a broker's position:

1. Conflicting interests
When we are in the stock market, we make our money from profits. A broker, on the other hand, presumably makes his or her money from commissions. We *only* make a profit when we have a successful transaction. The bro-

ker makes a commission *regardless* of whether or not our transaction was successful. In addition, the broker makes a commission each time we buy and sell. Thus, a broker makes a commission twice for each one time we can make a profit. This situation, of necessity, leads to conflicting interests.

Even when the broker is a totally honest individual (as most are), he or she must nevertheless feel motivated at some level to get us to buy or sell—or else, there's nothing in it for the broker. We, on the other hand, only want to buy or sell when there's a profit to be made. Thus, in the back of our minds there must always be the question, "Is the broker suggesting I make this move because it's in my best interests? Or is it because he or she needs a commission?"

When things don't go well, perhaps through no one's fault, it is only natural for us to question the motives of the broker. "Why did you get me into this transaction?" we demand.

It's hopeless for the broker to protest innocence. The inherent conflicting interest will always do him or her in. Ultimately the broker may throw up his hands and say, "It's your money. Do what you want!" In the fray a relationship can be severed and we can come away feeling cheated.

Some have suggested that to overcome this inherent problem in dealing with brokers, a new kind of commission structure be set up. The broker gets paid *only* a percentage of our profits. If it's 10 percent, then when we have a successful trade making, for example, a thousand dollars, the broker gets a hundred. On the other hand, if we don't make money or, what's worse, lose it, the broker gets nothing. This would tend to align broker motivation with our own.

However, for some reason, as of this writing I know of

no brokers who are jumping to adopt this new commission formula.

What is one to do, therefore? If you're a client, my suggestion is to be understanding. The broker does have to make a living, and if we only take up his or her time on the phone and never buy anything, that's a losing situation for that person.

On the other hand, we should also be prudent. If our broker moves us in and out of a lot of situations and we aren't making a profit along the way, he or she may simply be churning. In that case, it's definitely time to seek a new broker.

2. Broker inexperience

The title "stockbroker" tends to give an aura of professionalism to those who use it. In many cases the person is indeed a professional. Unfortunately, however, that's not always the case.

To become a broker, all one needs is a fairly reputable character and the ability to pass a less than awesome test. Having thus become a broker, one does not automatically also become a seer in the world of finance.

Typically a new broker is as awash in the world of stocks as is the new investor. When the two hook up together, likely as not it's a case of the blind leading the blind.

To overcome this problem, many brokerage firms these days offer their new brokers courses in stocks, bonds, and general finance. These courses are excellent, when they achieve their stated goals. Too often, however, the courses turn into sales meetings where, instead of financial knowledge, methods of manipulating the client are taught. Ultimately, for many brokers learning the ropes is done through hard trial and error.

It probably takes an individual broker with savvy between one and two years to learn the ins and outs of the market enough to be able to guide clients around the mine fields in penny stocks. Any less time than that and we as clients are in reality providing on-the-job training for the broker.

Therefore, a good rule with which to begin is this: If you're going to be investing your own money, never do it with a broker who's had less than about eighteen months direct experience in the field.

3. Compatibility

Finally, there is the matter of compatibility. I may be a daring investor, you a conservative one. Should we use the same broker? You may make quick decisions, I may take a long time. Will the same broker serve us equally well?

The point is that brokers have different styles. To be successful we need to find a broker whose style is compatible with our own. If, for example, we want to take a moderate approach, then we need a broker who is sympathetic to our needs and is a moderate him or herself. One who is radical and wants to take chances or who is too conservative will not fill our needs.

To find such a broker will take some searching. Just as you wouldn't want to be close friends with every person you'd meet on the street, you wouldn't want every broker to handle your money. We simply have to meet and talk with as large a number of brokers as possible before the right one will appear.

WHERE DO I FIND A PENNY STOCK BROKER?

If you want to find a broker who handles the Big Board, then any Smith Barney, Shearson, Merrill Lynch, etc. office will do. They are chock-full of brokers who will handle such transactions for you.

On the other hand, if you want to specialize in pennies, where are you going to find brokers? After all, most brokers handle only high-priced stocks.

There are sources, and we'll discuss them in a few paragraphs. But first, a word of explanation as to why this book does not contain a list of brokerage firms (if not brokers themselves).

My observation is that brokers move into and out of the field with amazing speed. Brokerage houses also seem to have relatively short life spans. Therefore, any list put into a tome that is long-term, such as this book, would probably be dated by the time it was in the bookstore. What's worse, a house "recommended" here could possibly turn sour in the future.

Thus, rather than provide you, the reader, with a list of brokerage houses and numbers to call, I am going to tell you where you can create a truly up-to-the-minute list for yourself.

It's easy. Chapter 5 contains a list of publications in this field. The larger of them, such as the *OTC Stock Journal* or the *Penny Stock Preview* or the *PennyStock News,* contain advertisements from brokerage houses specializing in the field. The house may be touting a new issue (asking you to send for a prospectus) or it may simply be promoting its services. In any event, from just a few copies of these publications you can put together a list of who's in the field as of the time you're searching. Then it's just a matter of calling around. (Many houses offer toll-free numbers.)

In addition, should this source fail, you may be able to contact some of the publications for a current list of brokers. They may have a recommended list they would be willing to share.

QUALIFYING A BROKER

Having thus commented in general on the broker/client relationship and where to find brokers, let's now turn our attention to the more specific subject of determining whether a broker knows what he or she is doing. Once we find a broker who we feel is fairly honest, experienced, and compatible, what else do we need to know? As it turns out, a great deal.

1. Is the Broker a Member of the NASD?

You'll recall from earlier chapters that the NASD is the self-regulating arm of the OTC market. *Any* broker with whom you deal should have, as a bare minimum, membership in the NASD. If the broker is not a member, then seriously reconsider doing business with him or her. (After all, if something goes wrong, with a member you can always threaten to take the problem to the NASD. If the broker isn't a NASD member, how much weight will your threat carry?)

Keep in mind that the NASD is a "voluntary" organization. Not every SEC-registered broker has to belong. The NASD provides an additional bit of assurance by conducting examinations of brokerage houses on a regular basis. The compliance department of the NASD will actually go to a brokerage house and examine records to see that SEC regulations are being enforced. Unfortunately, while this is helpful, it is still far from a guarantee that the house is completely honest.

2. How Long Has the Broker Been NASD Licensed?

This is a different question from the preceding one. If you ask about experience alone, the broker could answer,

"Several years." If you ask about NASD membership, the broker could answer, "Yes." But it could turn out that what was meant was that he or she has been slightly involved in the field as an investor for several years and got NASD membership yesterday.

A good rule of thumb is that the broker should be NASD licensed for at least eighteen months to two years.

3. Does the Broker Do His
Or Her Own Research?

This is a critical point. In the last chapter we discussed the house line, where brokers would repeat information and suggest stocks that were given to them by the brokerage house. For obvious reasons (if they're not obvious, reread the last chapter), we want a broker who thinks for himself or herself, one who goes out and does his or her own homework.

There are several ways to determine if a broker knows his or her stuff. The first is to ask if the stock being recommended is being underwritten or a market made in it by the broker's house. If every stock the broker recommends is underwritten or a market made in it by his or her house, then you know you're getting a house line. The broker is simply recommending what the house wants to push. Time to look for a broker who thinks for himself.

Another way to check is to ask the broker for 10K and 10Q reports. The 10K is the annual, and the 10Q the quarterly report that a company must file with the SEC. They are the bread and butter of research. Any broker who is doing his or her own work will surely have checked into these.

I have a friend who handles new brokers with a little test regarding these reports. When he's dealing with a new broker who recommends a company, he immediately says, "Send me a copy of the latest 10K and 10Q reports."

"It's positively amazing," my friend says, "how many brokers suddenly stop in their tracks. One minute they're pushing a company on me, the next they're anxious to hang up and, I presume, get to work on the next pigeon. Of course, every once in a while I get lucky and a broker really does send me the reports. And frequently it turns out to be a very good recommendation and broker!"

Alternatively, it's possible to ask the broker about the reports over the phone. Questions about recent income, liabilities, debt, and so forth should be easily answered if the broker has read the 10K and 10Q reports and/or is looking at them. (Alternatively, the broker should be able to quickly get hold of the reports to get the answers.)

On the other hand, if the broker can't produce the information, then why is he or she recommending the stock? Is it because the house has said it's a good stock to push?

(Note: It should be understood that just because a house is pushing a stock does not mean it's a bad investment. It could be an excellent investment. What we are concerned with is finding a broker who gives equal diligence to investigating both the house line as well as outside stocks before making a recommendation.)

4. Beware of Brokers Who Rely on Technical Analysis Alone.

Sometimes when I ask a broker about the 10K or the 10Q reports, I get a very quick and sophisticated reply. "Don't worry about those," the broker says. "They are irrelevant."

"What's important to know," the broker may say, "is that this company is in a hot field and the product it has is sizzling. People are scrambling to get the stock. The price has been hitting new highs almost every week. You're just lucky I have some available, and you'd better act quickly!"

What the broker is really doing here is relying on a sort of technical analysis (discussed at length in Chapter 7). The broker has probably looked at stocks overall and made a determination as to what field is popular and what stock within the field is likely to be a hit. Then the broker is telling me that based on past experience, stocks with sizzle in a field that's popular tend to do well. So I'd better buy.

Well, maybe it could be a good opportunity, and what the broker says could be right. But how does one judge? If you haven't known and dealt with the person over a long period, how do you know that his or her judgment about what's sizzling and what's going to do well is right?

Remember, this isn't a field where you can easily give your money to someone else and say, "Make my fortune for me." Rather, you have to do some homework yourself. It's one thing if, based on your own research, you think a field and a stock sizzle. Maybe you'd be willing to play a stock based on this alone.

But when a broker gives you this kind of information, then you'd better ask for a little steak to go along with the sizzle. After all, a broker should be listening to more than just rumors and testing more than just popularity. He or she should also be searching for the good, solid, fundamental stocks that will grow. Turning up the stock with both immediate and future potential is the real benefit that a broker can provide.

If the broker is a technician alone, watch out. You might be better off getting your information at the local soothsayer's office.

5. Does the Broker Buy the Stock
That He Or She Recommends?

For many of us, this is the acid test. We're sitting in a bar and a friend orders a drink for us that has a very weird name. When it arrives, it has smoke coming out of it, it's bubbling, and it's got a nasty odor. Our friend says, "Try it, you'll like it!"

We look at the drink and reply, "After you!"

What we're asking for is proof that it'll be good for us, that it will do us no harm. That proof takes the form of the other person taking the drink first. If our friend survives and smiles afterward, well then, maybe we will try it ourselves.

In ancient times kings would call their chefs out to personally taste the food that had been prepared to demonstrate that it wasn't poisoned. In the past the great researchers in medicine would frequently try out a new drug or treatment on themselves before risking it on a patient. Should we expect less from our stockbroker?

Look at it this way. You're in the market to make your fortune, right? Is your stockbroker in there for some totally different reason? No, he or she is out to get rich, too.

Thus, if a stock comes along that's really as good as he or she says, then your broker would be a fool not to buy it as well as recommend it to you. This is a truth that's solidly embedded in rock.

On the other hand, if your broker is recommending a stock but is unwilling to risk his or her money on it, should you? Would you take a medicine when the inventor wasn't willing to take it herself? Would you eat food that a chef wouldn't taste? Would you take a drink from a friend who wouldn't drink it himself?

Ideally the relationship you have with your broker should be one of mutual investing. You're both looking for a good deal. Your broker is out there finding them and making money two ways. The first is by buying stock. The second is by making commissions recommending that good stock to others. Anything less than this type of a relationship, and you should find another broker.

How do you know if the broker actually bought the stock? Ask to see a copy of his or her confirms, those little slips that verify a purchase. There's no reason in the world a broker would hesitate to send this to you, unless it didn't exist.

6. Is the Broker Too Busy for You?

In any house there will be one broker who's been around the longest, has the biggest clients, and is doing the best business. This is the broker with whom most of us want to deal.

However, this big producer may not want to take us on if we're starting out with a small amount of money to invest. He or she may already have several dozen clients who have hundreds of thousands of dollars to spend. Would this broker be as interested in us if we have five hundred dollars or a thousand?

This is a real problem when searching out a broker. Frequently we are ushered over to second (or third or fourth) best. While this "B" team broker we end up with may indeed have the time to spend with us, will he or she have the knowledge or experience to make us rich?

It's a common complaint and concern of new, small investors. Yet, upon examination it may prove to be unwarranted. If we go into a house, ask to see the manager, and then explain that we are a small investor, but that we plan to move up quickly and we want to deal only with the top producer in the house, we may very well get an entrée to the "A" broker.

Some top producers will take on all sincere investors, regardless of the size of their accounts. (Small investors can often recommend large investors to the broker.) If we don't insist on an unwarranted amount of time, make reasonable demands, and actively trade the market, we might very well get the attention of the top broker in the house.

Of course, if it doesn't work out this nicely, we can always try the next house.

It's important, however, that even after the first meeting, the broker continues not to be too busy for us. One sure way to check is to monitor the message direction. Are we always calling the broker? Are we always put on hold or told we'll be called back and then sometimes aren't? These are sure signs the broker doesn't have time for us. We shouldn't waste time with him or her, either, and should look elsewhere.

Ideally the message direction will be two way. The broker will call us with recommendations and suggestions as often as we call the broker. In addition, he or she should be sending us written materials on a regular basis so we can check out what's happening with particular stocks.

7. Does the Broker Have an Investment Philosophy?

While this may sound a bit esoteric, it can be very important. Both you and the broker should be operating on the same wavelength.

A good broker will begin a relationship by trying to find out as much as possible about you. She should ask whether you are interested in growth or just playing stocks. Long term or short? High risk or low risk? What is your personal market strategy? What fields do you prefer? What do you want to stay away from?

Armed with this information, the broker should explain her own philosophy. Does she prefer growth or playing? Long or short term? High risk or low? Does she have preferences in terms of fields and stocks? Does she play a "contrary" game? (Buy whatever the market says is bad?)

Now the two of you can stand off and look at each other. Are your philosophies compatible? If not, you'd better find a different broker.

8. Does the Broker Explain How
Your Account Will Be Handled?

This, of course, includes how much the commissions will be, but it's much more. The broker should explain her method of operating. Many brokers simply recommend stocks and put you in. But they don't recommend when to get out. Ultimately, if the broker doesn't have a sound investment outlook, you could pick many winners and still end up losing money.

You can tell if a broker really knows how to handle your account if she gives you a "plan." Usually this takes the form of a counseling session at the beginning of your relationship.

The broker may explain that she will recommend stocks. If you buy one of her picks, at the time you buy the two of you will determine when you will sell if the stock goes down and when if it goes up. Thereafter, she will execute the plan for you. If the stock looks like it's going to be a real winner, she will call and ask if you want to change the plan and let the stock run instead of selling it.

A broker who is able to work out a plan with you demonstrates clear understanding of the market. A broker who simply says, "Let's buy!" and doesn't have an escape plan for selling may really be incapable of dealing with the market. Remember, the broker must do more than just pick the stock. He or she must also know how to get you successfully into and out of the market.

9. Does the Broker Have
an Academic Degree?

Many investors would say, "Who cares if he has a master's or a Ph.D? What counts is, can he pick a winning stock!"

Indeed, that certainly is true. However, there's something about getting an academic degree that tends to instill a sense of respect for honest investigation in a person. Regardless of the field in which the degree was obtained (whether it be science or liberal arts), the degreed broker may tend to have a greater appreciation for true research.

Of course, that doesn't mean that a Ph.D. couldn't be an incompetent stockbroker. It's just that given a choice, I prefer to deal with someone who's waged the academic wars and succeeded than someone who has never been to that battle.

10. Does the Broker Have Connections?

This is important in a variety of ways. For example, if you are looking to play the new issue market, can your broker get new issues for you?

If you've explained what you want done and all you get from your broker are excuses, then perhaps it's time to consider a different broker. Some in the field simply don't have the connections to get the new issues. They don't know enough people, aren't respected by enough people.

The same holds true for growth stock. Some brokers have many connections in the field. A friend may tip them off about a great company. The broker may then research it and conclude it's a great buy and recommend it to you. But the whole chain might not have started without the broker's connection.

One way to check on a broker is to casually ask others in the field about him or her. Penny stocks is a small enough field that the top people tend to be known to others.

11. Can you Get a Friend to Recommend a Broker?

This can be an excellent place to start. I've put it toward the end of our list, however, because few of us tend to know others who are already involved in penny stocks.

Nevertheless, if you know an investor in the field, particularly one who's been around for a while and who's made some money, his or her recommendation of a broker can be invaluable.

12. Is the Broker's House Financially Sound?

They're all sound, you may think. Not so.

In terms of capital, all that a broker has to raise is a surprisingly small sum of money to open a house. For example, a house that is going to be a market maker could conceivably have less than fifty thousand dollars in net capital. (Net capital is net assets minus client indebtedness.) Of course, many houses have far more.

Nevertheless, the SEC requires that each house maintain a minimum amount of capital; this is called the "Net Capital Rule." When a house's capital drops below the minimum amount, the SEC may shut it down.

Shutdowns can and do occur because of insufficient net capital. They may occur for a variety of reasons. For example, the house may sell stock to an investor and then not receive the cash from that investor to make the purchase. The house has seven days to get the money. If it doesn't, then it is responsible for the money. This is called "Regulation T," and has been the undoing of some luckless houses.

In another instance a house might be shut down because it has speculated in the market and lost.

For whatever the reason, when a house is shut down, it means inconvenience at best and potential losses at worst. It could take weeks, perhaps months, to sort out the trades and ownership of stocks in a house that has been shut down. During that time you might be incapable of selling your stock.

It's important to ask your broker for a statement of the house's *current* financial condition. This statement should include a ratio of net capital to client indebtedness. The ratio can be any number, but if it's higher than eight (meaning the firm has less than one dollar for each eight dollars of client indebtedness), beware. Firms with ratios of ten or higher are getting into dangerous territory.

13. Who Is the Brokerage's Clearinghouse?

This question relates to the preceding one. Some brokerage houses clear their own accounts. Unless the house is very large, this is something to be wary of. (To see why, reread the previous section.)

Many houses, however, use other large firms to clear their transactions. Ask your broker what firm acts as the clearinghouse. Is that firm a member of the New York Stock Exchange?

The idea is to get a clearinghouse that's as big as possible. Remember, if the clearinghouse fails, as some have done in recent years, it can tie up your stocks for quite some time. On the other hand, if the clearinghouse is very large, a failure would cause such a market brouhaha that chances are the SEC would insist the mess be cleared up very quickly.

14. How to Interview Your Broker.

Thus far we have been looking at ways of qualifying a broker. Now let's try a different perspective. In a sense, getting a good broker is like hiring anyone else. We are going to be spending our money and we expect service in return. When we hire someone, we normally conduct an interview. The same should be true with a broker. We should interview him or her.

When you meet a new broker for the first time, whether on the phone or in person, you should have a series of questions to ask. Of course, you will form a general opinion by the way he or she acts and talks, but having those questions handy can help clear up matters quickly.

The actual questions you ask can vary enormously. I suggest you take a good number from those covered in this chapter. Just reword them to make them appropriate questions to ask a broker. For example, you can ask about the broker's affiliations, background, philosophy, and so forth.

In addition, to find out the broker's actual knowledge, sometimes it is useful to create a situation and ask what the broker would do. Perhaps it's something that has already happened to you in a stock transaction. You know how it actually came out. Does this broker have any suggestions or innovations that could have led to a more favorable resolution?

As personnel professionals know, the important thing when interviewing is to let the other person talk. Your job is to listen.

With a stockbroker this shouldn't be too difficult, as most are experienced in conversing. The trick is keeping them on a topic of your choice (or else you may find they are already trying to get you interested in a particular stock).

Go through the questions in this chapter, but always keep in mind that what you are ultimately trying to do is establish a business relationship. That means that you don't "grind" or "grill" the broker to the point where he or she begins to personally resent you. That's hardly the basis of a working relationship.

Rather, be friendly, informal, businesslike. Point out that it's to both your advantages if you can learn as much as possible as quickly as possible about each other. And remember, the broker is supposed to be the expert, so don't try to show off what you know. Try to learn what he or she knows. (If you don't know something, admit it and ask for an explanation.)

Don't be in a hurry to buy

Ultimately, the broker wants to sell you stock. A good rule to follow is never buy on the first meeting (which should be when you interview the person). There are two reasons. First, you really won't know what you think of the person until after the meeting, when you've had a chance to think it over.

Afterward you may come to the conclusion that this broker is terrific and really knows his or her stuff. On the other hand, you may realize that the broker is all hot air and intimidation. If it's the former, then you can go back and start trading. If it's the latter and you've already bought, however, think how sad you may feel.

The second reason is that it's a good idea to begin with a trial period. If at the first meeting the broker recommended three different stocks, wait and watch those stocks for a few days or even a few weeks. If the stocks move up, that tells you something positive about the broker's ability to pick winners. On the other hand, if the stocks move down, it tells you something else.

If you wait, you can learn about the broker's abilities without actually spending your cash. If you don't wait, you'd better be an excellent judge from the starting gate or be able to sustain a loss.

Remember, you can almost always go back and buy later.

15. Ongoing Trial Period.

I once had a friend who had a rather self-centered attitude toward his job. Once when his boss indicated that he was unhappy about something in my friend's performance, this friend replied, "I was looking for a job when I found this one. I can always keep on looking!"

Regardless of whether his boss was justified in reproaching him, I believe my friend's attitude was sound and is worth considering in penny stocks. We're looking for a good broker. We may temporarily stop looking when we find someone who fits the bill. But as soon as a problem develops, we can keep right on looking.

Finding a broker should be an ongoing endeavor. We may start out with a trial period. We invest a small amount and see how well the broker handles the transactions.

If we're satisfied, we may want to stick with this broker a while longer and make bigger investments. If he or she picks good stocks, we'll hang in there. As long as we're making profits, it's going to be hard to change.

But there may come a time when profits turn to losses, when the broker makes a foolish error or two in handling a transaction, when there is a personality clash, when there is a question of honesty. What do we do then?

Why, we continue on with our search for the good broker.

Remember, unlike marriage, which is a very deep and personal commitment, hiring a broker is strictly a business arrangement. If we become dissatisfied with the broker for any reason and feel that the arrangement is no longer beneficial to us, then we can and should bail out. One of the biggest mistakes we can make is keeping a broker long after we've decided that he or she is not working for us.

SPECIALIZING IN MINING AND ENERGY STOCKS
■

The world of penny stocks is often divided up into different areas of interest. For example, there's high-tech stock and medical stock. But no field has received more attention recently than mining and energy stocks. These have become the darlings of investors.

Entire markets are devoted primarily to these issues. The Denver OTC market, for example, is widely known as the home of oil and gas stocks. Spokane frequently fields silver mining issues. Vancouver (unique in that it is a penny *auction* market) has literally thousands of gold mining stocks.

With all the interest in mining and energy stocks, it is little wonder that this is one of the first areas that new investors tend to explore. With the fever pitch of a forty-niner many buy the stocks in the hope of finding the miner's dream, a "glory hole."

But are there really fortunes to be made in mining and energy stocks? Is it really the easy way to get rich quick?

These and other questions are what we'll examine in this chapter.

TIED TO THE EARTH

Mining and oil and gas stocks are directly tied to the earth. This is the first rule of low-priced stocks in this field. If you buy a gold stock, then the price of your stock, in general, will reflect the price of gold. If gold goes up, all other things being equal, so, too, should the price of your issue. The same holds true for silver and for oil and gas. (There are other mining stocks, such as copper or nickel, but we're only going to cover the big three in this chapter.)

Thus, when judging the field, it is important to look to how well the product is doing on world markets. For example, as this is being written, all mining shares in general have been down for at least a year. Silver prices have been low. Gold prices have inched up only modestly, and oil prices have plummeted. (Gas prices have fared somewhat better, primarily due to long-term contracts.) As gold, silver, and oil go, so, too, go the stocks of companies that are involved in these fields.

But having low prices seems not to daunt those who are excited about this field. In fact, many feel that low prices mean prime time to invest in these stocks. It depends on your perspective. If you want to buy low, then when prices are down may indeed be the best time to buy. On the other hand, if you like to wait until you see a definite trend, then waiting until prices rise will probably make more sense to you.

Overall, however, the rule remains that the price of mining and energy issues reflects the price of gold, silver, or oil.

PICKING INDIVIDUAL SHARES

Having thus disposed of the market, what can be said for picking individual shares? There are two vastly different schools of thought here.

No Room for Amateurs.

The first school looks at mining and oil and gas stocks from a fundamental perspective. It states in brief that it is just as difficult to find a good mining or oil stock as it is to find a good mine or oil well.

In other words, this is a field *exclusively* for experts. It takes individuals with dozens of years of mineralogical and geological experience to be able to truly evaluate the potential of a company in this field, so how can investors expect to do it in a relatively short time?

This school points out that there are all kinds of pitfalls in trying to buy these stocks. From the out-and-out fraudulent promoter who is trying to sell "fool's gold" to the sincere oil well owner who, because of economic reasons, hasn't a chance, the field is littered with hopeless companies and worthless stocks. The novice would have a better chance of picking a winning ticket in a lottery than wandering in among these treacherous stocks and being successful.

Every Stock's a Winner!

Then there's the other school of thought, which says something to the effect that "it doesn't make a darn bit of difference what stock you buy. When the market's hot, everyone's a winner!"

This perspective pays close attention to the linkage described earlier between these stocks and the prices of gold, silver, and oil. When prices for the product are going up, according to this viewpoint, any stock in the field will do well, at least for the short term. Therefore, just jump in with both feet and get rich! (This viewpoint is most clearly presented in a book titled *Small Fortunes in Penny Gold Stocks,* by Norman Lamb, published by The Penny Mining Prospector, 1096D, Coast Village Road, Santa Barbara, CA 93108.)

Growth Vs. Playing.
These two viewpoints are similar to two other perspectives discussed earlier: buying a fundamentally strong stock for future growth versus playing with a stock hoping for short-term profits. As noted, it is possible to make money either way.

However, to my way of thinking, it is better to be selective when buying a stock. I like to know something about the company. I want to know that it has at least a realistic chance for long-term success. I want some steak with my sizzle.

Therefore, for the remainder of this chapter we'll focus in on some of the fundamentals that affect these stocks. If you want to take a fling at playing a stock and pick it just by throwing a dart at a board, go right ahead. There's really not much more to say except that before you do, you ought to read the last part of this chapter, which will give some insights into when gold, silver, and oil are likely to see better days.

However, if you want to see some of what you're up against fundamentally with these stocks, read on.

MINING FUNDAMENTALS

The fundamentals for gold and silver are similar. Therefore, rather than repeat ourselves, we'll take just one example, gold.

As the old saying goes, "Gold is where you find it." Today, however, locating an ore-producing body is not quite as hit-or-miss as it was in the past. Today geologists have sophisticated techniques for determining the likelihood of finding minerals underground. Unlike in the past, today knowing where the gold is can often be the *least* critical part of a successful mining venture.

To put it another way, while today mine owners usually have a pretty good idea of where the gold is, they are faced with other problems. These other problems can be lumped into two categories: (1) Is the known gold in sufficient purity to make it commercially worthwhile to mine? (2) Does the company have sufficient capital and expertise to start up production and become profitable?

IS IT COMMERCIALLY MINABLE?

This often separates the experts from the novices. Those who are promoting mines will often point to "proven reserves." They will indicate that their mining claims are right next to another mine that is commercially producing gold. Further, they may point out that their proven reserves may be quite large. The promoters may even have genuine geological reports substantiating the reserves.

Armed with these proven reserves, the promoters are out looking for capital. All that they need, they say, is enough money to start production. Buy their stock and join them on the road to riches. Should we buy their stock? Is it a good deal when a company has proven reserves?

Maybe. But the real question is not how much proven reserve a company has. It's how much of that reserve is commercial.

It works like this. Gold may be near the surface or deep underground. It may be present in very small quantities, or in strong concentrations. Obviously, gold that is near the surface in strong concentrations is going to be cheaper to mine than gold that is farther down and thinly spaced out. A company might indeed have, for example, $100 million in proven reserves. But that gold might be a thousand feet down and it might cost $400 an ounce to extract from the ground. If the current price of gold happens to be $350, then no way is this company going to be successful. If it started production, it would lose $50 on each ounce it produced.

Having commercial reserves means that a company has gold that it can extract from the ground for *less* than the current price of the metal. A good commercial reserve, for example, would be extractable at $275 an ounce when gold was selling for $325. A commercial reserve worth $2 million might be far more valuable than only a proven reserve worth $200 million.

NOTE: What's commercial and what isn't depends on the price of gold. A company that has gold extractable at $400 an ounce might not be able to sell its stock for a dime a share when gold is $350. But if the price of gold suddenly goes up to $500 an ounce, that company's proven reserves suddenly become commercially developable. That stock can explode in value overnight. Thus, even companies with only proven reserves can be sleepers, good buys waiting for the price of gold to take off.

Finding Out.
How do you know if the reserves of a company are commercially worthwhile or just proven?

The truth is that unless you're a geologist and a mining expert, you probably don't. This is one of the biggest problems with mining stocks. As investors, we usually only have the word of the mining company as to the nature of its reserves.

Sometimes respected outside experts are called in who render opinions, and this can be helpful. Sometimes newsletter writers spend time investigating particular companies and give opinions, and this, too, can be helpful. Nevertheless, the fact remains that the average nonexpert investor can never really know if a mine's reserves are commercial or not . . . until production starts up. This is an important fact to keep in mind.

DOES THE COMPANY HAVE THE EXPERTISE TO MINE THE MINERAL?

Who are gold miners? Remember back to the last century when half the East Coast went West to strike it rich in California? What did those people know about mining?

Next to nothing. And things haven't changed all that much today. Miners remain dreamers. They go out looking for a strike, sometimes hit it, and think that everyone lives happily ever after. Unfortunately, that's not the way it is in the real world.

It takes a fortune to make a fortune in mining. With gold, it takes enormous capital to start up a mine and get it into production. Yet very often those who are in start-up mining companies either ignore this fact or simply are unaware of it. It's easy to make the mistake.

Small-Time Mining.
Weekend miners sometimes do very well with suction rigs floating on rivers digging up placer gold. Small companies sometimes do very well simply by using a process called "leaching."

Basically, leaching involves just dumping the ore on the ground in a giant leach pit. Then a solution of cyanide is poured over it and this draws out the gold, which is then refined.

Leaching can make it possible for a small company to get started. For example, the *company* buys the rights to an old slag heap. These are tailings left over from mines that may have operated a hundred years ago. Back then the miners were unsophisticated in the ways of removing gold from ore. They let a lot of the gold escape to remain in the tailings.

The *company* starts with the tailings and builds a small leach field around them. Almost from day one the *company* may be showing a profit. The owners may think that mining is easy. Now they're ready for the big time. All they need to do now is to raise a little capital and expand their business. So they issue stock, raise capital, and are on their way.

For the unwary investors, however, this company could really be a Trojan horse. Once the company raises capital, what is it going to do next? The old slag tailings are limited. Where is it going to get the next ore from which to leach gold?

It's one thing for a company to set up a small leach field and show a profit on old tailings. It's quite different for that company to mine ore, set up a giant leach field, and extract gold. The latter requires expertise and huge amounts of capital.

When the small company tries to expand, too often it finds that it is grossly undercapitalized. It may resort to borrowing, quickly use up its funds, and then fold. The investors, of course, are out their funds.

Thus, new mining companies, the ones that issue low-priced stock, tend to be extremely risky. Even when the owners are honest and sincere, there's the problem of experience and knowledge.

How do we avoid this pitfall? It's difficult, but one way is to be very careful of new issue mining stocks. Looking for a company that has already locked in production from other than tailings and other than leach fields is another hint.

Finally, looking for a company that has a track record of several years is also helpful. The trick, of course, is to find such a company that also has a low price for its stock.

GETTING STARTED IN MINING STOCKS

If after seeing the two problems noted above (there are others as well), you are still interested in pursuing mining stocks, you should spend some time finding a broker who specializes in the field.

We noted that there are brokers who specialize in penny stocks. A subspecialty is the penny stock broker who only handles mining stock. He or she should be in a position to familiarize you with the field and to offer research on what's currently available. (Of course, here you should apply the same criteria noted in the last chapter, as for any broker.)

Calling around to various houses will put you on the track of mining specialty brokers. Checking with the newsletters and advisories can also be helpful.

The bottom line, however, is that if you want to be successful in mining stocks, rather than throwing a dart at a list of stocks, you have to learn the field. Figure on spending years, not just weeks or months, in this endeavor. Yes, it may take a long time, but the rewards could prove it well worthwhile.

THE MINING MARKETS

The Spokane market tends to be a hotbed of silver mining stocks. However, most significant new mining issues in gold come out of Vancouver.

The Vancouver market is unique in the penny stock field. It is a true auction market, with volume as high as forty million shares a day. However, unlike the Big Board or Amex or other American markets, this Canadian market lists stocks in cents. It is a true penny market.

It does not, however, abide by the same rules as do American markets. Remember, in Canada the SEC does not oversee what's happening.

The Vancouver market is known for high-flying and highly speculative issues. The prices are typically between twenty-five cents and fifty cents a share. (Anything below twenty-five cents often indicates a stock with problems, perhaps on the way out.)

The Vancouver market typically has about half a dozen new issues a week. This attracts many investors from both near and far. (Interestingly, it has been estimated that roughly 40 percent of the investors in Vancouver are from the United States!)

To buy a new issue from Vancouver, however, an investor is supposed to be a resident of British Columbia. Stocks are sold to those who have B.C. addresses or to B.C. corporations.

It's important to note that U.S. laws governing stock purchases and sales may apply to investors who purchase stocks in Canada. One consequence here may be a double tax liability. If a profit is made on stocks *in Canada,* the investor may potentially be liable for tax on the gain to both the Canadian and the American governments. As a result, some Canadian brokers will only deal with American investors who actually come to the broker's office in Canada and sign statements releasing the broker from any liability in the sale or purchase of stock.

Commissions for buying stock in the Vancouver market vary depending on what country you are in. If you use a U.S. broker, you can expect to pay between 5 and 10 percent. On the other hand, if you use a Canadian broker, the commission can be only 3.3 percent.

OIL AND GAS

If investing in mining stocks looked difficult, keep in mind that it's child's play compared to investing in oil and gas. There are several reasons why, but two are most compelling. First, most oil and gas companies look alike. They have exploratory wells, developmental wells, and producing wells.

Second, most of these energy companies are linked. Each company seems to own a share of a field or well with another company. The whole industry specializes in spreading the risk, as well as the profit, around. Therefore, how do you separate the good companies from those that will fail?

The Wildcatters.

Most small oil and gas companies are piloted by individuals who have been in oil and gas for a long time. They often have worked for others, gained experience, and are now going to try to make it on their own.

Typically these "wildcatters" will locate desirable land and then try to raise money to get leases on the land and to put in an exploratory well. They are looking for investors who are true gamblers. The reason is that perhaps three-fourths of all exploratory wells are dry holes. They either produce no oil or gas or what they produce is commercially undevelopable.

Many wildcatters, however, will spread the risk around. They will share their lease with others in similar situations in the form of partnerships. Thus, if any one partnership strikes it, they all do.

Risk sharing does help, but it hardly eliminates the chance of losing. The investor should be aware that this remains a highly speculative area.

Developmental Wells.
After exploratory wells come developmental wells. Although they are promoted as "less risky," they must be considered high-risk ventures.

Developmental wells are drilled to "prove out" an exploratory well that showed oil. They may be dug from land adjacent to the exploratory well.

While the name "developmental" suggests that the risk is less, more than half of all developmental wells prove to be dry holes. Just because one exploratory well is successful does not in any way guarantee that wells dug nearby will also be successful.

Lower down in the level of risk are those companies that have producing wells. These wells actually are pumping oil (or gas) and producing revenues. Companies with these types of wells tend to be more mature and their stock tends to be higher priced. Nevertheless, it's important to note that even here there can be important distinctions. A company can have, for example, fifty "gross" wells. It may seem like a substantial amount. However, because companies share risks, it may turn out that although it owns *part* of fifty wells, its ownership is equal to 100 percent of only three wells. Thus, this company only has three "net" wells.

Difficult Evaluation.
Although we've covered some of the parameters in whirl-wind fashion, nevertheless we should be able to see that evaluating oil and gas companies has got to be difficult. While we can make some differentiation on the basis of exploratory versus developmental versus producing wells, this alone isn't going to help us come up with winners. Some of the best companies started out as wildcatters going for exploratory wells. Some of those that failed were companies with producing wells that tried to expand unsuccessfully or were poorly financed. Some of the more successful companies don't even do any work themselves, but instead buy pieces of other companies.

Just as with mining stocks, it takes an expert, someone who's directly involved in the field, to be able to do a realistic evaluation of a company. Again, finding a specialty broker and checking with newsletters and advisories will help. But ultimately, to succeed in picking good stocks, we're going to need to put in the time (sometimes years) to become our own expert.

THE PRICE LINKAGE

We noted earlier that the value of mining and energy stock is directly linked to gold, silver, and oil. As they go up in price, proven reserves become commercial, the profits of companies increase, and stock prices zoom. Thus, besides trying to pick the good companies from the bad, an investor in this area also needs to follow the price of metals and oil.

Interestingly, the prices of gold, silver, and oil are linked. They tend to rise or fall together. There hasn't been a time in recent memory when one was up while the other two were down.

Thus, the factors influencing them tend to be similar. Basically, what causes the prices of gold, silver, oil, and gas to fluctuate are supply and demand, inflation, and world crisis.

Here's how they work.

Supply and Demand.

Gold

Gold is supplied by over fifty countries worldwide, yet more than half of the entire new supply of gold comes from South Africa (roughly fourteen hundred metric tons per year). The world's second largest supplier is the Soviet Union, which sells upwards of four hundred metric tons per year.

Gold is very supply sensitive. Any major cut in supply tends to result in a significant increase in price. Thus, racial troubles in South Africa, which led to fears of mine closings, led to higher gold prices.

While most gold sales are relatively public, the Soviet Union tends to keep its selling clandestine. Thus, it is difficult to ascertain the effects of Soviet sales on the world market.

U.S. and Canadian producers of gold tend to be quite small, though growing. Mine production in both countries has been steadily rising since 1980.

On the supply side, gold is sensitive to the economy. The yellow metal's greatest use comes from jewelry. Since jewelry sales increase during economic expansion and contract during recessions, the well-being of the country is a strong factor in its price.

Other uses for gold include dentistry, electronics, and coinage.

When supply and demand are combined, we see that an expanding economy coupled with problems for South

Africa tend to be bullish for gold. Recessions and strong mine production tend to be bearish.

Silver

The tendency is to think of silver as a poor man's gold. Nothing, however, could be further from the truth. There is no single great supplier of new silver, as South Africa is for gold. Rather, dozens of countries produce silver. (Mexico is one of the largest producers.) In addition, silver is sometimes a by-product of other mining, such as nickel. Each year for the past several years, the amount of new silver mined has increased.

The supply of silver, however, is clouded by huge existing inventories. Since 1981 there has been an overabundance of silver, both domestically and abroad. Coupled with this immediate oversupply is an enormous overhang of "old" silver.

Old silver is metal, usually in the form of jewelry (previously this also included coins, but most silver coins have already been melted down), that comes onto the market whenever the price rises. India alone, for example, is reported to have some 300 million ounces readily available for melting and dumping whenever the price tends to go above seven dollars an ounce. (India has laws restricting the exportation of silver, but it nevertheless comes out in great quantities.)

As a result, there is enormous supply pressure to keep the price of silver low. On the other hand, there is relatively little demand pressure on silver.

Unlike gold, silver is primarily an industrial commodity. Its greatest use is in the photographic industry. However, with the advent of electronic video and fast film that uses less silver, this industry has cut back on its silver demand. Thus, while supplies of silver are large and increasing, demand is moving forward only modestly.

As a result, the price outlook of silver through the remainder of this decade remains clouded.

Oil

The 1970s was a period of oil shortage. OPEC (Oil Producing and Exporting Countries) effectively moved the price per barrel up from five dollars to nearly forty.

However, during the 1980s the oil-consuming countries significantly cut back on their demand for oil. This came about at the same time that many new oil sources (such as Alaska and Mexico) were brought on line.

As a result, the 1980s have proven to be a time of oil surplus. By 1985 OPEC's control over oil pricing had virtually disappeared and oil-producing countries were vying with each other for a diminished market. Saudi Arabia, the world's largest producer during 1984, kept production to less than 25 percent of its potential. During 1985 it moved up to 40 percent, still far below capacity.

Demand for oil is likely to remain relatively low through the remainder of this decade while supplies remain relatively plentiful. Thus, the outlook for a new oil shortage, unless caused by war, is not positive. Consequently, most experts are betting on low oil prices for some time to come.

Inflation.

Gold, silver, and oil prices are all related to inflation, but in different ways.

Gold and silver are reactors. They react to inflation. The reason is that they are seen as "hedges." Inflation means a loss of buying power for currency. A hedge is something that retains buying power. Gold and silver are perceived as having this power.

Thus, to hedge against rising inflation, investors buy gold and silver, and their prices move up, often rapidly. On the other hand, when inflation is low or declining, investors tend to stick the money in income-producing investments (which precious metals are not), and gold and silver prices tend likewise to go down.

Oil, on the other hand, is an affector. It affects the rate of inflation. The reason is quite simple—oil is used in the production of just about everything.

Besides directly affecting individuals at the gas pump, oil prices are factored into the costs of moving any commodity (whether by truck, rail, or plane) and producing any product (in the form of lighting and heating plants and operating machinery—and directly in many products, such as some fertilizers and plastics). Oil is ubiquitous in our society.

Thus, when oil prices rise, the price of just about everything else also goes up. When prices go up, we call it inflation. When oil prices go down and the cost of goods, thereby, drops, we call it disinflation.

An interesting sidelight to this is the fact that some monetarist economists refuse to recognize the direct relationship between oil and inflation. Rather, they feel that inflation is caused strictly by increases in the money supply without corresponding increases in productivity.

Thus, during the Reagan terms in office, the government's monetary policy was largely credited with reducing the rate of inflation. In reality, however, inflation was mainly brought down by a combination of falling oil prices and recession. (The lower oil prices allowed manufacturers to reduce costs; the recession prevented them from raising prices.)

World Crisis.
Finally, there is the matter of world crisis. This can directly and significantly affect gold, silver, and oil.

Oil is affected when the crisis centers around oil-producing countries. The war between Iran and Iraq, for example, produced important price jumps and slips, depending on how it went.

The war itself cut back production in both Iran and Iraq, thus keeping oil prices higher than they might otherwise have been. On the other hand, whenever the war tended to flare up and threatened to close the Strait of Hormuz, through which most of the Middle East's oil flows, the price of oil skyrocketed.

Similarly, any military or political crisis in any oil-producing country, from Saudi Arabia to Libya, is going to have a direct influence on world oil prices.

This will indirectly also influence the price of gold and silver. Remember, precious metal prices follow oil prices. While it might be months before an oil shortage produced any significant inflation, investors act on anticipation, and an immediate price hike in precious metal prices could be expected.

Additionally, gold (primarily) and silver (to a lesser degree) are seen as "coinage of last resort." In troubled times, when people are worried about war, they tend to convert their currency into bullion. It is for this reason that Middle Eastern investors tend to buy gold during crises in that part of the world. For the same reason, French farmers for generations have kept some gold coins hidden in the woodwork of their homes as a way of surviving during the repeated invasions of that country.

Though it's sad to note, political or military crisis in almost any part of the world is bullish for gold and, to a lesser degree, silver. On the other hand, periods of quiet tend to be bearish.

NOTE: Some so-called experts point to a so-called gold/silver relationship. They indicate that there is an almost mystical relationship between the two, which they frequently peg at around thirty to one (gold's price is thirty times that of silver). When the ratio is higher or lower, they then extrapolate that conditions are unstable and that the ratio will return to the thirty-to-one norm. Thus, when the relationship is high, investors should buy silver because it is underpriced. When it is low, they should buy gold because it is priced too low.

This is simply nonsense. Historically, the ratio between gold and silver has moved up and down enormously at different times. Only during one period, between the Great Depression and 1975, did the price tend to remain at roughly thirty to one for a long while. That, however, was because the government officially fixed the price of gold and unofficially determined the price of silver (by selling government hoards to keep prices artificially low). Prior to that time and since, there has been no historical "norm" for the ratio between gold and silver.

Yes, gold and silver do tend to move together. However, that is usually because they are influenced by similar fundamentals and because investors perceive a relationship between them, not because the two metals are in truth tied together in some magical manner.

THE BOTTOM LINE

Yes, there's plenty of money to be made by investing in mining and oil stocks. Unfortunately, there's also plenty of risk involved. The best advice, if you're determined to proceed, is to do so cautiously. Learn as much as you can and, until you become quite knowledgeable, invest as little as possible.

APPENDIX

■

National Association of Security Dealers
1735 K St. N.W.
Washington, D.C. 20006
202-728-8000

CRITERIA FOR
INCLUSION IN
QUOTATION LISTS

I. Composition of the Lists

There shall be two recommended lists of NASDAQ securities provided to the media: the "National List" and the "Additional List." Inclusion on the lists shall be determined semi-annually on the basis of information available to the Association on the selection date. All quotations released shall be Level I quotations.

II. National List

A. *Domestic Common Stock*
The financial criteria for domestic common stock are separated into two alternative categories detailed below. Issuers which meet either one of the alternative criteria will be included in the National List regardless of their dollar volume. Alternative No. 1 includes a net income requirement while Alternative No. 2 has no income requirement but establishes higher financial requirements for those development companies which have no operating income:

Alternative No. 1
1. 350,000 Publicly Held Shares
2. Market Value of Publicly Held Shares of $2,000,000
3. Minimum Bid Price of $3.00
4. Net Income of $300,000 in the previous fiscal year or in two of the last three fiscal years.

Alternative No. 2
1. 800,000 Publicly Held Shares
2. Market Value of Publicly Held Shares of $8,000,000
3. Net Worth of $8,000,000
4. Incorporated for 4 Years

B. *Foreign Securities*
Foreign issues and American Depository Receipts (ADRs) registered pursuant to Section 12(g) under the Securities Exchange Act of 1934, as well as issues for which all relevant information has been filed with the Securities and Exchange Commission pursuant to Rule 12g-3-2, shall meet the same criteria as domestic common stock ex-

cept that the publicly held shares requirement for ADRs shall be determined by the number of ADRs outstanding.

C. *Warrants*
Common stock of issuer must be in the National List and all criteria for domestic common stock apply except that the publicly held shares requirement is replaced with 450,000 warrants publicly held at the time of the initial distribution.

D. *Convertible Debentures*
Common stock of issuer must be in the National List and $100 million of the issue must be outstanding.

E. *Units*
All criteria for domestic common stock apply except that the publicly held shares requirement is replaced with 350,000 publicly held units at time of initial distribution.

F. *Rights*
Automatically included if common stock of issuer is quoted in the National List.

G. *Preferred Stock, Shares or Certificates of Beneficial Interest of Trusts, Limited Partnership Interests, Real Estate Investment Trusts and Closed End Funds*
Same criteria as domestic common stock.

H. *New Issues*
Securities that meet the above criteria immediately following an initial distribution or secondary offering will be added to the National List on the day of the distribution.

III. Additional List

All positions in the Additional List will be filled on the basis of dollar value of average weekly volume.

To monitor security volume data in NASDAQ a statistical moving average method called exponential averaging is used and is recomputed weekly. This technique gives more weight to the most current volume and less weight to the most distant past. For example, at present the weighting parameter is chosen to give 10 percent weight to the most current volume and less than 1 percent weight to the volume that occurred 23 weeks ago. Thus, the significance of the reported volume as maintained for more than 6 months is virtually nil.

INDEX

■